Sovereign Bodies

Sovereign Bodies

Citizens, Migrants, and States in the Postcolonial World

Edited by Thomas Blom Hansen and Finn Stepputat

PRINCETON UNIVERSITY PRESS

PRINCETON AND OXFORD

LIBRARY OF CONGRESS CATALOGING-IN-PUBLICATION DATA

Sovereign bodies : citizens, migrants, and states in the postcolonial world / edited by
    Thomas Blom Hansen and Finn Stepputat.
        p. cm.
    Includes bibliographical references and index.
    ISBN 0-691-12118-4 (cloth : alk. paper) — ISBN 0-691-12119-2 (pbk. : alk. paper)
        1. Political anthropology. 2. Sovereignty. 3. Human territoriality.
    4. Political violence. 5. Postcolonialism. 6. Power (Social sciences)
    I. Hansen, Thomas Blom, 1958– II. Stepputat, Finn.
    GN492.S68 2005
    305.5'122—dc22   2004054933

British Library Cataloging-in-Publication Data is available

This book has been composed in Palatino

Printed on acid-free paper. ∞

pup.princeton.edu

Printed in the United States of America

10 9 8 7 6 5 4 3 2 1

Contents

Preface

This volume started with a conference held at Sandbjerg Manor in Denmark in December 2000 around issues of sovereignty and citizenship in the postcolonial world. Many of the papers presented at the conference are included in this volume (Chatterjee, Fuglerud, Hindess, Jensen, Stepputat, Ong, Turner, and van der Veer). The conference was fruitful and stimulating, and our discussions benefited from presentations from Martijn van Beek, Luis Guarnizo, Ninna Nyberg Sørensen, Andre du Toit, Fiona Wilson, as well as a large number of Ph.D. candidates presenting work in progress at a number of workshops during the three days. We would like to thank the Centre for Development Research in Copenhagen and the Graduate School of International Development Studies at Roskilde University for funding and supporting the conference. As always, the professionalism of Mrs. Inge Jensen, the Graduate School administrator, was indispensible and highly valued by organizers and participants.

In the following years, the editors benefited from discussions with most of the contributors, and we decided to consolidate the collection by including a slightly broader range of contributions. Jean and John Comaroff, Ana Maria Alonso, Yael Navaro-Yashin, Achille Mbembe, and Lars Buur were willing to submit their contributions at relatively short notice. These additions made the collection broader in scope but also more ethnographically well-grounded. A special thanks to Achille Mbembe for organizing the seminar "Death, Bio-politics and Sovereignty" at the Witwatersrand Institute of Social and Economic Research (WISER) in Johannesburg in February 2003. The discussions at that seminar were important in reformulating and honing the Introduction to this volume.

THOMAS BLOM HANSEN
FINN STEPPUTAT

Contributors

Ana Maria Alonso is Associate Professor of Anthropology, University of Arizona.

Lars Buur is Research Programme Coordinator at the Nordic Africa Institute, Uppsala Sweden and Research Associate at Wits Institute for Social and Economic Research (WISER), Johannesburg, University of the Witwatersrand.

Partha Chatterjee is Director of the Centre for Studies in Social Sciences, Calcutta, and Professor of Anthropology, Columbia University.

Jean Comaroff is Bernard E. and Ellen C. Sunny Professor of Anthropology and Social Sciences, University of Chicago.

John L. Comaroff is Harold H. Swift Distinguished Service Professor of Anthropology and Social Sciences, University of Chicago.

Oivind Fuglerud is Research Director, Norwegian Social Research, and Associate Professor, Department of Social Anthropology, Oslo University.

Thomas B. Hansen is Professor of Anthropology, Yale University.

Barry Hindess is Professor of Political Science, Australian National University of Australia, Canberra.

Steffen Jensen is Research Fellow at Wits Institute of Social and Economic Research (WISER), Johannesburg and Roskilde University, Denmark.

Achille Mbembe is Senior Researcher at Wits Institute of Social and Economic Research (WISER), Johannesburg, University of Witwatersrand.

Yael Navaro-Yashin is Lecturer, Department of Social Anthropology, University of Cambridge.

Aihwa Ong is Professor of Anthropology and Southeast Asian Studies, University of California, Berkeley.

Finn Stepputat is Senior Researcher, Danish Institute for International Studies, Copenhagen.

Simon Turner is Senior Researcher, Danish Institute for International Studies, Copenhagen.

Peter van der Veer is University Professor at Utrecht University.

Sovereign Bodies

Introduction

Thomas Blom Hansen and Finn Stepputat

On Empire and Sovereignty

The attack on the World Trade Center in September 2001 aimed at what Al-Qaeda saw as the heart of America's global empire. The subsequent reactions in America and the rest of the world demonstrated that sovereignty and its ultimate expression—the ability and the will to employ overwhelming violence and to decide on life and death—have been reconfigured in the last decades of the twentieth century. The "war on terror" and the attacks on Afghanistan and Iraq demonstrated that underneath the complex structures of power in modern, liberal societies, territorial sovereignty, and the foundational violence that gave birth to it, still remains the hard kernel of modern states—an intrinsically violent "truth" of the modern nation-state that remains its *raison d'être* in periods of crisis. *Jus ad bellum*, the possibility of waging war against those one declares as enemies remains a central dimension of how a state performs its "stateness." At the same time, these reactions also vindicated Hardt and Negri's assertion that "imperial sovereignty" of the twenty-first century differs from earlier forms of imperial power (Hardt and Negri 2000, 161–204). As opposed to earlier eras, today's empire of global network-power has no outside. The enemies, or "deviants," within this space of moral-political-economic domination are all "within," and are often former allies of the U.S. government. In the simplified view of the Bush administration, these constitute an "axis of evil" that must be punished and disciplined in preemptive military strikes to secure internal peace in the United States and among its allies. The sovereign prerogative is to declare who is an internal enemy, and the "war on terror" is a war on internal enemies—within nation-states now policed under new stringent security acts, and within the global empire where legality and rights have been suspended for those declared "illegal combatants" and incarcerated in Afghan prisons, Guantanamo Bay, and other "spaces of exception."

The global transformations of politics, economy, and culture have been explored in various ways by theorists of globalization and international relations.[1] Their obvious merits notwithstanding, these works still maintain an unbroken link between state power, sovereignty, and territory. Sovereignty resides in the state, or in institutions empowered by states, to exercise sovereign power in supra national institutions and within the nation-state defined by its territory and the control of its populations. The emphasis in this body of literature remains on sovereignty as a formal, *de jure* property whose efficacy to a large extent is derived from being externally recognized by other states as both sovereign and legitimate. This taking effective sovereignty for granted is questioned by Stephen Krasner (1999) in his influential work, "Sovereignty: Organized Hypocracy." Krasner shows how international sovereignty and the principles of nonintervention are being breached in numerous ways by imposition as well as agreement, but in his account, sovereignty remains inherently linked to territory and the state power of states. It seems that sovereignty cannot be imagined independently of the state.

This volume questions the obviousness of the state-territory-sovereignty link. In tune with a line of constructivist scholarship in International Relations theory (e.g., Kratochwill 1986; Ruggie 1993; Biersteker and Weber 1996) we conceptualize the territorial state and sovereignty as social constructions. Furthermore, we suggest to shift the ground for our understanding of sovereignty from issues of territory and external recognition by states, toward issues of internal constitution of sovereign power *within states* through the exercise of violence over bodies and populations.

In the *Philosophy of Right*, Hegel remarks that during "the feudal monarchy of earlier times, the state certainly had external sovereignty, but internally, neither the monarch nor the state was sovereign" (Hegel [1821] 1991, 315). This "internal sovereignty" of the modern state was only possible under "lawful and constitutional conditions," in a unitary "Rechtsstaat" whose "ideality" would show itself as "ends and modes of operation determined by, and dependent on, *the end of the whole*" (316, emphasis as in original). Hegel makes it clear that this modern "ideality" of sovereignty can only be realized insofar as local and familial solidarities of "civil society" are sublated to expressions of patriotism through the state, particularly in situations of crisis (316). Even in this, the most systematic thinker of the modern state, sovereignty is not the bedrock of state power but a precarious effect—and an objective—of state formation.

Building on insights from a previous volume that sought to "denaturalize" the postcolonial state (Hansen and Stepputat 2001), and motivated

---

[1] Notably Sassen (1996); Ong (1999); Jackson (1999); Brace and Hoffman (1997); Held (2000), to mention but a few.

by global events, we propose in this volume to take a fresh and ethnographically informed look at the meanings and forms of sovereignty in the same postcolonial zones of the world. Our aims are threefold.

First, we suggest that sovereign power and the violence (or the threat thereof) that always mark it, should be studied as practices dispersed throughout, and across, societies. The unequivocal linking of sovereign power to the state is a historically contingent and peculiar outcome of the evolution of the modern state system in Europe since the Westphalian peace in 1648. The discipline of International Relations has for decades assumed states to be both normal, that is, with *de facto* legitimate control of their populations and territory, and identical, that is, with similar interests, strategies, and expected patterns of action.[2] To become a normal sovereign state with normal citizens continues to be a powerful ideal, releasing considerable creative energy, and even more repressive force, precisely because its realization presupposed the disciplining and subordination of other forms of authority. We suggest that sovereignty of the state is an aspiration that seeks to create itself in the face of internally fragmented, unevenly distributed and unpredictable configurations of political authority that exercise more or less legitimate violence in a territory. Sovereign power, whether exercised by a state, in the name of the nation, or by a local despotic power or community court, is always a tentative and unstable project whose efficacy and legitimacy depend on repeated performances of violence and a "will to rule." These performances can be spectacular and public, secret and menacing, and also can appear as scientific/technical rationalities of management and punishment of bodies. Although the meanings and forms of such performances of sovereignty always are historically specific, they are, however, always constructing their public authority through a capacity for visiting violence on human bodies.

Second, the chapters in this volume foreground the ethnographic detail and the historical specificity in studies of sovereignty and its correlate, citizenship and other forms of institutionalized practices belonging to a state and/or a community defined by, but not delimited by, a territory. All contributors, whether anthropologists or not, focus on the historically embedded practices and cultural meanings of sovereign power and violence, and the *de facto* practices of citizenship and belonging in a wide range of contexts. The focus is unequivocally on the performance of sovereign power within nations, and on the precarious construction and maintenance of localized sovereign power through

[2] For a good critique of these assumptions, see Bartelson's more philosophical critique of realism (Bartelson 1995, 12–52). Cynthia Weber's incisive study of sovereignty as simulation produced through acts of international intervention (Weber 1995), and Biersteker and Weber's volume on the social construction of sovereignty (1996).

exercise of actual or "spectral" violence—transmitted through rumors, tales, and reputations. The issue at stake is *de facto* recognition of sovereign power by local and discerning "audiences" who often pay their dues to several authorities at the same time. Taken together, the contributions make it clear that although sovereign power always seeks to project itself as given, stable and natural, it never completely manages to achieve the status of a "master signifier" that can stabilize a social order and a set of identities.[3]

Third, we believe that the complex history of the reconfiguration of sovereign power and citizenship in colonial and postcolonial societies demonstrates something important, and uncomfortable, about the permutations of these concepts. Colonial forms of sovereignty were more fragmented and complex, more reliant on spectacles and ceremony, and demonstrative and excessive violence, than the forms of sovereign power that had emerged in Europe after several centuries of centralizing efforts. These differences were rooted in indirect rule at a distance, to pragmatic reliance on local, indigenous forms of rule and sovereignty, and tied to the efforts at asserting racial and civilizational superiority. European states never aimed at governing the colonial territories with the same uniformity and intensity as were applied to their own populations. The emphasis was rarely on forging consent and the creation of a nation-people, and almost exclusively on securing subjection, order, and obedience through performance of paramount sovereign power and suppression of competing authorities. Demonstrative violence and short term economic exploitation were constitutive of colonial rule and took precedence over long-term economic rationalities.[4] As a result, the configurations of *de facto* sovereign power, justice, and order in the postcolonial states were from the outset partial, competing, and unsettled.

We believe that by zooming in on the historical production and actual practices of sovereign bodies—from states, nations, communities, self-appointed big-men and leaders, to mobile individuals and political outfits—outside the metropolitan hearts of empire, this volume can

[3] The poststructuralist questioning of a reasoning and unified subject and the Lacanian notion of the subject as irredeemably split has in International Relations been translated into an analogous critique of sovereignty and the sovereign state as a governing "master signifier" capable of stabilizing social identities. This critique aims at deconstructing the sovereign state as the privileged subject and actor in the international system, whose fragile constitution is concealed by formal recognition and a fiction of permanence (Edkins, Persram, and Pin-Fat 1999).

[4] For a succinct account of how European powers applied "Westphalian" norms of diplomacy and engagement in their approach to European states and "Christian nations" while applying other, more brutal and crude methods in dealing with African and Asian kings and with the Chinese and Ottoman empires, see Strang (1996).

qualify and complicate understandings of power and sovereignty both in the postcolonial world and in "the West"; it can open new conceptual fields in the anthropology of politics; and it can demonstrate the need for more embedded and "emic" understandings of what sovereign power actually means.

IMAGINING THE "MORTALL GOD": SOVEREIGNTY AND THE SECRET OF POWER

> "The main point of sovereign majesty and absolute power consists of giving the law to subjects in general without their consent." (Bodin 1992, Book 1, 23)

The modern notion of sovereignty as the ultimate and transcendent mark of indivisible state power emerged in Europe from the complex power struggles between the Vatican and the kings of northern and western Europe. As the idea of the ultimate authority vested in the Pope and the Holy Emperor began to crumble in the Renaissance and post-Reformation world, kings and their states increasingly became loci of both secular and divine authority. In his classic account, Laski argues that, "Luther was driven to assert the divinity of states, that the right of a secular body might be made manifest. [. . .] The state became incarnate in the Prince" (Laski 1950, 45). The rising urban bourgeoisie in many European states put their weight behind the kings in the protracted conflicts with the landed aristocracy, challenging the latter's rights to land, taxation, and eminence. The results were varieties of absolutist power, unification of territory, and centralization of the administration of the state, as well as elevation of royal power from being bestowed through acts of investiture by the political bodies of the estates, to become originary, indivisible, and above contestation. The sovereignty of the king now became the central principle of power, a mystical and metaphysical secret, beyond the reach or comprehension of ordinary men and only answerable to the divine law. As famously put by Thomas Hobbes: "The multitude so united in one person, is called a common-wealth. This is the Generation of that great LEVIATHAN, or rather (to speak more reverently) of that Mortall God, to which we owe under the Immortal God, our peace and defense" (Hobbes 1991, 120).

This configuration of power had roots in older conceptions of kingship, not least in the late-medieval political-theological notion of "the King's Two Bodies," analyzed subtly by Ernst Kantorowich. In the figure of the king, two bodies were united, the "natural body" of the living king, and the more eternal and encompassing "body politic" which expressed the office, the estates, and the majesty of the royal institution. The latter was superior to the former, and the body politic is often described as a *corpus mysticum*, a mystical body that was eternal and could not die along with the natural body. In spite of this articulation of theological concepts in the sphere of politics, there was a clear acknowledgment of royal power as not being sacred in itself, but being embedded in and dependent on the recognition of his subjects, as well as the blessings of the Church (Kantorowicz 1957, 7–23).

In contrast to this older acknowledgment of royal power as fragile and embedded, the notion of absolute rule posited a constitutive and unbridgeable distance between the sovereign and the subjects, and imposition of the will of the sovereign on the body politic. As Maritain puts it in his critique of sovereignty: "Either sovereignty means nothing, or it means supreme power separate and transcendent—not at the peak but above the peak—and ruling the entire body politic from above. That is why this power is absolute (ab-solute, that is non-bound, separate) and consequently unlimited" (Maritain 1969, 47). This configuration of sovereignty had been in gestation for a long time in Western Europe. Kings tried to carve out a space between the localized power of feudal lords, and the deeply entrenched notion of *imperium*—embodied in the Holy Roman Empire and the power of the Vatican to legislate, overrule and excommunicate disobedient kings.[5]

Hobbes's notion of the Covenant, by which subjects give up their right to rule themselves and grant it to the overlord in exchange for protection, defined the origin of sovereign power in acts of violence that were foundational exactly because they expressed an excessive and overpowering resolve to rule on part of the king. In spite of the imputed stability and self-evidence of the Covenant, most of Hobbes's argument circled around how sovereign power could be delegated and exercised in ways that would not undermine the status of the sovereign (esp. Hobbes 1991, 121–39). The most cursory glance at the violent constructions of centralized states of this era makes it plain that the preservation of the majesty of the sovereign king always was threatened by war and popular insubordination. The model of sovereign kingship was also from the outset challenged by other notions of legitimacy and representation of power.[6]

---

[5] The elaboration of a theory of the inalienability of sovereignty was at the heart of these efforts from the twelfth century onward. As shown by Riesenberg, both theorists of law as well as theologians contributed to a new idea of legitimate power and public office defined as a relationship between individual subjects and the king, rather than mediated by the estates or the *res sacrae*, the realm and property of the church (Riesenberg 1956).

[6] See, e.g., van Gelderen's recent account of how notions of *civitas* and *respublica* in the early Dutch republic in the sixteenth century challenged and undermined the idea of kingship as the only legitimate representation of the estates (van Gelderen 2003).

The violent and yet precarious character of sovereign power was expressed even more clearly in Jean Bodin's earlier discussion of what he called the "true marks of sovereignty." As Bodin puts it: "To be able to recognize such a person—that is, a sovereign—we have to know his attributes (*marques*) which are properties not shared by subjects. For if they were shared, there would be no sovereign prince" (Bodin 1992, 46). These marks were not necessarily bodily marks or forms of dress but first and foremost a specific type of actions that by their resolve and sheer force affirmed the status of the sovereign power as indivisible, transcendent, and self-referring. Bodin enumerates ten different marks, or abilities, that mark sovereign power: to give laws and change them at will (without consent of the subjects); to wage war against opponents or enemies of the state; to appoint the highest officials of the state only at its own will; to have the last judgment (*dernier ressort*) in legal disputes and thus also the power to pardon and grant freedom to prisoners irrespective of the law; to coin and validate money within the state; to impose tax on subjects or to delegate that right to officials or lesser lords; to confiscate land and assets; to use a royal seal to validate and authorize; to change the language of his subjects; and to reserve the exclusive right for himself to bear the title of "majesty" (46–88).

What is implicit but never spelled out in Bodin's text is that sovereignty is an *effect* of these actions, and that sovereignty needs to be *performed* and reiterated on a daily basis in order to be effective, and to form the basic referent of the state. Just like power only can be known through its effects, sovereignty also was here defined as a performative category, an ontologically empty category organized around a mythical act of foundational violence, or what Derrida has called a *coup de force*, a self-referential founding of the law as ground (Derrida 1992). If sovereignty is fiction, as Runciman has proposed in a similar vein (Runciman 2003), it is made real and reproduced through ritualized, everyday confirmations of this royal violence: the giving and enforcement of laws, the killing of criminals as well as enemies of the state, or of those who did not pay due respect to the king, and so on.

The absolutist and authoritarian states developed and matured in response to the insubordination, energy, and immense creativity released by the renaissance notion of the immanence of the world, that is, the independence of the human world from the divine and the transcendent (Hardt and Negri 2000–1, 97–101). These states sought to control increasingly mobile and literate populations and evermore restless and assertive estates within the body politic. The language of sovereign power now downplayed its self-born and self-referring character and turned to increasingly moralizing and inclusive registers, positing the sovereign as serving God's will, as well as the people by obeying the moral laws of society. In Pufendorf's classical treatise *On the Duty of Man and Citizen* (1673), sovereign power is described as founded on the consent of the people which can only be maintained if the sovereign provides safety to the people and rules in a virtuous and prudent way. The relationship between ruler and subject is described in terms of duties of the citizens but also of the sovereign who should enforce "public discipline so that the citizens conform to the precepts of the laws not so much through fear of punishment as by habituation" (Pufendorf [1673] 1991, 152).

Considering the rhetoric of sovereign power being exercised in the name and service of the people, the emergence of "the people" in the eighteenth century political debates as the ultimate source of sovereignty appears less discontinuous than sometimes made out to be. "The people" and notions of popular sovereignty were slowly invented in various forms in different states in Europe and in North America (Morgan 1988), but were never equated with what Spinoza termed "the multitude," that is, the actually existing mass of subjects. "The people" was made up of small groups of educated, wealthy, and propertied men, and of representatives of the estates—free peasants, artisans, burgers, and so on. By virtue of their control of property, of their domestic life and family, and of themselves (*qua* their Christian conscience and interiorized belief that supposedly controlled their actions), they were accorded a measure of sovereignty as individuals. Whereas the king and his *corpus mysticum* had symbolized and embodied sovereignty, the popular sovereignty was an even more abstract and transcendent principle and yet embodied in the ideal citizen, the man who is reasonable *qua* his reason, his self-control, and his property. As Lefort has remarked, democracy made political power and thus sovereignty into an "empty place," a mystical source of power that only could be temporarily manifested through representation of "the people" by "mere mortals" (Lefort, 1988, 17). The crucial marks of sovereign power—indivisibility, self-reference, and transcendence—were now embedded in the citizens. Violence was now fetishized as a weapon of reason and preservation of freedom of the citizens vis-à-vis the threats from outsiders, from internal enemies, and from those not yet fit for citizenship—slaves and colonial subjects.

The French and American revolutions did, however, open several disjunctures between people and state. The absolute monarch had represented sovereign power and the state encompassing "the people" within the body politic. Now the state and "the people" could no longer be identical and the state could become unrepresentative, illegitimate, and worthy of destruction. This crystallization of popular sovereignty did not curb the authoritarian possibilities inherent in the modern state but created the possibility of a new and more intensive merging of state and people. New intensive and "caring" forms of government of welfare, economy, and morality had developed in towns and cities across the German speaking Central Europe in the seventeenth century. This so-called *cameralism* and the strong local patriotism it engendered became a central inspiration for the emerging nation states.[7] As nation-states developed from the eighteenth century onward they engaged in a protracted labor to make the elusive "people" appear in tangible forms: in a shared history, in common sets of symbols emerging from everyday life (language, customs, religious life, etc.), clear boundaries, and not least, in rituals of death (punishment of traitors) and sacrifice (death and heroism in war and service of the nation) reproducing the national community. As George Mosse has pointed out, this paved the way for a direct representation of the people in mass-spectacles and the aestheticization of politics that characterized fascism. "The chaotic crowd of the 'people' became a mass-movement which shared a belief in popular unity through a national mystique. The new politics provided an objectification of the general will" (Mosse 1975, 2). Popular sovereignty became increasingly synonymous with national sovereignty and the people was now produced as citizens of the nation-state and their "political love" for the nation produced in schools, in the army, through innumerable institutional and disciplinary practices, pedagogy, art, songs, war, and worship (Weber 1977). The system of sovereign territorial states that had come into being after the Westphalian peace in 1648 only came into its full flourish on the European continent in the nineteenth century.

Domination of the non-European world, the race for commerce and territory, was intrinsic to this formation of sovereignty, just as the colonial world provided an essential ground for the formation of dominant ideas of nation, morality, domesticity, culture, and religion in the Western Europe. As Barry Hindess points out in this volume, vast colonial populations became integral to the international system of states as "noncitizen populations"; an illiberal and authoritarian parallel world whose subjects were permanently subordinated, serving as labor, soldiers and markets for proper and liberal European states. Similarly, the colonial territories only enjoyed a quasi-sovereignty by virtue of being the appendices to the metropolitan states.

As in the early modern period, the language of legality was the pre-

---

[7] These towns, both the *Reichsstaedte* formally under the Holy Roman Empire, and the *Landstaaedte* under the jurisdiction of local princes, enjoyed a wide array of rights and sovereignty in legal and economic matters. See Walker (1971) and Pasquino (1991). These rights and sovereignties all disappeared in the course of the rise of the unified German Reich in the nineteenth century.

ferred expression of sovereign power of the nation-state. "The people" began to acquire an altogether more stable, homogenized and orderly form as citizens were governed by law, and as states demanded primary and indivisible loyalties to the nation in return for a measure of rights. The twentieth-century history of the modern nation-state in the Western world revolved centrally around protracted struggles for recognition of citizenship rights to wider sections of the population—women, the working class, nonwhite individuals and communities, immigrants and so on—but also the granting of a wider and deeper set of rights and entitlements. In T. H. Marshall's classical account, the notion of citizenship began with civil rights, for example, rights to property and to a fair trial in which proper individual citizens could claim *habeas corpus* (lit. the right to claim and present one's body in front of a court), which curtailed the exercise of arbitrary state violence by defining the body of the citizen as an integral part of the sovereign body of "the people" and thus entitled to due process. The next phase was that of formal political rights to vote, to freedom of speech and assembly, in order to create political bodies representing the people and the nation; and the third phase was the social rights of the twentieth-century welfare states, in which citizenship meant access to an ever widening set of economic entitlements (Marshall 1977). As is well known, this politics of recognition (Taylor 1994) has continued to expand and proliferate, now including the recognition of a large number of cultural, religious, and sexual minorities in still more countries in the world. As we will return to later, this is a complex process with many forms driven by internal political compulsions, by increasing flexibilization of citizenship rights across national boundaries, as well as an ever more powerful discourse of human rights that impel states to grant rights, or resist from repressive measures in order not to damage their international reputation and standing within an elusive but effective "international community."

In this "age of rights" (Bobbio 1996), it seemed possible, until very recently, to claim that the exercise of sovereignty in its arcane and violent forms was becoming a thing of the past, that sovereignty now finally rested with the citizens, at least in liberal democracies. The world order after September 11, 2001, seems to belie this optimistic assumption, and it may be useful to revise the standard history of what Foucault somewhat reluctantly called "democratization of sovereignty." The languages of legality have, he argued, "allowed a system of rights to be superimposed upon the mechanisms of discipline in such a way as to conceal its actual procedures—the element of domination inherent in its techniques—and to guarantee to everyone, by virtue of the sovereignty of the state, the exercise of his proper sovereign rights" (Foucault 1994, 219). The crucial point is that, today, sovereignty as embodied in

citizens sharing territory and culture, and sharing the right to exc
and punish "strangers," has become a political common sense, or v
Derrida calls "ontotopology" (Derrida 1994), that defines the polit.
frontlines on immigration in Europe, on autochthony and belonging in
Africa, on majoritarianism and nation in South Asia and so on. In order
to assess and understand the nature and effects of sovereign power in
our contemporary world, one needs to disentangle the notion of sovereign power from the state and to take a closer look at its constituent
parts: on the one hand, the elusive "secret" of sovereignty as a self-
born, excessive, and violent will to rule; on the other hand, the human
body and the irrepressible fact of "bare life" as the site upon which sovereign violence always inscribes itself but also encounters the most
stubborn resistance.

Sovereign Bodies: Violence, Law, and Bio-politics

It was Foucault's *Discipline and Punish: The Birth of the Prison* that more
than any other work brought questions of the body to the center stage
of contemporary understandings of power. The first chapter analyzes
how the bodies of the condemned in their vulnerability mark "the sym-
metrical, inverted figure of the king" (Foucault 1977, 29), of the surplus
power or excess that, as we saw above, is the mark of sovereign power.
Analyzing how public torture and executions in the seventeenth and
eighteenth centuries were carefully arranged to symbolically punish
the limb that "committed the crime," often executing people at the
scene of the crime, Foucault argues that, "Its aim is not so much to re-
establish balance as to bring into play, as its extreme point, the dissym-
metry between the subject who has dared to violate the law and the all-
powerful sovereign who displays his strength [. . .] the punishment is
carried out in such a way as to give a spectacle not of measure, but of
imbalance and excess" (49).

The body of the criminal, naked and humiliated was, in other words,
the necessary double of sovereign power, its necessary surface of inscription. The tortured body transformed itself into something else, an
object of collective projections of the plebeian crowd whose presence
was essential to these performances of sovereignty. To some spectators,
the tortured body, purged of the evil at the moment of death, became
pure and almost sacred, as the sheer stubbornness of life in the bodies
that refused to die became a counterpoint to royal might. The condemned sometimes became popular heroes, symbols of the injustices of
the sovereign, and in many cases ineffective executioners were atta-l- 1
by crowds, prisoners freed, or the dead bodies of the condemne(

care of and given a decent burial by insurgent crowds. Foucault notes that these "disturbances around the scaffold" provided an important impetus to the rethinking of the system of prisons and punishments from the eighteenth century onward (44–69). Another motive driving the invention of the modern prison and correctional system was that the arbitrariness, the "archaic arrogance [. . .] exaggerations and loopholes" of the "super-powers of the monarch" allowed for a certain "right to illegality" at all levels of society (80) that accorded even the lowest strata a "space of tolerance" that was readily and obstinately defended. These two forms of excess, spectacular and arbitrary royal sovereignty, and the "infra-power of acquired and tolerated illegalities" of the common people came together in their most dangerous and unpredictable form around the spectacles of public executions (89).

The reaction was, as is well known from Foucault's subsequent work, the invention of modern prison system that concealed sovereign violence within thick walls, made the condemned into "the property of society, the object of collective and useful appropriation" (109). In the penitentiaries the criminals were supposed to exercise penance and cleanse their souls but, more important, to subject their bodies to a range of new correctional disciplines that unlike the marks of sovereign power left by torture, left "traces, in the form of habits, in behavior" (131). This was in Foucault's view a set of political technologies of the body whose functioning through minute and pedantic disciplines were fundamentally different from the archaic forms of sovereign power. This new political anatomy and its dispersed effects on individual bodies were, Foucault argued "absolutely incompatible with the relations of sovereignty," which always "encompasses the totality of the social body" (Foucault 1994, 218) and expresses itself through a language of law and legal codification.

It seems, however, that some of the manifestations of what Foucault saw as an archaic exchange between sovereign power and the simple life of condemned bodies are still very much with us. Prison revolts or, even more effectively, hunger strikes among prisoners are often used to great symbolic effect. Not unlike the sacralization and purity of the dying or tortured body on the scaffold, the emaciated body and the suffering of the hunger-striking prisoner destroying his/her own body, transforms the prisoner from a criminal to an almost sublime and purified figure. Allen Feldman provides another striking example of this in his analysis of the "Dirty Protest" among IRA prisoners who refused to wash their bodies or wear clean clothes. Through this use, if not suspension, of their own bodies initiated a broad and powerful protest against the prison authorities that only consolidated their moral leadership among inmates as well as outside the prison walls (Feldman 1991, 167–211).

There are other examples of similar uses of the body that defies ⟨ plinary power and challenges more conventional manifestation. sovereign violence: the civil disobedience campaigner who willin₂ submits his/her body to be beaten and put in prison and thus renders state power both excessively brutal and strangely impotent at the same time; or the more extreme case of the suicide bombers, whose determination to die make them manifestations of a sovereignty of will and of the individual body. Like other manifestations of sovereignty, such display of will, sacrifice and disregard of death appear both frightening and awe-inspiring as it thematizes the almost sacred character of life itself. Even in situations of total control, exception from legality, and psychological humiliation, as in the camps at Guantanamo Bay, it is imperative to keep the bodies of the prisoners alive and in good health in order not to be seen to violate the ultimate—biological life itself.

The "secret" of sovereignty seems, in other words, still to be defined in the tension between the will to arbitrary violence and the existence of bodies that can be killed but also can resist sovereign power, if nothing else by the mere fact of the simple life force they contain. If sovereign power originates in excessive and exceptional violence that wants nothing or sees nothing beyond its own benefit or pleasure, its object, but also its ultimate resistance, is found in the simple life of bodies that desires nothing beyond itself and the simple moments of pleasure of everyday life. This fundamental embeddedness of sovereignty in the body was at the center of Georges Bataille's exploration of the concept and its meaning in the modern world. To Bataille, sovereignty is not merely an archaic form of power and subordination but articulated more fundamentally in attitudes, or acts, beyond the realm of utility and calculation. "Life beyond utility is the domain of sovereignty" (Bataille 1991, 198).[8] Sovereign enjoyment is excessive and beyond the needs of those enjoying. A sovereign command does not calculate minutely what it wants, but inadvertently reproduces obedience *qua* its very gesture of disregard of danger and death (225–30). Sovereignty resides in every human being and shows itself in the desire to enjoy and revel in brief moments of careless freedom, in sexual ecstasy, in moments of simple nonanticipatory existence, when an individual experiences "the miraculous sensation of having the world at his disposal" (199). This was the original condition of man in "his non-alienated condition [. . .] but what is within him has a destructive violence, for example the violence of death" (214).

A part of Bataille's essay anticipates Foucault's work by arguing that

[8] Georges Bataille's work on sovereignty was written in the early 1950s but was not published until the 1970s as volume 8 (*La Souverainite*) in a series entitled *Ouevres Completes* (1970–1988). The text referred to here is the English translation.

modern bourgeois society, and communism with even more determination, have striven to eradicate the wastefulness, irrationality and arbitrariness at the heart of sovereignty: both as a mode of power, as a mode of subordination driven by the subject's projection of their own desire onto the spectacle of wasteful luxury of the court and the king, and as a space for arbitrary and spontaneous experiences of freedom and suspension of duties. The essence of Bataille's proposition is that because the exercise of sovereignty is linked to death, excessive expenditure (*depenser*) and bodily pleasure can neither be contained by any discipline, nor be fully "democratized" into an equal dignity of all men. Because sovereignty revolves around death, the ultimate form of expenditure beyond utility, it constitutes in Mbembe's words an "anti-economy" (Mbembe 2003, 15).

To Bataille, sovereignty has no positive existence but is a miracle intrinsic to human existence and can only be determined through what he calls a "negative theology" that captures the "miraculous moments" (241) in which sovereignty is experienced: in the awe of the leader or the king, in the disregard of death, of timidity, of prohibitions. Because sovereignty flows from the assertion of a basic life force that foregrounds the body and the senses rather than the intellect, it is ultimately connected with the will to take life, and to give up one's life but not in a calculated and rational fashion. Sovereignty is the opposite of "faintheartedness" and Bataille writes: "Killing is not the only way to regain sovereign life, but sovereignty is always linked to a denial of the sentiments that death controls" (221). In Bataille's view, the divine is the ultimate sovereign phenomenon, organized around an unknowable but indivisible void, a "deep unity of NOTHING" (234), that only can be known through its effects, the enchantment it generates, the imagination it fires and the objects it sacralizes.[9] To Bataille, the mystery of sovereignty has an irrevocably archaic quality, an "animality that we perceive in sovereignty" whose reappearance as various forms of irrational excess upsets and disturbs the ideals of equality and reciprocity forged in modern bourgeois societies (and those under communism). Echoing Mauss's notion of gift-giving as an inherently unequal form of reciprocity because the giver always retains more than he/she gives, Bataille argues that "the universal aspiration of the sovereignty of the gift giver" (347), that is, the desire to impress, assert and dominate through excessive expenditure inevitably presents a problem for the bourgeois sense of "proportionality" (348).

[9] The generative link between violence and the sacred in the act of sacrifice is well known in the anthropology and sociology of religion from Durkheim to Otto but received its most exhaustive and philosophically inflected treatment in the work of Rene Girard (1977).

Bataille tried to understand sovereignty as a common denominator for what we may call the "gift of power"—the mystery of the will to power of certain individuals, the charisma that violence, selfishness, and ruthlessness generate—and he identified its origins in elementary life force that expresses itself in extraordinary actions and moments. For all its subtle insights, it is not surprising that Bataille's work has been accused of rearticulating themes in the philosophical "vitalism"— from Nietzsche's ideas of the willpower of a future superior being, Bergson's biological ideas of the *elan vital* as an irrepressible life force, to Heidegger's much deeper ontological reflections, and even Merleau Ponty's writings on emotional and embodied intensities. But, unlike these writers, Bataille shifted the emphasis from searching for the sources of the will to understanding will as an effect that is deducted from violence and other sovereign acts. However, on the whole, vitalist thinking had a troubled and ambiguous relationship with rightwing politics and critiques of modernity throughout the twentieth century.[10] The crux of this problem lies in Bataille's somewhat impoverished analysis of modern bourgeois society as governed by lifeless, disciplinary and commercial logics, and his view of sovereignty, the sacred, and the elementary forces of life as residues of an archaic age.

The positing of sovereignty as a mark of something originary, of a will that is self-born and unaccountable and yet vitalizes the dull procedures of modernity, was even more pronounced in Carl Schmitt's earlier and controversial work on "political theology" from 1920. Written in the context of the upheavals following World War I, Schmitt's work on "the political" as an agonistic relation between friends and foes (Schmitt [1932] 1976) was deeply skeptical of parliamentary democracy and of rationalist or idealist notions of justice that in his view basically relied on only superficially secularised Christian ideas of mercy and salvation. Instead, Schmitt proposed the Hobbesian "decisionist" argument that law does not reflect the norms of a society but rather the will, the fortitude and authority of those who decide what is law. "For a legal order to make sense, a normal situation must exist, and he is sovereign who definitely decides whether this normal situation actually exists" (Schmitt 1985, 13).

The key concept for Schmitt was here the notion of the "exception"

---

[10] The fascination of violence and its capacity for purification and generating authenticity was along with celebration of fortitude and manliness mainstays in the cultural formations that led to Fascism. It was given literary expression by many, but most forcefully perhaps by Ernst Juenger (1996). The celebration of revolutionary violence also has a long history on the Left, from Sorel's fascination with the "clarity" of the confrontation of "the masses" with authority (2000), to Che Guevara's sublimation of guerilla warfare into acts of "love of the people" (MacLaren 2000).

(*Ausnahme*), which encapsulates what Bataille calls the "sovereign moment" in that it is a conceptual and normative void from where the law can be given but also where the vitality of the decision shows itself: "In the exception the power of real life breaks through the crust of a mechanism that has become torpid by repetition" (15). In Schmitt's view, sovereignty does not have the form of law; it lies behind, and makes possible the authority of the law. The specificity of the legal form lies not in content or style but in a certain excess, a surplus content that precisely is the trace of a decision: "That constitutive, specific element of a decision is, from the perspective of the content of the underlying norm, new and alien. Looked at normatively, the decision emanates from nothingness" (33).

Although Schmitt's decisionism on the surface may appear as hard-nosed realism, it is crucially dependent on a vitalist conception of modernity and democracy as weak, formalistic, and dull social forms. In the view of Schmitt and his many contemporaries who were sympathetic to Nazism, modern society remains dependent on the passion and intensity derived from archaic and premodern phenomena such as religion, war, the magicality of the decision, and the sovereign power of the leader.

Although sovereignty and state power is implicitly equated throughout Schmitt's work, his idea of the decision has a wider application and resonates in many ways with Bataille's idea of sovereignty as the sensual and embodied antithesis of the normative and customary. Both agree that sovereignty and its traces are ubiquitous and important in modern societies, always appearing under the sign of something excessive, or exceptional. Yet, for all the power attributed to the sovereign decision or moment, sovereignty is beyond definition, it is a "nothingness," a force or will that only can be known in the moment of its appearance.

In the recent work of Giorgio Agamben, one finds a highly creative attempt to combine the insights of Schmitt, Bataille, Kantorowicz, and others, and yet, through a Foucauldian optic, to get beyond the unmistakably metaphysical and vitalist tenor of their expositions. Agamben rejects Foucault's notion of sovereignty as an archaic form of power superseded by modern biopolitics and suggests that, "the production of a biopolitical body is the original activity of sovereign power. In this sense biopolitics is at least as old as the sovereign exception" (Agamben 1998, 6).

Instead of beginning with Hobbes, the absolutist state and the origins of sovereign power in Christian theology, Agamben argues that "bare life," or simple biological life, "has the peculiar privilege of being that whose exclusion founds the city of men" in the Western political tradition (7). In antiquity, the city and community proper consisted of free men and citizens—whereas women, slaves, outcasts, and other forms of life, that is, the majority of human beings, were excluded from the political community, and yet remained internal and crucial to society and economy.

This "inclusive exclusion" is captured in the Roman concept of *homo sacer*, the sacred man who is expelled and banished from the community and who may be killed by members of the community—but not sacrificed as he is not worthy of this gesture of honor before the divine. This figure, the outlaw, the *Friedlos*, or the convict, was historically the symbol of the outside upon whose body and life the boundaries of the political community could be built. The expulsion of someone who used to have rights as a citizen, or simply to categorize some individuals in a society as a form of life that is beyond the reach of dignity and full humanity and thus not even a subject of a benevolent power, is the most elementary operation of sovereign power—be it as a government in a nation-state, a local authority, a community, a warlord, or a local militia. At the same time, Agamben shows the figure of the sovereign to be ambiguous—a figure whose status and corporeality appears as fragile and ambivalent but also exempted from the rules of ordinary life as that of his double, the *homo sacer*, the figure symbolizing simple, mute and bare life (Agamben 1998, 49–103).

This logic of sovereign violence that founds the political community by excluding various forms of "bare life" has not disappeared with the emergence of modern biopolitical forms of governance. On the contrary. The essential operation of totalitarian power was to reduce the population to pliable bodies that could be improved, shaped, and regimented, but also exterminated if deemed unnecessary or dangerous. This operation, which aimed at containing and negating the "sovereign moments" and spontaneity of life that Bataille describes, had its counterparts in the rise of disciplinary institutions and welfare governmentality in Western democracies. In both cases this amounted to a "politicization of life" as well as a "medicalization of politics": a political rhetoric using metaphors of contamination and diseases of the body politics, and political rationalities that employ health, risk, balance, and prophylactic action as justifications for a range of interventions, from immunization programs to eugenics. Through these medical and corporeal metaphors, the body-as-organism popularized in nationalist ideology and political romanticism, returned once again as a privileged trope of society and community.

To Agamben, "the state of exception," the sovereign sphere deciding on the exclusion of "bare life" (*zoe*), has remained constitutive of the political community. It has acquired even more force as the empirical "multitude" of individuals have been incorporated into the political community of "the people" through franchise, citizenship, and universal entitlements in many nation-states in the twentieth century. The exception appears in three forms. First, as ideologies and institutions of improvement of "the people"—always haunted by the connotations of being poor, undisciplined and plebeian—seeking to produce good citizens and thus constitute proper life of the community and the state. Second, the exception appears as decisions on the status of life and death as new medical technologies blur and dissolve erstwhile definitions death and as genetic engineering undermine definitions of biological life. Increasingly, biological life subjected to the authoritarian and illiberal underside of liberal democracies (Hindess 2001b), is not merely in prisons and asylums, but within the citizen's own body—tissue, genes, or irrationalities beyond the control of the individual, legislated by the state or patented by corporations. Third, the exception is to be found in the camps of asylum seekers and refugees in many parts of the world. In this space, the displaced, the poor and the disenfranchised are governed as life outside the community while they are prepared for orderly entry into the *polis*. Agamben argues, that "the camp" has become an important, if not constitutive, metaphor of modernity, an ideal space of governance, order, categorization and discipline that in multiple forms functions as the necessary but uncomfortable and sometimes disavowed support of the reproduction of "normal" citizenship and community life (Agamben 1998, 166–80). Although immigration and accelerated movement of people around the world undoubtedly has brought the illiberal, exclusive, and sometimes openly racist dimensions of democracy and nation-states to the fore, it is equally clear that even the richest nations in the world are unable to contain and control these movements.[11]

The readings of sovereignty that we find in Bataille, Foucault, and Agamben go against the grain of the conventional canonical definitions of Western political discourse where the sovereign state is defined as the bedrock of a "civilized" international order. These readings afford us to understand the fragility and perpetually violent character of this order. They also afford us to understand the configuration of colonial and postcolonial sovereignties not as deformed or incomplete, but as polymorphous and yet vital to the so-called Westphalian system of nation-states by virtue of constituting almost permanent zones of "exception."

[11] The ambiguity of actual migration regimes are related to the continuing demands for cheap and flexible labor in the United States and Western Europe where border controls also are constrained by internationally codified rights and by public opinion.

Colonial and Postcolonial Configurations of Sovereignty

Over the last decade or more, a rich body of scholarship on colonialism has firmly established that the colonial world was integral to the formation of law, public institutions, cultural identities, and ideologies of rule in Europe. Technologies of public health management, crowd control, and urban planning were developed and experimented with in the colonial world (Mitchell 1988); consolidation of unitary sovereign rule in the European nation states was informed by experiments with sovereignty in the colonial world (Sen 2002); the disciplining and management of sexuality was prompted by the encounters with what was seen as an excessive sexual culture in the colonial world that would corrupt especially the lower classes in Europe (Stoler 1995, 2002); and notions of the self-restrained Western self, of literature, of "true" religion, and of the necessity of a cultural canon was prompted by the desire to present the West to the colonized people through modern education and missionary work (Asad 1973; Comaroff and Comaroff 1991, 1997; van der Veer 2001; Visvanathan, 1990, 1998). These efforts at rule, control, and generation of knowledge of the colonial worlds, as well as of the new unsettling realities of industrial modernity in the Western world, revolved around differences of culture, race, and civilization.

Colonial sovereignty defined itself in the mercantile and military logic of conquest, exploitation, and "civilization" by competing European states, and their encounters with local ideologies of rule and different notions of sovereignty. Local rulers or empires were sometimes defeated, but as often used as allies against other powers, especially in the seventeenth and eighteenth centuries when European presence in Asia and Africa was very tenuous. Colonial sovereignty was constructed slowly and piecemeal and oscillated between confrontation and alignment, between spectacular representation of European might and culture, and incorporation of local idioms and methods of rule. The establishment of a permanent administration and coherent territorial and economic control with the colonial territories, the fixing of borders and the extension of elements of metropolitan administration arrived rather late in the history of colonialism. By the late nineteenth century, the "Westphalian system" had become the dominant system regulating relations between so-called civilized nations and their colonies, while the uncolonized world of the Ottoman and Chinese empire, the kingdom of Siam, and so on were treated according to more brutal and "illegal" standards (imposition of fiscal control, conquest of mandate areas, confiscation of property, military punishment, etc.). These formally sovereign states were in practice treated like "nonstate" entities—pirates, privateers, mercenary armies—that for centuries had presented an onerous problem to the dominant European powers (Thomson 1989).

As a result of this gradual process, and the controlling principle of colonial legislation and colonial subjects as permanently exempted and different from rule "at home" in Europe, colonial sovereignties became (1) partial and provisional; (2) spectacular and yet ineffective in their exercise of territorial and social control; and (3) marked by excessive and often random violence. Our proposition, similar to that of Hannah Arendt (1951), is that colonial sovereignty remained a naked version of modern sovereign power, the raw "truth" and racist underside of the modern state.

Although the forms of colonial rule and their strategies of legitimization differed a great deal between Asia, Africa, and Latin America, there were nonetheless several commonalities across time and space: the constitutive differences of race, class, and status, the incorporation of small elites into the edifice of power, and the subjection of vast populations of "inferior" or "rude" civilization. Running the risk of making undue generalizations, let us briefly sketch the formations of colonial sovereignty, and its postcolonial progenies along the four broad themes that the contributions to this volume revolve around. First, the formation of public authority through the language and performance of "the law" and the creation of public domains and specified entitlements for various groups. Second, the marking of territories and populations as domains and properties of sovereign authority—nations, communities, and states—enacting their authority through violence and rituals. Thirdly, the inscription of sovereign power upon bodies of subjects, that is, production of a variety of "bare life" as objects of punishment and exercise of authority. Finally, we take a look at more recent reconfigurations of sovereignty and citizenship in the last few decades in response to the increasing transnational movements of labor, "experts," and refugees.

RACE, LAW, AND CITIZENSHIP

Sixteenth-century colonization of Latin America sought to construe sovereignty through a combination of rule of law and spectacular violence. In 1542, when "the New Laws" were introduced, "the time of the conquerors gave way to the time of the lawyers" (Sherman 1983, 175). Sweeping reforms undid the spatial and temporal organization of the pre-Columbian regimes by resettling the Indian population in strictly regulated towns for their administration and Christianization. Fully equipped with Church, council, prosecutor, and jail, the towns were meant to provide the Indians with "natural law, *policía* (good Christian customs) and government" (Viceroy Toledo, quoted in Abercrombie 1998, 247). Regulations dealt explicitly with "public" space as well as the design of Indian houses, which should facilitate surveillance. Indian authorities had certain judicial powers but major offenses and penalties, such as death penalty, amputation of limbs, and cutting off ears, was the realm of the Spanish judges (242–45). Indians and non-Indians were subjected to two separate systems of administration, the Two Republics, the obligation to pay labor services and tribute/tax being one of the major differences. Until the eighteenth century, non-Indians were not allowed to settle in Indian towns, while Indians had little access to cities and urban markets and could not occupy public offices. Legal, cultural, and educational institutions were under royal control, and the reign was highly legalistic, leaving less room for representation, even to creoles, than the contemporary regimes in Spain and Portugal.

Over time, the vastness of the empires, the geographical challenges, the demographic decline and the primacy of effective accumulation of wealth to fund the Crown's projects in Europe forced the administration to rely on existing indigenous elites, to reinvent pre-Colombian institutions for labor extraction, such as the *mita,* and to allow the creoles and settlers more room for private enterprise and encroachment on Indian land and labor. Territorial sovereignty was limited to a network of towns, cities, mines, haciendas, and plantations, and several regions remained unsettled until the late nineteenth century despite the efforts of military expeditions, by official or private armies, militias, or *bandeirantes.* The stifling fear of Indian or black slave rebellions was endemic throughout the colonial period and inspired extraordinary harsh measures of deterrence and punishment.

In the aftermath of the Independence wars, the territorial sovereignty of the new nations were less than self-evident. Towns and provinces were close to establishing a semblance of local sovereignty, and the notion of *patrias chicas*—small fatherlands—has remained meaningful well into the twentieth century. In the postcolonial landscape, the French centralizing tradition had little attraction compared to, for example, the Spanish 1812 Constitution, which provided increased power to provincial elites and some autonomy for municipalities (Mallon 2002; Thompson 2002). As much recent scholarship has shown, nineteenth-century nationalism in Latin America must be thought of in the plural as provincial elites and popular movements appropriated the ideas of nation and citizenship. The paradigmatic figure of postcolonial Latin America was the Caudillo, the military officer who forged alliances between local, popular movements, and factions of provincial or regional elites, engaging in struggles for regional autonomy or central power on the basis of private and official armies, militias, and guerillas (Walker 1999). This constant struggle over territorial control and social authority amongst local officials, local strongmen, and popular movements has remained a defining feature of Peruvian politics for more than a century.

As export economies advanced in the second half of the nineteenth century, state incumbents were enabled to establish permanent, professional armies and invest in infrastructural development which enhanced territorial and military control. The presence of army or police was episodic and everyday security and law enforcement was mainly taken care of by hacienda owners, voluntary police, and local strongmen with whom government representatives had to negotiate their presence and obligations. Throughout the nineteenth century, few governments in Latin America were able to generate statistics on population and economy (Centeno 2002).

The constitutions of the newly independent states in Latin America endorsed principles of popular sovereignty on the paper, but governmental practices were increasingly permeated by scientific racism and the idea that the country should be ruled by "a few good men." The undoing of colonial institutions and the gradual advance of liberal land and labor reforms removed the relative protection Indians used to enjoy. To the white elite they became the main problem of civilization and modernization to be solved by extermination, by improvement and whitening of the race through mixture with European migrant men as in the Argentinean case, or through education and culture of the indigenous population. Thus, rather than becoming citizens of the new nation-states, they were, as Stepputat shows in the case of Peru in this volume, often reduced to subjects of indirect government by local strongmen, landowners and others who took up local government offices. As indianness increasingly became associated with the rural hinterland of modernizing towns, the colonial bifurcation of the population along racial lines and the de facto exclusion of Indians from enjoying citizenship became an enduring feature of modern Peruvian history, even though racial categories vanished from public discourse in the twentieth century.

In postrevolutionary Mexico, the forging of citizenship took place through the rhetoric of *mestizaje* and a number of related state practices, as Ana Maria Alonso shows in her contribution to this volume. The celebration of *mestizaje* and the idea of "the cosmic race" emerged as a challenge to North American imperial sovereignty and a reversal of the negative stereotyping of Mexicans as mongrels. Although *mestizaje* ostensibly celebrates how racial mixing of Indians and whites has produced a new indigenous Mexican, it is still suffused by racial thinking. Its ideologues regarded the process as one of white blood uplifting and invigorating a stagnant and inferior Indian race thereby homogenizing and normalizing the national citizenry. However, distinctions based on color and other bodily marks remain powerful in Mexico.

The British and Dutch colonial empires in Asia were run by private capital for almost two centuries. Territorial control was only secured gradually through war or through alignments with, or subordination of local kings and notables. Questions of adjudication of conflicts, of taxation and of converting military conquest and predatory economies into quasi-permanent settlements regulated by what was regarded as civilized law, was a slow and gradual process. Both in the Dutch Indies and in British India, the arrival of white women and a growing number of poor whites meant that earlier paternalist forms of colonisation gave way to more systematic rule. The protection of the purity of races became more prominent, miscegenation was discouraged, and racial distinctions hardened. "Racist ideology, fear of the Other [. . .] were not simply justifications for continued European rule and white supremacy [. . .] but directives aimed at dissenting European underlings" (Stoler 2002, 25).

British India was undoubtedly a laboratory of colonial rule. Here, a range of legal forms, forms of punishment, control, models of competing sovereignties, and entitlements were tried and developed only to be applied later elsewhere in the colonial world. In his contribution to this volume, Hansen argues that despite its apparently august position, law, and an extensive system of legal regulation remained merely one of several forms of sovereignty in India. Adjudication within communities, reified by colonial rule, as well as local strongmen and other informal authorities were, and still remain, as important and enduring sources of authority in India as that of the modern legal form.

The colonial and postcolonial state has several faces: one was the benevolent face that allowed the proper, respectable and educated citizens to exercise certain rights, to form an embryonic civil society and a public sphere that allowed for a measure of criticism of both the state, its laws and its institutions. After independence, national citizenship was manufactured as the cultivation of a certain attitude and ethos of participation and responsibility among the educated vis-à-vis the life of the nation and the state.

The other face was more authoritarian and more violent, a more naked representation of sovereign power of the state—whether as police brutality against popular movements, or as robust bio-political interventions in the field of health, sanitation, and slum clearances. As in

the case discussed by Chatterjee in this volume, communities and individuals from the slums and the "popular" worlds negotiate and bar-
gain with the state authorities and politicians in order to secure livelihoods, or to prevent evictions. This sphere of direct encounters
between the state and the postcolonial subjects not yet ready to be fully
included in the life of the state and civil society as citizens constitutes
what Chatterjee calls "political society." Chatterjee characterizes this
sphere as governed by forms of community life and rationalities that
are radically different both from those of the Indian state, and those of
civil society.

Whereas colonialism in Asia generally had assumed the existence of
relatively codified, if decayed and decadent, forms of political authority among the colonized, the assumptions concerning Africa were
rather different. The people of the continent were generally seen as
being part of that awesome and cruel nature (Mudimbe 1988). Violence
was intrinsic to this world and the people of Africa were seen either as
subhuman or, at best, as unfinished and childlike human beings who
needed paternalist care and firm rule in order to evolve (Mbembe 2001,
173–89). The scramble for Africa after 1870 resulted in a quick and often
exceedingly brutal form of colonization. It was sovereignty exercised in
an almost elementary form upon populations that *a priori* were reduced
to the state of bare life. Colonization was a pure act of founding violence, a miracle in Bataille's sense, argues Mbembe: "That act consists
not only in ordaining without limits, but also in freeing oneself from reality's limits" (Mbembe 2001, 188). Colonial sovereignty in Africa was
organized around a perpetual violence that like in Asia and Latin
America exceeded earlier forms of sovereign might in terms of its brutality, scale, and systematicity. The use of indiscriminate force created,
in Mbembe's words, "infinite permutations between what was just and
what unjust, between right and non-right . . . (this) conspired to allow
an arbitrariness and intrinsic unconditionality that may be said to be
the distinctive feature of colonial sovereignty" (26).

Colonial administration certainly took place as a permanent, tropical,
exception from common law applicable in Europe. Administrators did
not have to comply with ordinary rules of bureaucratic rationality and
the colonial world was from the outset marked by corruption, random
and unaccountable violence, impunity, and systems of semifeudal patronage. Sovereign power was "circular," not aiming at constructing a
"public interest" or a colonial middle class like in India but merely "absolute submission" (32). The belief in living in a self-created world bred
a peculiar racial narcissism. Here aristocratic lifestyles, a "tropical
gothic," and notions of heroism and adventure of an archaic past could
be enjoyed and enacted by the petit-bourgeois colonial officer (Ander-

son 1990, 150). Brutal inscription of sovereign power upon bodies had also been a feature of precolonial African kingdoms but with colonialism a new idea of control of bodies and populations within precisely measured territories emerged. As Jeffrey Herbst has pointed out, precolonial kingship in Africa was defined as power over people and power radiated from centers of royal power whilst its efficacy faded as one moved away from these centers, into the almost infinite spaces of a sparsely populated continent (Herbst 2000, 40–55). Physical movement away from such centers was easy, and control of people, a scarce resource, was a perennial problem in large parts of Africa. The definition of states and sovereignty in terms of territorial unity evolved in the late colonial period but the linking of people to land, and of ethnicity to territory, only emerged as a powerful ideology of autochthony in the postcolonial states (240–42).

This form of sovereign power that Mbembe fittingly calls *commandement* was based on a deep and almost unbridgeable division of race inscribed in law, in economy and in (the absence of) rights. The result was what Mamdani has called an enduring bifurcation of the colonial state (Mamdani 1996). The urban areas were under direct rule, governed by law and bestowing rights on "civilized men" that is, white settlers and colonizers, whereas the natives living in the cities only enjoyed a limited set of civil rights, such as a right to property, but also often enjoying some opportunities of education and other forms of paternalist "grooming" and improvement. The vast majority of the colonized populations lived under indirect rule, or under the customary law that different colonial regimes over time codified if not invented.[12] This bifurcation was never complete and the proliferating mission stations in the countryside saw themselves as islands of order, aiming at imparting "civilization" by more benevolent means such as new disciplines of the body, obedience to the Christian God, and so on (Comaroff and Comaroff 1991, 1997). Using the example of the structure of kingship in the Zulu kingdom, Mamdani argues that precolonial kingship often was far removed from the despotic and arbitrary powers given to the chiefs under colonialism. In contrast to the centralized and violent assertions of royal power in Europe, the Zulu kings were elected among their peers, and disobedience to the king, even attempts at regicide or desertion of the king and tribe, was at the most punished with a fine of

---

[12] These systems gave rise to the legal pluralism that characterizes most African and other postcolonial societies and have been explored by a large number of studies. Native customary laws were for instance mapped in Zambia by Max Gluckman (Gluckman 1955, 1969) and "traditional" myths of power and kingship explored in a structuralist analysis by Luc de Heusch (Heusch 1982). Among the proliferating studies of legal pluralism, Sally Falk Moore's work still stands out as a classic (Moore 1978).

cattle (44). There were of course major differences between areas and colonial strategies. Territories as Congo, Angola, and Mocambique were scantily but brutally administered, whereas in settler colonies (Kenya, South Africa, and Rhodesia) the promotion of commercial farming and the allocation of "communal" land for African peasants played a key role in the evolution of a more intensive and morally inflected strategies aiming at incorporating and subordinating Africans within the economy and the state (Munro 1998).

In spite of vast differences between territories and continents, there is little doubt that the territorial control of colonial states generally was patchy and highly uneven; their monopoly of violence was at best incomplete—often farmed out to chiefs, community leaders, or other dispensers of indirect rule—but always excessive and spectacular; their biopolitical strategies mainly aimed at urban areas, seen as loci of law and civilization, aiming at producing subjects rather than citizens and always circumscribed by race and imperatives of order and economic frugality.

Postcolonial Anxieties, Death, and the Rituals of State

If the colonial state was built on the assertion of sovereignty without a referent, anticolonial movements strove to produce *national people* that could fill the void, and become the referent that made the power of the state legitimate. Once in charge of the erstwhile colonial administrative apparatus, the new national elites devoted enormous energy and pedagogical ingenuity to the task of converting colonial subjects into national citizens—capable of responsible public conduct, loyal to the state and prepared to accept their responsibility as the backbone of society in return for privileges and recognition from the state. To this day, the production of citizenship—understood as display of patriotic loyalty and of "civic conduct" in the public domain rather than formal or effective political rights—takes place as much in schools as in the streets, or at the ballot box, in societies like Mexico, India, Nigeria or Turkey. In schools, children are taught patriotism as a supreme value, and citizenship is not necessarily linked to freedom or rights.[13] Drawing on anticolonial ideology, the sovereignty of postcolonial nations have been rooted in the supposed autochthony of colonized people in "their" territories. The ostracization and killing of nonautochthonous "aliens"

[13] This marks another vast field of research but, to mention a few works on state formation and education, see for Mexico Morales-Gomez (1990) and Vaughan (1997); for Peru, Wilson (2001); for India, see V. Benei (2000) and N. Kumar (2001); for Turkey, see Navaro-Yashin (2002, 188–204).

have haunted postcolonial nations from Indonesia to India and East Africa. In their contribution to this volume, Jean and John Comaroff show that powerful notions of autochthony and naturalized ideas of origins have surfaced in an anxious postapartheid South Africa. Panics regarding "invasions of alien plants" into the country are metonymically related to, and fueled by, arrival of large numbers of migrants from the rest of Africa, derogatorily known as *makwerekwere*.

The traces of the colonial state, or the culture of colonialism, have not withered away, however. Sovereignty in the postcolonial world has in many ways remained provisional and partial, despotic and excessively violent. As Jackson (1990) has pointed out in his work on "quasi-states," the difference between legal and effective sovereignty was huge in the newly independent states. In many, territorial control has been heavily militarized often because of conflicts with neighboring states—as in South Asia, East Asia, and the Middle East—or in the name of national security when armed groups have challenged state sovereignty—as in many countries in Latin America. Often the internal cohesion and the monopoly of violence has remained as fictional and incoherent as during colonial rule. In parts of Africa, the territorial sovereignty of the postcolonial states has been eroded by to such an extent that it only exists in a formal sense, devoid of any monopoly of violence and replaced by zones of unsettled sovereignties and loyalties. These sovereignties are claimed and exercised by rebel armies, ethnic communities promoting powerful notions of autochthony, transnational Christian and Muslim organizations, vigilante groups, and economic networks, multinationals, and mining concessions governing large areas and numbers of people by what Mbembe calls "private indirect government" often including private security and police forces (Mbembe 2000, 2001, 66–101).

Interpreting the current "dispersion of state power and fragmentation of society" across Africa in Bataille's terms, Mbembe argues in this volume that sovereignty increasingly is performed through excessive expenditure of money, foreign goods, human life, and so on. This pattern has in turn given rise to a cultural repertoire of hypermasculine militarism that from Sierra Leone to Congo has literalized the notion of the political as a state of "generalized war."

The state still exists but merely as one of several possible dispensers of violence and coercion, and one of several instruments of taxation and exploitation. The often debated failure of post colonial states to develop into functioning bureaucracies that can underpin democratic rule has often been reduced to a relative absence of civil society and the preponderance of patrimonial structures and charismatic politics that have their roots in "traditional" African forms of power and prestige. But as pointed out by several scholars, the transference of already fictional-ized/utopian notions of civil society from European society to Africa fails to understand how the history of sovereignty on the continent has left it deeply fragmented and bereft of meaningful notions of shared publics, and impartial civilities.[14] For all its fragmentation, impotence, and the *de facto* regime of impunity it often protects, the state remains both a powerful and lethal instrument in the hands of repressive and dominant elites, as it can be a locus of utopian hopes for the future as in Uganda or South Africa, or a symbol of the armed ethnic and "racial-ized" community as in Rwanda or Zimbabwe.[15]

Although many states in Asia appear more in control of territory and economy, the authority of the state is neither uncontested nor compelling. Equally powerful forms of *commandement* construct eth-nic, national, or religious communities as sovereign entities that de-mand space, recognition, and annihilation of its perceived enemies in what is seen as a life and death struggle for the survival of the com-munity or the nation. Examples of such disjunctions between the sov-ereignty of the state and the sovereignty of the nation-community abound. They all revolve around the right to kill and punish and de-humanize the ethnic other with impunity in the name of a higher cause: the ongoing civil war in Sri Lanka, the recurrent anti-Muslim pogroms in India in the name of "protection" of the Hindu majority, the Islamic radicals who fight for the "liberation" of Kashmir, or the Is-lamists in Indonesia, Pakistan, or Malaysia who put loyalty to the Ummah and Islamic injunctions of the Sharia above that of the nation-state and its legal edifice.

One of the defining characteristics of "communal riots" and mas-sacres unfolding from Indonesia, over India to sub-Saharan Africa is that state agencies like their colonial predecessors, construct them as cataclysmic "events without actors." They are seen as spontaneous out-bursts of anger and irrationality of the masses. Only in very rare cases are rioters arrested and prosecuted as these events in practice are treated as collective imbalances in society, often as legitimate forms of revenge and inevitable political performances, not criminal offences, or challenges to the formal sovereignty of the law. Needless to say, this has rendered an enormous space for impunity for ethnic and religious mil-

[14] See J. Comaroff and J. Comaroff (1999a); Karlstrom (1999); Bayart (1986). For a clas-sical view of patrimonialism in Africa, see Clapham (1982) and Bayart (1993), for a more sophisticated view that stresses cultural repertoires of action and authority.

[15] For Rwanda, see, for example, Mamdani 2000; for Burundi, see Lemarchand (1996); and, for Zulu nationalist politics, see Mare (1992). For a highly interesting interpretation through the prism of sovereignty of the spectacular violence and anticolonial "racialisation" that char-acterizes Zimbabwe's current "suicidal governance" in Zimbabwe, see Worby (2003).

itants and *de facto* sovereignty of ethnic and religious communities within the state across Asia and Africa.

The presence of the state in Latin America is simultaneously highly conspicuous and clandestine, as Taussig argues. The presence of the notion of the state, of a ubiquitous and frightening power is linked to the way "violence and reason blend—of ghosts and images, and, above all, of formless, nauseating, intangibility. [. . .] the invisibility of security forces and strategic confusion as to numbers and force of bodies of armed men acting in the name of the state" (Taussig 1997, 121–22). Although the presence of the state in Latin America is manifested in competitive public spectacles and populist performances, perfected among others by Fujimori in Peru, the continent has a longstanding tradition of clandestine and deadly violence. Thousands disappearing in the night, wars on "social evils" from crime and drugs to migrants and people fleeing from rural violence, and so on are recurring elements in Latin American history. Whether the invisible and death squads operating in the dark of the night, actually work on behalf of state institutions, or against their will, is difficult to know with certainty. But given a long history of state-sponsored terror, ordinary people do not hesitate to name the state as being the actor behind such acts. Another "truth" of sovereignty—that its fragility that makes it dependent on being performed and reiterated through resolute violence in order to show its "true marks" as Bodin said—has left its mark on populations throughout the postcolonial world.

In this situation of fragile, eroding, and contested sovereignty, and faced with mounting expectations of high profile presence and benevolence, governments often stage high-profile spectacles to make themselves visible. The theater of conspicuous performance of power over life in the postcolony described by Mbembe for Cameroon (Mbembe 1992); the performance of the authoritarian possibilities of the state in India in the 1970s (Tarlo 2000); or the conspicuous display of state power and its roots in an autochthonous past by the Nigerian state through enactment of a modern version of the colonial durbar (Apter 1999a), or its obverse, the proliferation of scams and tricksters in the transnationalized Nigerian economy (Apter 1999b), have their roots in the peculiar colonial sovereignty.

The "weakness" of everyday stateness is often countered by attempts to make state power highly visible. In this endeavor, issues of security, crime, and punishment occupy a privileged arena for performance of sovereign power. The peculiar quasi-state of northern Cyprus, analyzed by Navaro-Yashin in this volume, exists because of a continuing Turkish military presence on the island. The regime seeks nonetheless to reiterate its own legitimacy through incessant parades, rhetoric and spectacular and excessive signs of its own existence—gestures that largely are ignored by the population. Yet, the anchoring of the unrecognized "republic" on a clearly demarcated territory and its exercise of control through a clandestine network of men—known for their excessive brutality and determination—rooted in the underground movement of the 1960s, has until now managed to reproduce an effective, if deeply traumatic, Turkish-Cypriot identity.

BODY, LOCALITY, AND INFORMAL SOVEREIGNTY

Colonial biopolitics shared many rationalities and modes of intervention with similar policies in Europe but the methods of disciplining, of persuasion and negotiation did not aim at creating responsible and self-governing individuals as Cruikshank points out in the context of the early twentieth-century United States (Cruikshank 1999). By contrast, colonial biopolitics took the form of generalized indirect rule and generally aimed at governing groups and communities at a distance. The worlds of the colonial subjects remained somewhat opaque and impenetrable and were always approached through what was assumed to be local and "natural leaders" of communities and localities. Motivated by important economic interests and the attempt to continue racial domination, colonial forms of biopolitics received their most comprehensive form in South Africa. As Steffen Jensen demonstrates in his exploration of a township in Cape Town in this volume, multiple government reports have in the course of the twentieth century diagnosed "colored" people as inherently criminal and thus in need of both paternalist care and firm regulation. In spite of this massive governmental regulation, actual power over life and death in the colored townships lies with local gangsters rather than a dreaded police force.

The colonial bifurcation of populations into educated, respectable quasi-citizens entrusted with governmental and civic responsibilities and the uneducated, innocent masses that could be turned into dangerous passion-driven mobs in need of strict policing, also persisted in many postcolonial states. The "multitude" still needed to be groomed, educated, policed and governed with a firm hand in order to evolve into a proper "people-nation." The relationships between the state and the popular world have often been violent. This "political society" is the locus public authority incarnated in the ubiquitous "big men"—the tough, self-made criminal-strongman-fixer-and politician who increasingly dominate the political life in slums and townships in South Asia, and many parts of Africa and South East Asia. These men command zones of local sovereign power not entirely "penetrated" or governed

Sassen notes, territories are being "denationalized," not by compulsion but by being literally farmed out to global capital as "special economic zones" of free trade and investment. This implies that states are willing to construct "graduated sovereignty" over territory, economy, and also labor, as Ong notes in the context of South East Asian states as Malaysia or Indonesia (Ong 1999, 214–39). But it also implies an expansion and flexibilization of the meaning of citizenship in several respects. First of all, a new type of citizenship, that of "economic citizenship," is emerging. It does not belong to citizens, Sassen argues, but to ". . . firms and markets, particularly the global financial markets, and it is located not in individuals, not in citizens, but in global economic actors" (Sassen 1996, 38). These global players can demand concessions and protection from states, tax holidays, disciplined labor, macro-economic stability, and so on, in return for investment, jobs, and hard currency. The highly skilled labor, consultants, and professionals who accompany, work for, and facilitate the work of such large "corporate citizens" have acquired unprecedented options in terms of mobility and flexibility of access to various nation-states—a process Ong traces in the context of the Chinese diaspora (Ong 1999, 110–58). In this world of fast information flows, effective lobbying, and the ability to generate capital across the globe, the nation-state appears weak, eroded, and increasingly porous.

States remain, however, crucial players in the transnational movement of people, labor, ideas, and loyalties. The expanding transnational spaces that now stretch across oceans and continents and also have become important targets for governmental intervention and attempts to retain or renew loyalty to the "old" country. In her contribution to this volume, Ong shows that alongside highly educated Chinese transpacific, multi-sited families, there is a large and impoverished and marginalized group of Chinese migrants seeking entry into North America. Such heterogenous groups have widely different relationship with the Chinese state and are treated very differently by North American authorities.

The notion of "diaspora," of loss of homeland and original culture, now proliferates among transnational populations. Upward mobile and politically conservative professionals and business people promote diasporic sentiments and sentimental attachments to the homeland. Proliferating "diasporas" crystallize in diverse transnational entrepreneurial networks, and cultural, religious, and political organizations and often receive handsome backing from governments in the nation-states of their origin. There are successful attempts not only to retain loyalty and secure remittances from transnationalized citizens but also to assert the sovereignty of the nation-state beyond its territorial boundaries. One obvious example is how the secular Turkish state for decades discreetly has supported the dispatching of religious teachers in order to retain and renew the loyalty of the large populations of *gastarbeitern* all over Europe. The Turkish government has discouraged Turks from taking up citizenship in their new countries of residence and has insisted on the obligation of young men who have grown up in Hamburg, Geneva, or Oslo to serve their time as conscripts in the Turkish military. Van der Veer's analysis in this volume of the recruitment of IT engineers in India to work in the United States provides another example of the crucial and continuing role of both state regulation and national imaginaries. Van der Veer shows that this process of "body shopping" goes hand in hand with the consolidation of conservative Hindu notions of Indian culture and the proliferation of support for militant Hindu nationalism among these affluent and successful expatriates.

The government of India now offers so-called People of Indian Origin cards, or dual citizenship to people of Indian origin as far as four generations back. These cards provide a type of quasi citizenship in India and constitute only a minor part of a larger effort by the right-wing Indian government to convert diverse, often wealthy populations of Indian origin into a permanently attached "expatriate nation," or a "global Indian family" (Hansen 2002). This practice has produced intransigent problems of racial or cultural determination of indianness and has in practice moved the definition of Indian citizenship away from the formal principle of *jus soli* toward a racially tinged *jus sanguinis* principle. In general, languages of blood have reemerged, which may be taken as a symbol of the resurgence of "long distance nationalisms" (Anderson 1994). Although diasporic dynamics and transnational nation-state formation were largely invisible in the post–World War II period, transmigrants were seen as important participants in nation-state formation in the late nineteenth century, in the countries they left, as well as where they arrived. Today, in a very different configuration of states, capital, ideology, and transnational movement, racialized national definitions of eligibility legitimate the actions of states of origin, but also of the attempts of host-governments to control human mobility (Glick-Schiller 1999).

The world of mobile and transnational citizens of the empire's global network capital is vastly different, and separated, from, the world of the ordinary labor migrant, the international refugee, or the illegal alien living in the large cities across the world. Toward these groups of people who perform essential low wage service-functions in the ever more informalized global economy, nation states appear as "hard" and impenetrable as ever. Often loathed among the more sedentary populations, as well as among highly paid mobile professionals, these groups are blamed for rising social costs and social unrest in Europe, for unemployment and destabilization of the nation in Southern Africa and in

South Asia, and so on. International migrants are subjected to the harshest measures available to contemporary nation-states.

In Western Europe, illegal migrants or asylum seekers are kept confined in camps and are the objects of much public interest. "Diasporic" loyalties, religious practices, and links to the homeland of the ordinary migrant are treated as a problem and a manifestation of disloyalty to their new country of residence. Oivind Fuglerud's contribution to this volume explores how the Norwegian authorities inscribe a hegemonic set of "cultural values" upon its territory and population as it seeks to control, know, and domesticate non-European refugees. Fuglerud demonstrates that such cultural and historical rhetoric is informed by the exercise of the sovereign right to decide on exclusions from the community. As Michael Walzer has argued, admission and exclusion "suggest the deepest meaning of self-determination" (1983, 62). Although the camp may be the implied rationality of much governance, or the attempts to govern, most encounters between migrants and the communities they live among take place beyond the control of the state, and beyond ordered camps or refugee centers.

Similar problems face the much larger populations of migrants and illegal aliens living in the large cities across the postcolonial world, although the capacity and will of governments to regulate and occasionally deport these groups vary a great deal. In countries in East Asia, in Malaysia, and in Saudi Arabia, the import, and frequent deportation of labor from neighboring countries take place with much determination and brutality. Countries such as India, Indonesia, South Africa, or Mexico are both unable and unwilling to exercise strict governmental control over the vast flow of bodies across their borders, and in and out of their cities. Instead, migrants are at the mercy of local forms of sovereignty and do frequently become the object of hateful pogroms and harassment by organizations claiming to protect the interests and culture of autochthonous citizens of the respective states. The migrant and the illegal alien is often linked to the anonymous and opaque dangers of the city and its underworld(s). Groups of "diasporic" young men are increasingly perceived as security threats in the heart of Western metropolises.

Migrants have, in other words, emerged as the "bare life" of our times—the in-between forms of life, uncoded substances without fixed belongings, unprotected by "their" states (unlike the skilled workers in the global knowledge economy), that is, a form of human life upon which the sovereignty of states, of ethnic/religious communities and local strongmen can be performed and "natured," as the Comaroffs put it.

These areas of exceptions are, in more than one sense, manifested by the refugee camps administered by the U.N. system that dot conflict-ridden parts of the non-Western world. Turner's contribution to this volume explores the complex and overlapping forms of sovereignty at work in a camp for Hutu refugees from Burundi. He shows that the "benevolent" and highly professional authoritarianism of the U.N. seeks to reduce the refugee to "pure victims"—an entire population in suspension—but also that this project constantly is pierced and undermined by the return of other, and older forms of sovereign power, such as exile political formations and local strongmen.

Modern states seek not only to produce citizens who are responsible and amenable to rational self-governance. They also seek to make these citizens bearers of the sovereignty of the nation and the state and thus, in a sense, produce their own ideal cause: the eighteenth-century idea, that the sovereignty of the state is the sum of, and expression of, the aggregate of each individual citizen. Thus, beneath the governance through reason and norms, lies the imperative of obedience to the rules, and further yet, the performance of violence and the armed protection of the community—Home Guards, civil patrols, the armed forces, and so on. The assertion in Western states after September 11 of the "hard kernel" of sovereignty is, among many other things, manifested in substantial expansions of these forms of domestic defense forces, or the huge Homeland Security program in the United States, many of which are based on voluntary commitments from citizens. These institutions—the armed heart of the sovereign nations—are both the instrument of national integration (as in the United States and Israel) and simultaneously closed to anyone considered culturally or religiously "alien."

The production of sovereignty through the nation and the state are, in other words, often exclusive projects that inadvertently presuppose and produce large numbers of poor, marginalized, or ethnic others as outsiders, people who are not yet ready to become citizens or included in the true political-cultural community. The state finds itself in constant competition with other centers of sovereignty that dispense violence as well as justice with impunity—criminal gangs, political movements or quasi-autonomous police forces that each try to assert their claims to sovereignty. In such situations, the state is not the natural and self-evident center and origin of sovereignty, but one among several sovereign bodies that tries to assert itself upon the bodies of asylum seekers, "terrorists," or mere criminals.

RACE, LAW, AND CITIZENSHIP

Territorializing the Nation and "Integrating the Indian": "Mestizaje" in Mexican Official Discourses and Public Culture

Ana María Alonso

Introduction

Robert Young maintains that theories of society, such as Spencer's Social Darwinism, are built on notions of hybridity that are "elaborated . . . about the issue of sexual interaction between the races." According to Young, "The races and their intermixture circulate around an ambivalent axis of desire and aversion: a structure of attraction, where people and cultures intermix . . . and a structure of repulsion, where the different elements remain distinct. . . . The idea of race . . . shows itself to be profoundly dialectical: it only works when defined against potential intermixture which also threatens to undo its calculations" (Young 1995, 19). What I argue here is that the converse also can be true: the idea of intermixture can be defined against a notion of potential purity that also threatens to undo it, to reduce it to dirt and degeneracy. As a

This chapter draws on fieldwork I did in Namiquipa, Chihuahua, in collaboration with Daniel Nugent in the 1980s, as well as fieldwork I did in Mexico City during the summer of 2001, funded by a Riecker Fellowship from the Department of Anthropology, University of Arizona. Different earlier versions of this chapter were presented at the 1999 and 2000 American Anthropological Association Meetings, and the 2000 Latin American Association Meetings. I also presented various earlier versions at the workshop on "Race and the Politics of Mestizaje," University of Texas-Austin (1999), at the conference on "People on the Move and the Territoriality of Nations," Oslo, Norway (2000), to the interdisciplinary discussion group on "Conflicts at the Limits of Mexican Cultural and Political Centralism" and the Duke-University of North Carolina Program in Latin American Studies (2001) and to the Department of Anthropology, University of Texas-Austin (2001). I thank Robin De Lugan, Charles Hale, Oivind Fuglerud and the Department of Social Anthropology at the University of Oslo, Ryan Long, and James Brow for these invitations to present the paper as well as the participants and audience members whose questions and insights informed the final version. I also thank Finn Stepputat for his insightful comments. David Killick very helpfully answered my questions about metallurgical processes and Gamio's metaphors. Patience MacIntyre provided me with a copy of Ramirez Vásquez (1968).

defense against this threat, the heterogeneity of intermixture can become reconfigured in the singular terms of purity: the hybrid becomes a thing-in-itself, the "mestizo," a new "cosmic race." My argument questions the widespread notion that hybridity is "always already" emancipatory. Instead, it indicates that the place of "intermixture" in the imagining of collective identity needs to be situated historically and ethnographically and examined not only with reference to counter-hegemonic formations but also in relation to statist projects of popular sovereignty and the creation of a disciplined citizenry.

I ground my theoretical argument in an examination of discourses of "racial and cultural mixing" ("mestizaje") in twentieth-century, post-revolutionary Mexican nationalism as well as some of the practices through which the state has orchestrated performances of mestizaje in everyday life. I focus on the early works of Manuel Gamio and José Vasconcelos, because these intellectuals were "founders of discursivity" who produced "the possibilities and the rules for the formation of other texts" (Foucault in Rabinow 1984, 114) key to the articulation of new postrevolutionary forms of governmentality. I go on to interrogate the extent to which state discourses and practices of mestizo nationalism actually have formed the self-representations of Mexican people and point to how new mobilizations from below as well as transnational projects from above are reshaping Mexico's political imaginary.

"Mestizo" and "Mestizaje"

Until recently, much scholarship on Latin America has used "mestizaje," commonly glossed as a process of "racial and cultural mixing," to refer to a real-life process rather than to a construct in political imaginaries of collective "peoplehood." Yet, as Marisol de la Cadena argues, mestizos "are not *simple, empirical hybrids,* a plain result of biological or cultural 'mixture' of two [formerly discreet] entities. Rather they evoke a complex conceptual hybridity inscribed in the notion of 'mestizo' itself" (de la Cadena 2002, 4). As a notion that has been central in Latin American political imaginaries, mestizaje has always had a polysemic character (Hale 1996, 2), as it has been a product of (unequal) dialogues whose meanings have depended on the changing relations of political forces in social fields of domination, exploitation, and subjectification.

"Mestizo" was a status category in the colonial New Spain ethnoracial hierarchy, applied to those who traced descent from both Indians and Spaniards—although in practice its meaning varied. This ethnoracial hierarchy lost its legal basis after Independence in 1821. During the nineteenth century, Latin American elites were greatly influenced by

Comptean positivism, Spencerian Social Darwinism—with its explicit condemnation of human hybrids—and pseudoscientific theories of race (Helg 1990, 37). Comparison between their own countries and the United States led some Latin American elites to attribute North American cultural, political, and economic development to Anglo-Saxon "racial purity" and to policies marginalizing Indians and blacks from the nation (38). Notions of the nation that positively valued the Indian past were espoused by a few nineteenth-century Liberal intellectuals (Portal Ariosa and Ramirez 1995, 51–60; Widdifield 1996, 10–13). Yet, the overall thrust of the Liberal project of nation-state formation was the erasure of local ethnicities (Gutiérrez 1999, 173) and the destruction of their basis in communal property and local political institutions. During the presidency of Porfirio Díaz (1876–1911), the presumed superiority of the European shaped state efforts to whiten the population through immigration and to incorporate the Indian into the nation through a model of development that resulted in the agrarian dispossession of rural communities, many of them indigenous (Knight 1990, 79).

The sovereignty of the Porfirian state in Mexico and the old alliance among state functionaries, white, European-oriented landed elites, and foreign capital was destroyed by ten years of revolutionary warfare (1910–1920). Mexican society was left sharply divided along lines of ethnoracial, regional, and class identity, fragmented by the multiple sovereignties of local communities and regional strongmen who could mobilize armed followings, and also vulnerable to North American imperial ambitions. The winning revolutionary faction was faced with a crisis of sovereignty on multiple levels.

First, the sovereignty of the postrevolutionary state was threatened by U.S. imperial ambitions, justified by notions of Mexico as a nation of "mongrels," of a "mixed" and hence "degenerate" race, purportedly incapable of governing itself. The mythohistory of mestizaje emerged as a challenge to North American imperial sovereignty, one that envisioned a Mexico that would play a sovereign role in world history and be something other than the backyard of the United States.

Second, the Revolution had made the disjunction between state and people only too clear. Lacking a monopoly of force, the new state tried to claim a monopoly of the authority to create social order out of revolutionary chaos and violence. This new order was to have a popular basis; state sovereignty was to be based on "the will of the *pueblo* (community)." Numerous *patrias chicas* had to be unified into one nation, creating a homogenous citizenry out of a divided multitude, and locating the sovereignty of the state in its ability to transcend social divisions and represent the indivisible will of this imagined community, now figured as mestizo. Official discourses promoted "racial and cultural intermixture" as the only way to create homogeneity out of heterogeneity, unity out of fragmentation, a strong nation that could withstand the external menace of North American imperialism and the internal menace of its own failures to overcome the injustices of its colonial past. Mexico would become "a normal sovereign state with normal sovereign citizens" (Hansen and Stepputat, introduction to this volume).

MESTIZAJE IN THE OFFICIAL DISCOURSES OF THE POSTREVOLUTIONARY MEXICAN STATE

One of the key figures in the development of mestizo nationalism was the Father of modern Mexican anthropology, Manuel Gamio (1883–1960), who obtained his Ph.D. from Columbia University under the supervision of Franz Boas. Gamio succeeded in carving out a central role for anthropology in the project of institutionalizing the Revolution. Named Director of Anthropology by Carranza's revolutionary government in 1916, he continued in this post until 1924, when he was appointed Subsecretary of Public Education by President Calles. President Cardenas named him the first Director of the Interamerican Indigenist Institute in 1942, a post he held until his death in 1960 (Nahmad and Weaver 1990, 294–316; Portal Ariosa and Ramírez 1995, 80).

Gamio's *Forjando Patria* ("Forging the Nation"), published in 1916, is the founding work of modern Mexican anthropology (Portal Ariosa and Ramírez 1995, 80) and one of the building blocks of mestizo nationalism. The text crosses genres: it is simultaneously mythology, history, scientific ethnology, and political commentary. The goal of the work is to contribute to forging a new nation—child of the Revolution of 1910—in relation to an external other—the imperialist United States—and to internal others—the Euro-American–oriented, white, prerevolutionary elite as well as the Indians who Gamio considered the shock troops of the Revolution but not its leaders. For Gamio, both whites and Indians were incapable of transcending the conquest, the originary act of foundational violence, and its colonial heritage. A new protagonist was needed for the "second Independence" (Gamio 1916, 121) of Mexico: the revolutionary mestizo subject would pave the way for a truly postcolonial national society.

The book proclaims itself to be a collective text because it is "inspired" by the author's "observation of the different social classes" (vii) and because its pages are made of "the flesh and soul of the people" (viii).[1] But, because "the people" had a high rate of illiteracy, the an-

---

[1] This and all other translations are mine.

thropologist is speaking for and not to them. The text's intended audience is probably those whom Gamio considered to be the leaders and victors of the Revolution (and with whom he was allied politically): not the Indians from the South but the members of the so-called mixed blood middle class from the North in whom "the European element" predominated (169). Gamio considered the latter class to be "the eternal rebel, the traditional enemy of the pure blood or foreign class, the author and director of uprisings and revolutions who has best understood the just laments of the Indian" (172). Indians, according to Gamio, had not reached a sufficiently advanced stage of cultural evolution to lead themselves out of slavery: their savior had to be the "intermediate" or "mestizo" race, the only possible bearer of a national culture (172).

The collection of essays is framed by an exhortatory mythohistory of "mestizaje."[2] The central metaphor, "forging the nation," links meanings drawn from the domains of metallurgy, sexuality and gestation, and landscape. "In the great forge of America, on the giant anvil of the Andes, the bronze and iron of virile races have been beaten out across the centuries" (3). In this opening moment of the mythohistory, the fusion of the bronze (or Indian) and iron (or Latin) races has not yet been accomplished. The second moment of the mythohistory narrates the making of the bronze race by Atahualpa and Moctezuma, but this process was interrupted by the conquest, and could not be "consummated." The failure of the Spanish colonists to forge the nation is told in the third moment: they "only used the steel of the Latin race, laying aside on the slag heap of society the hard indigenous bronze" (4). Subsequently, in a fourth moment, "Olympic men," the heroes of the Latin American independence movements, "grasped the epic and sonorous hammer and donned the glorious leather apron. . . . They were going to climb the mountain, to strike the divine anvil, to forge with blood and gunpowder, with muscles and intellect, . . . a pilgrim statue made from all the metals, all the races of America" (4). But the heroes died, and those who followed tried in vain to "sculpt the statues of the *patrias* with racial elements of Latin origin only" or else exploited the Indians, using them solely to "construct a humble bronze like pedestal." What had to happen happened: the "fragile" statue fell repeatedly, while the pedestal grew.

The exhortatory force of the mythohistory lies in its allegorical structure: the transformations of the narrative are an allegory of the historical process, of the key moments in the painful, prolonged, and frustrated birth of the nation. It is the mission of Mexico's new revolu-

---

[2] Gamio uses *sangre mezclada* [mixed blood] or *raza intermedia* [intermediate race] more often than mestizo, because of the latter term's negative connotations at the time he was writing.

tionary rulers to "grasp the hammer and gird the straps of the black-smith's leather apron so as to make surge from the miraculous anvil the new patria made of the alloy of iron and bronze" (1916, 6). The mytho-history concludes with an imperative that serves as a rallying cry: "There is the iron. . . . There is the bronze. . . . Forge brothers!" (6).

By identifying elements of the forge with the landscape, Gamio terri-torializes the modern nation. The metallurgical metaphor allows him to construe the birth of the nation as a progressive teleological process in which technology plays a privileged role. Gamio knew that the age of iron follows the age of bronze. He argues throughout the book that the new mestizo culture had to link the art of the Indian with the science and technology of the European in order for the nation to evolve.

Gamio's is a hybrid text that fuses the Greek myth of Hephaestus, the blacksmith of the Gods, who turned nature into culture by harnessing the creative fire of the forge, with Mexican history. In Greek mythology (and indeed in the myths and rituals of many other societies), the gen-erative powers of the blacksmith are obtained through a symbolic asso-ciation with (indeed, an appropriation of) the fertility of women. The blacksmith Hephaestus forged Pandora, the first woman. The reference here, I argue, is also to *Liberty Enlightening the World*, a monumental statue of a robed woman holding a torch, with a copper skin over an iron frame, given to the people of the United States by the people of France in 1884. The statue of the Mexican nation, however, is not the white Mother of Exiles but the mixed-blood mother of the new national subject. Gamio characterizes the mestiza as neither "servile" nor a "feminist" but, instead, as an "intermediate type" who embodies the "feminine" ideal (1916, 212); she "lives instinctively convinced . . . of her sacred and transcendent role in the generation and continuation of life" (227). Women's agency in the new society, according to Gamio, should lie in this sort of civic maternity and in mediating the polarities and reconciling the differences that had impeded the development of a unified, homogeneous nation (226). Indeed, Gamio's mestizophillia had an impact on the eugenics movement that emerged in postrevolu-tionary Mexico; inspired by neo-Lamarckianism, the theory that ac-quired characteristics could be inherited, this movement developed new, gendered forms of biopower on behalf of the postrevolutionary state, making women's generativity and child-rearing practices the ob-ject of increasing monitoring, in the name of the "health" of the nation (Stern 2002).

Despite his recognition of Mexico's heterogeneity, Gamio takes as his model European-derived understandings of the nation, which presume that a national public culture must be homogeneous. Moreover cultural homogeneity is held to presuppose racial homogeneity. The mestizo represents the transformation of heterogeneity into homogeneity, the bridge between the past and the future, the common origin point for the nation. The Indian element in the mestizo grounds the nation's claim to territory, provides a continuity of blood, and roots the nation's history in that of ancient, precolonial civilizations, whose art and mythology are expressions of the "national soul." By contrast, the European element guarantees the nation's future as it is associated with Enlightenment and science. Drawing a parallel to Indian nationalism as discussed in Chatterjee (1993), I hypothesize that the centrality of the indigenous element and, especially, its association with the aesthetic, mythological, and folkloric in Mexican and Latin American national imaginaries is linked to an identification of the interiority and timelessness of the nation, its "soul," with the "Indian."

If Gamio's text begins with myth, it ends with the science that he believes will redeem the Indian: anthropology. In this sense, Gamio's is a "mestizo" text. Yet, Gamio's work represents only the indigenist pole of the mestizophilliac project. The Hispanicist pole is articulated by the Oaxacan José Vasconcelos's (1882–1959) well-known work *The Cosmic Race*, first published in 1925. Vasconcelos was a philosopher, revolutionary intellectual, and political activist. He played a key role as secretary of education (1921–24), encouraging the development of public art for the masses, particularly in the form of the now famous murals of Rivera, Orozco, and Siqueiros; taking the Revolution to "every little village" by extending public schooling; and coining the motto of the National University, "The Spirit shall speak through my race" (Knight 1990, 102n1; Miller 1999, 46–50). Endowed with a relatively generous budget, the Secretariat of Public Education was Vasconcelos's stepping-stone for "establishing a comprehensive bureaucratic apparatus for the state administration of culture" (Miller 1999, 47). As secretary of education, Vasconcelos developed the institution of the so-called Cultural Mission: conceived through an explicit analogy to the Colonial Catholic mission and its civilizing project, this secular equivalent sent hundreds to preach the gospel of progress through Hispanicization to rural Indians. The Cultural Mission was a crucial component of the massive literacy and public hygiene campaign he initiated under the slogan "Alphabet, Bread, and Soap." Subsequently, in the 1940s, Vasconcelos became editor of the Fascist journal *Timón*. His writings were profoundly influential not only in Mexico but also elsewhere in Latin America. Contemporary Mexican elementary school history texts praise Vasconcelos's role in the "cultural revolution that led to a rebirth of the spirit and of faith in nationalist and universal values. The educational project of those years has not lost its force: today it serves as an inspiration for the educators and artists of Mexico and of the world."[3] His contributions were officially recognized during the year 2000, a year of national homage to his memory.

Most commentators mention in passing that Vasconcelos spent time as a child on the border in Piedras Negras, Coahuila, and Eagle Pass, Texas, without exploring the impact of this experience, and in particular, of Anglo racism, on his subsequent work. If, from an Anglo perspective, racist ideas about Mexicans served to legitimate the U.S.-Mexican War of 1848, in which Mexico lost half its territory, these ideas only grew more virulent during the course of the second half of the nineteenth century, especially along the U.S.-Mexico border. Anglo racial oppression of Mexicans "ran deepest where recurring international incidents spawned extreme nationalism and nativism among European Americans (Martinez 2001, 53). One study of Anglo stereotypes of Mexicans in nineteenth-century Texas points out that Mexicans were depicted as "inferior, . . . docile, ignorant, decadent, mediocre, indolent, immoral, hedonistic, cruel, vindictive, and bloodthirsty" (56). Significantly, Martinez links such pejorative stereotypes to the imperialist ideology of Manifest Destiny, which "impelled Americans to pursue territorial conquests aggressively and to seek the spread of 'civilization' among 'barbarians' and 'savages' (56). Manifest Destiny was predicated on the superiority of Anglo-Saxon stock over non-Nordic races and scientists declared that this stock had to be protected from the "degeneracy" and "mongrelization" that contact with Mexicans would bring (57). Scientists were fixated on racial mixing and saw the nonwhite and, specifically, Mexican woman as a threat to Anglo-Saxon purity, as "the wanton seductress who would cause the downfall of the nation" (Russell y Rodriguez 1999). They pointed to Mexicans themselves as exemplars of the perils of miscegenation, representing them as "a mixed-race people, who, although partly white, were doomed to racial degeneration and degradation" (Ibid.); theories of hybridity current at the time posited that "Mexicans could not be regarded as a racially stable population. Their mixedness would always anticipate a return to a primary, whole race, [in this case, the Indian] or to extermination" (Ibid.).

As a ten-year-old Mexican attending school in Eagle Pass, Texas, circa 1892, Vasconcelos experienced Anglo racism toward Mexicans on a daily basis. In his autobiography, *Ulises Criollo,* he paints a picture of the classroom as the site of a perpetual battle between Anglos and Mexicans: when "it was affirmed in class that one hundred Yankees could

[3] *Historia de México, Segunda Parte* (Mexico: SEP 1994), 82; my translation.

chase off one thousand Mexicans, I would rise and say 'That isn't true.' I would get even more angry when someone would assert, 'Mexicans are a semicivilized people.' . . . I would rise and say, 'We had a printing press before you did'" (in Martínez 2001, 105). Outside of class this battle was fought through blows, and Vasconcelos graphically describes his bloody struggle with a "sanguinary, aggressive, blond gringo" who took a "dislike" to him (105). Such childhood experiences, combined with an adult understanding of the United States as an imperialist power that threatened Mexico, shaped Vasconcelos's utopic vision of Mexico's future and of its place in world history, articulated in his famous work, *The Cosmic Race*.

The Cosmic Race is a bricolage of Nietschean, Bergsonian, Catholic, Hindu, Theosophist, and Spiritualist influences blended to provide millenarian predictions of the coming of a spiritual and aesthetic new age in which racial barriers will lose their force and ongoing mixture will lead to an Iberoamerican cosmic race that will play a leading role in world history (Vasconcelos 1979). Vasconcelos inverts the Spencerian assumption of the superiority of pure races over hybrids (which shaped Porfirian policy). However, his notion of a cosmic race reconfigures heterogeneity in terms of purity and, thus, reproduces much of what he critiques. History shades into myth as the workings of Spirit become manifest in the struggle of Iberoamericans against imperialist Anglo-Saxons. With his "practical talents," the Anglo-Saxon might excel at industry; but these accomplishments would be transcended by the Iberoamerican mestizo.[4]

For Vasconcelos, the mestizo is a product of "a mandate from History . . . first noticed in that abundance of love that allowed the Spaniard to create a new race with the Indian and the Black, profusely spreading white ancestry through the soldier who begat a native family, and Occidental culture through the doctrine and example of the missionaries who placed the Indians in condition to enter the new stage" (Vasconcelos 1979, 17) of civilization. As in Gamio's text, men's virility symbolizes the capacity to reproduce social order, whereas women's generativity only reproduces social subjects. Begetting is marked by the ambivalence of desire and aversion that Young has noted, but, accord-

---

[4] Note the parallels here with Negritude, a movement of the 1930s and 1940s among Francophone Africans and Caribbean people of African descent. In response to white racism, the exponents of Negritude argued that whites might be superior in science and technology but blacks were superior morally, aesthetically, and spiritually. Like Negritude, Vasconcelos's cult of mestizaje was not a parochial "nationalism." Rather, Vasconcelos espoused a universalistic, pan-Latin racial "patriotism," which had to find its "root" in Cuahtemoc and Atahualpa as well as in its "Hispanic fountainhead" (Vasconcelos 1979, 11).

ing to Vasconcelos, love overcomes "the repulsion of one blood that confronts another strange blood" (1979, 20).

However, love is only one pole of this ambivalent axis. Between desire and aversion lie seduction, betrayal, and rape. Miguel León-Portilla, one-time director of the Indigenist Inter-American Institute, writes that "children of Spaniards and indigenous women," were "frequently born of women seduced and later abandoned. . . . [t]he unhealed trauma of the vanquished was bound to become inflamed with the awareness of one's descent from a fleeting union, perhaps one of violence, and certainly not one of equality" (1990, 109). This is the argument of Ocatvio Paz's controversial essay on Mexican national character, "The Sons of La Malinche," originally published in 1950. Paz locates the origins of the Mexican in the violation of Indian women by Spanish men as symbolized by the relationship of the Spanish conqueror, Hernán Cortés, to his Aztec mistress and translator La Malinche.

In official nationalism and public culture, Cortés and La Malinche are represented as the prototypical father and mother of the first mestizo. This is evident as early as the 1920s. For example, *Cortés and La Malinche* is the title of a mural commissioned by the Secretary of Public Education (SEP) and painted by José Clemente Orozco in the National Preparatory School between 1923 and 1926. In this mural, which "represents mestizaje in the New World,"[5] a naked Cortés restrains as well as comforts a nude and seemingly impassive La Malinche, while at his feet lies the prostrate body of the conquered Indian man; here the colonial violence that marks the birth of the mestizo is displayed in all its postcolonial ambivalence.

Forced violation and freely chosen love are the two poles within which official nationalism has configured the origins of the mestizo. Through metonymic displacement, ethnoracial hierarchy is represented as gender hierarchy: the rhetoric of mestizaje reconsolidates patriarchy. When the trope of rape is used, the inequalities and violence on which mestizaje rests are tacitly acknowledged—but only as gender inequalities: the feminine remains the "'historically muted subject of the subaltern woman' who only becomes a productive agent through an act of colonial violation" (Young 1995, 19). By contrast, when the trope of "free" sexual union is used, ethnic inequality is denied. The predominance of mestizo children, and of a continuum rather than an absolute polarity of color, is said to undermine ethnic hierarchy. This is the basis for the official myth of "ethnic democracy"—held to charac-

[5] Description of the mural *Cortés y la Malinche*, <http://biblioweb.dgsca.unam.mx/san_ildefonso/html/cortes.html>. I have seen this mural on several occasions, most recently the summer of 2001.

terize Mexico as well as other Latin American countries such as Brazil (Twine 1997), Venezuela (Wright 1990), and Columbia (Wade 1993).

The mythohistory of mestizaje in Mexico, as in Nicaragua (Gould 1998), and elsewhere in Latin America (Smith 1996), symbolically effaces the Indian man as subject by erasing his virility. Paradoxically, although the blood of the heroic Cuahtemoc (versus the "cowardly" Moctezuma) is held to run in the veins of the cosmic race, the Indian man's role in fathering the nation's prototypical citizen is never mentioned. Finding little to value in contemporary indigenous culture, the Hispanicist Vasconcelos asserts "the red men . . . from whom Indians derive, went to sleep millions of years ago, never to awaken" (Vasconcelos 1979). Although Gamio finds aspects of indigenous culture—such as the arts and mythology—valuable, he argues that Indians' cultural evolution was halted by the conquest and by subsequent centuries of oppression. The task of leading them out of the slavery associated with social relations and ideas that had colonial origins was to fall to the postrevolutionary state and its scientific mestizo intellectuals, above all to indigenist anthropologists. Indigenismo became a top-down applied science that accorded little agency to Indians themselves (Dawson 2000; de la Peña 2000; Saldívar 2000; Sesia 1995). How could it do otherwise when its very goal, turning Indians into mestizos, was to "integrate" those it had itself expelled?

FORJANDO PATRIA IN EVERYDAY LIFE: STATIST PRACTICES OF POPULAR SOVEREIGNTY

Since the cultural revolution initiated in the 1920s, statist practices have made the meanings of mestizaje manifest in national public culture. This has entailed the continual appropriation of indigenous culture, monumentalized as national patrimony and folklorized as "'national traditions' that all citizens are encouraged to practice so that they cannot become a gesture of separation" (Hill 1991, 77).

Schools have been important sites for the construction of "national sovereignty" and the transformation of "the multitude" into "the citizenry," which in Mexico has involved not only discourse and violence but also state redistribution of resources. The institution of the school and the role of teachers as cultural and political brokers between the state and people have been key to the clientelist party politics of postrevolutionary Mexico.

There is a large literature in Spanish and in English on schooling in postrevolutionary Mexico (see Vaughan 1997). Recently, Natividad Gutiérrez has analyzed elementary school textbooks dating from 1960 to 1992 to determine how *mestizaje* is represented to children (Gutiérrez 1999). I have examined the year 2000 textbooks (copyrighted 1993 and 1994). In the 2000 school texts, Mexico is explicitly and repeatedly characterized as a mestizo nation. The origin of the mestizo in these texts is represented through the narrative of Cortés and La Malinche. I agree with Gutiérrez's conclusion that "the texts' exegesis of mestizaje favors the Hispanicist legacy . . . and minimizes the indigenous heritage" (1999, 77). Although the achievements of precolonial indigenous cultures are recognized, little is said about indigenous people in the present. Rather than being represented as a vital part of contemporary society, indigenous culture is displaced to a peripheral realm of difference. For example, the third grade text states that "indigenous ethnies often have their own customs and authorities. They also dress in their own way. But what really distinguishes them and unifies them is that they speak their own languages."[6] Situated in the frontier spaces beyond national culture and development, Indians are repeatedly characterized as being in need of "integration." For example, the second part of the same text adds, "In general, the conditions of life of Mexican indigenes are poor. They need work, food, health services, schools, security and respect. Much has been done to integrate the indigenous population into the development of Mexico but much more is left to be done."[7] This is very much in line with the redemptive vision of integrationist indigenism and mestizaje already discussed.

Interestingly, the iconography of textbook covers may have shaped images of the nation as much as the text between them. The anthropologist Rossana Reguillo recalls, "The patria was that mestiza woman of generous breasts and defiant gaze, wrapped in the white, green and red cloth of the Mexican flag, who years ago looked out at the children we were then from the cover of each one of our school books" (Reguillo 1998, 1). Mestizo nationalism has not only been inculcated through discourse; since the 1920s, the state has worked to develop a public visual culture of nationalism, articulated in public art, in cinema, in public space, in public rituals and folkloric spectacles, and in the huge network of museums run by the National Institute of Anthropology and History (INAH). Anthropologists have played a key role in the production of this public visual culture of nationalism.

In the Introduction to this volume, Hansen and Stepputat make a compelling argument for deconstructing Foucault's opposition between premodern forms of power organized around sovereignty and modern forms organized around supposedly new articulations

[6] *Historia de México, Primera Parte* (México: SEP 1993), 120.
[7] Ibid., *Segunda Parte*, 93.

of power/knowledge/discipline. Tony Bennett's work on the "exhibitionary complex" is relevant here (1999). Bennet argues that if modern carceral institutions transformed the premodern, public performance of punishment by withdrawing the bodies of the condemned from the public gaze, the "public dramaturgy of power" nevertheless continued to be important, articulated in the institutions of the "exhibitionary complex" that deployed new technologies of vision (Ibid.). The museum was the key institution of the exhibitionary complex, "involved in the transfer of objects and bodies from the enclosed and private domains in which they had been previously displayed (but to a restricted public) into progressively more open and public arenas where, through the representations to which they were subjected, they formed vehicles for inscribing and broadcasting the messages of power" (333). Although Bennett focuses on art museums in Europe, ethnographic, archaeological, and historical museums have become key components of nation-building or of ethnic revindication in many postcolonial societies (e.g., see essays in Kaplan 1994). In Latin American nation-states, such as Peru (Poole 1997) and Mexico, the exhibitionary complex became central because of the importance of spectacles of "Indian" arts and crafts, music, dance, rituals, costume, and mythology in constructing the "soul" of the nation. Spectacles and performances of mestizo nationalism were not only located between the covers of textbooks or the confines of schools but also became integral to the public spaces of the city.

Museums, above all the National Museum of Anthropology, inaugurated in its current form in 1964, have been key locii of appropriation of the indigenous and *lieux de memoire* for postrevolutionary public memory. According to García Canclini, this "staged synthesis of the national" is considered one of the most compelling materializations of Mexicaness (García Canclini 1995, 127). Museum Director Ignacio Bernal, explained that the purpose of this monument to the national cultural patrimony[8] was to materialize the vision of the mestizo nation:

> Since the Revolution of 1910 Mexicans have begun to see their double cultural legacy much more clearly, recognizing the importance of

[8] The removal of objects from indigenous pueblos—where they may not be considered "national patrimony"—for display in museums has not always met with indigenous people's approval. For example, the inhabitants of the pueblo of Coatlinchan resisted the removal of what was thought to be a giant sculpture of the pre-Hispanic rain god Tlaloc, by sabotaging the trailer that was to transport it to the National Museum in Mexico City. According to the creators of the museum, "Superstition held that if Tlaloc were removed, the rains—and thus life itself—would cease. . . . To avoid further resistance, federal forces were called in" (Ramirez Vásquez 1968, 36). Currently, national versus ethnic rights to "cultural patrimony" are a hotly debated dimension of the reconfiguration of sovereignty in Mexico.

both of its components. It is widely acknowledged that modern day Mexico is the result of a fusion of two old and diverse cultures, and that it is this indissoluble mixture which gives Mexico its unique national character. But how could this meaningful fusion, and particularly the qualities of the indigenous culture (for the Hispanic element has long been well known), be understood and given contemporary validity . . . ? It was absolutely essential, then, to create a museum such as this. (Ramirez Vázquez 1968, 12)

The dedication plaque of the museum features Mexico's national emblem, an eagle perched on a cactus devouring a serpent, which is derived from the Aztec legend of settlement. This emblem "encourages an imaginary association between the figure of presidential authority and the mythical Aztec narrative of settlement" (Gutiérrez 1999, 78), symbolically territorializing the contemporary nation and rooting it in the time and space of the primordial inhabitants of the center. Above the title, Adolfo López Mateos, president of Mexico (1958–1963), inscribed the following text: "The Mexican nation erects this monument in honor of the great cultures that flourished during the pre-Columbian era in regions that now form part of the Republic of Mexico. In the presence of the vestiges of those cultures, contemporary Mexico pays tribute to indigenous Mexico, in whose expression it discerns the characteristics of its national identity."[9] This dedication (reproduced on the museum's contemporary Web site) provides an interpretative frame for one of the central contradictions of modern mestizo nationalism, which is negotiated within the museum; namely, that the grounding of "a national consciousness in the Indian cultures" has at the same time promoted "their disappearance in the 'name of national unity'" (Gutiérrez 1999, 108).

Since 1964, this contradiction has been expressed and mediated through the spatial layout of the museum. The dramatic, monumental displays of pre-Colombian cultures are located on the first floor, which is a giant rectangle that runs from the outer courtyard and culminates in the Mexica (or Aztec) room with the Sun Stone at its center. The

---

[9] For the earlier history of the museum, see Morales-Moreno (1994). This and all other quotes are from Ramirez Vazquez (1968); this is a text put together by the anthropologists, museologists, art historians, and so on who created the 1964 National Museum of Anthropology. The text and its accompanying photographs is structured so as to evoke the prototypical experience of visiting the museum and provides a virtual tour. The exhibits have been changed since 1968. The most recent transformation of the ethnographic exhibits on the second floor reflects the crisis of the project of mestizo nationalism, a crisis that was evident by the 1990s. The older narrative of mestizaje now shares space with the newer narrative of the pluricultural nation. I am currently doing research on museums as sites where ethnoracial and place-based identities are being reformulated, and a new national imaginary is being shaped in Mexico.

Aztecs are privileged in the museum, as well as in mestizo nationalism more generally, because they are represented as the creators of the most synthetic, splendid, and expansive pre-Columbian civilization, one whose center was located in the site of today's capital.

The ethnographic exhibits are on the second floor and, whenever possible, they are located right above the corresponding archaeological exhibits (Ramirez Vázquez 1968, 38). In the early 1960s, indigenous people were themselves invited to the museum and "asked to build their own habitats" within it; modern objects were deliberately excluded from their simulations (Ramirez Vázquez 1968, 39). The spatial separation of archaeology and ethnography distances contemporary Indians from their heritage, whose true heir becomes the nation. Simultaneously, contemporary Indians become marginalized from the national project of modernization; they become vestiges of the past, objects, not authors, of science. Hence, the spatial separation is at the same time a division between past and present: if the Indian past is located at the core of the nation, the Indian present is at its margins (García Canclini 1995, 129–30).

When the museum was built in 1964, the last room the visitor was to see was "The Synthesis of Mexico Room," presided over by a portrait of the "acculturated Indian," President Benito Juarez. This room no longer exists. As described by Alfonso Caso (founder and director of the National Institute of Anthropology from 1939 to 1944, founder and director of the National School of Anthropology, and founder and director of the National Indigenist Institute from 1949 until his death in 1970), this room offered "the visitor a panoramic view of the pre-Columbian and European elements that combine to give Mexico its characteristic unity as a nation and a culture" (Ramirez Vázquez 1968, 251). The room showed the presence of the past in the present, above all in art, architecture, music, dance, and literature—in short, in the realms of the aesthetic and folkloric. At the same time, according to Caso, it demonstrated that "the Indian has ceased to be a man attached to his old pre-historic traditions": they were now patrimony of the mestizo nation. And it was the state, in the service of that nation, that had redeemed the Indian from his vestigial existence and "brought him quickly into the twentieth century" through its indigenist programs (Ramirez Vázquez 1968, 251).

This same paradoxical relationship between the traditional and the modern is expressed in the architecture of the museum building as a whole. The architect, Pedro Ramirez Vázquez, explained that he searched for "an architectural expression that was to be contemporary yet not alien" to the pre-Columbian legacy (15). In order to do this, he tried to uncover the underlying concepts shared by pre-Hispanic, colonial, and modern architecture, which he believed had a common core in the persisting influence of the landscape on the built forms of the past and present.

If architecture territorializes the nation, it is because both indigenous stylistic elements and the perduring influence of a "timeless," originary landscape have rendered it "native." Nationalist architecture from 1920 to 1930 sought to materialize the new national synthesis through the neocolonial style, developed from native materials and styles during the three centuries of colonial rule, a style conceived as a fusion of the Spanish and the Indian. An ardent supporter of the neocolonial style, Vasconcelos was convinced that buildings were key sites for conveying meanings and he went to great lengths to materialize his vision of the cosmic race in the construction of the Palace of Public Education in Mexico (Vasconcelos 1979, 40).

Space is a key boundary marker of ethnoracial identity in Mexico. The rural is coded as Indian, whereas the urban is coded as Mexican. As Lomnitz-Adler (1992) argues, the organization and representation of public urban space has been colonized by state practices and has been key to the spectacle of nationalism; the exhibitionary complex is not confined within the walls of museums. Indigenous terms are used to name streets, neighborhoods, plazas, and parks. The names of the heroes of the struggles to birth the nation baptize public space. The heroic Cuahtemoc, the last Aztec emperor, now considered the first Mexican to symbolize the struggle for national sovereignty, frequently lends his name to thoroughfares. However, Moctezuma, who let himself be taken prisoner by the Spanish conquerors, does not. Every city of any size has streets commemorating Hidalgo, Morelos, Guerrero, Juárez, Madero, Carranza, Obregón, and Zapata, the *Benmeritos* or distinguished heroes of Independence, the "Fathers of the Patria."

The equation of the dominant ethnic category with the core of the nation and the location of subordinated ethnic identities at its internal frontiers is secured partly through differential power over private and public spaces. The Plaza of the Three Cultures in Mexico City, also known as the Plaza of Tlatelolco, is a case in point.[10] A bronze plaque in one corner provides an interpretative frame for the space: "Valiantly defended by Cuahtemoc, the city fell into the power of the conquistadors in this place. It was neither a triumph nor a defeat but, instead, the painful birth of the mestizo pueblo, today's Mexico" [my translation]. Three structures—an Aztec pyramid, a seventeenth-century colonial church, and the modern foreign ministry—serve as icons of Mexico's heritage. The mestizo synthesis is produced by the state as agent of modernity and as custodian of the past of the great indigenous civiliza-

---

[10] As is the Zócalo, Mexico's central plaza, on which I am writing a paper.

tions, which make Mexico a nation unique among other nations, one worthy of their respect. This plaza is the site for spectacular, commemorative performances of "the indigenous" thorough "traditional" dances and costumes on national holidays such as the anniversary of the defense of Tenotchtitlán, the Aztec capital, against the Spanish conquerors, which have as their intended audience not only Mexicans but also foreign dignitaries and tourists.

If public urban space is represented as the space of a modernity that has integrated and transcended tradition, rural space is represented as the space of a tradition that has resisted modernization. Applied indigenist anthropology sought to modernize the Mexican countryside, at times reorganizing rural space. Casey Walsh's work on Manuel Gamio provides a case in point (Walsh 2000). Gamio believed that acculturation to U.S. society led Mexican migrants to progress, but that they often descended to the level of their compatriots after returning to their home communities. Hence, he hit on the idea of setting up isolated colonies of repatriated migrants in rural areas that would function as sites of cultural, ethnoracial, and economic progress in the rural frontier. Such colonies would be organized by the state, which would provide needed resources, technology, and credit (Walsh 2000). A somewhat different notion of rural development was instantiated in the INI's Centros Coordinadores Indigenistas, the first of which were built in the 1950s. According to Emiko Saldívar, the function of the CCIs was to transform the indigenous community "from several different angles, promoting the establishment of federal schools, different hygiene practices, introduction of new crops and working skills" as well as reinforcing "the links to the federal government" (Saldívar 2000, 4). The role of anthropologists in these centers, as Saldívar adds, was to act as "cultural brokers," working to eradicate such "bad" aspects of Indian culture as monolingualism while reinforcing "good" aspects such as the making of arts and crafts (Ibid.). In other instances, indigenist anthropologists were instrumental in coordinating the forced displacement of rural, indigenous people to make way for so-called capitalist improvements such as dams (Gutiérrez 1999, 103–5). Many of these reforms of the Indian were more or less explicitly inspired by Spanish colonial strategies. Ironically, although anticolonial, postrevolutionary nationalism "strove to produce the national people in whose name the struggle against colonialism had been fought" (Hansen and Stepputat, Introduction to this volume), a colonialism that purportedly persisted after formal Independence as the mark of illegitimate social institutions and practices as well as of the condition of the "Indian," it drew on the social memory of colonial techniques of subjectification in its attempt to forge postcolonial, postrevolutionary subjectivities.

The Mestizo National Subject in El Norte: The Case of Namiquipa, Chihuahua

What has been the response of Mexicans, particularly those living in the northern borderlands where the Mexican state's sovereignty over its territory has been most questionable because of U.S. imperial ambitions as well as northern regionalism, to the mythohistory of mestizaje? In Gamio's vision, the northern revolutionaries and their heirs were to spearhead the mestizo national renaissance; have Norteños, including the descendants of revolutionaries, embraced this vision? Collaborative historical and ethnographic research in the revolutionary pueblo of Namiquipa, located in Chihuahua's Sierra Madre, done during the 1980s by myself and Daniel Nugent, provides some insight into this underresearched question (Alonso 1995; Nugent 1993). The self-representation the Namiquipans conveyed to us then was that they were the largely "white" (*blancos*), "civilized" members of a community in which people strove to "progress."

Established by the Spanish colonial state in 1778, Namiquipa was one of several subaltern military colonies whose "civilized" peasant inhabitants were accorded social honor in return for fighting "barbaric Indians." In order to advance projects of territorial conquest and domination, the colonial and Mexican states actively produced and enforced distinct forms of social identity. These forms of subjectivity made the reputations of men contingent upon their degree of civilization and their performance in warfare, and linked female reputations to ethnic and sexual purity. The main ethnic distinction that emerged during the Apache Wars (which only ended in 1886) was that of "gente de razón" and "indios bárbaros." "Gente de razón" (people of reason) was a category that blurred distinctions between "españoles," and "castas" or "mixed bloods," a status that could be attained by Hispanicized social actors prepared to uphold a sedentary, civilized style of life and become agents of the state's colonizing mission. The blurring of distinctions between españoles and castas was the product of a process of whitening of the civilized population that took place on the frontier. Because reason, or the capacity for civilization, was identified with Spanish blood, many Hispanicized mestizos and mulatos were able to "bleach" themselves and become de facto whites (*blancos*). But, paradoxically, at the same time that they whitened their categorical identity, and sharpened the opposition between Self and Other, the gente de razón were engaged in a process of intercultural exchange with the indios bárbaros, which transformed their own cultural practices (see Alonso 1995 for a detailed discussion).

Mestizo in Namiquipa is used in Namiquipa today as an insulting term of other-identification and as a term of self-identification only when making a self-deprecatory comment or joke. For example, one of the few times I heard mestizo used as a term of self-identification was when a well-respected farmer jokingly commented after a few drinks: "We are mestizos. We descend from the Indians who are lazy and from the Spaniards who are thieves."

Although the late-eighteenth-century church records identify the pueblo's early settlers as "mulatos," "mestizos," and "indios"—of several different *naciones*—as well as "españoles," Namiquipans today say that, as a group, they have mostly "Spanish blood" (*sangre española*). The only admixture of "Indian blood" (*sangre india*) they tend to recognize is Apache, as they consider themselves to be "*muy bravos*" like the *bárbaros* whose blood they carry.

Namiquipa was a stronghold of Pancho Villa's popular movement during most of the Revolution of 1910–1920. Interestingly enough, Norteño perceptions of ethnic differences between themselves and other Mexicans became more sharply drawn at this time. In 1916, Ciro B. Ceballos, a prominent propagandist for the Norteño revolutionary Venustiano Carranza, extolled the benefits of the revolutionary triumph of the frontiersmen, "unless it were to turn out that on putting themselves in intimate contact with the rest of the Mexican population . . . the former [Northeners] were to acquire the vices of the latter, leading to the degeneration, if not the transformation, of the essential conditions of their present indisputable racial superiority'" (cited in Knight 1990, 107n64).

"Whiteness" is a central trope in Chihuahuan's sense of Norteño identity. Pointing to their region's distinct history of conquest and colonization, Norteños frequently comment that they are "whiter" than the *Chilangos* or Mexicans of the South and Center, whom they perceive as "browner." Relative to other Mexicans, Norteños consider themselves to be brave, independent, rebellious, self-sufficient, and hardworking. Norteños perceive their region to be more democratic, egalitarian, and open to individual achievement than the rest of Mexico. All of these qualities, from their point of view, are indexed by the relative whiteness of their skin.

The historian Raquel Rubio Goldsmith conducted oral history interviews over a four year period with with ten Norteñas who moved to *el otro lado* after the 1910 Revolution. She notes, "All of the women I interviewed who came from the *sierras* of Chihuahua and Sonora, calling themselves Mexicanas, grew up proud that they were of Spanish heritage—not mixed" (Rubio Goldsmith 1998, 277). Indeed, in my own research I found that skin color was a central criterion of feminine beauty.

Whiteness has other sources besides the frontier past. At least some Namiquipans believed that migration to the United States, in which they regularly engage, literally made them whiter (*mas blancos*). Some people even speculated that it had something to do with the water. Namiquipans' interest in purchasing North American rather than Mexican commodities was based in part on the whiteness that such commodities would symbolically confer on them. On the border, commodity fetishism has acquired a specific ethnic character.

The results of Pablo Vila's (1999) six-year study of identity formation in the Cd. Juarez-El Paso area, conducted during 1991–1997, suggest that Namiquipans's understanding of what it means to be Norteño might be more broadly shared. Vila found that Mexican origin residents of the Juarez-El Paso area think of themselves as Norteños and that they define this category of collective identity in much the same way as do Namiquipans, with "whiteness" playing a central role. These findings put into question the degree to which Norteños draw on official notions of mestizaje to construct their own identity and indicate that further research on this question is needed.

Perhaps the twentieth-century rhetoric of mestizaje and indigenism has been most credible to those who have been its authors, functionaries of Mexico's state apparatus, artists, and intellectuals. Indeed, as Miller has argued, Latin American intellectuals have been crucially dependent on the state, because a mass reading public for their work did not emerge until after the middle of the twentieth century; moreover, in Mexico, the postrevolutionary state developed an efficient apparatus of "containment" to discipline the institutions of intellectual life (1999, 43–44). Yet, since the 1970s, Mexico's indigenous movement has posed a challenge to the integrationist vision of the nation. Although indigenism had been critiqued by Mexican intellectuals for a number of decades (e.g., Bonfil 1987; Medina 1996; Warman et al. 1970; Villoro 1979 [1950]), questioning of the mestizo nationalism to which indigenism was linked is more recent and can be seen in the work of nonindigenous as well as indigenous intellectuals. The verdict of Bartolomé Alonzo Camaal, an indigenous intellectual interviewed by Gutiérrez, is no longer so controversial: "When Indian knowledge is appropriated, it is called mestizaje. . . . [this] does not benefit the indigenous people at all" (Gutiérrez 1999, 153).

CONCLUSION

Bakhtin argues that authoritative discourse is "incapable of being double-voiced; it cannot enter into hybrid constructions" without losing its authority (1981, 344). This chapter problematizes Bakhtin's arguments, and, by extension, a notion of cultural hybridity as "always already" contestatory. Hybridization, whether linguistic or cultural, can be a key strategy for constructing forms of national-popular sovereignty, which, as in the Mexican case, are exclusionary in their very pretensions to be inclusionary. The dialectic of structures of attraction and repulsion is as easily linked to a politics of domination, exploitation, and subjectification as it is to a politics of protest.

Modern forms of state surveillance and control of populations as well as of capitalist organization have depended on the homogenizing, rationalizing, and partitioning of space. Both Gamio and Vasconcelos despaired of homogenizing the "land of contrasts" that is Mexico. Paradoxically, it is the constant iteration of the statement that "Indians" have to be integrated into the nation that has served to secure the official conceptualization of mestizos as living within a single, shared spatiotemporal frame, the time and space of those entering modernity. By situating Indians in the space-time of tradition, both behind and at the frontier of the national, the state has turned autochthonous people into a national minority.

Carol Smith has argued that state projects of nation-building centered on myths of mestizaje have been "much less successful than we previously assumed. Most . . . new [social movements] have arisen to represent the identities and issues (race, ethnicity, religion, gender) suppressed by the nation-building *mestizaje* process. A notable feature of these movements is that many of them came into existence to protest what *mestizaje* meant to them" (1996, 161). Toward the end of the twentieth century and into the twenty-first, efforts by Mexican indigenous rights activists to challenge the relationship between the traditional and the modern that has characterized the official conflation of Mexicanidad and "La Raza Cósmica" acquired greater public visibility and began to have a national impact (Gutiérrez 1999; Stephen 2002). Mexico signed Convention 169 of the International Labor Organization in 1991. Indigenous mobilizations prompted the revision of the Federal Constitution in 1992: Article 4 now recognizes that "[t]he Mexian nation has a pluricultural composition, originally based on its indigenous pueblos." Beginning in 1994, the indigenous organizing that had been going on at local and regional levels for years was given further impetus by the EZLN (Mallon 1996, 1998; Stephen 2002). The 1996 Accords of San Andrés signed by the rebels and the government proposed a new relation between the state and native peoples, one that would have recognized rights to culture, territory, and self-determination. Yet, the so-called *Ley Indigena* passed by the Mexican Supreme Court in 2002 has been widely denounced by indigenous groups as a watered-down version of these accords.

Indigenous mobilizations from below and transnational pressures for democratization, including a "powerful discourse of human rights which impels states to grant rights, or resist from repressive measures in order not to damage their international reputation and standing within an elusive but effective 'international community'" (Hansen and Stepputat, introduction to this volume; see Speed and Collier 2000), have been among the key factors in putting into question the official myth of mestizaje (see essays in Reina 2000). Currently in Mexico, a number of national projects—tied to different visions of national and ethnic sovereignty—vie for hegemony, ranging from the older project of mestizaje to the newer official multiculturalism to more radical forms of inter- and multiculturalism from below, which do not split the right to culture from struggles for socioeconomic rights. The redefinition of Mexican nationalism is still incomplete and contested.

Violence, Sovereignty, and Citizenship in Postcolonial Peru

Finn Stepputat

CITIZENS AND SUBJECTS IN THE POSTCOLONY[1]

The closure of the third presidential campaign of the once beloved President Fujimori took the form of a huge party in the central Plaza of Lima. The main attraction was the queen of Peruvian *techno-cumbia,* Rossi War, who helped mobilize many women from the "Mothers' Clubs" in the city's popular neighborhoods. The president himself moved in a dancelike fashion to his campaign *schlager,* "the dance of the Chinese" (*el baile del Chino*), cheering the huge public at the plaza and the rest of the population who could not help watching the wall-to-wall transmission of the event on five TV channels. The party was almost void of political messages, but one message slipped out, loud and clear: "In Peru, we will not accept there being first and second class citizens."

This message became the trademark of Fujimori's policy after he had wiped out the Maoist guerrilla, Sendero Luminoso, and brought inflation under control in the early 1990s. Through presidential programs, many of them funded by international agencies, "he" provided numerous rural districts with schools, clinics, water systems, roads, bridges, community halls, central parks, and electricity, in addition to the subsidized food, milk and popular soup kitchens for "vulnerable groups." The action did not go unnoticed, although the gulf between the rural and the urban districts in terms of human development continued to widen (Franke 2000). Fujimori won in most rural districts in the poorest parts of the highland, and popular discourse hailed him for being the first Peruvian president who had "taken us into account."

This chapter will look into how the image of first- and second-class citizens has become so powerful in Peruvian national and local politics

---

[1] The ideas and empirical data in this article owe much to the long-standing and very inspiring research collaboration with Fiona Wilson as well as with Ninna Nyberg Sørensen and Henrik Rønsbo at the former Centre for Development Research in Copenhagen. Thomas Blom Hansen, Steffen Jensen, and Lars Buur also have given valuable comments on earlier drafts of this chapter.

despite the fact that more than two hundred years have passed since the dismantling of the colonial segregation between the subjects of "the Indian Republic" and the citizens of the "Spanish Republic" began. As we will see, the Spanish Bourbon reforms in the late eighteenth century and the liberal reforms during the nineteenth century undercut the logics and privileges of the Indian Republic in general and of the Indian elite in particular, while the Constitution of the liberated country turned colonial Indians into Peruvians. But the liberties and rights promised by the first postcolonial regimes have been slow in coming to the former Indians who were caught in "the postcolonial limbo between tributary subjects and citizen tax payers," as Thurner has put it (1997, 53).

This chapter explores the postcolonial limbo with regard to struggles for citizenship and sovereignty during what we may call the "long nineteenth century," the formative period of the modern Peruvian nation-state between the late eighteenth and early twentieth century. Inspired by Agamben's (1998) argument that political and moral communities are founded upon the exclusion of "bare life," bodies subjected to biopolitics but not involved in politics,[2] this chapter analyzes practices of sovereignty and citizenship at the intersection of state, (bio)politics, and race during the long nineteenth century, when the colonial Indians became included in the new nation-state and yet disenfranchised at its margins. The analysis shows that the internal exclusion of (former) Indian and Indigenous bodies received a spatial expression through the bifurcation of the rural and the urban and the institutionalization of "indigenous communities" in the rural habitat.

How do we conceptualize the political phenomena related to the transitions from colonial to postcolonial societies? In his analysis of colonial Africa, Mahmood Mamdani (1996) makes the fundamental distinction between the citizens who are subjected to and participating in direct government, and the subjects who are incorporated in the colonial administration by means of indirect rule. Although direct government is linked to a more or less liberal governmentality and the idea of a more or less sovereign citizen, a number of nonliberal practices are found in the realm of indirect government, as evidenced by the corporal punishment in institutions of "customary law," and the importance of forced labor recruitment or common usufruct to land. Many of these practices become vilified in the postcolony when all inhabitants, in principle, are liberated and incorporated into the same state, under the same law, and with the same constitutional rights. But many postcolonial states have been unable to do away with the existing bifurcation. As Mamdani suggests in the case of African states, ei-

[2] See the Introduction to this volume.

ther "tribal rule" has been incorporated into patron-client relations between the rural and the urban, or the tribal authorities have been undone, while the rural areas have been subjected directly to the (undemocratic) urban elites. The question is how these ideas apply to Latin American cases. Among other differences, the emergence of colonial indirect government analyzed by Mamdani coincided historically with the emergence of ideologies of indigenist advocacy (*indigenismo*) in formally sovereign nation states in Latin America, which were incorporated by some regimes through the institutionalization of special arrangements for indigenous populations during the first decades of the twentieth century. But the memories of colonial relations between rulers and the ruled also were different in, for example, the Andean countries, where, as we will see, memories of a "colonial pact" seemed to influence the political agency of the former Indians in the nineteenth century.

Although in principle the former subjects became citizens and the states sovereign in postcolonial societies, this was far from the reality in Latin America. Even as liberal political doctrines became increasingly dominant in the nineteenth century, they coexisted with deliberately discriminatory practices. In this doctrine, access to the class of "citizens" was conditioned upon certain assets, such as being male, and having formal education, registered property and proven commitment to the sovereign political body to which the citizen belonged, as also Partha Chatterjee writes in his contribution to this volume. Although access to education was severely limited and intimately tied to urban culture, many males had ample occasion to prove commitment through military or labor services to local and provincial elites, or to the central state. Hence, contestations over land, labor, education, and military service should not only be regarded as struggles over resources and immediate interests, but more broadly as struggles over emerging ideas and practices of the conditions of belonging to a political community, in other words, of citizenship, nationhood, and sovereignty.

In this volume, Barry Hindess makes the point that the coexistence of liberalism and discriminatory exclusions of segments of the population is less a question of hypocrisy than a liberal attempt to deal with a reality, which does not appear to present the necessary conditions for liberal government to function. Rather than giving liberty and citizenship to all and basing government on the autonomous individual, liberal projects in postcolonial states have tended to establish a distinction between (1) populations that were suitable for liberal (self-)government; (2) populations that could be improved, or could improve themselves, to a point in which they could manage autonomy; and (3) populations judged to be beyond the scope of improvement. The latter would hence be exterminated, excluded, incarcerated or turned into pliable subjects by other means (Hindess 2001a).

However, through most of the nineteenth century, the new states could only implement regulations and exercise sovereign practices through alliances with regional and local elites, strongmen, and formally disbanded colonial authorities, all of whom filled the "void" between the dismantled colonial system of administration and law enforcement, and distant central state apparatuses. The following analysis gives a schematic overview of 150 years of transition in the Central Peruvian Andes, from colonial indirect government of "Indian towns" under the sovereignty of the Spanish King before 1780, to the 1920s, when principles of popular sovereignty were appropriated by broader social movements, when modern biopolitics came to characterize central state governance, and the government institutionalized "indigenous communities" at the margins of the postcolonial state.

The following sections look into the dynamics of the dismantling of indirect colonial government, including the ensuing conflicts and the vestiges of colonial institutions, mainly the Indian Mayors (*Alcaldes*), who remained, for all practical purposes, brokers between rural communities and public office holders and local elites, despite being abandoned and even prohibited upon Independence. One section deals with other forms of authority and interstitial sovereignty that fill the void between the dismantled colonial institutions and the emerging and centralizing state apparatus, in particular local bosses known as *gamonales*, who were essential for local state formation, and the *montoneras*, armed highland communities emerging during the war with Chile in the late nineteenth century. The last sections of the chapter analyze the changing discourses of race and the emerging biopolitical regime, which together had the effect of transferring indianness from the former Indian towns to their rural hinterlands where the population was submitted to particular forms of government.

One of the most enduring legacies of the nineteenth-century transformation seems to be the association of the rural (and, by implication, the provincial, as seen from the center) with coercive and violent forms of power and noninstitutionalized forms of negotiation (Poole 1994). Elsewhere in this volume, Partha Chatterjee develops the notion of *political society* in opposition to the notion of civil society, which he reserves for bourgeois society engaged in a field of formalized practices and institutions between "state and society" and, in practical terms, inhabited by a relatively small and clearly identifiable social group.[3] Political society then denotes the kind of political engagement that is

---

[3] See also Chatterjee (1993) for a critique of "civil society."

generated when state representatives negotiate directly with groups within the population over issues of welfare, behavior, and entitlements in a way that does not fit the formal institutions of liberal democracy.

As is evident from scores of current policy papers and academic writing, representations of this political otherness are permeated by romantic images and/or images of pathological behavior and pollution. Mamdani's analysis of postcolonial politics is no exception. Describing the political effects of rural-urban migration after the lifting of colonial (and apartheid) restrictions on mobility and settlement, he notes that migration has brought the legacies of indirect government to the city where the rural authoritarianism tends to "pervert civil society" and give rise to "urban champions of the customary" (e.g., Inkatha in South Africa) (Mamdani 1996, 297). Thus, the rural/urban divide is depicted as a divide between legitimate politics and more violent forms of imposition or negotiation, a divide that furthermore is racialized, as we will see in the following analysis of the central Peruvian highland (de la Cadena 1998a).

INDIRECT COLONIAL GOVERNMENT

When the Spaniards conquered the region, they sought to change the spatial organization in order to control the population and facilitate the extraction of tributes. They concentrated the Indian population in Indian communities or towns (*Pueblos de Indios*), where several *Ayllus*[4]— or clans—were gathered around the central square and the Church. However, as has been documented in other parts of Latin America, the reductions were not very successful in concentrating people. Apparently, shepherds and peasants continued to inhabit their high-lying and/or distant places, while participating in clan-based exchange relations between different niches in the vertical range (Fabre 1977; Silverblatt 1995; Smith 1989).[5]

The Indian towns developed at the seats of the old *Ayllus*. The ancient ethnic nobility, the *Kuraka* families, were given special privileges. The *Kurakas* concentrated the powers of political representation, tribute collection, and judicial authority in certain matters, not including the

[4] The *ayllu* may be defined as a group whose members regard themselves as "brothers" who owe one another aid and support, in contrast to others outside the group (Spalding 1982).

[5] Many social relations go back to pre-Inca societies, in which chiefly families in the valleys and poorer clan members at high-lying pastures were involved in exchange institutions in which the latter herded the animals (cameloids) of the chiefs in exchange for access to food and/or agricultural land at the lower altitudes. Some of these institutions continued to work in different incarnations well into the twentieth century (Smith 1989).

authority to take life (Abercrombie 1998). The *Kurakas* had political legitimacy in both Republics, the Spanish and the Indian. They managed an indirect government through the council, the Mayor (*Alcalde Mayor*), and village headmen, the ordinary *Alcalde Varayoccs*.[6] The office of *Alcalde* was created by the Toledo-reforms in the late sixteenth century as a rotating office, filled by election on the basis of merit and respect, and often occupied by lesser, but literate, nobility. The *Alcaldes* organized communal labor turnouts, crop rotation, managed the calendar of communal festivals, and had responsibilities for public order and judicial services, the *res publica* of the Indian Republic. These offices were intended to check the power of the hereditary chiefs (Thurner 1997), and have continued as important institutions in some form and in some places until the end of the twentieth century.

The relationship between the Indian communities and the Spanish king has been characterized as a "colonial pact" (Platt 1982, 40). Maintaining institutions of the Inca Empire, the Spaniards linked tribute payment and land rights in what was perceived as an asymmetrical but reciprocal pact that guaranteed the access to land for the community of tribute-paying Indians (40). As Walker (1999) has noted, "Indian" was ultimately a fiscal category that defined rights and obligations and in this way anchored otherwise blurred racial identities. Although representatives of the king assigned unalienable but territorially ill-defined land to the *Ayllus*, the *Kurakas*, and their tributary communities, Spaniards and *mestizos* were excluded from the reductions. They were not allowed to establish commercial agriculture if this would threaten the welfare of the Indian communities, the tribute-paying golden hen of the Crown. However, after 1712, a different category of land could, if "vacant" or "extra" be transferred to Spaniards and *mestizos* who formed private haciendas at the higher altitudes. (Thurner 1997, 50).

Although the categories of *Indios, mestizos,* and Spaniards formed as distinctive social identities with different links to the colonial administration, they were never absolute, closed, or marked by clear-cut ethnic divisions (Smith 1989). Over the centuries, Spaniards, Indian elites, and Indians of different ethnic groups moved in and out of positions in relation to communities, haciendas, and colonial/postcolonial administrations: Spaniards married into *Kuraka* families to have access to land, and small flock owners sometimes "found it suitable to be humble Indian *comuneros* [community members], at other times Indian aristocratic nobles, and at still others, Spanish feudal lords, in the struggle for

---

[6] From *Vara*, the truncheon or staff that symbolized the authority of the mayor in the neo-Mediteranean system of governance.

the recognition of legal title to land" (50). In general, the principle of spatial segregation between Indians and others gradually eroded during the eighteenth century, and *mestizos* started to mix with the Indian elites in the Indian towns.

The linkage between tribute payment and access to land, wood, and water as framed in the colonial pact between Indians and the Spanish king became central for the Indians' imagination of citizenship when the indirect government of the Indian Republic was dismantled from the late eighteenth century (Thurner 1997; Walker 1999; Wilson 2003a).

Dismantling Indirect Government

The dismantling of colonial indirect government began during the Bourbon reforms towards the end of the eighteenth century, in particular in the early 1780s. The reforms were intended to increase the revenue from the colonies by modernizing and centralizing the administration, increase Spanish control, and integrate the Indians further into the Spanish Republic. The central administration levied new taxes on Indians and others, removed tax exemptions and collected taxes more rigorously. These changes were difficult to balance with local legitimacy for the *Kurakas* (Walker 1999) and in 1783, the king decided to remove the hereditary privilege of overseeing tribute collection from the *Kuraka* families and transfer it to *mestizos* or even Spaniards (Jacobsen 1993).

The latter reform was a reaction to the largest rebellion in Spanish America, which took place between 1780 and 1783. The increasingly coercive and less negotiated character of government sparked off a complex cycle of social movements directed toward the Spanish regime and its supporters (Jacobsen 1993). Under the leadership of Tupac Amaru II, a diverse, but mainly Indian, Pan-Andean movement engulfed the region from Northern Argentina to Colombia, threatening to overthrow Spanish domination. The rebellion was quelled in blood by the Spaniards who performed a spectacularly cruel execution of Tupac Amaru II in Cuzco in 1781, thus restating the sovereignty of the Spanish Crown.

The meaning of the rebellion has been much debated (see Stern 1987). Although the Bourbon reforms were an immediate cause of rebellion, it seems that their aims were wider than the reestablishment of a previous balance. The rebellion drew upon the image of the Inca and incorporated demands by descendents of the Incas for more privileges, while broader utopian ideas of a simple, egalitarian, and just world were projected back in time upon the Inca Empire (Flores Galindo 1994). But the rebellion was clearly based in the contradictions of the colonial regime and the colonial Indio identity and may be seen as proto-nationalist (Silverblatt 1995). Although the rebellion was definitely anticolonial in its aims, the alternative to the colonial regime was unclear (Walker 1999); the Tupac Amaru rebellion occurred before the enlightenment revolutions that fed into the later, Creole dominated nationalist movements that eventually achieved independence from Spain in the 1820s.

The rebellion left enduring marks in the region. It increased the fear and horror of the Indian among the Spaniards, and precipitated an onslaught on the *Kuraka*-families and their privileges. In 1825, after Independence, Simón Bolivar finally abolished the "title and authority" of the *Kurakas* and decreed that henceforth, "the local authorities will exercise the functions of the extinguished *caciques.*"[7] Although potentially contending sovereigns were thus undercut, the disappearance of the literate Indian elite also facilitated the future "national myth" of the Indian as an inferior being. As argued by Cecilia Mendez, the colonial Indian was respected for his capacity for political organization and other qualities which were "crucial to rescue, conserve, and cultivate in order to facilitate their exploitation" (Mendez 1996, 220). But without an Indian aristocracy, it was easier to equate the Indian with poor, ignorant, and inferior beings and deny any relations between the present and the glorious past of the Inca Empire. Prohibiting the use of Inca-names in the Peruvian nation, the Creole nationalists sought to prevent subalterns from forging their own nationalisms (Mendez 1996).

The dismantling of indirect government continued with the nineteenth-century liberal land reforms, which tended to dissolve the colonial pact, or the land-tax nexus (Gootenberg 1989; Thurner 1997). When the Republican regime substituted a personal "contribution" to the state treasury for the colonial tribute the Indians were linked directly to the state, which took the place of the king and before him, the Inca. But the other side of the pact, access to land, underwent more serious changes because of the land reforms: the land of the communities was turned into state property with the purpose of selling off and privatizing the land. The Law of 1828 tied citizenship to property and declared Indians to be owners of the communal land they possessed.

As property owners, Indians could now, in principle, sell their land in the market. However, a "literacy clause" in the same law barred illiterate Indians from property rights. This was justified partly in terms of the need to protect Indians from undue alienation and transfer of land to non-Indians, and partly as a way of upholding tax revenue from the Indians that henceforth would pay tax for the simple usufruct of the

---

[7] Quoted from Thurner (1997, 25). Cacique is the Nauahtl word for chief, used across the continent by the Spaniards.

state's land (Thurner 1997). In practice, the literacy clause excluded most Indians from full citizenship and left them in limbo between tributary subjects and propertied citizens. This "subaltern form of Indian citizenship" was, according to Thurner, wrapped up in the hybrid, Indian notion of *republicano*, which harked back to the colonial pact of reciprocity of the Indian Republic, now transposed upon the new "Peruvian" polity (34).

The *republicano* tax-land nexus was undermined as reforms proceeded under President Castilla in his mid-nineteenth-century "liberal revolution." In 1855, Castilla put an end to the "literacy clause," and under influence of the Guano-boom revenue that poured into the treasury of the central state, he removed what he saw as the last remnants of colonial society. The "contribution," leveled only upon the Indians, was abolished in the name of progress: ". . . thenceforth they will not contribute except in the same way that the rest of the inhabitants of Peru do . . . Emancipated from the humiliating tribute [. . .] and elevated by the natural effect of civilization, Peru will gain a numerous and productive population in the indigenous race which will undoubtedly offer her a richer contribution" (quoted in Thurner 1997, 44).

As in the case of legal protection of communal land, the Indian communities lost land through privatization. A closer look at sections of the central Andes reveals a more complex picture, however. In the valleys, in the former Indian towns, the former *Kuraka* families lost power, disappeared, or mestizized. *Mestizos* took over control of public offices which gave them ample opportunity to lure fertile agricultural lands away from their neighbors with the result that landed property increasingly became concentrated in the hands of a few "petty local notables" (Fabre 1977, 258). In the highland above the towns, haciendas encroached upon communal land as commercial possibilities grew from the mid-nineteenth century, but the need for labor gave scope for negotiation for the shepherds who lived at some distance from the former Indian towns in the valleys. Gradually they became less dependent on the town elites and more dependent on the hacienda owners, who captured the labor and the pastures at the high frontier, partly through purchase of land, and partly by emulating the reciprocal relations that formerly tied town elites and dependent Indians together in the Indian communities (Manrique 1987; Samaniego 1978; Smith 1989).[8] In a fascinating study of land-labor-relations in Tarma, at the eastern slopes of

[8] Hacienda owners sponsored food, music, and alcohol for *faenas* (collective work turnouts) and religious fiestas. For other institutions, see Smith (1989). Engaging the shepherds in debt relations by forwarding goods to them was another way of securing access to labor, but, as described by Manrique (1987), the shepherds maintained a certain scope for negotiation.

the Andes, Fiona Wilson has documented a very similar process taking place toward the end of the nineteenth century (Wilson 2003a).

CONTESTED SOVEREIGNTIES: CAUDILLOS, GAMONALES, MONTONERAS, AND THE STATE

Although the structures and authorities of indirect government of the Indian republic were dismantled over a period of one hundred years, the state was only one of several effective sovereignties within the ill-defined boundaries of Peru. During the better part of the nineteenth century, regional strongmen—*caudillos*—and regional elites fought over central government or the conditions under which they would ally themselves with central government. Caudillos commanded regional armies based on their ability to forge alliances between different segments of elites and subaltern groups, and had the reputation of being capable of wielding violence (Walker 1999).

In the mid-nineteenth century, after decades of struggles between Lima-based and provincial caudillos, Lima reemerged as the prosperous and self-contained center of Peru, but it was not until after the Pacific War with Chile (1879–1883) that a national army was organized under the supervision of a French military commission (Nunn 1983). Before the war, the central state apparatus had little interest in the interior of the country, and the inability of state institutions to establish and defend effective territorial sovereignty, to penetrate society, safeguard rights, and carry out governmental policies was characteristic of the postcolonial limbo. Republican institutions were set up for the direct government of every settlement within the territory, but the central state was not even remotely in a position to effectively enact direct government. Government depended on alliances with provincial elites that won the "power of appointment" of public officials within their regions of interest (Nugent 1997). Race, defined in terms of purity of blood, was a mayor legitimizing principle of exclusive aristocratic rule, and elite alliances for the territorial extension of domains were built on the basis of intra-elite marriages (Nugent 1997).

Alongside the landowning, but mainly urban-based, white elite, a new social phenomenon appeared, associated with precarious state rule at the rural frontiers of the nation: the *gamonal*. The term emerged in the 1860s (Poole 1988), signifying landholding *mestizos* or "'whites' of tainted social origin" as well as their allied authorities, merchants, and intermediaries who controlled relations between the Indians, the market and the state (Stern 1998, 16). As such, they took over the place of the Indian aristocracy as mediators between Indians and the central administration. The name *gamonal* refers to a parasitic plant in the Andean region, which is able to survive under the harshest conditions, and the image of the *gamonal* was often associated with the idea of ill-achieved wealth (de la Cadena 2000).

In Poole's interpretation, the nineteenth-century rural frontier was characterized by "a culture of violence" in which masculinity, honor, and theatrical violence were key elements (Poole 1988). Without institutional backing from the state apparatus "out there," *gamonales* engaged in highly personalized and symbolic acts of violence, usually victimizing people with whom he (and sometimes she) had social relations, such as fictive kinship ties. Unlike the absentee *hacendado*, the *gamonal* shared the habitat, the women, and the (drinking) culture of the highlanders (de la Cadena 2000). Comrade and master, protector and perpetrator, mainly maneuvering beyond state control and able to perform violence without punishment, the *gamonal* was the trickster of the frontier. He controlled the wilderness and the wild Indian on behalf of the state, but he also represented the Indians of his area *vis-à-vis* state institutions, including the courts. The power of the *gamonal* rested on the ability to monopolize relations to the judicial system and to produce unpredictable violence with impunity in the name of the state. Construing a kind of interstitial sovereignty, the notion of *gamonal* served to disassociate the foundational violence from the state.

A third concept related to the exercise of sovereign practices is the *montonera* movement, an indigenous movement that emerged in the highlands during the Pacific War (1879–1883). The war with Chile illustrates the fragility of Peruvian territorial sovereignty in the nineteenth century. As the Chilean army occupied the better part of central Peru, large factions of the Limeño elite opted in favor of joining forces with the Chileans who were seen as representing a more advanced and civilized state, among other reasons because they had solved their "Indian problem" through wars of extermination.

In the occupied highlands, the Peruvian general Cáceres soon realized that he could do little with his fifteen hundred men. Sacrificing tight control over the armed forces for an effectively extended army, he opted for a *guerrilla,* literally, in his words, a "small-scale war," using the *montoneras* (Smith 1989, 68). Although other groups either supported the Chileans directly, as did some of the large landowners, or vacillated between support and resistance, such as the *mestizos* in the former Indian towns, the shepherds of the dispersed settlements at the high altitudes of the central highland constituted the backbone of resistance to the Chilean army during the occupation, also when considered at a national scale (Mallon 1995; Thurner 1997).[9]

---

[9] The following is based on information on the *montoneras* who ruled between the Vilca and the Mantaro valley, southwest of Huancayo.

The *montoneras* mobilized up to five thousand men in the area. They received 200 rifles from Cáceres in 1982 and purchased another 550 rifles during the next two years (Smith 1989, 70–72). Initially mobilized through loyal landowners or by townsmen in the valley communities, these soon lost control of the highlanders under the command of Thomas Laime. The guerrilla force was structured on the basis of "confederations of villages" and their indigenous authorities, the *Alcaldes*. The *montoneras* ambushed and disturbed the Chilean army, and followed the orders of Cáceres to punish collaborators, including the hacienda owners who supported the Chileans. They invaded and sacked several haciendas—following the example of the Chileans—and executed their owners. Some one hundred thousand sheep disappeared into the war economy. They were eaten, distributed, or sold on the coast in exchange for weapon and ammunition.

After the Peruvian president had signed a peace treaty with the Chileans, the *montoneras* continued their regime in the highland where they sacked and occupied haciendas and engaged in an increasingly violent regime against uncooperative villagers and townspeople. Reminiscent of Spanish colonial customs of punishment, they cut off the ears of enemies and killed several authorities whom they accused of being spies. According to inhabitants of the valley towns, the highlanders were bloodthirsty bandits who pretended to be fighting in the name of the nation (Mallon 1995, 199).

Whereas the *montoneras* fought for the nation, they were increasingly countered by agents of the state and a regional alliance of merchants and landowners. In 1884, Cáceres invited Thomas Laimes to come to Huancayo for a meeting. Laimes arrived with his leaders and a guard of *montoneras*, confident that they would be respected for their contribution to the liberation of the *patria* and that they could strike a deal with Cáceres regarding the hacienda land they occupied. "Tell Cáceres that I am as much a general as he is and if he wants me to go to Huancayo he must treat me as equal to equal."[10] Laimes was arrested, tried before a council of war, and executed together with three leaders. Despite the loss of their leaders, the *montoneras* upheld a liberated zone for several years (Ibid.). In the Central Andes such groups still, in 1888, occupied forty-five haciendas (Smith 1989, 76). Gradually, an army expedition ("the Pacifier of the Centre") brought the widespread movement under control through a mixture of high handed repression including massacres, and negotiations with representatives of local segments of the movement (Mallon 1995). The aim of the army was to replace the indigenous *Alcaldes* with republican authorities, but state representatives had to negotiate directly with the *Alcaldes*.

[10] Tello, quoted in Smith (1989, 75).

The insubordinate movement has been interpreted as an emerging class movement which turned against the increasingly exploitative hacienda owners and town elites as patron-client relations were breaking down (Smith 1989, 74). On the basis of Pratt's analysis of the colonial pact, Thurner (1997) interprets the movement as a movement for (land-) rights precipitated by the rupture of the reciprocal land-tax nexus between the state and its postcolonial subjects, which left community resources unprotected. The fact that indigenous village *Alcaldes,* on behalf of the movement, occasionally formulated political appeals to state authorities in the current language of liberal governance, referring to their property and social rights as citizens of the nation, supports Thurner's argument (99, 108, 150).

To these partly complementary interpretations, we may add that the *montonera* movement may be seen as a case of outsourced sovereignty[11] where the movement, in the name of the nation and armed by the state, emitted death sentences and performed corporal punishments (cutting off ears) that used to belong to the domain of the Spanish colonial authorities rather than the domain of Indian indirect government (Abercrombie 1998). The posterior violent manifestation of autonomy within the nation and against the state led to repression but also to a *de facto* (but not *de jure*) recognition of the *Alcaldes* as representatives of rural indigenous communities, acting independently of their former masters in the Indian towns. We may see these rural communities as an incipient political society that achieved, for a moment at least, a direct line to the central government, thus bypassing the Republican authorities in the former Indian towns (Mallon 1995). Although they were not accorded any rights to land, the autonomous communities and their understanding of a hybrid, *republicano* citizenship, fed into the development of a special status for rural communities in the emerging biopolitical state.

BIOPOLITICS AND THE RURAL-URBAN DIVIDE

In the aftermath of the Pacific War, large parts of the indigenous population were effectively and explicitly excluded from full citizenship despite the fact that a liberalist political doctrine became increasingly influential in Peru, as in so many other areas of Latin America. The political debates in Peru at the turn of the nineteenth century were centered on the question of the capabilities and moral standards of the (former) Indian and *Mestizo* populations as well as the scope for their improvement and eventual inclusion in the nation-state. Although ideas

---

[11] See Lars Buur's contribution to this volume.

of race and hybridity provided the idiom for these debates, the meaning and usage of the concepts tended to change from being associated with blood and phenotypes, to being associated with, and even substituted by, "culture," which was understood as education, rational reasoning, and civilized behavior. Thus, when the Indians were excluded from citizenship in the early 1890s, it was not because of their race but because they were illiterate and uneducated. As a Special commission argued in 1892: "The making of a good electoral law, in conformity with the democratic principles that serve as a base for our constitutional system, comes up against the frustration presented by the lack of culture among our popular masses, the majority of whom do not know how to read and write and do not understand the most trivial of the citizen's rights and responsibilities" (quoted in Mallon 1995, 218).

This argument raises the question of the possibility of educating the "popular masses." From one position in the debate, the "racial pessimism" of extreme Conservatism (de la Cadena 2000), a Limeño intellectual wrote in 1897 that "the Indian race is an old and degenerated branch of the ethnic trunk from where all the inferior races emerged. They have all the characteristics of decrepitude and ineptitude for the civilized life. Without character—endowed with almost no mental life, apathetic, without aspirations, inadaptable to education."[12] A similar pessimist view was presented by a German witness to the indigenous rebellion in Huaraz in 1885 who held that "[t]he conflicts between different races cannot be solved on the basis of justice, and the racial wars are always wars of extermination."[13] Hence, the rebellious Indians cannot be subjected to the law.

In the dominant view however, propagated by the *civilista* government between 1893 and 1919, education was redemptive and seen to be the key of the homogenization of races and the formation of a true nation-state. Although education had been an explicit task of the provincial councils since 1870, the central state administration and the Lima elite reclaimed the domain around 1905 when free and obligatory education was turned into a responsibility of the central state (Wilson 2001). For many decades, however, education could only be accessed in the towns, and was intimately associated with urban life and modernization.

Education was not the only domain of increased state presence, which deepened the difference between the rural and the urban in terms of citizenship. In a brilliant analysis, Wilson shows how health and hygiene became a field of intervention through which identity and

---

[12] Clemente Palma (1897), "El Porvenir de las Razas en el Peru," quoted in Flores Galindo (1994: 231; my translation).

[13] Ernst Middendorph, quoted in Flores Galindo (1994, 231).

the status of citizenship in provincial Peru was reworked at the turn of the nineteenth century (Wilson 2003b). The town elites' preoccupation with modernization and the creation of a proper public, urban space coincided with the spread of worldviews and causal explanations based on the new natural science. Hence, new regulations for the combat of epidemics generated new distinctions and requirements that tended to bar the rural, indigenous population from urban space, such as the market and the cemetery. One example was the law in 1896 that demanded families of deceased persons to present an official document within twenty-four hours in order to give them access to the cemetery of the town (Wilson 2003b). In practice, this meant that the rural population was barred from access, quite contrary to the colonial scheme of governance, when the town was the ritual centre of the *ayllus* that had been congregated around the "Indian town" (Wilson 2003b).

In general terms, the late nineteenth century seems to displace indigeneity or Indianness to the rural hinterlands as new indexes of modernity, stateness, and citizenship are introduced, such as property, hygiene, and education. As Wilson (2003b) suggests, the rural-urban dichotomy seems to be sharpened as, on the one hand, urban subalterns are de-Indianized, defined in class terms and associated with the will and scope of betterment and modernization,[14] whereas, on the other hand, the rural population is indianized and defined in increasingly abstract racial/ethnic terms. The difference in institutional, physical presence of the state in the forms of schools and other institutions was of course marked, but the divide was reflected in other ways as well.

Deborah Poole gives the example of the "criminal anthropology" spreading in Peru around 1900, which linked certain forms of violence—in particular cattle rustling—to the Indian highlanders (Poole 1988). Inspired by European theories concerning the climatic and racial origins of criminal behavior, an identity was constructed between the harsh, open space of the high agricultural frontier, the Indian race inhabiting these empty, uncivil (prehistorical and prepolitical) spaces, and the frequent occurrence of violence and criminal behavior. The identity was so marked that, in some cases, the mere fact that the accused lived isolated, outside urban space, was sufficient evidence of criminal behavior. By contrast, in the interest of liberal equality in law, the pure, uncivilized Indian could not be held as responsible for his acts as the "half-civilized," while the latter should be judged "prudentially," that is, according to the habitat and mental development of the individual in question (386). As such, rural Indians could be seen as exceptions in regard to the national law.

[14] See also de la Cadena (2000).

The rural-urban divide was also at the heart of ideological struggles over citizenship and indigeneity in the early twentieth century when provincial intellectuals began to react against the progressive centralization and aristocratic nature of the *civilista* government. This "regionalist" movement became particularly important in the "Indian South"[15] where it developed into a distinct form of *indigenismo*, which was a pan-Latin American movement with the purpose of defending the Indian population and constructing regional or national political cultures based on indigenous culture (Poole 1997, 182).

The *indigenistas* reacted to ideas of biological racism and embraced the new ideas of the environment—geographical as well as social—as determining social types (de la Cadena 1998b). Although *indigenistas* shared with other groups of intellectuals the rejection of bioracism and national projects of "whitening" through cross-breeding, they did not join the celebration of the cultural *mestizo* as a national ideal (de la Cadena 1998b; 2000). Unlike in Mexico, where cultural hybridization or "*mestizaje*" became official policy after the revolution (see Alonso in this volume), the Peruvian *indigenistas* condemned the cultural-racial hybridity as much as they celebrated indigenous purity. They saw the *mestizo,* and in particular the *gamonal* and the literate Indian of the rural towns, as degenerated, ignorant, abusive, and misplaced, a disdain that harks back to the colonial elite's disdain of the *mestizo* caste (de la Cadena 1998b, 35). The indigenist ideologue Valcarcél described the *mestizo* town as a sleepy place with the inhabitants hiding away in the shadow: "What do these troglodytes do? They do nothing. They are the parasites, the scum of the sewer [T]he master of the wretched *mestizo* town is the quack lawyer [who] is secretly feared and abhorred [. . .] He exploits the whites and the aborigines equally. Lying is his job." The *ayllus* on the other hand, "breath happiness," "enkindle pure beauty," and are "pieces of pure nature."[16]

Thus, the *indigenistas* produced a romantic image of the Indians as predestined to develop in the rural habitat where they rightfully belonged, but where they were exploited by *gamonales.* As analyzed by de la Cadena, the *indigenistas* in this way cleared the middle ground between the illiterate, rural Indians and the well-educated urban intellectuals of dark complexion who experienced being treated as *mistis (mestizos)* by the Indians in the highland and despised as *cholos* in Lima (de la Cadena 1998a).[17] Although the Lima elite regarded provincialism as

<hr/>

[15] The "Indian South" referred in the beginning of the twentieth century mainly to the departments of Cusco and Puno, which were important economic centers for the booming wool production (de la Cadena 1998b).

[16] Valcarcél (1925), quoted in de la Cadena (1998, 148–49).

[17] *Cholo* is usually a derogative term for the urbanized Indian but also can have positive connotations when used in diminutive.

the problem of development of the nation, the *indigenistas* regarded the violent and ignorant *gamonales*—to be distinguished from good, educated hacienda owners—as the main problem (de la Cadena 1998b). Politically, the *indigenistas* came to occupy the space that, in Thurner's (1997) interpretation, had been opened by the indigenous imagination of a *republicano* citizenship, somewhere in between the colonial tax-land pact, and the revolutionary idea of equal citizenship rights for all, including the former Indians. The most explicit product of *indigenista* influence in Peruvian politics came in the first part of President Leguías government (1919–1930) with the provisions for the recognition of "indigenous communities" in the Constitution of 1919.

POPULAR SOVEREIGNTY AND INDIGENOUS COMMUNITIES

When President Leguías came to power in 1919, he launched his "new fatherland" (*Nueva Patria*), an authoritarian, populist project for the modernization of Peru, under heavy influence from anti-aristocratic and *indigenista* intellectuals. He presided over what may be described as Peru's first modern, normalizing state (Poole 1997, 213), which made a tangible investment in health, education, and infrastructure (Slater 1989). He abolished municipal elections and appointed local and regional authorities as part of an unprecedented centralization of government. With a brief exception in the 1960s, municipal elections were not resumed before 1980 (Degregori et al. 1998).

Although the centralization undermined provincial elites and the remnants of the city-states, and removed the fora in which Indians could have a minimum of influence on politics (Wilson 2003a), a new regime of government was installed for rural populations. Recognizing the rights of "Indian communities," the new Constitution gave the state explicit responsibility for the protection, development, and culture of "the indigenous race" for which a specific set of laws was defined (Winder 1978). In 1921, Leguías established an Office for Indigenous Affairs under the Ministry of Development, and from 1926 communities were recognized and given titles to land. Communities achieved juridical personhood (*personería jurídica*) and were represented by the *personero* who dealt directly with the state administration and the courts. As such, the community was a modern form of organization.

The *Alcalde* system, which had functioned as a kind of shadow government of the former Indian communities, was never recognized as representative of the Indigenous communities. The *Alcalde* system was abolished by decree in 1828, but *Alcaldes* continued to serve the republican administration in many ways, in particular by embodying relations between towns and their dependent neighborhoods and villages, where the *Alcaldes* were used for tax collection and mobilization of voluntary workers for *faenas*—the general turnouts for public works and other tasks—in the town (Ramos and Ramos 1983). During and after the Pacific War, the *Alcaldes* appeared to provide the organizational glue and political edge of rural communities. Authorities negotiated with them, but they remained publicly unrecognized and were prohibited again and again. In 1933, for example, more than one hundred years after the first abolition, Law No. 479 declared that "[I]n an absolute manner, the appointment of 'Alcalde de Vara' or 'Varayoc' among the indigenous of the Central region is abolished" and that "[T]he authorities which in any manner break this law by intervening in, or permitting, the appointment of 'Alcaldes de Vara' or 'Varayoc' will be substituted immediately."[18] Nevertheless, the *Alcaldes* still, toward the end of the twentieth century, had a role to play in many highland areas in Central and Southern Peru (Degregori et al. 1998).

Far from being a reinvention of the indirect government of the colony, it may be useful to consider the indigenous communities in the perspective of Mamdani's discussion of the forms of indirect government, which developed in colonial Africa in the first decades of the twentieth century. The Indian communities of the colony were "detribalized" during the long nineteenth century—the *Kuraka* families lost their privileges, the *Alcalde* institution was abolished by law, the land-tax nexus was disarticulated, and the labor services prohibited. However, the new indigenous communities tended to "retribalize" parts of rural society, framing what Mamdani would call an "ethnic citizenship" (Mamdani 1996; 1998). Emphasizing social rights rather than the civic and political rights of "civic" citizenship, the Constitution entitled poor rural dwellers to state owned land *qua* their nativity and their assumed belonging to an ancestral cultural community, the precolonial *Ayllu,* so celebrated in the indigenist literature.

The indigenous communities seem, to a certain degree, to live up to the perception of citizenship that guided the political agency of the former Indians in the second half of the nineteenth century. This perception was based on ideas of social rights and a reciprocal relationship between the state, providing land, and the former Indians providing taxes, labor, and military service. But, as defined in the Constitution, the special regime for *comuneros* constituted a biopolitical program for the improvement ("development") of the indigenous race, which in due time and in an appropriate environment should enable them to live up to national standards for citizens and to assume full responsibility. In

[18] Quoted in Ramos and Ramos (1983, 140). As they mention (120), the law of 1933 was not respected, either. Even public documents from governors calling for labor service demand the *Alcalde Varayocs* to mobilize labor.

this sense, the communities resembled the North American reservations (Biolsi 1995) and the South African homelands.

It has been argued that the indigenous communities were supposed to serve as labor reserves from where cheap migrant labor could be recruited for export agriculture, mining, and the construction of roads and cities. Drawing on Agamben's analytical perspective it may, however, also be argued that the special status for racially marked rural populations is related to the development of national sovereignty and the national political community (Agamben 1998, 2000). In other words, the communities constituted an attempt to contain an unruly rural population, which was to be subjected to a biopolitical regime without being recognized as a political actor and incorporated as such in the political body of the nation. Agamben's image of the camp, the space of the permanent state of exception, as a basic structuring principle of liberal society may seem far fetched. But considering the fearful memories and violent repressions of the Tupac Amaru rebellion and the *montoneros* movement, as well as the contemporary rural mobilizations that formed the background for the indigenist movement in early-twentieth-century Cusco (de la Cadena 2000), the interpretation of the indigenous communities as a kind of counterinsurgency program cannot be dismissed that easily.

SOVEREIGNTY, RURAL GOVERNANCE, AND SECOND-CLASS CITIZENSHIP IN PERU

This chapter has given an account of the dismantling of the colonial indirect government of the Indian Republic and the incorporation of the former Indians in the Peruvian Republic that took place between the late eighteenth and the early twentieth century. We have seen how the former Indian towns and communities were gradually weakened and undermined as their privileges were removed and haciendas encroached upon the land and labor supplies of their dependent settlements. Far from being able to establish effective territorial sovereignty, the Peruvian state depended on a new figure, the *gamonal*, who controlled public offices and established sovereign domains through a combination of paternalist practices, control of the law, and violent spectacles. Together with the unrecognized *Alcaldes* the *gamonales* filled the space between what Carlos Fuentes has called "the legal" and "the real" country,[19] between the formal structures of governance and the deeply contested sovereignty of the state at local level, thus generating a kind of interstitial sovereignty.

[19] Carlos Fuentes: "Latin America at war with itself," quoted in Lowell (1990, 99).

During the second half of the nineteenth century, the (colonial) conception of race, which was based on blood and lineage and served as an exclusive weapon of the aristocracy, gave way to a biological concept of race. This served as a scientific language through which Indians could be described, classified, and treated as morally inferior people and subjected to biopolitical techniques and programs of improvement (Poole 1997; Stoler 1995). It seems, however, that it was the event of the Pacific War and in particular the Indian social movements in its wake that generated the push toward the development of biopolitical programs, in the provincial capitals as well as in the center of the nation.

In Peru, nationalist projects of modernization became associated with an increasingly dichotomous and racialized distinction between the urban and the rural. The urban became the locus of modernization and projects of self-discipline as described so vividly by David Nugent (1997) in the case of Chachapoyas where nonelite urban classes embodied the movements for popular sovereignty between 1910 and 1930. These movements excluded the indigenous inhabitants of the rural hinterland to where indianness was increasingly confined as described above. In this way, the de-Indianization of the urban nonelite classes was accompanied by the Indianization of the rural Andean population (de la Cadena 1998b, 2000).

What we may regard as an incipient political society forming around the *Alcaldes* who sought to negotiate conditions of citizenship with state incumbents was quelled or disregarded after the *montoneros* had been pacified, whereas urban-based social movements—first *indigenistas,* later unions and political parties, including the Shining Path—saw it as their responsibility to represent the rural communities and defend them against the violent and ignorant *gamonales.*

With the legislation that provided for the "indigenous communities," the racialized split between the government of rural communities and the government of urban populations was institutionalized in the Peruvian state. Subject to the sovereign state, the community tended to become a quasi-sovereign, in the name of which members could be punished and excommunicated in case they did not live up to the obligations and moral standards decided upon by the communal authorities. The rural communities were (in principle, if not effectively) subjected to a biopolitical regime, which, protecting them from the forces of the market, was meant to control and civilize them in a space and speed, which coincided with their *habitus.* With the institutionalization of the differentiated government between rural communities and urban populations the Leguía regime constituted a distinction between first- and second-class citizens. Whereas the government of the urban emphasized self-discipline, the government of the rural Andean population was particularly authoritarian (Poole 1994). Thus, there seems to be a line from the fear of the insubordinate colonial and post-colonial Indian since the late eighteenth century; from the conviction of *gamonales* that violence and authoritarian management was necessary for the control of the rural Indian; to the unleashing of violence upon the Andean rural communities by the Peruvian army as well as the Shining Path in the late twentieth century; and the authoritarian politics of President Fujimori (1990–2000), who tended to present himself as the only representative of the second-class citizens while tending to reproduce the rural populations as biopolitical rather than political subjects. The disturbing fact in this regard is the support he received from exactly this part of the population who saw him as their ally in the struggle against the national Peruvian elites. As his slogan went: *Cholitos y Chinitos en contra los Blanquitos* (Cholos and Chinese against the Whites) (Oleart 1998).

Sovereign Violence and the Domain of the Political

Partha Chatterjee

I

It is modernity that I will talk about. And also violence, which is a theme that etches itself so strongly on the stories of Saadat Hasan Manto, one of the greatest writers of modern South Asia. As is well known, the question of violence lies at the very heart of the concept of sovereignty. The modern state's claim to unchallenged territorial sovereignty is in fact identical to the Weberian definition of its claim to a monopoly of legitimate violence. Manto often describes with pitiless irony the devastating hollowness of these claims. But because I do not have the facility to draw large conclusions from the singular familiarity of fictional narratives, I need a different site to ground my thoughts. I will do so in the much-talked-about field of Indian democracy. I will speak about state and society in India as they come together in the democratic process. On that ground, I will talk about modernity, religion, and the sovereign violence of the state.

There is now a large literature examining the relation between state institutions and society in India. Lloyd and Rudolph (1987) have suggested that the balance has shifted periodically from a "demand polity" in which societal demands expressed as electoral pressure dominate over the state and a "command polity" where state hegemony prevails over society. The late M.S.A. Rao, in his last work done jointly with Francine Frankel, had suggested that public institutions such as the bureaucracy and organized industry, which had previously been the centers of dominance, were now under pressure from the rising power, especially of the lower castes, in political institutions such as the legislatures and the political parties (Rao and Frankel 1990). From the periodic swings of the Rudolphs' model, the narrative here has become one of the decline of a political order. Further underscoring the theme of decline, Atul Kohli (1991) has described the recent history of Indian politics as one in which, by surrendering to the immediate electoral pressures exercised by various social groups, democratic state institutions have been allowed to decay, leading to an all-round crisis of governability.

One problem I have had with the existing literature, framed as it is largely within the confines of a modernization narrative, whether of a Weberian or a Marxian type, is that the conceptual domains of state and society have either had to be sharply distinguished, with the central state institutions carrying the burden of an interventionist project of modernizing traditional social institutions and practices, or collapsed entirely so that state practices become completely molded by the pulls and pressures of prevailing social institutions. With the unquestioned spread and deepening of electoral politics in India in the last three decades, it has become difficult to locate the sites, if any, of an interventionist project of changing society, or indeed of the transformations that have been brought about by the expansion of democracy itself.

In a series of recent papers, I have attempted to sketch out a conceptual field where some of these questions could be tackled (Chatterjee 1998a, 1998b, 1998c, 2004). One move I have suggested is to think of a field of practices mediating not between state and citizens in civil society but between governmental agencies and population groups.[1] I have favored retaining the old idea of civil society as bourgeois society, in the sense used by Hegel and Marx, and of using it in the Indian context as an actually existing arena of institutions and practices inhabited by a relatively small section of the people whose social locations can be identified with a fair degree of clarity. In terms of the *formal* structure of the state as given by the constitution and the laws, all of society is civil society; everyone is a citizen with equal rights and therefore to be regarded as a member of civil society. The political process, then, is supposed to be defined by the interaction of the organs of the state with members of civil society in their individual capacities or as members of associations. In actual fact, this is not how things work. Most of the inhabitants of India are only tenuously, and even then ambiguously and contextually, rights-bearing citizens in the sense imagined by the constitution. They are not, therefore, proper members of civil society and are not regarded as such by the institutions of the state. But it is not as though they are outside the reach of the state or even excluded from the domain of politics. As populations within the territorial jurisdiction of the state, they have to be both looked after and controlled by various governmental agencies. These activities bring these populations into a certain *political* relationship with the state. But this relationship does not always conform to what is envisaged in the constitutional depiction of the relation between the state and members of civil society. Yet these

---

[1] The most complete statement of this argument is to be found in Chatterjee (2004).

are without doubt political relations that may have acquired, in specific historically defined contexts, a widely recognized systematic character and perhaps even certain conventionally recognized ethical norms, even if subject to varying degrees of contestation. How are we to begin to understand these processes?

It is to tackle questions of this kind that I proposed the idea of a *political society* encompassing the relations between governmental agencies and population groups that are the targets of government policy. Political society in this sense consists of a set of practices different from those constituted by relations between civil society and the state. Faced with similar problems, some analysts have favored expanding the idea of civil society to include virtually all existing social institutions that lie outside the strict domain of the state.[2] This has become rampant in the recent rhetoric of international financial institutions, aid agencies and nongovernmental organizations among whom the spread of a neoliberal ideology has authorized the consecration of every nonstate organization as the precious flower of the associative endeavors of free members of civil society. I have preferred to resist these unscrupulously charitable theoretical gestures, principally because I feel it is important not to lose sight of the vital and continually active project that still informs many of the state institutions in India to transform traditional social authorities and practices into the modular forms of bourgeois civil society. That civil society as an *ideal* continues to energize an interventionist political project, and that as an *actually existing form* it is demographically limited, are both facts that, I think, must be borne in mind when considering the relation between modernity and democracy in India.

It may be recalled that in the early phase of the Subaltern Studies project, we talked about a split in the domain of politics between an organized elite domain and an unorganized subaltern domain. The idea of the split, of course, was intended to mark a fault line in the arena of nationalist politics in the three decades before independence during which the Indian masses, especially the peasantry, were drawn into organized political movements and yet remained distanced from the evolving forms of the postcolonial state. To say that there was a split in the domain of politics was to reject the notion, common in both liberal and Marxist historiographies, that the peasantry lived in some "prepolitical" stage of collective action. It was to say that peasants in their collective actions also were being political, except that they were political in a way different from that of the elites. Because those early experiences of the imbrication of elite and subaltern politics in the context of

---

[2] For arguments of this kind, see Cohen and Arato (1992).

the anticolonial movements, the democratic process in India has come a long way in bringing under its influence the lives of the subaltern classes. It is to understand these relatively recent forms of the entanglement of elite and subaltern politics that I am proposing the notion of a political society.

In illustrating what I mean by political society and how it works, I have earlier used the example of a squatter settlement in the city of Calcutta and the efforts of the members of this settlement to assert their presence in urban life.[3] This they do through a body that has the form of a voluntary association but that uses a moral rhetoric of kinship and family loyalty. Because the settlement is premised on the illegal occupation of public land and therefore on the collective violation of property laws and civic regulations, the state authorities cannot treat it on the same footing as other civic associations following more legitimate social and cultural pursuits. Yet state agencies and nongovernmental organizations cannot ignore it either, because it is but one of hundreds of similar bodies representing groups of population whose very livelihood or habitation involve violation of the law. These agencies therefore deal with the settlers' association not as a body of citizens but as a convenient instrument for the administration of welfare to a marginal and underprivileged population group.

The squatters on their part accept that their occupation of public land is both illegal and contrary to good civic behavior, but they make a claim to a habitation and a livelihood as a matter of right. They profess a readiness to move out if they are given suitable alternative sites for resettlement. The state agencies recognize that these population groups have some claim on the welfare programs of the government, but those claims could not be regarded as justiciable rights as the state did not have the means to deliver those benefits to the entire population of the country. To treat those claims as rights would only invite further violation of public property and civic laws.

What happens then is a negotiation of these claims on a political terrain where, on the one hand, governmental agencies have a public obligation to look after the poor and the underprivileged and, on the other, particular population groups receive attention from those agencies according to calculations of political expediency. The squatter community I talked about has to pick its way through this uncertain terrain by making a large array of connections outside the group—with other groups in similar situations, with more privileged and influential groups, with government functionaries, with political parties and leaders, and so on. In the course of its struggles over almost five decades,

[3] This example is discussed in Chatterjee (1998b).

the squatters have managed to hold on to their settlement, but it is an extremely insecure hold as it is entirely dependent on their ability to operate within a field of strategic politics. I make the claim that this is the stuff of democratic politics as it takes place on the ground in India. It involves what appears to be a constantly shifting compromise between the normative values of modernity and the moral assertion of popular demands.

Civil society then, restricted to a small section of culturally equipped citizens, represents in countries like India the high ground of modernity. So does the constitutional model of the state. But in actual practice, governmental agencies must descend from that high ground to the terrain of political society in order to renew their legitimacy as providers of well-being and to confront whatever is the current configuration of politically mobilized demands. In the process, one is liable to hear complaints from the protagonists of civil society and the constitutional state that modernity is facing an unexpected rival in the form of democracy.

I further explore this theme by giving you one more example from the domain of popular politics in the Indian city.[4]

II

On May 5, 1993, in the early hours of dawn, a man died in a Calcutta hospital. He had been admitted a few days before and was being treated for diabetes molutus, renal failure and cerebrovascular accident. His condition had deteriorated rapidly in the previous twenty-four hours and, although the doctors attending him struggled through the night, their efforts were in vain. A senior doctor of the hospital signed the death certificate.

The name of the man who died was Birendra Chakrabarti, but he was better known as Balak Brahmachari, leader of the Santan Dal, a religious sect with a large following in the southern and central districts of West Bengal. The sect itself is no more than fifty years old, although it probably has its antecedents in earlier sectarian movements among the lower caste, especially Namasudra, peasants of central Bengal. Its religious doctrines are highly eclectic, consisting entirely of the views of Balak Brahmachari himself as expressed in his sayings, but they are characterized in particular by a curious involvement in political matters. The sect's mouthpiece *Kara Chabuk* (The Strong Whip) regularly published its leader's comments on current political subjects in which

[4] I am grateful to Ashok Dasgupta and Debashis Bhattacharya of *Ajkal* for their generous help in researching the story of Balak Brahmachari's death.

there was the recurrent theme of "revolution," a cataclysmic churning that would surgically cleanse a corrupt and putrid social order. The sect, in fact, first came into the public spotlight in the period 1967–1971 when it participated in political demonstrations in support of the Left parties and against Congress rule. The Santan Dal activists, with many women in their ranks, some in saffron clothes, holding aloft their tridents and shouting their slogan "Ram Narayan Ram,"[5] were an incongruous element in Leftist demonstrations in Calcutta at the time, and could not but attract attention. But no one accused the sect of opportunistic political ambitions, because it made no claims to electoral representation or recognition as a political party. Since then, many of the followers of the sect have been known to be sympathizers and even activists of the Left, especially of the Communist Party of India (Marxist) (CPI(M)), a leading partner in the Left Front, which has ruled West Bengal since 1977.

On this particular morning in May 1993, the followers of Balak Brahmachari refused to accept that their spiritual leader was dead. They recalled that several years ago, in 1960, he had gone into *samadhi* for twenty-two days during which, from all outward appearances, he was dead. But he had woken up from his trance and returned to normal life. Now once more, they said, their Baba (spiritual leader) had gone into *nirvikalpa samadhi*, a state of suspension of bodily functions that could be achieved only by those with the highest spiritual powers. The members of Santan Dal took the body of Balak Brahmachari from hospital to their *ashram* (sanctuary) in Sukhchar, a northern suburb of Calcutta, and began to keep what they said would be a long vigil.

Soon the matter became a cause célèbre in Calcutta. The press picked it up, publishing reports of how the body was being kept on slabs of ice under heavy air conditioning and of the defensiveness of the Dal spokesmen against hostile criticism. One Bengali daily, *Ajkal,* pursued the story with particular vigor, turning it into a fight for rational values in public life and against obscurantist beliefs and practices. It accused the local authorities and the health department of the West Bengal government of failing to implement their own rules regarding the disposal of dead bodies and of conniving in the making of a serious public hazard. Soon the authorities were forced to respond. On the thirteenth day of the vigil, the Panihati municipality clarified that it had served the Santal Dal leaders with a notice asking them to cremate the body immediately, but that under the municipal laws it had no powers to carry out a forcible cremation (*Ajkal*, May 18, 1993). On behalf of the Santan Dal, Chitta Sikdar, the secretary, kept up a regular defensive campaign

---

[5] A chant invoking Ram and Narayan, the two incarnations of Vishnu.

in the press, maintaining that the spiritual phenomenon of *nirvikalpa samadhi* was beyond the understanding of medical science and that Balak Brahmachari would soon resume his normal bodily life.

The standoff continued. *Ajkal* raised the tempo of its campaign, opening its columns to prominent intellectuals and public figures who deplored the persistence of such superstitious and unscientific beliefs among the people. Groups of activists from progressive cultural organizations, the popular science movement and the rationalist society began to hold demonstrations in front of the Santan Dal headquarters in Sukhchar. *Ajkal* spared no efforts to provoke the spokesmen of the Dal and to ridicule their statements, refusing to refer to the dead leader by his sectarian name of Balak Brahmachari and instead calling him "Balak Babu"—a nonsensical "Mr. Balak." There were some heated confrontations at the gate of the Santan Dal ashram, with the Dal activists reportedly stocking arms and preparing for a showdown. One night, some crackers and handmade bombs exploded outside the ashram and a group of Dal activists came out and shouted over their loudspeakers: "The revolution has begun" (*Ajkal*, June 21, 1993).

Nearly a month after the official death of Balak Brahmachari, his body still lay on ice slabs in an air conditioned room with his followers waiting for him to break his *samadhi*. *Ajkal* claimed that there was an unbearable stench in the entire neighborhood of Sukhchar and that the residents of the area had had enough. Now it began to be openly alleged that it was because of electoral reasons that the government was reluctant to intervene. The elections to the local government bodies in rural West Bengal, the crucial panchayats, which had become the backbone of Left Front support, were scheduled for the last week of May. Any action against the Dal could antagonize a lot of Left Front supporters in at least four districts of West Bengal. It also was suggested that some important leaders of the CPI(M) were sympathetic to the Santan Dal and that one minister in particular, Subhas Chakrabarti, minister in charge of tourism and sports, was regarded by Dal members as a fraternal supporter.

On June 25, 1993, fifty-one days after the official death of Balak Brahmachari, the health minister of West Bengal announced that a medical team consisting of leading specialists in medicine, neurology and forensic medicine would examine the body of Balak Brahmachari and submit a report to the government. The Indian Medical Association, the apex professional body of medical practitioners, immediately protested saying that to call for a new examination implied a lack of confidence in the death certificate issued from the hospital. It pointed out that no scientific grounds had been furnished to question the original judgment of the hospital doctors. The government doctors went ahead nevertheless and returned from Sukhchar to say that they had not been allowed to touch the body. They reported that the body had been putrefied and carried signs of mummification and that it had not decayed completely because of the extremely low temperature at which it had been kept (*Ajkal*, June 26, 1993).

By this time, Subhas Chakrabarti had been given charge by the CPI(M) leadership to devise a solution to the impasse. Accompanied by the local CPI(M) leaders, he visited the Sukhchar ashram and later told journalists that he was trying to persuade the followers of the Baba to cremate the body. He agreed that there was no scientific reason for doctors to reexamine a body that had been certified as dead, but insisted that this was a necessary part of the process of persuasion. He pointed out that "Babadom" was still prevalent in the country and that thousands of people were followers of these religious leaders. He warned that it was dangerous to take religious fanaticism lightly. It was the government's view, he said, that applying force could provoke fanaticism. When asked if he was aware of the health hazard that had been created in the neighbourhood of Sukhchar, he claimed that he had smelt nothing, but that was probably because he was a habitual inhaler of snuff (*Ajkal*, June 26, 1993).

On June 30, in a four-hour operation beginning at two in the morning, a force consisting of five thousand policemen stormed the Santan Dal headquarters, took charge of the body and removed it to a nearby crematorium. *The Telegraph* reported that the last rites were performed by the guru's brother as the security cordon pushed back wailing women who still believed their departed cult leader would be resurrected. The state government, severely criticized for soft-pedaling the issue, heaved a sigh of relief.

The police force, which was attacked by Dal activists with acid bulbs, knives, tridents, glass bottles, and chilli powder, used tear gas shells to immobilize the defenders and gas blowers to make its way through window grilles and collapsible gates into the heavily fortified headquarters. But it did not resort to shooting. Many Dal activists as well as policemen were hurt, but, as the official press release put it, "there were no casualties" (*The Telegraph*, July 1, 1993; *The Statesman*, July 1, 1993).

The minister Subhas Chakrabarti congratulated the police and the local administration for carrying out a very difficult and sensitive operation. He referred to the popular Hindi film *Jugnu* and said the job was more difficult than what the actor Dharmendra had faced in that film. "Of course," he said to journalists, "you think all that is lumpen culture, but I think it is an apt example." The following day, *Ajkal* in its editorial announced: "We have come to the end of that age in West Bengal when lumpen culture could be called lumpen culture. Progressive West Bengal has seen the end of the age of reason. Now begins the age of *Jugnu*" (*Ajkal*, July 2, 1993).

Despite the relatively smooth and successful conclusion of the matter, the controversy did not die down. Chitta Sikdar, the secretary of the Santan Dal, protested to the chief minister against what he described as an authoritarian and undemocratic action of the government. He said the treatment received by Balak Brahmachari at the hands of the rulers of society would be remembered in history in the same way as the trials of Jesus Christ, Galileo and Socrates. By contrast, opinions such as that of *Ajkal* condemned as opportunistic the attempt by sections of the government and the ruling party to target the second-rank leaders of the sect for misleading their innocent followers and profiting from their over-excited religious sentiments but not criticizing the sects and the so-called godmen themselves for spreading unreason and superstition. Twelve days after the cremation of Balak Brahmachari, the secretary of the Santan Dal and eighty-two others were arrested and charged with rioting, assault, obstruction of justice and other offences (*Ajkal*, July 13, 1993).

Members of the Santan Dal continued for several months to write letters to newspapers portraying themselves as victims of an undemocratic and illegal police action. They asked what laws of the land the Baba's followers had broken by believing that he would come back to them. Did a religious belief in extraordinary spiritual powers deserve blows from the policeman's truncheon? And was it not the case that the Dal followers were finally subjected to police action because most of them were low-caste peasants whose marginal political value had evaporated after the local government elections were over? Although public memory might be short, one letter warned, the memory of victimhood was merciless. The perpetrators of injustice would one day meet their day of judgment (*Dainik Pratibedan*, February 5, 1994).

The case illustrates, I think, several of the points I have raised so far about the relation between modernity and democracy in a country like India. Modernity is a project that is located in the historical desires of certain elite sections of Indians. The specific story of the emergence and flowering of those desires and their sources in colonial projects has been much discussed. There was a time, when the country was under colonial rule, when it was believed by these elites that the crucial transformative processes that would change the traditional beliefs and practices of the people and fashion a new modern national self must be kept out of the reach of the colonial state apparatus. With the end of colonial rule and the coming to power of these classes in the postcolonial state, that transformative project became firmly located in the dynamic potential of the organs of the new national state. That those organs were now part of a constitutional system of representative democracy made the modernizing project an expression of the will of the people and thus gloriously consistent with the legitimizing norms of modernity itself.

Religion came under the sway of this transformative project in a major way. In the colonial period, the transformation was carried out through a variety of social institutions, including new sectarian movements of reformed religion, both Hindu and Islamic, using all of the new cultural technologies of print and pedagogy. In the process, a certain cultural consensus emerged among the elite sections of Indians on the norms of religious practice in modern life. These norms made it possible for the leading groups in society to make distinctions between acceptable ritual behavior or doctrinal belief, and unacceptable superstition and irrationality. Following independence, the normalizing of religious practice was carried out most ambitiously through the legal organs of the state in the constitution itself and also in the set of legislations known as the Hindu Code Bill. The minority religious practices were left largely untouched by this exercise, not because they were not thought to be in need of reform but because of the uncertainty as to whether the will of the people as expressed by a parliamentary majority carried an adequate measure of legitimacy for the minority communities. In other words, there was already a nuanced and differentiated notion of representation built into the idea of democratic legitimacy, even though the idea of separate representation of minorities was anathema.

This project of cultural transformation through the powers of a democratically constituted state has become considerably muted in the last two decades. A crucial experience that, I think, defined the new limits of state action in Indian democracy was that of Indira Gandhi's emergency regime in 1975–1977. That brought home to India's elites the fact that modernizing agendas could be made the political pretext for setting up an authoritarian regime that was little more than a perversion of the so-called will of the people. Such a regime put at risk all of the legal-political guarantees for a large, complex, and differentiated bourgeois civic life, even if it did not directly threaten the well-being of the bourgeoisie as a class. Moreover, the emergency regime also failed to prove that it could sustain itself as a self-reproducing structure, as in other authoritarian systems in the postcolonial world, in the face of the various impediments it faced from both within and outside the country. Following the collapse of the emergency regime in 1977, a consensus emerged among modernizers of both the Left and the Right that it was unwise to push through projects of social change by means of forcible state intervention unless these were first negotiated through certain mediating processes between state and society.

Although many of the sites and activities characteristic of the arena I have called political society can be shown to have emerged within the spectrum of nationalist political mobilizations in the colonial period, I would say that it has taken on something like a distinct form only since the 1980s. Two conditions have facilitated this process. One is the rise to dominance of a notion of governmental performance that emphasizes the welfare and protection of populations—the "pastoral" functions of government, as Michel Foucault called it—using similar governmental technologies all over the world but largely independent of considerations of active participation by citizens in the sovereignty of the state. This has enabled the mutual recognition by state agencies and population groups that governments are obliged to deliver certain benefits even to people who are not proper members of civil society or of the republican body of true citizens. The second condition is the widening of the arena of political mobilization, even if only for electoral ends, from formally organized structures such as political parties with well-ordered internal constitutions and coherent doctrines and programs to loose and often transient mobilizations, building on communication structures that would not ordinarily be recognized as political (for instance, religious assemblies or cultural festivals, or more curiously, even associations of cinema fans, as in many of the southern states).

The proliferation of activities in this arena of political society has caused much discomfort and apprehension in progressive elite circles in recent years. The comment about "lumpen culture" in the *Ajkal* editorial I cited earlier is typical. The complaint is widespread in middle-class circles today that politics has been taken over by mobs and criminals. The result is the abandonment—or so the complaint goes—of the mission of the modernizing state to change a backward society. Instead, what we see is the importation of the disorderly, corrupt and irrational practices of unreformed popular culture into the very hallways and chambers of civic life, all because of the calculations of electoral expediency. The noble pursuit of modernity appears to have been seriously compromised because of the compulsions of parliamentary democracy.

Given a history in India of more than a hundered years of modern representative institutions, we can now see a pattern of evolution of this familiar Tocquevillian problem (Kaviraj 1998). Early liberals like Dadabhai Naoroji or Gopal Krishna Gokhale or even Muhammad Ali Jinnah in the early phase of his political life were entirely convinced of the inherent value of those institutions, but they were also hugely circumspect about the conditions in which they could function. As good nineteenth-century liberals, they would have been the first to specify requirements such as education and a proved commitment to civic life that would have to be met before a people could be considered fit, in their language, "to receive parliamentary institutions." If we look at it from another angle, we might say that for men like Naoroji or Gokhale, democracy was a good form of government only when it could be adequately controlled by men of status and wisdom. With the rise of the so-called Extremists in nationalist politics, especially with the Khilafat and Noncooperation movements, there came into organized political life in India many forces and many ideas that did not care too much about the niceties of parliamentary politics. It was Gandhi, of course, who in this period, intervened decisively in the political arena created by the new representative institutions of the late colonial order. Even as he claimed to reject parliamentary institutions along with all of the other trappings of modern civilization, he was more instrumental than anyone else in bringing about the mobilization that would in the end make the Indian National Congress the ruling political organization of independent India. As has been shown in many studies, Gandhi's words and actions are shot through by the parallel themes of unleashing popular initiative and controlling it at the same time.[6] With the formalization of Congress rule in the first decade and a half after independence, control became the dominant motif in the close interweaving of state initiative and electoral approval in the so-called Congress system of the Nehru period.

The journey from the Nehru period to the crisis of the mid-1960s to the reestablishment of Congress dominance in the state populism of the first Indira Gandhi regime is a trajectory that is not unfamiliar to the historical experience of many Third World countries. What was distinctive in the life of Indian democracy is, I think, the defeat of Indira Gandhi's emergency regime in a parliamentary election. It brought about a decisive shift in all subsequent discussion about the essence and appearance of democracy, its form and content, its inner nature and outward appearance. Whatever may be the judgment of historians on the "real" causes of the collapse of the emergency regime, the 1977 elections established in the arena of popular mobilizations in India the capacity of the vote and of representative bodies of government to give voice to popular demands of a kind that had never before been allowed to disturb the order and tranquility of the proverbial corridors of power. One cannot but wonder if this is not the momentous experience that separates the popular understanding of democracy in India from that in Pakistan where it is possible today for both elites and subalterns to say in unison that electoral democracy is a fake and that the path to true democracy may have to pass through a spell of military dictatorship.

But before we in India are too quick to congratulate ourselves, let me restate what I have been arguing so far in this talk. The contrary themes

[6] The writings of the Subaltern Studies group of historians have explored these themes most elaborately. See, in particular, Guha (1998).

of popular legitimacy and elite control remained embedded in the conception of Indian democracy from the very beginning. They have not gone away, nor have they been resolved or superseded. They have only taken new forms as a result of the ongoing struggles between elite and popular conceptions of democracy. They are being played out once again in the recent debates over democratic modernization in India. The uncertain demands of popular ratification have led committed modernizers to throw up their hands and lament that the age of reason had been brought to an end by the political surrender to the forces of disorder and irrationality. They read the many compromises with electoral compulsions as signs of the abandonment of enlightened politics. Generally less noticed are the transformative effects of these contrary mobilizations among the supposedly unenlightened sections of the population. Because this is an area that is only beginning to be studied, I can only make certain preliminary remarks on it. But this constitutes, I believe, the most profound and significant set of social changes that are being produced by the democratic process in India today.

In one of my recent writings dealing with the question of minority rights and the secular state in India, I had suggested that the more democratic strategy would be to promote representative processes *within* the minority communities themselves (Chatterjee 1997). It has been objected that this is "too strong" a requirement, that it is a concession to religious-communitarian politics itself, and that it smacks of the "separate electorates" system in British India or even (some have said) to the *millet* system in Ottoman Turkey. I could give a range of answers to these objections, but the one that will be most pertinent here is the following. All of these objections spring from the inability to recognize a domain of politics that is located neither within the constitutional limits of the state nor in the orderly transactions of bourgeois civil society, even though it is *about* both. The encounter with the constitutional state and the normative requirements of civil society has engendered a certain demand for representativeness within the various communities that *are* the social forms of populations in India. This is the most tangible effect of democratization in India. Even as population groups both engage with and resist the agencies of the state, they give rise to an internal process in which community leaderships are criticized, new voices are heard, other examples of other communities are cited, and the demand raised for greater representativeness within the community. These processes have occurred most visibly in recent years in the mobilizations among the dalits and the so-called other backward classes. But they have also occurred among tribal populations and indeed among the religious minorities. And if one looks to the immensely rich and productive debate coming out of the women's movement in

India, one cannot fail to notice the importance of the strategic question: legal reform through state initiative from the top or mobilization of initiatives within the relatively unmobilized spaces of the communities themselves? To choose the former is to underscore the moral primacy of the modernizing state and the legitimacy of its claims to sovereign violence. To advocate the latter is to accept the risks of walking through a normatively uncertain political terrain. If my critics demand that I state my preference between the two, I would say that although the former strategy has not necessarily exhausted itself, I believe that the real challenge lies in exploring the possibilities of the latter.

Let me also say that there has already evolved among the governing classes in India one response to this strategic choice. I see this as a variant of the colonial strategy of indirect rule. This involves a suspension of the modernization project, walling in the protected zones of bourgeois civil society and dispensing the governmental functions of law and order and welfare through the "natural leaders" of the governed populations. The strategy, in other words, seeks to preserve the civil virtues of bourgeois life from the potential excesses of electoral democracy. I am convinced that this was the attitude taken by the economically dominant groups in Bombay, the industrial and financial capital of India and the apex of its urban cosmopolitan culture, toward the political leadership of the Shiv Sena, the most overtly fascist element in the Hindu right-wing formation that, until a few years ago, ruled the state of Maharashtra.

The other response is less cynical, even as it is more pragmatic. It does not abandon the project of enlightenment but attempts to steer it through the thicket of contestations in what I have called political society. It takes seriously the functions of direction and leadership of a vanguard, but accepts that the legal arm of the state in a country like India cannot reach into a vast range of social practices that continue to be regulated by other beliefs and administered by other authorities. But it also knows that those dark zones are being penetrated by the welfare functions of modern governmental practices, producing those effects on claims and representation that I have called the urge for democratization. This is the zone in which the project of democratic modernity has to operate—slowly, painfully, unsurely.

In bringing up the example of the negotiations over the disposal of a dead body in Calcutta, I was not trying to provide a narrative of the correct handling of contradictions among the people. Nor am I saying that the specific form in which a local crisis of modernity-versus-democracy was resolved on that occasion flowed out of a conscious political project of social transformation in which the ruling parties in West Bengal are engaged. Rather, my intention was to point out the possibilities that exist in that normatively nebulous zone that I have called political society. When I use that term, I am always reminded that in the *Prison Notebooks*, Antonio Gramsci begins by equating political society with the state, but soon slides into a whole range of social and cultural interventions that must take place well beyond the domain of the state. I have tried here to emphasize that even in resisting the modernizing project that is imposed on them, the subaltern classes embark on a path of internal transformation. At the same time, in carrying out their pedagogical mission in political society, the educators—enlightened people like us—might also succeed in educating themselves. That, I submit, will be the most enriching and historically significant result of the encounter between modernity and democracy in a country like India.

III

Finally, I come to the subject of sovereign violence. Manto's distinctness, as has been pointed out many times, lies in his merciless, sometimes brutally unsentimental, handling of the theme of violence. His English translator, Khalid Hasan, has remarked: "He alone of the writers of his time was able to turn the bloody events of 1947 into great literature" (Hasan 1987, 8). Few will quarrel with this judgment. But it is worth asking why others did not even try to do what Manto did. Is there some mystery here about the nature of the violence of 1947 that defied representation? I think it is useful to consider this question in the context of the complicated relationship of modernity to democracy and of the role of the violence of the modern state.

In August 1954, seven years after partition and a year before his death, Manto is supposed to have written an epitaph for himself. "Here lies Saadat Hasan Manto," it said. "With him lie buried all the arts and mysteries of short story writing. Under tons of earth he lies, wondering if he is a greater story writer than God" (Hasan 1987, 9–10).[7] Some may read these lines as one more example of Manto's penchant for shocking his readers by an exaggerated display of his bloated ego. What vulgar insolence, they might say, to compare the creativity of a story writer with that of god! But others—an unfortunate few, perhaps—will recognize here the condition of the modern secular mind, trapped under tons of political doubt. If ever there was poignancy in irony, I think it is here. It expresses the predicament of a creative human spirit that must continue the work of creation in a world that, it believes, has been permanently abandoned by God. How does it do its work?

[7] I was drawn to this epitaph by Aamir R. Mufti's reflections on it in Mufti (in press).

Let us note, first of all, that the condition we are talking about here is not one that belongs to the world of the popular. The latter is suffused with the idea that the act of making the world requires powers that are much larger than what belongs to ordinary humans. The violence of human life is also made sense of, more often than not, as the violence of the gods, sometimes transparent, sometimes inscrutable. I once spent many months scouring the archives for eyewitness accounts of communal riots in Bengal. I came away with the lasting impression that even as ordinary people often described in vivid detail the disastrous things that happened to them, they tended to attribute the reasons to some externalized cause, something that was purposive but beyond themselves. In one his many famous disagreements with rationalists, Gandhi insisted after the Bihar earthquakes of 1934 that these were a "divine chastisement" for the sin of untouchability. Deliberately taking up a position located in popular beliefs, he said in effect that this was a violence of God. When asked why God should inflict a punishment that did not distinguish between upper castes and untouchables, Gandhi said, "I am not God. Therefore I have but a limited knowledge of his purpose" (Gandhi 1958, 87). On the basis of what I know about the subject, I am not persuaded that there exists in popular consciousness a notion of violence that is fundamentally without reason. Violence may be committed for vengeance, for punishment, for justice, for practicing an occupation, for a host of other reasons including possession by spirits, demons, gods, but rarely, perhaps never, as a senseless act without deliberate cause.

It is the modern secular consciousness, for whom—famously—the world has become a disenchanted place, that faces this peculiar problem of making sense of violence in human life. At the risk of grossly oversimplifying a huge history to which the greatest minds of the modern world have devoted their attention, let me say that at least as far as the world of modern political life is concerned, there have been two strategies that have been followed to bring reason and order to the facts of violence. One is to create a transcendental umbrella of ethics under which to shelter and domesticate the use of violence. This produces certain notions of goodness and justice that are believed to be true and, in the appropriate conditions, the use of violence is considered a legitimate instrument to achieve those transcendentally established moral goals. Justice, punishment, discipline, progress, science—there have been many notions of the just and the good that have legitimized violence in the modern world. The other strategy is to devise an economy of violence. The question here is not whether to use violence, but how much? Of what kind? To what purpose? With what results? It is not an ethical imperative that works here, but one of costs and benefits, of matching causes to effects, of efficiency.

Modern political life makes sense of violence either by measuring it against an ethical imperative or by reducing it to the grid of an economy. We can see both moves being made in the story I narrated earlier about the death of Balak Brahmachari. The protagonists of rationality were complaining about the squeamishness of the government, hemmed in by electoral pressures, in imposing its own rules of public order and morality. If the government had to use force, the rationalists were saying, it should have used it, because it would have been justified. The government, in the end, did use violence, but within a carefully deployed economy of forces and effects so that it could say that no more violence was used than was necessary to produce the desired results: "there were no casualties," it declared. The members of the Santan Dal, to the extent that they participated in this discourse of modern politics, protested against what they believed was an illegitimate use of force that violated their right to hold and practice their religious beliefs. Everyone participated in making sense of the violence of the modern state.

To the extent that I know the history and literature of the violence of 1947, I believe there is a similar eagerness on all sides to make sense of it in terms of the logic of the modern nation-state. There are considerations of ethics—and of praise or blame—in the demands and concessions of different parties—the Congress, the Muslim League, the British. What is the loss of partition for Indians is the success of independence for Pakistanis. And then there are the considerations of economy. Was the violence inevitable? Could it have been avoided? Were the British too hasty in wanting to get out? Could a little more state violence at the right time have avoided the uncontrolled explosion of communal violence? It is not that nothing has been said about 1947. In fact, a great deal has been said, and is still being said. They have been said within the twin parameters of ethics and economy.

Manto's uniqueness lies in the fact that he refused to accept the parameters of either ethics or economy in talking about the violence of 1947. He had no recourse to a morality that was given to him either by God or by transcendental reason. Nor would he allow himself to be seduced by the economic calculations of governmental violence. For him, the violence of partition called for a response that was, if I may put it this way, an act of pure politics, where morality and economy had to be created all at once, all by oneself, *de novo,* from the bare elements of human interaction. It was at such a moment of pure politics that Bishan Singh "stood in no man's land on his swollen legs like a colossus." Pure politics, grounded in nothing other than its own domain. But this moment of pure politics cannot be sustained. The scope of its creative promise is too enormous, the burden of its responsibility too great. Bishan Singh, also known as Toba Tek Singh, screamed and then collapsed to the ground: "There, behind barbed wire, on one side, lay India and behind more barbed wire, on the other side, lay Pakistan. In between, on a bit of earth which had no name, lay Toba Tek Singh" (Manto 1987, 18). Perhaps, it is only after the fact—after the fact of life itself—buried under tons of earth, that one can contemplate if, at that moment of pure politics, one was a greater story writer than God. But it is not a risk many will take. In fact, my hunch is that this is the reason why no one other than Manto has even tried doing what he did. To embrace politics in its pure uncertainty, its unrelieved dangerousness, without the security of an anchor in some pregiven idea of the good, without the technical instruments of measuring costs and benefits, is terrifying. To seek refuge in history and statecraft is to return to the comfort of the familiar. That is what most of us prefer to do. We are not great story writers.

The discomfort that many feel with the goings-on in what I have called political society is, I think, because it raises the specter of pure politics. This is a zone where, I have said, the certainties of civil-social norms and constitutional proprieties are put under challenge. The claims of sovereign power are shaken by an ambiguous legitimacy and a hesitant will. Rights and rules have to be, seemingly, negotiated afresh. Only those voices are heard that can make the loudest noise and can speak on behalf of the largest numbers. There is violence in the air. Not everything that happens here is desirable or worthy of approval. But then, how can we be sure that what we desire or approve is what is truly good? Who can decide that except those who go through the dangerously creative process of politics itself? I think Manto would have recognized these people. Those who dream of building the new democratic society must aspire to be greater story writers than god.

I do not know if in those fervid, disorderly zones of what I have called political society, the foundations of a new democratic order are being laid today. That is for historians of a future generation to analyze and describe. What I do know is that the practices of democracy have changed in India in the last four decades, that the project of state-led modernization has been drastically modified, and that the forms of involvement of the subaltern classes with governmental activities as well as with representative institutions have both expanded and deepened. There are new efforts to garner popular legitimacy in favor of elite dominance, such as the political formation that goes under the sign of Hindutva, which has sought to demonstrate to the ruling classes of India that it can create an alternative and more viable structure of class rule than the decrepit Congress. On the side of those who are governed, they have succeeded, in the teeth of severe opposition from the dominant sections, to bend and stretch the rules of bourgeois politics and rational bureaucracy to create forms of democratic practice that, even as they retain the names given to them by Western sociology and political theory, have become unrecognizably different. These are the creations of the Indian people. Perhaps some day, a great story writer will appear to give them new names and a new language.

DEATH, ANXIETY, AND RITUALS OF STATE

Confinement and the Imagination: Sovereignty and Subjectivity in a Quasi-State

Yael Navaro-Yashin

Sovereignty as Excess

It is the 20th of July, the date to commemorate the arrival of Turkish troops in northern Cyprus in 1974 when the island was partitioned. Imagine twenty-five years after this incident, an army still in command in a foreign territory, orchestrating massive ceremonies on the memorable date with tens of thousands of soldiers marching through towns and cities, passing by with tanks and armor, saluting the leader of the administration in northern Cyprus and the commanding generals of the army, and chanting in unison: "Every Turk is born a soldier!," "Everything is for the Motherland!" Picture such grand military ceremonies organized every July 20, with much investment to create a "public" to stand by in aura and applause. Figure the insignificant participation of the "public" in such ceremonial, in spite of the incitement to attend. Only the parents and grandparents of school children attending the compulsory ceremony stand idly by to accompany their children, procedurally waving flags. "Shoot, hit, and take pride!" cry the soldiers as they tramp down the streets of Nicosia, the capital city of Cyprus, divided with a border since Turkey's commemorated invasion. Such slogans are inscribed by the army over the mountains and hills of northern Cyprus, readable from a distance. A giant flag of the "Turkish Republic of Northern Cyprus," the contemporary name for the internationally unrecognized polity, colors the mountains, positioned in such a way as to be visible from the south, the Greek side of the island.

"Klerides [the Greek-Cypriot leader] can see our flag from his window," said Cevat Bey, a man closely aligned with the administration of

For comments provided on earlier drafts of this essay, I would like to thank Caroline Humphrey, Thomas Blom Hansen, Mehmet Yashin, and the anonymous reviewers for this volume, as well as participants in the University of Cambridge, Department of Social Anthropology seminars on the theme of authoritarianism. The research for this essay was conducted with the support of a grant from the John D. and Catherine T. MacArthur Foundation.

the quasi-state in northern Cyprus and active in several of its propaganda bodies. He and his associates have recently founded what they called "The Organization to Light up the Flag on the Besparmak Mountains," aiming to generate a fund in the amount of one million British pounds to project light onto the flag so it will be visible even at night. "First the star and crescent in the middle will be lit up, in red, to symbolize the flag of Turkey," said this man who owns a nuts and sweets shop in the Nicosia marketplace, "then, after 5 seconds, suddenly the two stripes at the top and the bottom will lighten up, to symbolize the flag of the TRNC. . . . This flag is the symbol of our sovereignty. It is visible even from Larnaca, the very south of the island, the Greek-side." Then, exhibiting the excessive mode of the discourse of sovereignty in northern Cyprus, he continued: "You know what I say, even if we go totally bankrupt and hit the bottom, we are sovereign here. Nobody can touch our sovereignty. We have power, the Greeks have understood this!"

The economy of Northern Cyprus has gone bankrupt in the last few years, with repercussions from Turkey's vast economic crisis. The offshore banks which kept the accounts of Turkish-Cypriots collapsed in the year 2000, swallowing the savings of their customers. There is vast unemployment and deep-running discontent. The absurdity and the excessive factor in Cevat Bey's statements and endeavors can only be appreciated with knowledge of this context. The more the regime loses its legitimacy in the domains of providing for its subjects, the more it resorts to political symbolism. But if the regimes' excesses were mirrored and mimicked by their populations in the last century, in contemporary northern Cyprus this is not the case. Only the very few allies of the army and the administration are moved by declarations of unsurrendering and uncompromising sovereignty for its own sake. Slavoj Zizek writes of the element of "surplus-enjoyment," coined by Lacan in the model of Marx's "surplus-value," which "implies a certain renunciation of 'pathological,' empirical use-value" (1989, 82). He refers, in this context, to Mussolini's Italy, where a rationalizing economism for or against facism was looked down upon (e.g., "empirical use-value"), in favor of the pure purpose of sovereignty in Italy for its own sake (what Zizek calls "surplus-enjoyment"): "And Fascism is obscene in so far as it perceives directly the ideological form as its own end, as an end in itself—remember Mussolini's famous answer to the question 'How do the Fascists justify their claim to rule Italy? What is their programme': 'Our programme is very simple: we want to rule Italy!'" (Ibid.). Remember Cevat Bey's words: "We are sovereign here. Nobody can touch our sovereignty. We have power, the Greeks have understood this!"

The Spirit of Terror

Unlike political regimes which have been transformed or turned over in the last decades, whether it be in Europe, in the postsocialist world, or in the Third World, a specific regime of authority has been more or less maintained in Turkish-Cypriot enclaves and territories in Cyprus, now, for almost forty years. Here, it is interesting to study the workings of an old-fashioned regime in the contemporary period. Indeed, an old political ethos haunts the contemporary in northern Cyprus, "the spirit of the TMT" ("TMT ruhu"), as Turkish-Cypriots call it.

The TMT (Turk Mukavemet Teskilati), the Turkish Resistance Organization, was a guerrilla group founded underground in 1958 by Turkish-Cypriot community leaders in collaboration with Turkey's Special War Unit (Akkurt 2000, 35; Tansu 2001, 27–29). It took its inspiration from the Greek-Cypriot EOKA[1] that was fighting the British for independence and for union with Greece (ENOSIS).[2] The mimicry and mirroring between these two underground organizations and the administrative practices they engendered is significant. Now, as they generated what is problematically called the "inter-communal conflict between Turkish-Cypriots and Greek-Cypriots," the members of EOKA and TMT also became community administrators early on. They took their place in the administrative body of the Republic of Cyprus, when declared independent (from the British) in 1960. When in 1963 EOKA attacked Turkish-Cypriot communities, the whole island was parceled into ghettolike enclaves with complicated borders guarded by the United Nations. Turkish-Cypriot administrators defected from the bicommunal Republic of Cyprus and under the organizing initiative of the TMT began to form their own separate statelike system. The kernels of the contemporary unrecognized state in Cyprus (the "Turkish Republic of Northern Cyprus") and its specific culture of politics[3] were planted in that period.

The structure of the TMT and its political spirit was what organized the successive administrative entities under which the Turkish-Cypriots became subjects. A Turkish-Cypriot lawyer explained: "The TMT was protecting the Turkish-Cypriots from attacks by EOKA. And the Turkish-Cypriots had to recognize this force that was protecting them."

[1] Ethniki, *Organosis Kyprion Agoniston* (National Organization of Cypriot Struggle).

[2] Enosis means "unification" in Greek.

[3] With the term "culture of politics," I refer to a whole set of experiences inscribed in collective memory, a network of common political reference points, an enduring political system with a specific style of government, as well as an unarticulated and unconscious experience of the political shared by a group of people who have been subjects of a specific kind of polity under a definite historical conjuncture or context.

Now, Turkish-Cypriots still speak of what they call "the spirit of the TMT" as metaphor for the culture of politics in northern Cyprus. The old guerrilla fighters are now leaders and members of the administration, more than forty years onward after the formation of the TMT. There is still a taboo around discussing the culture of terror inflicted by the TMT on its own subjects, the Turkish-Cypriots. And in official representations (in the administration's newspapers and in propaganda speeches delivered in national ceremonies, school textbooks, and programs on TV), TMT fighters are represented as "heroes" who saved Turkish-Cypriots from being exterminated by the Greek-Cypriots. If this interpretation is partially accepted by Turkish-Cypriots, it is also complicated, by most who are not associated with the establishment, in spaces where people feel they can speak their mind. In the most intimate encounters, among close friends and family, people tell stories "of Turkish-Cypriots murdered by the TMT," commonly speculating whether their "martyred" relatives may have been assassinated by the TMT and not, as officially claimed, by EOKA or by Greek-Cypriots. Numerous stories are circulated in private quarters about TMT atrocities against its own subjects, the Turkish-Cypriots.

Cemil, who was born around the time when the TMT was created, said:

> The system that has, to this day, continued to govern this country is the TMT system. The TMT was founded in 1958 and started to administer the Turkish-Cypriots. Even the postal service was in TMT hands in the period of enclaves between 1963 and 1974. Now we have the continuation of that administration, only under a different name, the "Turkish Republic of Northern Cyprus."
>
> The spirit of 1958 still haunts us. People who have grown under this system learned to be discrete, to watch their words and speech. I never learned to be this way; this is why they sacked me from a number of jobs. Somebody heard that I was saying something critical about the administration to somebody else. And that was the end of that.

"The TMT spirit" could be studied and analyzed as the political unconscious of Turkish-Cypriots. With the old guerrilla-fighters still in power, if in civilian or administrative garb, and offshoots of the old organizational circuits springing up under new names, the TMT is alive not only as a culture of politics but also as actual and implemented political organization. But when Turkish-Cypriots refer to what they call "the TMT spirit," they are referring to the culture of terror, tacit fear, and enforced secrecy that was the order of the day at the height of conflict with Greek-Cypriots, between 1963 and 1974, a culture of politics that has remained as practice and precipitation since.

A former guerilla, Savalas Bey gave an account of the culture of politics spread through the TMT:

I joined the Organization at the age of eighteen. During the day, I used to work in the village cooperative. But in the nights, I used to leave home and go underground. There was secrecy then. You couldn't tell anything even to your mother or father. My old man was a bit slow. One time, two times, he didn't understand what I was up to. But one night, again he saw me returning home very late. He asked me: "What are you up to?" "I was tying the donkey to the tree," I told him. When he saw that I kept returning late, he got mad. I was married then. I realized this wouldn't work. I spoke with my wife; I said to her, "Look, I am in the Organization, that's why I am constantly going out at night. But don't tell anybody, or they would have me killed." My wife went to my parents and told them I need to work in the cooperative at night and everyone locked their mouths. They never asked me anything again. Anyway, our language was coded then; we spoke with passwords so nobody would understand.

People almost viscerally remember the fear instigated by the TMT. Pembe Hanim, in her sixties, said:

The TMT came to our village and made a "guerrilla" out of every thief and idle man. These men became the leaders of the TMT in our village. We used to be afraid of both Greeks and Turks. The TMT spread fear amongst us; that fear remains. They killed many Turks, you know. For example, they killed the husband of our neighbor Behice Hanim who was a policeman in the British bases. One night the TMT came to his house and said he should leave the gate to the bases open for them to go in and smuggle guns. But if he were to hide this from his British employers, he would be left without a job, so of course he told the British. The following day, the TMT called him up to the village square. There they beat him up violently. His bones were broken. He was practically lynched. He died soon after.

If subjects of the administration in northern Cyprus speak of the endurance of "the TMT spirit," that culture of fear they refer to with periodical lynchings and terrorization is relatively less intense today than it was at the height of conflict. The difference is that people have become used to being administered under such a system and have been inhabiting its culture of politics.

In 2001, an organization was founded under the name of "the National Peoples' Movement" ("Ulusal Halk Hareketi") commonly referred to as the UHH. An offshoot of the society of retired TMT guerillas or of "veterans," the UHH was founded as a reaction to the "This Country Is Ours" ("Bu Memleket Bizim") movement mobilized by forty-one trade unions and two left-wing political parties. In the years 2000 and 2001, people had begun to join this movement in protest of the economic crisis and the restrictions that the regime had been imposing on civil rights. Under this emblem and movement, people walked several times to the border, demanding that it be lifted. The UHH declared itself a "civil society organization" in response, claiming to represent "the voice of the Turkish-Cypriot people."

The activities of the TMT veterans were received with a mixture of worry and irony on the part of Turkish-Cypriots. There was tacit knowledge that the UHH had been founded by Denktash, the leader of the regime, as an underground organization which would work as a supplementary secret service for the administration. But Mustafa, in his forties, said: "I am not afraid of the UHH. It's obvious who they are: the same group of men who are everywhere. Denktash's men, members of the Nationalist Justice Party (MAP), and the UHH are one and the same thing. Has anything changed with the foundation of the UHH? No." An old member of the TMT, Ahmet Bey, now eighty-seven years old, was very frank in his account of the culture of politics he had lived in: "In the old days [referring to the height of conflict in the 1960s], there was fear of the Organization. The TMT had spread fear, so that the Turkish-Cypriots would obey them. The TMT threatened people, killed many. Often the TMT didn't even hide that they were behind the murder of Turkish-Cypriots. Otherwise, if they hadn't spread this terror, they wouldn't have been able to make people submit to their authority." I asked Ahmet Bey if he felt there was more of a culture of fear in the past than in the present: "Of course in the past," he said. "Now they have sprung up under a different name, 'the UHH,' and they try to scare people. But nobody is scared; everyone laughs at the UHH." The UHH was received with bitter humor and nonchalance on the part of Turkish-Cypriots because it was an old and familiar story with the same characters at play. More than forty years into the sovereignty of "the TMT spirit" in Turkish-Cypriot enclaves and territories, a culture of terror has survived. People have been socialized to manage their lives under this, now, institutionalized order. So the UHH is no big news. Pembe Hanim said, in reflection: "Anyway, we have always only talked in our backyards. We lock our mouths in other places. Now, with the UHH, what is going to change? We will continue to operate the way we have done."

MENTAL BORDERS

The border, demarcating a zone separate from the south, is probably the single most important mechanism and symbol of sovereignty in northern Cyprus. The idea of "partition" (in Turkish, "taksim") had been at the center of the TMT's visions for Cyprus, countering EOKA's quest

for ENOSIS (union with Greece). A "border" dividing the island between its so-called Turks and Greeks was the central most important
icon in the political imaginary of Turkish-Cypriot administrators, from
the days when they were fighters under the TMT. "Partition or Death"
was the slogan of Turkish-Cypriot and Turkish nationalists in the 1950s
and 1960s ("Ya Taksim, Ya Olum"). Borders which were erected in 1963,
as barricades, barrels, and barbed wires, between community enclaves
and units, were revised in 1974, with the Turkish army's invasion, this
time dissecting the island through a complicated line right down the
middle, passing through towns, neighborhoods, and villages. The
TMT's dream of "partition" was realized and implemented as plan and
project. The border, guarded by the Turkish army since 1974 (as well as
by Greek-Cypriot soldiers on the other side) would physically as well
as symbolically mark the dividing line between the south of the island,
assigned to Greek-Cypriots, and the north, where activities ensued for
the further creation of a separate political reality under a new polity.

Old residents of Nicosia remember the day a wall was forcefully
erected in the middle of their street, at times detaching the entrance
doors from the balconies of their houses. They sit outside, in front of
their homes, with backs turned against the now half-remembered, half-
forgotten walls. The market area, which, according to old craftsmen
and shopowners, used to be busy and buzzing with life even between
1963 and 1974, in the time of the ghettolike enclaves, is now marked by
military no-go areas at the end of every street leading to the south of the
city. The space on the other side of the border is an actual "dead zone,"
in the hands partly of the Turkish army, partly of the United Nations,
and partly under Greek-Cypriot sovereignty. The northern side of the
border is half-dead, too. Most of the workshops, stores, and ware-
houses on the streets bisected by the border have been shut and closed,
now, for years.

This border that marked a separation in lives and life histories is defended by the administration in northern Cyprus as the mark and
marker of sovereignty.[4] The army has erected several monuments, des-
ignating complicated no entry and no access zones. In several places
along the barricades, walls have been decorated with nationalist slogans, inscribing the border with its officially designated symbolic
meaning. From the point of view of the northern Cypriot administra-

[4] Readers should note that the material for this article was researched and gathered in
2001 and 2002 when the border dividing Cyprus since 1974 was still intact and the Turkish-
Cypriot administration barred people from crossing it. There has been an unexpected development since April 23, 2003. The Turkish-Cypriot administration has decided to open
a few gates at the border for access to both Turkish-Cypriots and Greek-Cypriots for the
first time. Developments deserve another study.

tion and, at least partially, from that of Turkish-Cypriots, the border is there to protect Turkish-Cypriots from attacks by Greek-Cypriots, of the sort that took place in 1963 and 1974. So, the slogan "Ey Turk, don't forget the massacres" highlights the end of a street, blocked by barricades in the north-looking side of the border in Nicosia, assigning to the border how it ought to be perceived and interpreted. Rauf Denktash, the leader of the "TRNC" is commonly quoted for saying "We will not return with a pen what we obtained with blood," associating the line across Cyprus with the blood of martyrs spilt on the ground and refusing to negotiate with Greek-Cypriots.

The actual border between north and south, highly loaded symbolically, is not the only medium through which access is prevented to subjects of the regime in northern Cyprus in their everyday lives. Many parts of divided Nicosia as well as whole villages and areas in the countryside have been designated first-degree military zones and are off-limits to "civilians." Fences and barbed wires all over the country separate areas allocated to "civilians" from those strictly assigned to soldiers. So anyone living in northern Cyprus as a categorized "civilian" has to operate within this confined habitus.

But a border is no border in and of itself, even if enforced through military means and emblematized as the central motif of sovereignty. What interests me is the mark this border has left on the psyches and subjectivities of Cypriots who are subjects of the political entity in the north, the side, covert, or unseen effects of a specific kind of sovereignty. If people experience suffocation and entrapment in the north, the same border, viewed from the south, does not generate similar experiences or subjective responses. Subjecthood under different polities and social realities engenders different subjectivities in the counterfaces of the same wall. Although the border is coined "a problem" by subjects of the regime in the south of Cyprus—that is, most Greek-Cypriots would say they would like the border to be lifted, as it was imposed by Turkey's invasion—the border is experienced as less of a problem by south Nicosians than it is by subjects of the regime in the north. For Greek-Cypriots, the border marks a separation from their past lives in villages and towns left in the north, a bifurcation of their life histories. It does not symbolize entrapment or a block on access to the world. Subjects of the regime in the south, the Republic of Cyprus, are citizens of a recognized polity whose access to international economic, political, and cultural transactions is not barred or prevented. In the north, in contrast, the border is experienced as more poignant and emblematic of having been turned into subjects of a regime with little if no international connections. So, if for administrators and the army in the north, the border is not a problem (but a good thing), for subjects of the regime in the north, "the border" is the single-most symbol and reality of the experience of enclosure, entrapment, and confinement.

Spatial metaphors are at the center of Turkish-Cypriot ways of expressing their experience of living as subjects of the polity in northern Cyprus. "This is an open air prison," is one of the most common expressions, in a nutshell describing how it feels to live and manage one's existence in a bordered habitus. The "open-air prison" ("acik hava hapishanesi") metaphor weighs heavy with its implication and intrinsic paradox. Indeed, people who are trapped and subjects in the north experience the "outside" (outdoors, the air, the mountains, the sea, the sky, the landscape) as "indoors," as an enclosed and framed space, as a no escape zone. "The prison," as metaphor, is in the political imaginary of Turkish-Cypriots, because their habitus is physically and forcefully marked by barricades. Under the undeclared martial law in northern Cyprus, the gravest offence is crossing the border, either to the south or into military barracks. Many people have been brought to military court for crossing the border either accidentally or willfully, and punished with actual prison terms. Expressing, again, the experience of confinement, Turkish-Cypriots also describe northern Cyprus as a "camp for prisoners of war" ("esir kampi"), experiencing themselves as prisoners kept inside by administrators of the regime and by soldiers.

The metaphors are multiple and creative, but they all communicate an experience of enclosure. "It's as if they locked us in a cage," said Atiye, a woman in her fifties. "From my neighborhood, I look one way and see the barricades; I look the other way and see the dry mountain; in the middle we live in cement constructions. It's as if some people have taken us and put us in here, inside a prison." "It's as though they took us and put us in a zoo like an endangered species," said Selen, in her twenties. "This place is like an asylum," said Kemal, in his forties, commenting on the madness of confinement or mapping madness and confinement onto one another. "This is our concentration camp," said Ali, employing a reference to one of the utmost symbols of total human subjection.

The border is so central to the Turkish-Cypriot political imaginary because it symbolizes the limit and limitations of the polity. It is the brink. I will argue that "the border," in this context, is the self-created fault-line of the northern Cypriot regime. It is where the psychic-political effects of sovereignty are acted out and experienced.

Within the borders is a legal-political system that, if unrecognized by the United Nations (and therefore "illegal" under international law), functions under the name of "legality." The TRNC's domain of power is as much one of governmentality as it is of sovereignty. It is significant that the northern Cypriot administration operates on a notion of "citizenship." Turkish-Cypriots are "citizens" of the illegal state and under the laws and statutes of northern Cyprus, they have certain "rights." However, the same regime which presents itself under the symbols of "citizenship" and procedural democracy, also suspends them by deciding on states of emergency. It is ironic that TRNC administrators should have turned the suspension of rights into a "law" or rule as much as their original provision. The constitution of the TRNC can be analyzed as an anthropological object, something I do elsewhere. But for the purposes of this discussion, suffice it to know that the TRNC constitution negates (in clauses 4 of every article) the rights provided by clauses 1. Clause 1, for example, grants the right to form a trade union to all "citizens" of the TRNC; clause 4 of the same article negates this, defining states of emergency when forming trade unions will be considered dangerous from the point of view of the state's indivisible sovereignty. Therefore, as much as it is a constitution based on a notion of "citizenship," the constitution of this state-system also enforces subjection. At the moment when, in Carl Schmitt's sense, the sovereign (here, the leader of the TRNC in Council with generals and the ambassador from Turkey) decides on the state of exception, the rights of the "citizen" are suspended or cancelled. Then, I will propose that Turkish-Cypriots and settlers from Turkey living under this regime are neither just "citizens" nor just "subjects," but subjected citizens.

Here, neither Foucault's analytical notion of "the prison" (1979), a domain of governmentality, nor Agamben's notion of "the concentration camp as nomos of the modern" (1998), a zone of sovereignty where the state of emergency is the order of the day, exactly capture the structural position that subjected citizens of the "TRNC" regime have been under. Here, there is not the total subjection of the actual concentration camps. What is curious is that there is a sophisticated state system operating through the symbols and transactions of "citizenship." But there is undeclared martial law. And at moments decided by the sovereign National Coordination Council, the domain of "citizenship" and "rights" are canceled.

So spatially articulated is this particular form of "subjected citizenship," that "the border" has been conceived as the precipice between subjection and citizenship, the symbol of that moment of emergency when the rights are disaggregated from the exceptions, or, that line when the state of emergency, in Agamben's sense, becomes the rule. In recent years, many Turkish-Cypriots have been breaking through the borders upon reaching breaking points in their lives in northern Cyprus. As long as they are able to operate, maintain a living and certain rights under the "citizenship" laws of the "TRNC," the subjected citizens remain within the borders. But as the state system has no longer been able to sustain its domain of citizenship, either by cancel-ing rights under clauses of exception or having gone bankrupt under the economic crisis of the past two years, many Turkish-Cypriots have found ways to cross the border to the south. I will suggest that those who have reached the traumatic breaking point in their lives, crossing the border in search of jobs in southern Cyprus (the Greek side), have done so when they have experienced, in an enduring sense, their exis-tence in northern Cyprus as "bare" rather than "political life," in Agam-ben's sense: when their citizenship rights have been limited or their economic livelihood challenged under the present bankrupt order.

The story of Omer Bey who has considered and attempted several times to cross the border to the south is instructive. The following ex-cerpt is from my fieldnotes dated March 11, 2002:

> Omer Bey has reached the breaking point for some time. He used to sell clothes piecemeal, but with the economic crisis, he was left un-employed. His wife Sevgul Hanim does house cleaning in Nicosia six days of the week and the family (with two children) barely manage to maintain a living on her income. Omer Bey has been looking for a job for more than two years, without results. Meanwhile, he has been searching for a way to get out of northern Cyprus to work abroad. He tried to get a British visa on his TRNC passport, but he was refused three times by the British High Commission in Nicosia. His intention was to find access to the U.K. and therefore to some form of work. In order to gain access to Europe, he then tried to get a Republic of Cyprus (Greek-Cypriot) passport. He applied through a middleman operating from Pile, the mixed village on the border, but he is still waiting. Last week, he heard that he might not be able to obtain his Republic of Cyprus papers, which was his only hope for an exit from northern Cyprus. He reached his limit. He could take it no longer. He had been feeling terrible over the long term, jobless, deep in debt, and not able to maintain his family. He went to his wife's workplace and told her: "If I return home tonight, I return; if not, I will be on the Greek side." He said he would try to cross the border to the other side and find a job in the south. And he left.
>
> Sevgul Hanim, his wife, was deeply distressed. "If he crosses to the other side, it's finished. He won't be able to return. If he returns, they would bring him to military court." In the end, Omer Bey wasn't able to cross the border: he worried that he would be spotted by a soldier. Having reached his breaking point, he tried, but seeing the dangers, with soldiers on duty by the barricades, he returned.

The border with the Greek side is the limit. And when one reaches the limit, one hits the limit. It is as if Omer Bey, having reached the limit in his life wanted to put his chest against the border as the symbol of his entrapment, the ultimate limitation. He knew he could be killed attempting to cross the border and that he might not be able to see his family again even if he successfully crossed. But that was it; he had reached his breaking point. If there was an element of economic rationalization in Omer Bey's decision to cross to the south (i.e., no job in the north, debt, and the prospect for a well-paid job in the south), there was as strong an element of a nonrational hitting of the border where Omer Bey could have been killed, kept from returning, or brought to military court.

I would like to suggest that Turkish-Cypriots like Omer Bey, who have hit the border in attempts (sometimes successful) to cross it, reach this point when their "political life," in Agamben's sense, has been eliminated to the point of reaching "bare life." On the border, there is nothing but "bare life." Crossing means either consigning to death or to giving up one's rights to citizenship under the "TRNC." But it is precisely when these rights, economic among them, turn nil that Turkish-Cypriots hit the border with aspirations to jobs and certain, if limited, citizenship rights under the Republic of Cyprus in the south. Crossing that threshold is a turning point. It is enacted under intense existential trauma. People tell stories of catharsis once having crossed the border. What is interesting is that most Turkish-Cypriots still do not cross and that is what I study in the final section of this chapter.

BORDERS ON THE IMAGINATION

"Borders on the imagination" is my tentative analytical metaphor to study the marks or effects of sovereignty on the consciousness and subjective experience of political subjects. I am referring to a more quiet domain, the backroom of consciousness, where authoritarianism has born a deep mark. If spatial confinement has been one of the centermost domains through which social control has been implemented and experienced, it has to be centered in a study of this kind of sovereignty. Physical borders and their rationalization through propaganda is a domain through which a political entity has been able to constrain not only the lives, but also the consciousness and the imagination of its subjects.

The reflections and commentary provided by Turkish-Cypriots living along the borders are instructive. Taylan spent his childhood in Famagusta, which had been carved up into enclaves even before 1974:

We lived right on the Green Line in Famagusta. Between 1963 and 1974, this line used to divide the Greek and Turkish sides of the city.

My whole childhood passed with my mother warning me not to pass to the other side, saying "there are Greeks there." There wasn't a fence or barricades on the green line. We just knew that the other side of our street was "the Greek side" and we didn't pass. After 1974, when the other (Greek) side of the green line was attached to this side too, for many years I was unable to visit the coffeehouse that used to be Greek; I couldn't pass to the other side.

Serhat, who was listening to this conversation said: "We imprisoned ourselves. And now we are unable to get out of our own prison." Taylan continued to recount his experience:

People who have lived within borders for thirty years are unable to imagine that these borders will be lifted if Cyprus becomes a member of the European Union. Our vision is so narrow and limited. People are still asking whether the Lokmaci barricade in Nicosia [the most symbolic barricade] will be cancelled. They cannot imagine a borderless world. Look at people from Turkey, how broad their imagination is. They play with the idea of going to England, to America for one year. People inside this place [in northern Cyprus] cannot imagine such things.

"Inside this place" or "within this place" (in Cypriot Turkish, "bunun icinde") is the most common way of expressing, in a stream of consciousness manner, the experience of living as subjects of the regime in northern Cyprus. Those who live their everyday lives in the areas that are permissible and accessible, within the limits and borders, experience their whole space as "an indoors." Taylan reflected on the lives of his relatives and other Turkish-Cypriots who had immigrated to the United Kingdom and were living in London:

Cypriots who have lived in London for many years never go to the center of the city, don't learn English. . . . They live between two streets. As if they were still in Cyprus between 1963 and 1974, or Cyprus after 1974.

Now, one could be led to think that for people who so fundamentally experience their subjection through the medium of space, who so consciously articulate their experience of confinement, and whose rights to "political life" and economic livelihood have been constrained, that a crossing or annihilation of the border (the idea of a "borderless world") would be desirable. But this is not so simple. I will argue that the state of mind of those who remain within the borders and of those who attempt to cross is part of the same reality. Borders leave marks on the conscious and unconscious worlds of people who have experienced spatial segre-

gation for such a long term. What is articulated or expressed has to be
put in the context of (or compared with) what is unconsciously felt, desired, or enacted. Those who trespass or cross the border without permission are, in Giorgio Agamben's terms, in sovereignty's domain of
"bare life." There have been incidents, well known to Cypriots on both
sides of the divide, of shootings of people who have crossed the border
willingly or by mistake. Here, the border is the utmost symbol of sovereignty and crossing is considered defecting. Turkish-Cypriots who
have crossed to the south (through various means like the help of middlemen) have been declared "traitors" ("vatan hainleri") by the regime
in the north and faced serious consequences under military courts
when they have tried to return.

Listen to the words of Olgun, a young man born in 1978, four years
after the demarcation of Nicosia's present border: "What can we do, we
young people," he complained, "locked between walls and barrels. We
have had enough; we have reached our boiling point, our point of explosion." I reflected on his frustration, saying, "it would be great
wouldn't it, if there were an agreement and you could pass to the other
side of your own city?" Olgun's response was not what I had expected:

> Look, my map ends where the border begins. . . . I once got permis-
> sion to cross to "the other side," to attend a number of bicommunal
> activities for young people. But when I pass the border, I don't feel
> like I am in my own city. When I am on the Greek side, I feel like I am
> in another country. When people look at me, I think they are looking
> at me because I am Turkish, even though they are just looking at a
> human being. When I cross to the Greek side, I feel scared, I get very
> anxious. Once I was in a car with a few Greek friends. We stopped at
> the traffic lights and I felt a rush of panic, as if something was going
> to happen to me. I felt unsafe. When I return to the border and see the
> flag of the TRNC, I say "oh" [in relief], I relax. When I cross the bor-
> der back to this side, I feel back at ease. I feel like I have returned to
> my country. I grew up here.

"Here," for Olgun, is the northern side as spatial as well as administrative zone. Olgun was expressing relief not only for having returned to
his space of familiarity, but also for returning to his proper polity, the
"TRNC," with its flag as symbol. Commenting on refugee feelings of
longing for villages and houses left on the other side after the exchange
of populations in 1963 and 1974, Olgun said: "There is nothing that I
miss on the other side, because I was born in this side. My family has a
house and a field in a village now in the south. And I don't feel like we
should claim our property back. Why should I? What do I have to do
there?"

Olgun is a citizen of the "TRNC," a status that gives him no right to access or recognition internationally. Like many Turkish-Cypriots, he arranged to obtain a Republic of Cyprus passport so he can travel out of Cyprus more easily. But Olgun's feeling about this passport that could, if need be, allow him access (without visa or restrictions) to Europe was interesting: "I have a 'Greek passport,' but I don't like having it. I don't feel like its my own passport. I feel like I am taking advantage for having a passport like this." Olgun felt uneasy about being outside the designated area of the polity he had grown subject to. If he complained, with his friends, of feeling confined, of being bored and lacking energy, he also felt at ease within the political reality he was brought up in. The border and the idea of crossing it to the mythisized "other side" was so dominant in his imagination that the actual experience was scary. He felt relief once he stepped back into the zone of the very regime, which had determined the subjection and confinement that he so complained about.

Like Olgun, I spoke with many young people who have known no other political reality but the successive administrations of northern Cyprus. To the children of parents who longed to see their villages and towns left on the other side, the borders were not disturbing. I asked Dervish, born in 1987, what he thinks about the border. "It doesn't effect me," he said. "Because I don't know; I haven't seen the Greek side." The symbolic weight loaded onto "the border," standing, in official Turkish-Cypriot representations, for "peace," "freedom," and sovereignty, the physical blocks as well as ideological bombardment, have had a toll on the consciousness and unconscious of subjects of the regime, and especially on young people who have experienced nothing else firsthand. Twelve-year-old Secil said, "I don't want there to be a peace agreement with the Greeks." "Why? What would happen if there were an agreement?" I asked. "The Greeks would come to cut us again, I feel scared of that. They would do to us what they did between 1963 and 1974. If there is an agreement, the Greeks will start coming to this side. I fear this, I wouldn't want it." "Should it remain like this?" I asked. "Yes, I'd like this place to remain as it is. . . . A friend of mine was saying, "I want peace; I want peace." I told her, "what are you going to do with peace? Should the Greeks come and cut you again?" She stopped and thought and said: "You are right, let there be no peace then." Secil's parents and family are peace supporters and critics of the regime in the north, but she goes to school where the main component of the curriculum is a standard account of the massacre of Turkish-Cypriots by Greek-Cypriots in the years between 1963 and 1974. I asked Secil if she is curious to see the other side of Cyprus. She said, firmly, "No."

The ideas of "partition" and separate "sovereignty" and the project of creating a new political reality have been partially successful, we could argue, given the mental and psychic worlds they have created even in subjects of the regime who would critique the experience of confinement that ensued. An enduring, if manufactured, political reality leaves marks deeper than would be evident in its subjects' consciously articulated worlds.

We have to remember that we are studying a polity that presents its domain of sovereignty as an arena of "peace and freedom." The most important national holiday of northern Cyprus, celebrating the arrival of troops from Turkey in 1974, is called the "20 July Peace and Freedom Holiday." And symbolically, on this and other occasions, Turkish-Cypriots are told that being on this side of the border means being "free." "You are free to live," I would argue, with its intrinsic paradox, is what could be read between the lines. It also could be read as "We are free to give you your life," with the authoritarian undertone and the implication of the opposite. The regime in northern Cyprus, having gone politically and economically bankrupt, still expects twenty-eight years after a ceasefire with the Greek side, that its subjects be "barely" happy to be in life, i.e. to be have been spared from murder by Greeks. Remember the statement of the man close to the establishment, "We will not give up our sovereignty, even if we go totally bankrupt." There is no rationale here, only excess. Sovereignty in northern Cyprus, after almost forty years of rule under the TMT and its offshoots, still attempts to maintain its legitimacy on the grounds of having granted Turkish-Cypriots their "bare life," in Agamben's sense of the term (1998), having saved them of attacks by the Greek-Cypriots. But it is only if they could conceive themselves as "bare" human beings that the Turkish-Cypriots could remain content. And, of course, they do not. Turkish-Cypriots are constantly referring to the "rights" that they deserve, of the absence of "justice," of wanting a "legal order." And the ideological rhetoric of "peace and freedom" is quite a contrast to peoples' experiences and expressions of confinement. Nobody is deluded by the regime's ideological apparatus. The systematic propaganda defining this side of the border as a zone of "freedom" for Turkish-Cypriots does not have the Orwellian effect of having its subjects really believe that "confinement is freedom" or that "war is peace."[5] In northern Cyprus people sit in their homes and backyards, in spaces of utmost familiarity, with TVs turned on to incessant programs and speeches of propaganda, but confiding with one another in the most

[5] This is how this study differs from social psychology in the 1930s and 1940s, when it was argued that populations were brainwashed by the policies to which they were subjected (see, for example, Adorno 1998).

counterideological mode. The critique of ideology is ordinary here. At no point does the nationalist rhetoric with its imitation of old regime oratorical styles move Turkish-Cypriots to flock to the streets and join in celebrations of the numerous and excessive national holidays.

However, I am wondering, given what I have observed, whether the buzzing TV in the background presenting Denktash's memorized speeches repeated over and over again does not, even if ignored, leave a quiet mark on the subjective unconscious of subjects of this regime, even on those who most readily oppose or critique it. The "borders on the imagination" metaphor I proposed refers precisely to that domain of what we could call psychic-political experience.[6] If the excessive mode of sovereignty is unable to incite the masses to movement and participation, its buzzing omnipresence as intervention in everyday life leaves wounds, if not in consciously articulated expressions, certainly in the backroom of consciousness.

[6] For a discussion of "psychic-political experience," see Navaro-Yashin (2002).

Naturing the Nation: Aliens, Apocalypse, and the Postcolonial State

Jean Comaroff and John L. Comaroff

PROLEGOMENON

The White Heat of Apocalypse, or "The Week the Cape Burned"

Helicopters scampering over the blazing vineyards of
Constantia became the "motif" of the Cape of Storms this
week as the Peninsula burst into flames producing scenes that
could have been staged for a mega disaster movie. From the
beaches of Muizenberg columns of smoke rising above the
mountains . . . looked like Mount Vesuvius in full rage
burying the fleeing victims of Pompeii. . . . Overhead the tiny
helicopters buzz mosquito-like against the sky, heroic in
purpose, but only adding to the sense of helplessness as they
dash their toyish . . . waterbombs against the . . . advance of
the lunatic flames. (*Mail & Guardian,* Johannesburg, January
21–27, 2000, 6[1])

What might "natural" disasters tell us about the ecology of nationhood? How might the flash of environmental catastrophe illuminate
the meaning of borders and the tortured politics of belonging? How
and why, to be more specific, do plants, especially foreign plants, become urgent affairs of state? And what might they disclose of the shifting relations among citizenship, community, and national integrity in
an era of global capitalism? Pursuing these questions in South Africa,

Earlier, rather longer, and somewhat different versions of this essay have been published in *Hagar: International Social Sciences Review,* 1, 1 (2000), 7–40; *Journal of Southern
African Studies,* 27, 3 (2001), 627–51, and *Social Identities,* 7, 2 (2001), 233–65. It also has been
published in Spanish translation in *Revista de Antropologia Social,* 1, 1 (2002). See those
versions for our acknowledgments to the various people implicated in its original production. We also should like to thank Thomas Blom Hansen for undertaking the task of
abbreviating this version, which he did both with consummate skill and with sensitivity
to the substance and spirit of the text.

[1] M. Merten, "The Week the Cape Burned," *Mail & Guardian,* January 21–27, 2000, p. 6.

we run up against two faces of "naturalization" in the politics of the postcolony: one refers to the assimilation of alien persons, signs, and practices into the received order of things; the other, to the deployment of nature as alibi, as a fertile allegory for making people and objects strange, thus to forge critical new social and political distinctions.

We begin our narrative with the fire.

Apocalypse, African Style

The turn of the millennium came and went in South Africa without incident; this despite public fears of violence and mass destruction. Then, two weeks later, Cape Town caught fire. On a hot, dry Saturday afternoon the veld flared up suddenly in a number of places across the greater metropolitan area. Gale-force southeast winds carried walls of flame up the stately mountain spine of the Cape Peninsula, threatening historic homes and squatter settlements alike. As those in the path of the inferno were evacuated, SATV showed disjunctive images of civic collaboration: of the poor helping each other carry paltry possessions from doomed shacks; of the wealthy dropping their valuables in swimming pools and lining up to pass buckets of water. On Monday, as the bush continued to burn, helicopters dumped thousands of tons of water on the flames. Volunteers aided emergency fire-fighters brought from as far afield as Pretoria, more than 1,500 km to the north. The Mother City sweltered under a blanket of smoke as ash rained down on her boulevards and beaches. Many major roads were closed. In total, some nine thousand hectares burned. The mountains smoldered on sullenly for weeks. So, too, did the tempers of the population; one man, for example, was charged with viciously assaulting a youth whom he suspected of starting a blaze along a rural road.[2] Attributions of blame flew in many directions, none of them politically random. Fire is endemic to the region and to the regeneration of its vegetation; those who profit from its bounty have no option but to live with the risk. But this, a conflagration of unprecedented scale, raised fears about the very sustainability of the natural kingdom in the "fairest Cape." For weeks, the blaze, some termed it "the holocaust," dominated public discourse. This vernacular divination—the debate in the streets, the media, the halls of government—laid bare the complex social ecology whence the fire itself had sprung, enabling it to cast penetrating light on conditions-of-being in the postcolony.

In the initial heat of the event, stray cigarette ends and abandoned

---

[2] N. Joseph, "Man Arrested For Beating Up Young Fire Bug," *Cape Argus*, February 2, 2000, p. 5.

cooking fires were blamed for the blaze. But this was rapidly overtaken, in "official opinion," by talk of arson, a theory supported by a smattering of circumstantial evidence; some even detected a new front in the campaign of urban terror, widely attributed to Islamic fundamentalism, that had gripped the Cape Peninsula for several years.[3] Then the discourse abruptly changed direction, alighting on an etiology that took hold with extraordinary force: whatever sparked it, the calamitous scale of the blaze was a result of invasive alien plants, plants that burn more readily and fiercely than native flora. Fire might be a "natural part" of the Cape ecosystem, government advisors attested, but the presence of invasive aliens had changed that system significantly.[4] Outrage against these intruders grew steadily, particularly in the English-speaking press; the Afrikaans media had a somewhat different agenda (see later). Landowners who had allegedly allowed these interlopers to spread unchecked were denounced for putting life and limb, even "our natural heritage" itself, at risk.[5]

Heritage has become a construct to conjure with as global markets erode the distinctive wealth of nations, forcing them to redefine their sense of patrimony. Not coincidentally, South Africa is currently engaged in a bid to have the Cape Peninsula declared a "World Heritage Site" in recognition of its unparalleled biodiversity. This heritage is embodied, above all, in *fynbos* (Afrikaans, "fine bush"; from the Dutch *fijn bosch*),[6] the sclerophyllous or small-leaved, evergreen shrubs and heath that dominate the vegetation of the mountains and coastal forelands of the Cape (Kruger 1978; Day et al. 1979). In recent decades, *fynbos* has become the prime incarnation of the fragile, wealth-producing beauties of the region; and, as it has, local environmentalists have become ever more convinced that it is caught up in a mortal struggle with alien interlopers, which threaten to reduce its riches to "impenetrable monotony" (Hall 1979, 134). Efforts by botanists to cool the hysteria—to insist that "fire in fynbos [is] normal," not a "train smash in terms of biodiversity"[7]—had little effect on the public mood. A cartoonist, allowing a

[3] B. Jordan, "Ash City: Why the Fires Were So Bad," *Sunday Times,* January 23, 2000, p. 7.

[4] Guy Preston, special advisor to Ronnie Kasrils, Minister of Water Affairs and Forestry; quoted in J. Yeld, "Force Landowners to Clear Invading Alien Plants," *Sunday Argus,* January 22–23, 2000, p. 7.

[5] Yeld, "Force Landowners," p. 7; L. de Villiers, Chair of Peninsula Mountain Forum, "Take Decisive Steps to Avoid Future Fire Disaster," letter to the *Cape Times,* January 28, 2000, p. 11.

[6] Cowling and Richardson (1995, 21) suggest that the name might reflect the fact that early Dutch settlers found this species of Cape vegetation too slender to harvest as timber.

[7] Richard Cowling, distinguished scholar of the Cape fynbos biome, cited in "The Peninsula's Fynbos Will Flourish Again," *Sunday Argus,* January 29, 2000.

rare moment of irony to flicker amid millennial anxiety, drew a UFO hovering over Cape Town as the city sank into the globally warmed sea, its mountain tops covered by foreign flora. Peering down, the occupants of the space ship declare: "They seem to have a problem with aliens."[8]

Whether or not he knew it, the satirist had touched a deep nerve: the anxiety over foreign flora gestured toward a submerged landscape of civic terror and moral alarm. Significantly, when the fire was followed some two weeks later by ruinous floods to the north, another headline quipped: "First fires, now floods—next frogs?"[9] By then, it was not altogether surprising to read that "huge forests of alien trees" were being held by experts to have "caused all the trouble" in the water-logged Mpumalanga Province.[10] In this, one of the poorest regions in the land, "large stands of invading aliens," the vast plantations of powerful logging corporations, were blamed for thwarting the capacity of indigenous plants to act as "natural sponges."[11] What exactly was at stake in this mass-mediated chain of consciousness, this litany of alien-nation? Why the propensity to "blame it on the weeds," as one journalist put it?[12] Observers elsewhere have noted that an impassioned rhetoric of autochthony, to which alienness is the negative counterpoint, has edged aside other images of belonging at the end of the twentieth century; also that a fetishizing of origins seems to be growing up the world over in opposition to the liberal credo of *laissez-faire* (Geschiere and Nyamnjoh 2000). But why? Why, at this juncture in the history of postcolonial nation-states, and of South Africa in particular, has nature presented itself as a persuasive alibi for the conception of nationhood and its frontiers? And how, in turn, does the naturalization of nationality relate to the construction of older identities framed in terms of history, culture, race, ethnicity? Could it be that the anxious public discourse here over invasive plant species speaks to an existential problem of nation-states everywhere: in what does national integrity consist, what might nationhood and belonging *mean*, at a time when global capitalism seems everywhere to be threatening sovereign borders?

These questions are not meant to cast doubt on the danger actually posed by fire or flood; nor on the effort to explain and manage them with reference to the effects of foreign flora. It is precisely *because* these

[8] Chip, "They Seem to Have a Problem With Aliens," *Cape Argus,* January 27, 2000.

[9] I. Powell and H. Hogan, "First Fires, Now Floods—Next Frogs?," *Mail & Guardian,* February 11–17, 2000.

[10] F. Macleod, "The Trees That Caused All the Trouble," *Mail & Guardian,* February 11–17, 2000.

[11] Most notably Guy Preston, the expert said to have linked alien vegetation to the Cape fires (see note 4); F. Macleod, "The Trees That Caused All the Trouble" (see also later).

[12] M. Merten, "Blame It on the Weeds," *Mail & Guardian,* January 21–27, 2000.

matters are so real and urgent that they carry the charge that they do. But the extent to which aliens of all kinds became a public preoccupation in South Africa just after the millennium went far beyond the usual bounds of botany, far beyond the concerns of the environmental sciences, beyond even the imperatives of disaster control. It is with this excess that we are concerned here. For, as we have already hinted, the explosion of events, emotions, and arguments "after the fire" has a compelling story to tell about citizenship, identity, and nation-building in this and other postcolonies.

THE POSTCOLONIAL NATION-STATE IN PERSPECTIVE, RETROSPECTIVELY

The postcolonial nation-state—and here we write specifically from an Africanist perspective—is not a definite article. It refers to a labile historical *formation*, a polythetic class of polities-in-motion. South Africa, famously, is the latest country to join the class. As such, it reveals, with harsh clarity, many of the contemporary obsessions of postcoloniality. Those obsessions reach into diverse realms of collective being-in-the-world: into the struggle to construct a moral and material community in circumstances that privilege difference; into the endeavor to regulate sovereign borders under global conditions that not only encourage the transnational movement of labor and capital, money and goods, but make them a necessary condition of the wealth of nations; into the often bitter controversies that rage as people assert various kinds of identity to make claims of entitlement and interest; into troubled discourses on the proper reach of twenty-first-century constitutions and, especially, their protection of individual rights; into the complicated processes by which government, nongovernmental organizations, citizens acting in the name of civil society, and other social fractions seek to carve out a division of political and social labor; into the implications of *angst* about the decay of public order, about crime both organized and random, about corruption and its policing.

Such issues have not always dominated the discourses of postcolonial nation-states or saturated their public spheres. These polities have long entertained mass flows of human, animal, and vegetable migrants across sovereign borders (Crush et al. 1991); but never before has the presence of aliens occasioned the same sort of alarm as it seems to nowadays (Reitzes 1994, 7). As this suggests, many things have changed since the dawn of the postcolonial age, an age still uneasily defined by a prefixation upon what it is not. Even at the most gross of levels, postcolonies have moved through two epochal phases.

Epochal Shifts: From the Past to the Postcolony

The first was born, historically and figuratively, in India at midnight on August 14, 1947. It lasted forty years or so. This period is conventionally associated with the *de*colonization of the Third World. It is also a period in which the new states of Africa found the promise of autonomy and growth sundered by the realities of *neo*colonialism, which freighted them with an impossible toll of debt and dependency. In the upshot, the received narrative goes on, the idyll of European-styled democracy—the "black man's burden" according to Basil Davidson (1992)—gave way to ever more authoritarian rule, itself buttressed by the Cold War imperatives of the First and Second worlds. The details need not detain us. What is important for now is that, in its formative years, postcoloniality was a product of the "old" international political order, of its organization of sovereign nations within the industrial capitalist world system. In that order, people, plants, commodities, and currencies moved across frontiers under more-or-less tightly enforced, normatively recognized state regulation. Every so often, alarmists in Europe called for the repatriation of immigrants or for rigorous control over foreign flora and fauna. But cross border movement, mainly along the coordinates of former colonial maps—the British Commonwealth, greater France, the Black Atlantic—was regarded as a routine part of the bureaucratic work of governments everywhere.

The second epoch in the genealogy of postcolonial states, the epoch with which we are more immediately concerned, is very different. Its point of origin, says Bayart (1993, x), may be dated to 1989, when "most sub-Saharan African countries" began to experience a "wave of demands for democracy." These events were a product of the same world-historical process that transformed Central Europe and reverberated across the planet at the time: the *political* coming of age—its economic roots and its ethos, patently, long predate the 1980s—of neoliberal capitalism as a global phenomenon. This world-historical process, the recitative now goes, metamorphosed the old international order into a more fluid, market-driven, electronically articulated universe: a universe in which supranational institutions burgeon; in which space and time are recalibrated; in which geography is perforce being rewritten; in which transnational identities, diasporic connections, ecological disasters, and the flow of human populations challenge both the nature of sovereignty and the sovereignty of nature; in which "the network" returns as the dominant metaphor of social connectedness; in which liberty is distilled to its postmodern essence, the right to choose identities, subjectivities, commodities, sexualities, localities, and other forms of collective representation.

As this suggests, the second postcolonial epoch has been marked by a great deal more than just a move "back" to democracy. Indeed, although the renaissance of participatory politics *has* reanimated some of the institutions of governance eclipsed in Africa during the years after "independence" (Harbeson et al. 1994), its promise to empower "the public" in affairs of state came at a juncture when institutional state power was dispersing all over the place: into transnational corporations and associations, into nongovernmental organizations, into syndicated crime, into shadowy, privatized parastatal cabals (Korten 1996; Roitman 1998). This may, in part, explain why there has been a strong countervailing stress on the reconstruction of civil society since 1989. We have argued in another context (Comaroff and Comaroff 1999a, 2000) that, as a call to action, the force of latter—of "civil society," that is—exists in inverse proportion to its density and content as a concept; that its appeal is largely underwritten by its inchoateness, its vacuity. We also have argued that its return as a dusted-off fetish in the late twentieth century bears strong parallel with its first rise in the eighteenth. In each case, it has come to the fore under conditions of rapid transformations in economy and society, in community and family, in selfhood and the social division of labor.

For its part, "the" state, an ever more polymorphous entity, is held, increasingly, to be in perpetual crisis (Worby 1998), its power ever more dispersed, its legitimacy tested by debt, disease, and poverty, its executive control repeatedly pushed to the limit and, most of all, its hyphen-nation—the articulation, that is, of the state to the nation, of *the* nation-state—everywhere under challenge.[13] In the circumstances, notes Mbembe (1992, 3), "the postcolony" tends to be "chaotically pluralistic," even when it evinces a semblance of "internal coherence." This is why, it is often said, postcolonial regimes evince a strong predilection to appeal to magicalities, especially, to anticipate what is to come, under the sign of autochthony. That ruling cadres rely on magical means to do the work of hyphen-nation is not new, of course. But resort to mass-mediated ritual excess—to produce state power, to conjure up national unity, and to persuade citizens of the reality of both—*does* feature prominently in the second postcolonial age; in rough proportion, maybe, to populist perceptions of crisis. Thus, says Worby (1998, 560–62),[14] in those parts of Africa where government is stretched, its authority has become ever more dependent on the performance of quotidian ceremonial, extravagant in its theatricality; citizen-subjects, he

[13] Note, in this respect, Appadurai's (1990, 14) observation, now a decade old, that the hyphen linking the nation-state is less an icon of conjunction than an index of disjunction.
[14] After Mbembe (1992, 3f).

goes on, live with the state in a promiscuous hybrid of accommodation and refusal, power and parody, embodiment and alienation.

Belonging, Borders, Autochthony, Antipolitics

Although these symptoms of the second age of postcoloniality are the stuff of anxiety across Africa, the stereotypically bleak portrait of states falling apart, of nations drifting—into Hobbesian chaos—is overdrawn; the political sociology of Africa is much more complex, more diverse than it allows. What is more, both the contradictions and the crises evinced by many postcolonies are part of a broader condition. We refer to the changing character of "the" nation-state under the impact of globalization. We have offered a commentary on this historical process elsewhere (Comaroff and Comaroff 2000). Here it is enough to note just three things about it.

The *first* arises out of the refiguration of the modernist subject-citizen. The neoliberal age, especially after 1989, has seen an explosion of identity politics. Not just of ethnic politics. Also of the politics of gender, sexuality, age, race, religion, lifestyle, and, yes, class. As a result, imagining the nation rarely presumes a "deep horizontal fraternity" any more (Anderson 1983). Although most human beings still live as citizens *in* nation-states, they tend only to be conditionally, partially and situationally citizens *of* nation-states. Identity struggles, ranging from altercations over resources to genocide, seem immanent almost everywhere as selfhood is immersed—existentially, metonymically—into claims of collective essence, of innate substance and primordial sentiment, that nestle within or transect the polity. In short, homogeneity as a "national fantasy" (Berlant 1991) is giving way to a recognition of the irreducibility of difference; so much so that even countries long known for their lack of diversity—Botswana, for example—are now sites of ethnic conflict. And culture, at once essentialized and open to constant reinvention, becomes yet another possession, a good to be patented, made into intellectual property, merchandised, consumed (Coombe 1998; Hegeman 1991). All of this puts even greater stress—in both senses of the term—on hyphen-nation. The more diverse nation-states become in their political sociology, the higher the level of abstraction at which "*the* nation-state" exists, the more urgent appears the threat of its rupture. And the more imperative it becomes to divine and to negate whatever is perceived to endanger it. States, notes Harvey (1990, 108), have always had to conjure up "a definition of public interests over and above . . . class and sectarian" concerns. One solution that has presented itself in the face of ever more assertive claims on society and the state, of claims made in the name of different sorts of identity, has come to lie in autochthony: in elevating to a first-principle the ineffable interests and connections, at once material and moral, that flow from "native" rootedness, and special rights, *in a place of birth*. Nor is this merely a strategic solution that appeals to those caught up in the business of government. It resonates with deeply felt populist fears—and with the proclivity of citizens of all stripes to deflect shared anxieties onto outsiders.

Autochthony is implicit in many forms of identity, of course. It also attaches to places within places, parts within wholes. Citizens *in* contemporary polities do not find it difficult to reimagine nationhood in such a way as to embrace the ineluctability of internal difference: *multiculturalism, rainbow nation,* and terms of similar resonance provide a ready argot of accommodation, even amid bitter contestation. However, when it comes to the limits of that difference, autochthony constitutes an ultimate line. Whatever other identities the citizen-subject of the twenty-first-century polity may bear, s/he is unavoidably either an autochthon or an alien. Nor only s/he. It too. As we have seen, and will see further, nonhumans also may be ascribed the status of indigene or other.

The *second* follows closely: it concerns the obsession of contemporary polities with policing borders—and, hence, with the limits of sovereignty. Much of the debate over the "crisis" of the state hinges upon the contention that governments can no longer control the flow of currencies or commercial instruments, labor or commodities, flora or fauna, information or unwanted aliens. National frontiers, of course, have always been porous. But technologies of space-time compression *do* appear to have effected a sea-change in patterns and rates of global mobility. This is why so many states act as if they were constantly subject both to invasion from outside and to the seeping away of what should properly remain within. South Africa, for one, laments its brain-drain and the pull of the market on its sports stars[15]—while anguishing, xenophobically, over the presence in the country of millions of immigrants.

Xenophobia, as we all know, is on the increase in Western Europe, too. Much of it focuses on "unassimilable" migrant workers. But not always. Recall the British fear that the Channel Tunnel would open England up to rabies, that the coming of the Euro would herald the end of sterling as its sovereign currency, that the authority of the European courts would destroy its legal dominion (Darian-Smith 1999); or the phobic French reaction against the infiltration of U.S. cultural products. Both express anxiety, in the face of transnational flow and global

---

[15] See, for example, "Official Figures for Brain Drain Released," *The Star,* March 14, 2000.

(de)regulation, about borders and their breach. Globalization, after all, has provoked antagonistic responses not only among peoples of the former "Third World," for whom it represents itself as colonialism in new, largely North American guise. Given the logic of the neoliberal capitalist economy, *all* nation-states find themselves in a double bind. In order to partake of that economy, to garner the value that it spins off, governments require at once to open up their frontiers *and* to secure them: on one hand, to deregulate as far as possible the movement of currencies, goods, people, and services, thus to facilitate the inflow of wealth; on the other, to regulate them by establishing enclaved zones of competitive advantage so as to attract transnational manufacture and media, investment, information technology, and the "right" kind of migrants—among them, tourists, skilled personnel, nongovernmental organizations (NGOs), development consultants, even laborers who will work more cheaply than locals. In this way, the state is transformed, in aspiration if not always in reality, into a mega-management enterprise, a licencing authority even, for the benefit of "stakeholders" who desire simultaneously to be global citizens and yet corporate subjects with shares in the commonwealth of a sovereign polity. The corollary is plain. The border is a double bind because national prosperity appears to demand, but is also threatened by, *both* openness and closure. No wonder the *angst* about what ought or ought not to be allowed in, what is or is not in the collective interest.

The *third* feature of the predicament of the nation-state is, baldly stated, the depoliticization of politics. The argument goes like this: neoliberal capitalism, in its triumphal, all encompassing global phase, offers no alternatives to *laissez-faire;* nothing else—no other ideology, no other economic system—seems even plausible. The primary question left to public policy is how to succeed in the "new" world order. Under its hegemony, the social is dissolved into the natural, the biological, the organic. And the political into the technical. "Political choices," as Xolela Mangcu puts it for South Africa,[16] "are depoliticized and given the aura of technical truth. Public policies that get implemented are those backed by "growth coalitions" which span government, business, the media and other interest groups. . . . [These] shape national consensus on priorities."

Politics, then, are reduced either to the pursuit of pure advantage or to struggles over "special" interests and issues: the environment, abortion, health care, child welfare, rape and domestic abuse, human rights, capital punishment, and the like. Witness how long-standing lines of ideological and social commitment are increasingly set aside, as the

[16] X. Mangcu, "The Score So Far: Poverty Alleviation 0, Soccer World Cup 10," *The Sunday Independent,* March 12, 2000.

basis of collective action, in favor of coalitions formed to deal with urgent questions of the moment—often, significantly, "crises" sparked by ecological catastrophe or violent threats to order. These crises are, by their nature, short-lived: they burst into the limelight, flare into public awareness as "hot issues," and then burn down again.

Our evocation here of the imagery of fire—now situated within in the imperatives of the postcolonial nation-state, its location in the global world of neoliberal capitalism—returns us to the apocalyptic events in Cape Town at the turn of the millennium.

NATURING THE NATION

> . . . Ralph Waldo Emerson once commented on the impact of immigration: "A nation, like a tree, does not thrive well till it is engraffed [*sic*] with a foreign stock." Hopewell Radebe, *The Star*, March 16, 2000[17]

A Lesson from Fynbos

It is possible to read the burning bush as an epic instance of nature's deadly caprice. Many "white Africans" did. But the full impact of the blaze, we shall argue, arose from the capacity of those flowers and flames to signify charged political anxieties, many of them unnameable in everyday discourse. Before we make this argument, however, a question: How, exactly, did those flowers and flames come to mean so much?

First, the flora. Flowers have long served as signifiers of modern states, of course. *Protea cynaroides* (Giant/King protea)—the bloom that most typifies *fynbos*—has been South Africa's emblem for many years. *Sui generis,* as an inclusive category, however, *fynbos* is associated primarily with the autochthonous identity and patrimony of the Western Cape; it is the distinctive mark, the "rich cloak," of the region.[18] Also with Cape Town, whose emergence as a global city it has come to symbolize. To both, it stands in a relationship resembling that of classic African totemism: in a relationship of humans to nature, place to species, in which each enriches the other so long as the former respects, and does not wantonly consume, the latter. Thus, although the export of *fynbos* plants has grown into a huge industry since the 1960s—market demand has stimulated the development of many new "wild"

---

[17] H. Radebe, "Time We Became a Bit More Neighbourly," *The Star*, March 16, 2000.

[18] J. Yeld, "The Peninsula's Fynbos Will Flourish Again," *Saturday Argus*, January 29–30, 2000.

cultivars (Fraser and McMahon 1988, 155)—Cape Flora have simultaneously become the focus of ever greater conservationist concern. Even passion (Bond 1993). This vegetation, the object of ever widening state protection, is commonly described by researchers as being under serious threat—a threat born increasingly by invasive aliens (Richardson and Cowling 1992), whose destructiveness, say some environmentalists, has overtaken that of human beings (see Stirton 1978, 8). It was not always so. None of it.

For a start, the use of *fynbos* to refer to the indigenous plants of the southwestern Cape—the "Fynbos Biome"—is quite recent. Described by early naturalists as "Flora Capensis" (Harvey 1859–1865) or "Cape Flora" (Bolus 1886), this vegetation was "officially christened" as the "Cape Floral Kingdom" in the early twentieth century (Fraser and McMahon 1988, 119), and was known as such for decades (Adamson 1958; Levyns 1936). *Fynbos* does appear in Acocks's *Veld Types of South Africa* in 1953, but only as the Afrikaans translation for "Coastal Macchia" (Acocks 1953, 13). Sometimes used colloquially used at times to refer to the narrow-leaved, evergreen plants of the region, the term did not become established, either in popular or botanical parlance until the late 1960s and early 1970s.[19] Note that this was precisely the time when international demand for Cape Flora began to take off, and a national association was formed to market them. It also was the point at which politicians began to dub *fynbos* a "natural asset" and a "treasure-chest" (Munnik 1978, 7)—and at which botanists began to argue that it merited conservation as a "unique biome type" (Kruger 1977).

In sum, for all the fact that *fynbos* has come to stand for a "traditional" heritage of national, natural rootedness, it emerged as unique, and uniquely threatened, at a particular moment in the history of South Africa. Before then, Cape Flora seem to have been resilient (Adamson 1929). As recently as 1953, an authority on the subject actually described *fynbos* as an *invader* whose expansion threatened the mixed grassveld of the southwestern Cape (Acocks 1953, 14, 17). What is now said of aliens was being said, not long ago, of this "national treasure."

Admittedly, the vegetation of this ecological niche *has* altered much since then. But so have the values that inform our perceptions of it. Where, once upon a time, farmers saw Cape Flora as useless, as poor grazing on barren soil (Cowling and Richardson 1995, 21), a *"fynbos*

[19] This was confirmed by botanists working on the Fynbos Biome, although "fynbos" seems first to have appeared in a publication in 1916 (Dave Richardson, personal communication). Regular academic usage begins in the early 1970s. The term appears on a list of Summer School lectures at the University of Cape Town in 1972, for example, and in Kruger (1977). We certainly do not recall it being in circulation while we were growing up in the Cape.

landscape" is now widely taken for granted as the "climax community" (Cronon 1983, 10); that is, an evolutionary end-point to be achieved and conserved. This despite the fact that other views are possible. One has it that a "*fynbos* landscape" might be less an end-point than "a stage in succession to forest" (Manders et al. 1992). In this light, the ideal of sustaining such a landscape in perpetual equilibrium might be seen as an instance of the kind of functionalism that, Cronon argues, "remove[s] ecological communities from history" (Cronon 1983, 10).

Encounter with Aliens

But it is not just as fragile heritage that *fynbos* has captured the imagination of the public in the postcolony. It is also as a protagonist locked in mortal struggle with alien invaders that threaten to colonize its habitat and choke off its means of survival. Foreign "plants currently use . . . 3300m cubic meters of water each year, . . . 7 per cent of South Africa's mean annual runoff," declared the Minister of Water Affairs and Forestry at a high level symposium on invasive species, held in Cape Town after the blaze.[20] Anxiety about these invaders is not limited to South Africa. The issue has become urgent in other Western nations as well. Ironically, in Australia, it is South African flora that are demonized (Carr et al. 1986; Wace 1988); ironic because it was Australian species, vegetation that "grows taller and burns easier than *fynbos*," that bore the brunt of blame for the Cape fires of January 2000,[21] the "chief nasties" being wattles (including the infamous rooikrans), pines, bluegum, and hakea—this last, to close the ironic circle, a "Protea-type shrub."[22] Alien plant *do* seem to have become the stuff of melodrama, of resonant allegory, on a worldwide scale. This, we shall see, is because they transform and represent diffuse political terrors as natural facts.

Time was when there was great enthusiasm at the Cape for plant imports. Already by the opening decades of the eighteenth century, species such as Mediterranean cluster pine had to be introduced to the mountain slopes in large numbers to cater for the timber demands of the settlers (Fraser and McMahon 1988, 147). By the mid nineteenth century, interest in horticultural borrowing had turned to Australia— the other antipodean British colony and South Africa's enduring rival—whose heathlands constitute a Mediterranean biome so similar

[20] Ronnie Kasrils as quoted in J. Yeld, "Invasive Plants are Costing SA Dearly," *The Star*, February 24, 2000.

[21] B. Jordan, "Ash City," *Sunday Times*, January. 23, 2000.

[22] M. Merten, "Blame it on the Weeds," *Mail & Guardian*, January 21–27, 2000.

to the southwestern Cape that some posit an evolutionary convergence between them (Cody and Mooney 1978). By 1875, the government was encouraging large plantations of cluster pine and other imports, including hakea and Port Jackson, to shelter them. So eager were the authorities to see these exotics take root that they distributed millions of seeds and awarded prizes for the greatest acreages planted (Hall 1979, 134). This is in stark contrast to the present day.

What happened in the intervening hundred years? How did desirable imports become invasive aliens, "pests," "colonizers," even "green cancers"?[23] For one thing, exotic species spread beyond the confines of plantations and gardens—both spontaneously and through human effort—establishing themselves with great success among Cape Flora. Experts note that, until quite recently, this evoked little interest among botanists, government, or the population at large. It was only in the late 1950s and 1960s that the Botanical Society of South Africa appointed a committee to promote awareness of the problem and voluntary "hack groups" first took to the veld to cut out the malignant growth.

During the 1970s and 1980s, plant invasion at the Cape came under increasing scrutiny. Botanists, noting that foreign "infestations" were visible even on satellite pictures (Hall 1979, 135, 139), concluded that invasive weeds had "outgrown any merits they might have had in the *fynbos* region." In 1978, the Department of Nature and Environment Conservation published a popular source-book, *Plant Invaders: Beautiful but Dangerous*, and additional hack groups were founded in upper-middle-class rural white areas, although the efficacy of their efforts remained uncertain. At the same time, local expert opinion still had it that exotics, in *controlled* populations, did have some utility; that, in any case, it was impossible to eliminate them altogether; and that, even if it were, "other species might appear as weeds in the future" (140). All of which implied a sense that botanical categories shift over time. At this juncture, too, threats to the Cape Flora were described in multidimensional causal terms, terms that embraced fire, climatic change, and human intervention (Cowling et al. 1987; Day et al. 1979; Fraser and McMahon 1988).

It was not always to remain so.

The 1990s witnessed a marked tendency to reduce multidimensional causes to monolithic agents—above all, to alien plants—in accounting for the fragility of Cape Flora. This becomes abundantly clear from the way in which attitudes to fire in the *fynbos* shifted over the decade, culminating in the "holocaust" of January 2000.

---

[23] See Anonymous, *The Green Cancers in South Africa* (no publisher given, 1959).

Playing with Fire

As we have said, fire has long been recognized to be endemic to the Cape floral ecology (Adamson 1958; Marloth 1924); as even the earliest colonial observers noted, "natural" blazes consume large expanses every year, their intensity varying with the state of the vegetation, with topography, and with the weather. Much burning is also intentional: African views of regeneration set great store on it, for instance—despite the fact that colonial authorities, unnerved by the prospect of natives playing with fire, applied harsh sanctions.[24] Official disapproval persisted until relatively recently, when new research began to paint a more complicated picture of the forms and functions of *fynbos* combustion (Kruger 1979; van Wilgen et al. 1992). Thus, although the media almost always label these fires "devastating," expert opinion acknowledges that species diversity is "at least partly dependent" on burning (Kruger 1979, 44; van Rensberg 1987, 41). But these caveats were muted by the popular debate that raged after the millennial conflagration in Cape Town.

Most salient to our concerns here is the changing place accorded to aliens in arguments about the connection of fire to *fynbos*—not to mention in the politics and the perceptions that inform those arguments. True, it has long been said that certain imports burn more intensely than Cape Flora, which *is* itself quite flammable. But foreign vegetation was, in the past, only one of several factors held to produce fires of distinct kinds, scale, and effects. One authoritative report (Kruger 1979), for example, does not even discuss invasive plants; van Rensberg's more recent popular guide to *fynbos* (1987, 41) lists exotics only at the very end of a diverse list of possible combustible agents. As we have seen, not even the public discourse after the fires of 2000 alighted immediately on aliens. When it did, however, they became a burning preoccupation.

Not everybody blamed them. But dissenting voices were drowned out as the dialectic of disaster gained momentum. One view attributed the conflagration to global climatic change. It was given remarkably short shrift;[25] this was a calamity that seemed to demand an explanation rooted in *local* contingencies. Another line of argument was to be read in the Afrikaans press, which dealt with the same events very differently. Indicative, here, was the stance of *Die Burger*, then the major organ of the New National Party, which glossed the whole event as indictment of the African National Con-

---

[24] A law passed at the Cape in 1687 imposed a "severe scourging" for unauthorized veld burning; second offenders merited the death penalty (Kruger 1979, 43).

[25] See M. Feris, "Scientists Pour Cold Water on Global-Warming Claim," *The Star*, February 17, 2000.

gress (ANC) regime, of its inefficiency in government and its wanton neglect of the Cape.[26]

But many others were excluded entirely from the public debate. For some of them, alien plants had another significance altogether. We refer to the large numbers of poor and unemployed of the Peninsula—in particular, those living in informal settlements.

Squatter "camps" have loomed ever larger in the Cape metropolitan area since the late apartheid years. During those years, migrants to the city resisted forced removal to impoverished "homelands" and, in so doing, brought the savagery of the ruling regime to the attention of the world. Africans have long felt unwelcome in the Western Cape, which has long been predominantly the preserve of whites and coloureds. But, since the transition, black in-migration has become a veritable flood. Informal communities have burgeoned along national roads and on mountain sides, many in close proximity to healthy populations of combustible alien trees—like the Australian rooikrans (*acacia cyclops*), fuel of choice for the *braaivleis* ("barbecue"), a key rite of white South African commensality.

What is extraordinary about many recent migrants to the Cape is the degree to which their lives are provisioned by alien timber.[27] Unelectrified settlements in the hollowed-out bush comprise row upon row of square houses, most of them built of laterally laid logs of rooikrans and other Australian wattles. Threading between these abodes walk women and children, heads piled high with kindling of "imported" provenance; the search for fuel is a permanent feature of the lives of squatters, wherever they reside. Along the roadsides men sell small bundles of *braai* wood to commuters and tourists, the majority of them white and middle class. Used in domestic food fests, these condemned aliens are the stuff of a hallowed cultural practice.[28]

It is not surprising, then, that the first reaction to the blaze by wood vendor Thami Mandlana—perhaps the only squatter camp resident interviewed by the press at the time—was to exclaim that "the price of logs will soar!"[29] He was right. The cost of rooikrans went up 50 percent. But

[26] "Totaalplan Teen Brande," *Die Burger*, January 21, 2000; "Regering en Dienste Moet Beter Koördineer—Minister," *Die Burger*, January 22, 2000; "Bokkie se Trane," *Die Burger*, January 22, 2000.

[27] No wonder, then, that they were quick to ask early hack groups what uses were envisaged for the felled trees. Efforts have since been made under the *Working for Water* program (see later) to develop secondary industries using alien wood (<http://www-dwaf.pwv.gov.za/idwaf/Projects/WFW/Secondary%20Industries.htm>).

[28] In the national campaign to extirpate invasive plants, burning alien wood for domestic fuel has been suggested as a patriotic duty; see "Hack Day 2000," special supplement to mark Water Week, *The Star*, March 20, 2000.

[29] B. Jordan, "Ash City," *Sunday Times*, January 23, 2000.

the longer-term implications for these woodcutters were more alarming. Mandlana again: "[L]ots of people . . . cut wood around here and now there won't be enough to go around. Our hearts are sore because of this fire. . . . This is our only livelihood and now we hardly have any left."

This is the other face of the story of alien vegetation in the Western Cape. That vegetation has long been an integral part of the local economy—the underclass part, which is all but invisible to the more fortunate who touch its roadside edges. But in the postcolony, where wealth is ever more polarized and state provision is largely absent, it is a vital part. A recent survey of "people's plants" estimates the value of rooikrans as fuel in the Cape at thirty million Rand per year (van Wyk and Gericke 2000, 284). But this touches hardly at all on the interests of those for whom aliens are anathema, those by whom they are seen to imperil the future of a shared natural, national heritage. Where, in fact, imported flora *do* feed mainstream commerce, those who publicize their dangers have run into difficulty: Guy Preston (see 11n4), quoted as having blamed huge forests of nonindigenous trees for exacerbating floods in poverty-stricken Mpumalanga—where giant logging corporations are major employers—was later prompted to "clarify" his remarks. He went to some lengths to acknowledge that the planting of these forests was "usually acceptable," that it provided much needed jobs and yielded foreign currency.[30] The discourse of invasive aliens clearly has its limits. Still, as we shall see further, its ideological scope has become strikingly broad, encompassing the integrity and regeneration of the nation-state itself.

As Preston's "clarification" makes plain, scholarly experts find themselves playing a delicate role as the drama of alien-nature has caught fire, fanned by an avid press. With the conservation of "natural heritage" being sucked deeper and deeper into a space of intense public passion, botanists are invoked as never before, their work taken to be a matter of urgent national import. But, as their research becomes the stuff of political mobilization, nuances—like the fact that not *all* imported plants are aggressive invaders—are lost. To wit, polite protest to the media has added little subtlety to the escalating excitement.

ALIENS AND THE AFRICAN RENAISSANCE

Until a few years back, the term "alien" had rather archaic connotations in South Africa, being enshrined in laws—like the Aliens Act (1937) and Aliens Registration Act (1939)—intended to prevent an influx of European refugees prior to World War II. This legislation remained largely

[30] G. Preston, "Loving the Alien," letter to the *Mail and Guardian*, February 18–24, 2000.

intact until the 1990s,[31] when aliens again became a charged political issue, now in the "new" South Africa. It was at about the same time that foreign plants became both the subject of ecological emergency and an object of national renewal (Hall 1979, 138). Perhaps the most telling evidence of this was the *Working for Water Programme* (WFW), launched in 1995 by then Minister of Water Affairs and Forestry, Kader Asmal. Part of the postapartheid government's Reconstruction and Development initiative, the scheme centered on the eradication of alien vegetation. Billed as a flagship public works project to create jobs and combat poverty, the program envisaged twenty years of bush clearing. Its tone was urgent: "[Alien plants] are similar to a health epidemic, spreading widely out of control," declared the WFW home page;[32] laws would be promulgated to prosecute landowners who failed to curb nonindigenous flora. Concerted intervention would not merely restore the productive potential of the land. It would also invest in "the most marginalized" sectors of South African society, thus to promote social equity. Unemployed women and youth, ex-offenders, even the homeless would be rehabilitated by joining eradication teams and by working in industries that made invaders into marketable products. Meanwhile, the public was exhorted not to buy foreign plants—and to inform the authorities of anyone who encouraged their spread.

Alien-nature, in other words, was to become the raw material of communal rebirth. At first, the scheme met with mixed success. Financing eradication units in any sustained fashion proved difficult, although stirring pictures of the formerly unemployed hacking away at unwanted growth appeared in the media. In July 1997, the *Cape Argus* reported that the Cape Metropolitan Council, had refused to fund the clearing of invasive plants on Table Mountain.[33] Efforts to pass legislation were equally controversial and the eradication plan was made to "tread water" for a year or two. Meanwhile, public anxiety about foreign species became ever more audible.

Thus, by the time the apocalyptic fires broke out in January 2000, there was no half-heartedness about attacking the alien. *Ukuvuka*, Operation Firestop, was launched within days, and media and corporate sponsors stepped in to bolster WFW.[34] Even the powerful Forestry Owners Association, formerly on "collision course" with the program, came to an un-

---

[31] It was replaced by the Aliens Control Act 96 of 1991 and subsequent amendments.

[32] <http://www-dwaf.pwv.gov.za/idwaf/projects/WFW/Default.htm>.

[33] A. Weiss, "Alien Plants Plea by Asmal Rejected: Dispute Over Water Supply," *Cape Argus,* July 3, 1997, p. 4.

[34] *Ukuvuka,* Xhosa, "to wake up"; as we have seen, the image of the alarm call was ubiquitous in this discourse. See B. West, "'Firestop' Launched to Save Mountains," *Cape Times,* February 7, 2000; J. Yeld, "Four Fire-Hit Hotspots Get Top Priority in R3,6m Rescue Effort," *Cape Argus,* February 21, 2000.

easy compromise about clearing foreign flora from river banks.[35] With popular feeling ever more sharply focused on attacking the "scourge," public commentators seemed intent on coaxing "a spirit of community"[36] from the ashes. A new Minister of Water Affairs and Forestry put it succinctly:[37] "The fire has united us all. All key stakeholders—the authorities, the commercial interests, the landowners and the general public—now can come together to ensure that we are never again placed at such risk. And the key to it all is the clearing of these alien plants." There now appeared to be widespread faith in the fact that a purge of foreign flora had "huge potential for job creation," itself a nation-making priority. A national Water Week and Hack Day was announced, with special newspaper supplements illustrating the most offensive aliens, calling on the public to report those who harbored them, and appealing, in the name of patriotism, for recruits to voluntary hack groups.[38]

As time went by, politicians made ever more overt connections between the war against aliens and the collective prosperity of the nation. A symposium to discuss international cooperation in the control of invasive species, held in Cape Town a month after the blaze (see earlier), drew no less than four government ministers. "We are all in this together," pleaded the Minister for Water Affairs, "for alien species do not respect lines drawn on maps."[39] Global trade and tourism, it was noted, had created a class of "unwanted international travelers" like foreign flora and disease-bearing insects.[40] But the most portentous words of all came in a message from President Thabo Mbeki himself: Alien plants, he avowed, "stand in the way of the African renaissance."[41]

FOREIGN OBJECTS: THE POLITICS OF ESTRANGEMENT
IN THE POSTCOLONY

And so, in rhetoric that both mirrored and magnified the public mood, invading plants become embroiled in the state of the nation. What un-

[35] J. Soal, "Working for Water Has Deal with Forestry on Alien Plants," *Cape Times*, February 22, 2000.

[36] de Villiers, *Cape Times*, January 28, 2000.

[37] Yeld, "Wake Up Cape Town," *Sunday Argus*, January 22–23, 2000.

[38] See "Hack Day 2000," special supplement for Water Week, *The Star*, March 20, 2000.

[39] Address to International Symposium on Best Management Practices for Preventing and Controlling Invasive Alien Species, Kirstenbosch (Cape Town), February 22–24, 2000 (proceedings forthcoming).

[40] M. Merten, "Eradicating Invasive Aliens," *Mail & Guardian*, March 3–9, 2000.

[41] Message from President Mbeki, read by Valli Moosa, Minister for Environmental Affairs and Tourism, at the International Symposium on Best Management Practices for Preventing and Controlling Invasive Alien Species, Kirstenbosch, February 22–24, 2000; see also K. Bliksem, "Only the Truly Patriotic can be Trusted to Smell the Roses, and Weed Them Out," *Sunday Independent*, February 22, 2000.

derlies the ideological inflation that began with the burning bush, went on to inflame patriotic passions, and flared so fiercely as to endanger the African renaissance? An answer is to be found in a cluster of implicit associations and organic intuitions that, as they surfaced into the public sphere, gave insight into the infrastructure of popular consciousness-under-construction; in particular, into the way in which processes of naturalization made it possible to speak the unspeakable, and to assail the unassailable, thus to deal with the contradictions inherent in the making of postcolonial nationhood under post-1989 conditions. Take this comment by a noted newspaper columnist, satirist, and self-confessed cynic:[42] "Doubtless there are gardening writers who would not think twice about sounding off in blissful praise of something as innocent . . . as the jacaranda tree. . . . But . . . you may be nothing more than . . . a racist. Subliminally that is. . . . Behind its blossoms and its splendid boughs, the jacaranda is nothing but a water-hogging . . . weed-spreading alien." As *natural*ized immigrants, plant imports used, in the past, to grace the nation. Until recently, the jacaranda (*Jacaranda mimosifolia*) was "almost . . . South Africa's national tree" (Moll and Moll 1994, 49). Now, in a bizarre drama in which flora signify what politics struggles to name, they are becoming objects of estrangement, even racination; this in a land obsessed with who is or is not a citizen, with constitutional rights and wrongs, with routing out all vestiges of racism from within the body politic, not least in the liberal press.[43] A second columnist made this yet more explicit in speaking of the "ethnic cleansing" of the South African countryside. For centuries, she wrote, people enjoyed the shade of oaks, the smell of roses—aliens all. Now, "floundering in the complacency of democracy," they blame all evil on those aliens.[44] But it was a wry letter to the *Mail & Guardian*, a widely read weekly, that made the political subtext most brutally plain.[45]

It is alien-bashing time again. As an alien . . . I am particularly prickly about criticisms of aliens even if they are plants. . . . Alien plants cannot of course respond to these accusations. But before the Department of Home Affairs is dragooned into investigating the residence permits of these plants I, as a concerned fellow alien, wish to remind

---

[42] Bliksem, *Sunday Independent*, February 22, 2000.

[43] A controversial investigation of racism in the mainstream press, both overt and "subliminal," was being conducted by the Human Rights Commission at the time; see, for example, E. Rapiti, "Journalists Must Do Their Jobs Without Interference," letter to the *Mail & Guardian*, March 10–16, 2000.

[44] C. Lazar, "Forget Alien Plants, What About Guns?," *The Star*, March 7, 2000; for a reply on behalf of the Working for Water Program, see B. van Wilgen, letter to *The Star*, March 14, 2000.

[45] M. Aken"Ova, "Loving the Alien," *Mail & Guardian*, February 18–24, 2000.

one and all that plants such as maize . . . soybean, sunflower . . . originated outside of the continent of Africa. In any case, did the fire-and-flood-causing alien plants cross the borders and establish plantations . . . by themselves?

For this interpolated alien, himself under no illusions, the allusions are obvious. They flow from the naturalization of xenophobia. Barely displaced in the kingdom of plants is a distressingly familiar crusade: the demonization of migrants and refugees by the state and its citizenry alike.

It has been noted that the migrant, and more recently the asylum seeker, is the specter on whose wretched fate the triumphal neoliberal politics of the "new" Europe has been founded. In South Africa, too, a phobia about foreigners, above all from elsewhere in Africa, has been the illicit offspring of the fledgling democracy—waxing, paradoxically, alongside appeals to the African Renaissance and to *ubuntu*, a common African humanity. That this is occurring among a people themselves familiar with exile, who in the past lived reasonably peaceably with inmigrating labor, seems all the more ironic—and all the more in need of explanation. Of late, the phobia, which started out as a diffuse sense of misgiving, has congealed into an active antipathy to what is perceived as a shadowy alien-nation of "*illegal* immigrants"; the qualifier has become all but inseparable from the sign, just as, in the plant world, *invasive* has become locked, adjectivally, to alien. Popularly held to be "economic vultures"[46] who usurp jobs and resources, who foster crime, prostitution and disease, these doppelganger anticitizens are accused—in uncanny analogy with nonindigenous flora—of spreading wildly out of control, and of siphoning off the rapidly diminishing wealth of the nation (Sinclair 1996).

Aliens are a distinctive species in the popular imagination. In a parodic perversion of the past, they are marked by skin color and "native" culture. This is most dramatically revealed, as such things often are, at moments of mistaken identity—when South Africans are themselves thought to be outsiders and treated accordingly. Like the national volleyball star, apprehended by police because she looked too dark, or the son of a former exile, arrested eight times over the past few years because his "facial structure" and accent marked him as foreign.[47] Once singled out, "illegals" are seldom differentiated from bona fide immigrants or refugees.[48] All are referred to as *makwerekwere*, a disparaging Sotho term for incompetent speech—and, by implication, for exclusion

[46] H. Radebe, *The Star*, March 16, 2000.

[47] H. Radebe, "Persecuted For an Incorrect Facial Structure," *The Star*, March 16, 2000; L. Madywabe, "My Four Hours as an Illegal Immigrant," *Mail & Guardian*, March 3–9, 2000.

[48] Madywabe, "My Four Hours."

from the moral community. Many live in fear of violent attack, detention, or repatriation.

The fear is well founded. With the relaxation of controls over immigrant labor, previously secured by intergovernmental agreements and
electrified borders,[49] South Africa has become the destination of choice
for unprecedented numbers of people from countries to the north; estimates vary from two to eight million.[50] This influx has occurred amid
transformations in the domestic economy that have significantly altered relations of labor to capital (Comaroff and Comaroff 1999c). Not
only has drastic downsizing, euphemized as "jobless growth," cost
some five hundred thousand jobs in the past five years, most of them
held by blacks;[51] even more noteworthy, over 80 percent of employers
now opt for flexible, "nonstandard" labor (Adam et al. 1998, 209), much
of it done by lowly paid, nonunionized "illegals," whom farmers and
industrialists see as essential to their survival in competitive markets.
Small wonder, then, that unemployment is a ubiquitous anxiety; that it
is seen as a major impediment to postcolonial prosperity; that routing
the alien, who has come to embody the threat to work and welfare,
presents itself as a persuasive mode of confronting economic dispossession. Thus it is that foreigners—in particular, black foreigners—are
the object of consternation and contestation across the new nation, from
politicians and their parties, through the media and trade unions, to
street hawkers and the unemployed.[52] In September 1998, a crowd returning by train from Pretoria, where they had been protesting the loss
of work, threw three *makwerekwere* to their deaths.[53] A few months later
came reports of a gang in Johannesburg dedicated to the "systematic
elimination" of aliens.[54] Immigrants and their property have regularly

[49] These agreements laid down terms of contract and reimbursement, and decreed that
foreign workers could not join unions; Reitzes (1994, 8).

[50] See the findings of the South African Migration Project, summarized in C. Carter and
F. Haffajee, "Immigrants are Creating Work—Not Taking Your Jobs," *Mail & Guardian*,
September 11–17, 1998; also J. Matisonn, "Aliens Have Many Years' Respite in SA," *The
Sunday Independent*, March 19, 2000.

[51] See P. Salopek, "Mandela Stresses Success, Struggle," *Chicago Tribune*, February 6,
1999, p. 3.

[52] For example, the African Chamber of Hawkers and Informal Business claims that illegal immigrants imperil the commerce of their members, the South African Congress of
Trade Unions has threatened to strike over the hiring of nonunionized aliens, and the
Inkatha Freedom Party has warned that it will take "physical action" if the state fails to
"take drastic steps" (see Reitzes 1994, 8). The press, moreover, has been repeatedly
charged with encouraging xenophobia; see, for example, P. Dube, "Media Berated for
Stoking Xenophobia," *The Sunday Independent*, February 27, 2000.

[53] "Jobless Mob Goes on Death Rampage," *Cape Argus*, September 4, 1998.

[54] T. Amupadhi, "African Foreigners Terrorized," *Mail & Guardian*, December 18–23,
1998.

been attacked by local communities, forced into "ghettos," criminalized and scapegoated.[55] A survey conducted in 1997 by the South African Migration Project, under the aegis of the Institute for Democracy, ranked the hostility of South Africans toward newcomers as one of the highest in the world. So acute is it that the Human Rights Commission has launched a Roll-back Xenophobia Campaign and various agencies of government are actively supporting cultural projects aimed at combating discrimination against outsiders.[56]

Yet the state is itself an ambiguous actor in this drama. On the one hand, it strives volubly to uphold the standards of liberal universalism, insisting on the uncompromising protection of human rights; on the other, it sometimes contributes, wittingly or not, to the mood of xenophobia. Thus its law enforcement agencies have been unable to resist the temptation of attacking the foreign specter. As its ability to maintain public order has increasingly been questioned, the Ministry of Safety and Security has grown proportionately more active in its war on noncitizens: although anxiety about invasive plants was escalating in the opening weeks of 2000, government announced a "US-style bid to rid SA of illegal aliens" (*The Star*, February 14, 2000) and to penalize those who knowingly employed them. The parallel could not have been more clear. Not long after, police around the country carried out high profile raids on "gentlemen's clubs" suspected of trafficking in undocumented sex workers.[57] Onslaughts on "illegals" in show business, the media, and the music industry followed.[58] Then, within weeks, the Minister of Safety and Security personally initiated a "blitz" in Johannesburg on strongholds of immigrant business, vowing to "thoroughly ventilate all criminal elements and illegal immigrants out."[59] Police in

[55] Sinclair (1996, 16). Our observations in the North West Province confirm this. A letter to the *Mail* (Mafikeng) from a "concerned villager," for instance, reported on two "illegal aliens" running businesses on the outskirts of the town, and accused them of "robbing hard working South African citizens"; "Illegal Aliens—Where"s the Justice?," *The Mail*, July 23, 1999.

[56] This campaign is a joint initiative of the Human Rights Commission, the National Consortium on Refugee Affairs, and the United Nations High Commission on Refugees; M. Kebede, "Don't Let this be a Curse," *Cape Argus*, January 12, 2001. An exhibition entitled *Kwere Kwere: Journeys into Strangeness*, held at the Castle of Good Hope in Cape Town in March–April 2000, was supported by the Arts and Culture Trust of the President and the National Arts Council of South Africa.

[57] "Brothel Raided," *Pretoria News*, March 3, 2000, p. 1; P. Molwedi, "Brothel Owner Granted Bail of R10 000," *The Star*, 7 March 2000, p. 2.

[58] E. Maluleke, "Bitter Informants Flush Out Successful, but Alien Celebs," *City Press*, February 13, 2000, p. 3.

[59] M. Tsedu, "Illegals Deserve Better Than This," *The Star*, March 20, 2000, p. 12; H. Radebe, *The Star*, March 16, 2000.

Pretoria followed suit. Panic ensued as over fourteen thousand people—many of them "honest, taxpaying citizens"[60]—were searched and some one thousand arrested.[61] Reports reminiscent of the apartheid era told of violence on the sidewalks. Foreign nationals, held at a deportation center, were said to have been harshly beaten, their property looted.[62] Then began the reaction: amid accusations of excess, respected commentators maintained that the clamp down had seriously backfired, putting human rights at risk. They and others voiced urgent calls for a more adequate, enforceable immigration policy.[63] Meanwhile, suspicion started to surface, just as it did in the case of invasive plants, that the zeal for weeding out aliens was misplaced. Why this harassment of strangers? asked one "appalled citizen." It was not as if *they* were guilty of the "rape, murder, hijacking and bank robberies" that South Africans perpetrated on each other.[64] The answer seemed plain, at least to Steven Friedman, Director of the Centre for Policy Studies in Johannesburg.[65] Arresting immigrants may do "nothing to reduce crime." But it *does* create "the impression of activity and effectiveness" on the part of government, an illusion "as important as reality." Here, in short, is an instance of the kind of symbolic activity of which we spoke earlier: of the mass-mediated ritual excess, directed at producing state power and national unity, that features so prominently in the second postcolonial age. It appears to work. According to a Human Sciences Research Council poll, noted Friedman, most citizens believed, in December 1998, that the regime had lost its capacity to contain crime and to assure public order. Now some 60 percent think that it actually *does* have some control—despite no change in the incidence of serious felonies.

[60] Madywabe, *Mail & Guardian*, March 3–9, 2000; L. Mitchelson, "Anti-Crime Blitz Should be Extended to All Suburbs," letter to *The Star*, March 17, 2000.

[61] "121 Illegal Immigrants Held in Swoop East of City," *Pretoria News*, March 3, 2000; "Police Raid Sex Club," *Sunday Times*, March 19, 2000.

[62] Reports of violence at the center, owned by a consortium that includes members of the "struggle elite," are not new. In this case, the Cameroonian embassy lodged a formal protest to the South African government (*The Star*, March 17, 2000). See also Tsedu, *The Star*, March 20, 2000.

[63] See "We Should See Human Rights Body as Our Ally," special comment by the editor, *The Sunday Independent*, March 19, 2000. The Aliens Control Acts of 1991 has garnered its share of criticism, and government officials have acknowledged that its application is "arbitrary and subjective" (Sinclair 1996, 15); J. Matisonn, "Aliens Have Many Years' Respite in SA," *The Sunday Independent*, March 19, 2000.

[64] Mitchelson, "Anti-Crime Blitz Should be Extended to All Suburbs," letter to *The Star*, March 17, 2000.

[65] S. Friedman, "Action With Too Little Discussion," *Mail & Guardian*, March 24–30, 2000.

ENDS AND MEANINGS

Geschiere and Nyamnjoh (2000, 423–25, 448) argue that the growing stress in Africa on autochthony—and, concomitantly, on the exclusion of the *allogène*, the stranger—departs in important respects from older ontologies of being, belonging, and difference; most notably from ethnicity, with which it shares many features, among them a capacity to arouse strong affect and to justify the construction of unambiguous social boundaries. Autochthony, they suggest, is less specific, more protean in its substance. Its supple discourses readily accommodate "a switch from one Other to another." It is thus more readily open to political manipulation on many levels at once; not least in reaction to the kinds of social and economic processes set in motion by "seemingly open-ended global flows."

Yet more may be said about the salience of autochthony as a naturalizing allegory of collective being-in-the-world; about its salience, to return to the Introduction to this volume, in the production of sovereign power by contradistinction to "bare life"; also about its salience as a motor of collective action. But it is undeniable that, in postapartheid South Africa, outrage against aliens *has* provided a versatile call to arms, uniting people long divided by class, color, and culture: it *is* enthusiastically mobilized by those who seek to conjure a new nation not merely by bridging familiar antinomies but by erecting finite frontiers under conditions that, by all appearances, threaten to dissolve them altogether. And, with them, the coordinates of material and moral community. We have spelled out those conditions. They lie in the particular historical circumstances of postcolonial nation-states at the close of the twentieth century: specifically, their absorption into a global capitalist economy whose neoliberal ways and means have altered Fordist patterns of production and consumption, the articulation of labor to capital, the nature of sovereignty and civic identity, geographies of space and time, and much else besides. Hence, the insistence earlier on, situating our understanding of those nation-states not in a comfortable sociology of ideal-types, but in the hard-edged specificities of their second, post-1989 coming.

Here, then, lies one theme in the theoretical counterpoint that animates this essay: the conceptualization of postcolonial polities. It is beyond our present scope to "theorize" those polities—whatever that might mean at this moment in the history of Western social thought. However, because of the manner of their insertion into world history, we have argued, they evince three notable features. Each is an intensification of the predicament of the contemporary nation-state *sui generis*,

each a corollary of the changing face of capitalism, all of them interconnected. The first is the transfiguration of the modernist political subject:
a move away *from* a sense of belonging in a homogeneously imagined
community of right-bearing persons *toward* one in which difference is
endemic, irreducible, and diversely constituted; *from* the idea of citizenship based on "horizontal fraternity" *toward* one in which each national is a stakeholder vertically rooted in a body corporate; *from* a notion that attachment may be acquired equally by ascription, residence,
immigration, and naturalization *toward* the primacy of autochthony,
making it the most "authentic," the most essential, of all modes of connection. The second is the contradictory logic of sovereign borders: the
simultaneous necessity that they be open to various forms of flow—of
finance, workers, commodities, consumers, infrastructure—and yet enclaved enough both to offer competitive advantage for global enterprise and to serve the material interests of a national citizenry; in other
words, to husband the kinds of difference, the kinds of distinction between the local and the nonlocal, from which transnational capital may
profit. The third is the depoliticization of politics, its displacement from
the realm of the social and the cultural, the moral and ideological, into
the technical, apparently value-free dictates of the market—and its at-
tendant forms of economic and legal "rationality." Also into the imperatives of nature, however those come to be constructed, disseminated,
taken-for-granted. Put these things together, and the moral panic about
strangers becomes overdetermined. Take human aliens. Their very existence embodies the contradiction of borders and boundaries in the
age of global capital. On the one hand, by crossing those borders they
import value into the heart of the polity, be it as cheap, manageable
labor for agribusiness or industry, as traders who undersell indigenous
merchants to the advantage of local consumers, as people with skills in
short supply, or whatever. On the other, they are held to take away jobs
and benefits from nationals, to undercut the struggles of local workers,
to bring contagion, and, by trafficking in drugs, bodies, and contra-
band, to commit the kinds of crime that unravel the social fabric. Moreover, their presence raises difficult questions about the changing nature
of political citizenship in the postcolony: given that South Africa, like
other nation-states, fetishizes human rights—rights, that is, which transcend parochial identities and borders—should outsiders not enjoy
them like any autochthon? What precisely ought to separate the entitlements of the citizen from those of any other human being? On what
basis is discrimination against foreigners justified in a society dedicated
to "nonracism," in a nascent national culture that speaks the language
of *ubuntu*, a common Africanity? Why, with the apotheosis of the free
market, should strangers be the target of local protectionism? This, in

sum, is where the liberal ideology of universal inclusion runs up against a politics of exclusion whereby identity is mobilized to create "closed" spheres of interest within "open" neoliberal economies. Note here, too, the depoliticization of politics in the treatment of the alien-as-specter, of its displacement into a technicist discourse about demography and economic sociology, about health and disease, about social pathology and criminality.

Much the same may be said of alien vegetation: *Is* the jacaranda, the almost-national-tree, a naturalized South African? Or a hateful interloper? The fact that it has become the subject of ironic comment about subliminal racism and ethnic cleansing—something almost unthinkable a short while ago—makes clear how much the concern with borders, belonging, autochthony, and alien-nation has imploded. Who, exactly, *is* a South African? As this suggests, the transference into the floral kingdom of profoundly political questions is itself a dramatic instance of the process of depoliticization of which we have spoken. Although there is no doubt that real issues of ecology *are* raised by the effect of imported vegetation on fire and flood, the effort to construct a nation with reference to a rhetoric of exclusion, a rhetoric validated by appeal to the apparent value-free exigencies of botany and the environmental sciences, is a cogent instance of naturalization—to which, now, we return.

One remaining question has not yet been resolved: Why *nature*? Here lies the other strand of our theoretical argument. Central to our analysis are the claims (a) that the apocalyptic fire in Cape, underdetermined by the proximate events themselves, became the lightning rod for a panic about nonindigenous vegetation; a panic (b) that crystallized inchoate fears about alien-nature, named them, and called them into the heart of public consciousness; (c) that this is owed to the fact that the anxiety concerning foreign flora, although real enough in and of itself, was, at the same time, also a metonymic projection of more deep-seated questions facing the postcolonial state about the nature of its sovereign borders, about the right to citizenship within it, about the meaning and the passion inherent in national belonging—and, in particular, about the tendency to invoke autochthony in answering those questions, both pragmatically and figuratively.

This is where naturalization enters the picture. Recall that classically, as we noted, it has had two connotations. One is the assimilation of alien persons, signs, and practices into a world-in-place; its prototype is the metamorphosis of outlanders into citizens of the liberal nation-state. The other, whose genealogy stretches from Marx through Gramsci to Foucault, is the deployment of nature as alibi, as a fertile allegory for rendering *some* people and objects strange, thereby to authenticate the limits of the ("natural") order of things; also to interpolate within it new social and political distinctions. It is tempting, in the South African case, to invoke yet another connotation—one owed to Durkheim—according to which processes in nature are taken to be a direct reflection of processes in society. Some did just this, as we have seen, finding in the panic about invasive plants a mirror for the angst about immigrants. But such a reading of the events in question is insufficient. Nature is everywhere more directly, more dynamically implicated in the social practices by which history and ideology make each other. The unfolding controversy about indigenous plants and alien-nature became the vehicle for a public debate, as yet unfinished, over the proper constitution of the polity, over the limits of belonging, over the terms in which the nation, the commonweal, and the stakeholding subject are to be constituted in the age of global capitalism and universal human rights. In so doing, it permitted a vocalization of concerns and conundrums not easily addressed by politics-as-usual. Even more, the displacement of the argument about outsiders into the floral kingdom made it possible, by analogy, to contemplate and legitimate discrimination against those humans not embraced in the body of the nation, those cast adrift on the currents of the new world order. And it sanctioned, if unwittingly, a new, postracist form of racism; a form of racism that, by concealing itself in the language of autochthony and alien-nature, has come to coexist seamlessly with a transnational culture of universal rights.

As this implies, discourses of nature cast a sharp light on the everyday actions and events through which definitions of belonging and citizenship—and their dark underside, the politics of exclusion—are being reframed in the postcolony. In particular, they illuminate the question of why it is that autochthony—a form of attachment that ties people to place, that natures the nation, that authorizes entitlement—has become so central in an epoch when nationhood seems at once critical and yet in crisis, when borders everywhere present themselves as paradoxes, when a beleaguered political imagination strives to make sense of social being in a world of *laissez faire*.

Sovereignty as a Form of Expenditure

Achille Mbembe

The object of this study is to analyze conceptions of the political that, in present-day Africa, articulate power as a theory and practice of war. As it is employed here, the notion of "war" does not refer purely and simply to those moments of the dramatic enactment of conflict that present themselves in terms of the confrontation of forces of men followed by scenes of destruction involving the loss of human life on the field of battle. This form of ordeal has already been thoroughly investigated in his own day by Clausewitz. In the case of Africa, too, it has formed, over the past ten years, the subject of a range of increasingly sophisticated historical studies.[1]

These studies do, however, underestimate the centrality that war has come to assume in the mental representation that contemporary African social actors hold of politics in general, and of sovereignty in particular. In the recent history of several countries, war has become just as much the means whereby one creates a world, as well as the life-world that is itself created. African wars have given rise to at least two different logics of expenditure.[2] The first type of expenditure relates to the ability of the human psyche to invest heavily in—and to sublimate—objects, resources, and even indeed human beings—and then to release an extraordinary quantum of energy whose function is to ensure their serial and systematic destruction—a destruction from which there comes to be derived a corresponding satisfaction. This work of destruction—which consists in its essence of a "putting to death"—is a striking manifestation of absolute, sovereign power, whether this is expressed at the level of intention, of action, or of fantasy (cf. Mbembe 2003). Although the impulse to death and the passion for destruction revolves around self preservation in the first type of expenditure, the second form of expenditure opens the way to the possibility of getting oneself killed in the name of that for which one is prepared to live (sovereignty as self-sacrifice). In the fullest acceptance of this risk, the principle of destruction is on an equal footing

---

[1] See, recently, Ellis (1999); Allen (1991); K. Wilson (1992); Geffray (1990).

[2] Concerning the notion of "expenditure/consumption" (*dépense*), see Bataille (1967).

with the will to exercise power over the unknown that is represented by death.

As Castoriadis (2002) reminds us, what a society, a community, indeed particular individuals are prepared to live and to die for "isn't in most cases either material or "real." Very often, the politics of life and death take shape around "imaginary social symbolizations." These imaginary social symbolizations are made concrete in and implemented by institutions in which force and violence are constituted and organized as struggles "about power, through power and for power" (Foucault 1976, 16–17). In this respect, times of war are not so different from the times of politics, or that war is politics continued by other means, as Clausewitz put it. Inverting this proposition and understanding politics as war continued by other means, Foucault was able to show how the role of political power was to "reinscribe continuously that power relationship in institutions, in economic inequalities, in the language, even in the very bodies of one group and another," through a whole panoply of technologies and contrivances.

If the true purport of power rests, in the final analysis, in its capacity to continue the conduct of war by other means, is it possible, then, to interpret democracy and the movement for democratization as straightforward incidents in a war? As the broken-down elements of war? As a radical change of locus of war itself? If war is as much a means to the achievement of sovereignty as a means of exercising the right to kill, what place do the new African forms of politics-as-war accord to life, death, and the body?

In order to address these questions, I shall first identify certain structuring elements of the material conditions of life in the Africa of the last quarter of the twentieth century. I shall then investigate two structures of the imaginary that describe and define just as many forms of political struggle and warfare considered in the light of their hold on bodies, on things, and on life.

FRAGMENTATION AND DISPERSION

Three major events have, in the course of the last quarter of the twentieth century, profoundly affected the material conditions of the production of life in Africa. These events are as follows: (1) the increasing rigor of monetary constraint, and its effects in revivifying long-distance imaginaries; (2) the simultaneity of democratization and of the deregulation of the economy and the structures of the state; and (3) the dispersion of state power and the fragmentation of society. These three events came about at the same time. From this simultaneity derives the fact that they sometimes substituted for each other, that their effects sometimes canceled each other out or, on the contrary, that one such development would spur on another, to the extent of bringing on a mutual involvement of individual and social experience.

Let us take first monetary constraint that has weighed down society in at least two different ways. At first, the general drying-up of liquidity,[3] and thereafter its progressive concentration in specific channels and networks whose control of access, and policing of debt and obligation, have been growing ever more draconian.[4] The capture and immobilization of individuals through indebtedness have become central to bonds of political loyalty.[5]

It is also through the means of such obligations and bonds that the value of people (as opposed to things), and the assessment of their usefulness, or even their status as disposable, nowadays take place (Bales 1999). Consequently, the controlled influx and the restriction of the movements of money around zones of the extraction of mineral resources has allowed the formation of isolated enclaves at the heart of a devastated economy (oil-bearing, diamond-mining, tourist enclaves). The extraction of these valuable resources in such enclaves has, in return, made these areas zones of conflict and war.

In thus contributing to the emergence of a new geography of conflict and to the creation of a new type of trading-post economy, the movements of capital have accentuated the fragmentation of national and regional economic spaces. Although certain areas exhibit a reversion to practices of barter and self-subsistence, others undergo the experience of a dollarization with unforeseen side effects (see de Boek 1998). The new dynamics of acquiring profit and making a living from the scarcity of money have consequently led to an unprecedented revivification of the imaginaries of the far-away and the remote.[6] This revivification has been reflected in an unparalleled increase in private agent's ability to operate over broad areas. Such also have been the case of violent attempts to immobilize and spatially fix entire categories of population, notably in the interests of waging war.

This has given rise to a new form of governmentality. The latter con-

[3] If we do have economic analyses of monetary politics over this period, such is not the case for studies on relations between money and the social imagination in general. See, however, Stiansen and Guyer (1999); Guyer (1994); Vallée (1989). On certain historical aspects of imaginaries of the far-away, see, for example, Boahen (1962); Johnson (1976); Stewart (1976).

[4] See, for example, Marie (1995) and Brydon (1999).

[5] On the dilemmas created in particular by inflationary pressures and the way in which these pressures have in turn structured struggles for money and survival in urban milieux, see Guyer, Denzer and Agbaje (forthcoming).

[6] Compare the studies by Simone (2001), and Diouf (2000).

sists of the control of the mobility of people—individuals or even multitudes—by jurisdictions or armed formations of an extra- or quasi-statal character. What is more and more at work in the exercise of power is to a large extent the same thing that is at work in war itself: the maintenance of a social identity and the possibility of the production and reproduction of bare life. This new form of governmentality, based on the proliferation of extreme situations and predatory practices, attacks bodies and lives only in order the better to control the flow of resources, objects, and commodities released by the process of economic informalization.

Because they rest in very large part on the values of transience as opposed to those of sedentary living, the new dynamics of profit and livelihoods through migration have contributed to a profound change in the forms and the nature of social belonging. How, in fact, can one continue to belong to a community in a context in which one is physically removed from it and in which one can no longer directly take part in the rituals that a sedentary life renders possible? The scattering and dispersion imposed by the necessities of long-distance livelihoods have certainly not abolished the old definitions of "community." In many cases, the "community" has remained that place of birth, concrete and geographically situated, that one appropriates to oneself and defends, and that one seeks to isolate from the contact of those who have no part in it; and in the name of which one kills and gets oneself killed at need. Considerable variations have nonetheless appeared in the relation between "what belongs to more than one person, to many people, to everyone" and what, by being in a narrower sense "private," is susceptible of being enjoyed in an entirely individual manner. A chain of "intermediaries," brokers and specialists in the negotiation over objects, stories, and identities, have seen a great enhancement in their statuses. The enhancement of these statuses has benefited from the breakdown and shifting of existing frontiers (cf. Mbembe 2000). The result has been not only an increase in the speed of migrations but also a proliferation of networks that have specialized in exploiting faraway resources (Fall 1998).

In another register, the possession of financial resources (or the lack of them) has caused a profound shift in the framework of the formation of individuality and in the realms of subjectivity. On the one hand, the dominant perception has become that according to which money, power, and indeed life are all equally subject to the rule of chance. Nothing being certain and everything possible, one takes the same sort of risks with money as one does with power and life. On the other hand, among the social categories that experience no difficulties in amassing fortunes, the relations between desire and its objects have changed into a sensualist and hedonistic obsession with expenditure, an idolatrous possession and an ostentatious enjoyment of material goods becoming the locus for the staging and enactment of novel lifestyles and ways of living (Warnier 1993).

In both cases, however, the cultural content of the process of differentiation has been the same, namely, on the one hand, an acute consciousness of the volatility and frivolity of money and fortune, and, on the other, a "live for today" conception of time and of value. Power just as much as fortune and enjoyment, poverty as much as violence have first been experienced in material forms. Hence the emergence of subjectivities at the center of which is found the need for tangibility, palpability, tactility. One finds these characteristics as much in the ways in which wars are fought, as in the forms in which pleasure and sensuousness are experienced.

Next, let us examine the effects of the concomitance of democratization, of the deregulation of the economy, and the informalization of state structures. Throughout the last quarter of the twentieth century, the deregulation of the economy and the dissipation of state power have proceeded in tandem. In some cases, the two phenomena crosscut each other. In others again, their effects canceled each other out. Very often, they reinforced each other. For example, at the beginning of the 1980s, the material conditions of the exercise of power and of sovereignty in Cameroon had deteriorated in proportion to the aggravation of the constraints linked to the repayment of debt and the application of the politics of structural adjustment. And as the continuing economic crisis did not let up, this unravelling continued throughout the 1990s, and the crumbling away of the structures of state sometimes took on unexpected forms (Bayart, Mbembe, and Toulabor 1993).

Because the drying-up of liquidity (general insolvency) affected the state as much as it did society, it contributed to a substantial change in the systems of reciprocity and exchange that were at the foundation of state socialization during the period of authoritarian rule (Mbembe 1999). The chain of deficits and unmet debts extended itself to society at large. Social actors then responded either by intensifying practices of the circumvention of rules and of embezzlement, or by expanding their practices of false accounting and default. The distinction between struggles for subsistence properly so called and struggles for survival pure and simple evaporated (Harts-Broekhuis 1997; Lugalla 1995). In both cases, daily life comes more and more to be described in terms of a paradigm of menace, danger and uncertainty.

Far from putting an end to the crisis or leading to the "rule of law" and "good governance" expected by international financial institutions, the double demand—characteristic of the 1990s—for political and economic liberalization was to accentuate, almost everywhere, the emasculation of the public power. Because the state had lost its ability to manage risk and the unexpected by any means other than those of naked force, it was consequently in a context of societal violence and a general dispersion of power that the attempts to break free of authoritarianism took place.

The weakening of the state's administrative capacities went hand in hand with the privatization of certain of its sovereign functions (Hibou 1999; Mbembe 1999). The primacy accorded to deregulation converted itself, on the ground, into a generalized movement of deinstitutionalization, which itself provided an atmosphere propitious to irregular, or informal, activities. This informality was to be found not merely in the economic domain but at the very heart of the state and the administration, and in all aspects of social and cultural life bearing any kind of relation to the struggle for survival. Conduct seeking to "bend" or infringe regulations with a view to accruing rent and deriving the maximum benefit from the failure of state institutions was to prevail as much among the representatives of the state as among private actors (Niger-Thomas 2000).

Still more important is the fact that democratization is occurring at a time when, as a result of the brutal effect of monetary constraint, the process of the fragmentation of society had reached hitherto unsuspected depths. In the context of the struggle for survival that marked the last quarter of the twentieth century in Africa, social fragmentation has taken on widely differing forms. In addition to the extreme atrocities of genocidal wars, forcible uprootings of populations, and massacres, it can also be seen in people's recourse to a plurality of repertoires of action and a parallel entanglement of conflicting codes of legitimation. More than hitherto, practices of informalization are no longer confined to the economic sphere alone and to strategies of physical survival. They have become, little by little, the paramount forms of the social and cultural imagination.

The consequences of this new cultural condition for the constitution of social movements and the formation of coalitions and alliances, has been considerable. The short term temporality, marked out by improvisation, immediate, and informal arrangements and the imperatives of the immediate conquest of power, are privileged at the expense of long-term "projects" and the search for alternatives. Alliances are constantly being made and unmade. The provisional and continually renegotiable character of contracts and agreements emphasizes the fundamental reversibility of political processes. The divergences of interest, multiple allegiances, and multiple relations of authority work against cohesion and durable crystallizing of social movements. The result is an unending particularization of conflicts, and a fragmentary and fissiparous mosaic of organized struggle.

POLITICS AS FEAR OF DEATH AND THE WILL TO SURVIVE

Among the dominant imaginaries of sovereignty in contemporary Africa is that which posits the fear of death and the will to survive as critical to any political practice. The belief is that political power cannot find any other reliable foundation for itself than in threatening the security of its subjects as individuals. From this stems the necessity for those subjects to immunize themselves against it in advance, by measuring, at every stage, the risks that such a challenge would involve for the preservation of life itself.

In this configuration, the angle from which politics, its object, its limits, and its uncertainties, are measured, is the desire at all costs to evade death. It is this desire that the state manipulates in the calculus of subjection. Nothing gives a better idea of this configuration than those regimes that, at the height of protest movements of the 1990s, reluctantly agreed to kick-start a process of national refoundation and renewal, by means of "sovereign national conferences." Far from calming such conflicts, this mechanism actually only served to stir them up still more. There followed a bumpy and contested transition that soon was brought to an end. In most of these cases, the failure of negotiated transitions led to fraudulent elections and a vigorous process of authoritarian restoration (Togo), or a series of coups d'état, some of them drenched in blood (Niger), or by a descent into civil wars that often took a regional dimension followed by the partition of the country into numerous fiefs controlled by various warlords supported by neighboring states (Congo-Kinshasa).

But the concern to avoid death at all costs and the instinct for self-preservation have also been productive of new imaginaries of politics in regimes in which the elites have successfully resisted the pressure of the opposition's forces and have been able, unilaterally, to gradually open up the political system. In being the only ones who determined the scope, the nature, and the content of any such openings, these elites have laid down a set of rules that enabled them to keep their grip on the main levers of the state and the economy and guaranteed their continuance in power. Fundamental disagreements between those in power and the opposition in these countries persist, while at the same time there continues a situation of conflict in which periods of latency alternate with periods of violence. Such is notably the case in Cameroon, in

Zimbabwe, in Guinea, in Togo as well as in Chad, and the Central African Republic.

In the majority of these cases, the reaction to popular opposition was to *contain* the thrust of protest, exerting as necessary a repression that was sometimes improvised, brutal, and unrestrained (imprisonments, shootings, suppressions of opposing parties, proclamations of states of emergency, press censorship, etc.). The regimes in power sought to depoliticize social protest, to give an ethnic profile to confrontations, and to attribute to street protests the character of hooliganism. These regimes also extended the role of the army to the tasks of the maintenance of law and order. In certain cases, entire regions or cities, were placed under a dual administration, both civil and military, as it happened in Douala in Cameroon in 2000.

Wherever the established regimes felt themselves most under threat, they fostered the emergence of gangs or militias controlled either by party zealots operating in the shadows or by military or political leaders. The role of the so-called war veterans in Zimbabwe is the best-known example. In some cases, the militias won themselves greater and greater autonomy, and transformed themselves into veritable armed formations, with their own independent chains of command distinct from those of the regular armies, notably the case in Congo-Brazzaville. Three consequences have followed from this breakdown in the monopoly of physical force and the unequal distribution of the means of terror through society: (1) the dynamic of informalization has speeded up; (2) a new form of social division separates those who are protected (because they are armed) from those who are in no way protected; (3) political struggles have developed a tendency to be settled by force as the access to arms regulate dynamics of insecurity, self-preservation, and access to property.

More important, no change to a more peaceful state has taken place in any of these countries. Some segments of the opposition have been coopted by the ruling parties. Forms of violence and technologies of subjection have taken on hitherto unheard-of forms. Urban criminality and rural brigandage have become more accentuated (Mburu 1999). Huge swathes of national territories are carved out, while entire geographical areas (rural or urban) escape from the control of central government (Mitulla and Kibwana 1998). Conflicts over land ownership have grown more exacerbated, as in the Ivory Coast and Zimbabwe. At the same time, violent forms of the appropriation of resources have increased in complexity and links have appeared between the armed forces, the police, the justice system, and criminal milieus. Loci of enduring conflict make it possible to occupy part of the military permanently with tasks of internal repression (notably in frontier towns), or in wars on the frontiers, or on tasks of pacification in rebellious regions situated within the confines of the national territory.

When changes at the head of states are not the consequence of coups d'état (Ivory Coast), they are the result of rebellions supported from outside (Congo-Kinshasa). Whether it takes a natural form (illness) or a criminal one (murder, assassination), the death of the autocrat, his disappearance or his flight, or in brief his eviction from power by violent means, remains the central point in the cultural configurations examined earlier. Because the possibility of the overthrow of power by electoral means has proved to be out of the question, only assassination can counter the principle of an uninterrupted retention of power.

POLITICS AS THE WORK OF DEATH

Another imaginary of sovereignty is the one that, in its definition of the political, accords a large role to the possibility that anyone may be killed by anyone else. Furthermore, this possibility is perceived, if not as legitimate, at least as constituting a general rule or even a commonly accepted practice. Although certainly displaying some continuities with the configuration discussed earlier, this one also presents us with characteristics of its own. First, it rests on a pyramid of the destruction of life, whereas the former was concerned with the conditions of its preservation and the price that had to be paid to achieve that end. Second, in establishing a relationship of relative equality in the ability to kill and its corollary, the possibility of being killed—a relative equality that only comes to be suspended by virtue of the difference between being or not being in possession of arms—this configuration lends authority to the idea that politics can effectively be translated, at base, into a "work of death." Third, in escalating violence into forms that are sometimes paroxysmal, sometimes virtually self-parodic (as in Sierra Leone and Liberia), this cultural configuration accentuates the functional character of terror, dread, and panic and renders possible the destruction of every social bond other than that of enmity. It is this bond of enmity that justifies the active relationship of dissociation of which war constitutes a particularly violent version. It is also this bond of enmity that allows the routinization of the idea that power cannot be acquired or exercised except at the price of someone's life; and that, ultimately, the death of the Other is the precondition for the constitution of political community.[7]

[7] In establishing this set of categories, I have availed myself of the assistance provided by Esposito (2000).

Three processes have played, in this respect, a critical role. The first was the forms of differentiation inside military institutions during the last quarter of the twentieth century. The second relates to a change in the distribution of arms in African societies during the period under consideration. The third relates to the emergence of militarism, a political culture founded on the application of force and an ethic of masculinity resting on the violent expression of acts of virility.

PAUPERIZED ARMIES

It is important to note that the military as an institution have undergone important transformations in the course of the last twenty years. These years coincided with the end of anticolonial struggles and the appearance of a new generation of wars whose chief targets have been civilian populations and the control of resources. In order to legitimate them, the participants in these wars no longer have recourse to antiimperialist rhetoric or to any emancipatory project, as was the case during the 1960s and 1970s. They appeal rather to moral categories whose peculiarity is to blend a language of modern utilitarianism with the remnants of indigenous philosophies of evil, as in the case of Liberia and Sierra Leone. Hence the prevalence, in the discourse of the warriors, of metaphors and dichotomies pertaining to ontology, degeneration, and redemptionist theologies: death and corruption, evil and sorcery, wealth and consumption, sickness and madness.

The last decades have witnessed an accentuation of internal inequalities in the ranks of the military institutions themselves. Conditions of life in barracks have deteriorated. In many countries, the pauperization of the troop and the lack of wages has lain at the root of violent incidents and public disorders. Breakouts from the barracks have multiplied, notably on the occasion of various operations labeled as "maintenance of law and order" and of organized pillaging operations. Later, the practice of racketeering became widespread, the soldiery showing no hesitation in setting up roadblocks on the highways, or indeed in organizing actual raids against the civilian population with the aim of seizing or confiscating property. With the end of the systematic confinement of armed force in the barracks, the technologies of political control have become more and more physical, not to say anatomical. As physical mobility has become ever more central to livelihood and survival, the exercise of control has taken the form of a frantic and unbridled proliferation of *passe droits*. In the most elevated ranks of the army, numerous colonels and generals were able to set up their own networks of accumulation—when they hadn't invested purely and simply in the resale of arms, trafficking in minerals, and other lucrative operations, as was the case of the modus operandi of the armies of Rwanda, Uganda, and Zimbabwe in the war in Congo. In parallel, there have been in operation a relatively rigid insulation between the various branches of the armed forces and the various units of the security forces (presidential guard, special forces, police, gendarmerie, etc.), contributing to the general dispersion of the means of repression.

RULE OF THE DISTRIBUTION OF ARMS

The second process that played a direct role in the generalization of warlike relations was a shift in the "rule of the distribution of arms" in most of the countries at war. By the "rule of the distribution of arms" should be understood simply the quality of the power-relation established when political differences and other disputes could be settled by one of the parties having recourse to force of arms. As already indicated, the last quarter of the twentieth century is characterized by the progressive loss of the state's monopoly over the means of violence and their gradual devolution to a multiplicity of units of private armed formations operating, sometimes outside the framework of the state, and sometimes within it, but with a certain degree of autonomy. The breakup of this monopoly also set its seal on the appearance of entrepreneurs of violence, of whom some acquired little by little certain capabilities for the organization and mobilization of human and material resources with a view to war. It is in the capacity for the acquisition and remobilization of the resources of violence that the rule of the distribution of arms in society develops.

This has given rise to a hitherto unencountered form of governmentality. Both the exercise and the object of power changed fundamentally. It is no longer so much a matter of repression or discipline as of mass death. In place of a simple caesura between state and society, a different economy of power characterized by multiple capillary relations of force, as much at the level of the state as at that of society, has emerged. There is no locus more significant for the breakdown of the distinction between state and society than that of the techniques of war-making. War no longer necessarily pits armies or sovereign states against each other. It increasingly pits against each other armed formations operating behind the mask of the state and armies without a state, but controlling distinct territories, both having as their targets of choice civilian populations that are either unarmed or have been constituted into militias.

The sphere of war itself, consists more and more in the singling out and appropriation of the resources necessary to the reproduction of life.

The forces that shape life, organize it, and manage it are, essentially, armed forces or forces acting through the means of arms, whether in situations of combat or in the banal situations of everyday life. In these conditions, power is infinitely more brutal than during the period of authoritarian rule. It is more physical, and more anatomical. It no longer aims at obedience as such. If it still has a taste for bodies this is not so much in order to discipline them, but, to inscribe them into the order of that supreme economy of form that is the massacre.[8] The general spread of insecurity has also, in its turn, deepened within society the distinction between the bearers of arms (who are at the same time the generators of insecurity and the purveyors of protection from it) and those who, because they are bereft of them, are at permanent risk of seeing their lives and their property placed in hazard.

In cases in which they have ended by the military victory of one of the conflicting parties, the wars of our time have rarely been followed by a democratization of the regimes thus set in place. On the contrary, these social formations combine the characteristics of military principalities exerting control over long-distance commerce and the exploitation of natural resources. In other cases, such internal wars have produced authoritarian regimes decked out with masks of "developmentalism" (Uganda, Rwanda, Liberia, Eritrea, Ethiopia). In the cases in which armed revolts have failed to conquer the totality of the state power, they have provoked territorial secessions and have succeeded in controlling whole regions that they administer on the model of the societies of the colonial "concessions" (cf. Coquery-Vidrovitch 1972), especially where there are mineable mineral deposits (such as the diamonds in Sierra Leone or Angola).

Sometimes there exists no military or state administration as such. The conduct of public affairs is effected by means of groups of clans, while the creation and circulation of riches is left in the hands of private actors (Prunier 2000). The fragmentation of territories then comes about in various forms: the emergence of regional fiefs controlled by different forces, receptacles of commercially exploitable resources backed by neighboring states (such as Congo-Kinshasa, Sierra Leone, Somalia); war zones on the borders of neighboring states (Uganda, Eritrea, Ethiopia, Sudan, Rwanda); dissident provinces or regions in the interior of national states (Angola, Uganda, the Casamance region of southern Senegal); security cordons around capitals and the adjacent areas (Congo-Brazzaville); internment camps for civil populations judged to be on the verge of rebellion (Burundi, Rwanda); economic predation with the support of mercenaries summoned from afar (Ukraine, Roma-

---

[8] See, for example, Law (1985).

nia, Bulgaria, South Africa); and generalized practices of dehumanization in war zones (Liberia, Congo-Kinshasa, Angola, Sierra Leone, Sudan).

In order to legitimize their actions, contemporary African warriors mobilize the rhetoric of the eradication of corruption, of the protection of the environment, or of the rights of minorities—the common and unifying elements of the international lexicon. In so doing, they assign to current conflicts the connotations of a fundamental moral conflict. The warriors' discourse freely mixes the desire for sacrifice, the wish to liquidate existing tyrannies, ideologies that aim to dissolve social differences, and considerations linked to race or to the survival of ethnic groups that consider themselves under threat, as in Liberia, the Delta region in Nigeria, and in parts of Uganda. Other discourses draw their central categories from indigenous interpretations of the social world in terms of sickness, misfortune, and cure.

War, under these conditions, takes on the appearance of a vast therapeutic liturgy. Others again, rely on nuclei of meanings derived from monotheistic religions or messianic eschatologies of a religious type, when they do not borrow their mental and symbolic structures from autochthonous imaginaries of the occult. Others claim to inscribe themselves within the horizons of a modernity from which they retain above and beyond all other elements the materialist, utilitarian, and hedonist dimension.[9]

Whatever may be their ideological underpinnings, their translation into politics occurs through the medium of incessant and debilitating warfare, in the course of which thousands, even hundreds of thousands, of victims are massacred, and hundreds of thousands are either made into refugees or confined in camps. The "modes of execution" of mass death in themselves vary little; the sequelae of death little more. In the case of massacres in particular, the corpses despoiled of life are rapidly reduced to skeletons. Their form nowadays inscribes them in a register of undifferentiated generality: mere remnants of an uninterred grief, empty and unmeaning corporealities, strange deposits buried in a cruel stupefaction. In the case of the Rwandan genocide, where a great number of skeletons was able, if not to be exhumed, at least to be preserved in a visible state, it is the tension between the petrification of the bony remnants with their strange coldness, on the one hand, and, on the other, their obstinacy in wanting at all costs to mean something that is striking. There does not seem to be, in these bits of bone marked by their impassivity, any kind of supramundane serenity: just the illusory refuse of a death that has already overtaken people.[10]

[9] On various readings and critiques of these dimensions, see Bataille (1991); see also D. Bennett (1999); Comaroff and Comaroff (1999b); and Goux (2000).

[10] For a representation of these states of mind in the contemporary African novel, see Diop (2000) and Monenembo (2000).

In other cases where physical mutilation replaces outright and immediate killing, the prior removal of certain limbs opens the way to techniques of incision, ablation, and excision that also in their turn have for their object the human skeleton. The traces of this "creative" surgery persist long after the event, in the form of human figures that are certainly alive, but whose bodily integrity has been replaced by lumps, stumps, and fissures, and even huge wounds that are difficult to close, and whose function is to place constantly under the gaze of the victims and of those who are around them the morbid spectacle of their dismemberment and their passage into the categories of meat and of flesh, of being reduced to mere and simple life.

The Relationship of Reciprocal Negation

The third process directly connected with the spread of warlike relationships is the emergence of a culture of militarism that, as we have already said, rests on an ethic of masculinity according a large role to the violent expression of acts of virility. The successive crises of the last quarter of the twentieth century have in various ways affected the relations between men and women, and then again between men and children. In certain cases, they have contributed to deepening the already existing inequalities between the sexes. In others, they have brought with them a profound change in the general terms in which and through which both male domination and femininity are expressed (see, for example, Ashforth 1999; Sindjoun 2000). Among the most deprived groups of the population, the role of "head of the family" generally held by men has undergone a loss of status, most obviously in cases in which the role of "provider" could no longer be entirely fulfilled for lack of resources. Ultimately, the new cycle of struggles for survival generated by the crisis has, paradoxically, opened various possibilities of social "mobility" for a numerically small but influential group of women, in particular in certain spheres of material life related to irregular or frankly illegal activities (Niger-Thomas 2000). These growing possibilities of social mobility have gone along with a renewed challenge to masculine prerogatives and a growth in relations of violence between the sexes.

These processes have had consequences for two different forms of domination. One, based on the notion of social debt within the family, has been severely shaken and has from now on become a bone of contention. In effect, it was around this notion that there was tied, until very recently, the knot that bound together the relation between men and women and between men and children within the family. One of the cornerstones of the African systems of phallocracy was, in effect, the idea of the indebtedness of sons to fathers and that of the unequal complementarity of male and female roles. The conception whereby because they "come from" their fathers and are considered to be engendered by them, children—and particularly sons—are in the nature of their fathers' possessions was closely tied in to the dominating ideology of the African forms of patriarchy (Berry 1985).

Relations between men and women within the family, in their turn, proceeded according to a logic centered around two pivotal conceptions: that of appropriation and that of a reciprocal instrumentality between unequal parties. With regard to women as with regard to children, the masculine prerogative consisted in nourishing, protecting, and guiding, in return for which there was exercised a form of domination founded on the narcissistic constitution of the male self (ideologies of seduction and virility) and discrimination in respect of rules of inheritance. In large part the culture of militarism is supported by these same frameworks, which it reproduces in the domestic sphere and, above all, which it extends into the civil and political sphere: armed men playing, in relation to those who are definitely not armed, the same roles and disposing of the same attributes as does the father within the family unit. In these conditions, the military prerogative becomes the masculine prerogative in an even higher register. An active process of demasculinization strikes at the whole of the civil population, the pleasure of male domination becoming the exclusive privilege and preserve of "military" society.

As for the other form of domination, one could call it domination of a "phallic" type.[11] This form of domination was all the more strategic in the crystallization of power-relations in that it not only rested on a mobilization of the subjective foundations of masculinity and femininity but also had direct and precise links with the overall economy of sexuality. From this point of view, it referred back to the inner psychic life of power as such (Butler 1997). Effectively, at the heart of certain African constructions of power and masculinity was to be found the phallus (Mbembe 2001). Male domination derived a great part of its power and theatrical effect, not so much from the hazarding of life in the course of war as from the capacity of the individual male to demonstrate his virility at the expense of woman, to obtain its validation from that very woman who was subjugated by it.[12]

From this point of view, the phallus was not merely the emblem of

[11] Phallic domination expresses itself in many forms. All that I study here is the version that relies on physical attributes and anatomical arrangements to produce the effects of subjugation. On other aspects, such as seduction, pleasure, and eroticism, compare Biaya (forthcoming). In more general terms, see the note by Butler (1999).

[12] On this ideal of the "beautiful death" and its relations with forms of glorification of virility, see Rauch (2000, Ch. 2).

masculinity *par excellence,* or even what was supposed to exhibit its essential attribute. A veritable "living statue" of the masculine self, it also constituted a locus of evaluation of the self and of power. This is the reason why it formed the object of a more or less openly avowed cult. The penis was, in its own right, that part of the body that in postulating and defining the masculine as such, worked to assign each sex its proper place in the order of things (Lallemand 1986). After all, the measures of male enjoyment were all ranked around the turgescence of the male member, and inability to achieve erection evoking the menace of vulnerability, in short, of emasculation and impotence. And, for the rest, the production of the insignia of power and representations of politics were so tied to the emblem of the phallus that the setting to work of power was related metaphorically to the setting to work of an erection, the ideal image of the autocrat becoming, thereby, the completed and fulfilled symbol of *homo erectus* (Mbembe 1996).

Sexual fulfilment itself was expressed in two different fashions. First, in the to-ing and fro-ing of what presented all the characteristics of a conquest: alternating movements of intromission, of withdrawal and then of repenetration into the feminine interior; and then, in the explosive operation: the evacuation and expulsion of the reserve of semen, that major symbol of every orgasm that is to be considered virile. In both cases, the phallus had to operate as an instrument of the subjugation of women. This subjugation took place, in the one case, in a conscious act of the scission, possession, and physical domination of one body by another, by means of one of its more privileged members. In both cases, equally, the element of the display of "male credentials" and the active and even aggressive demonstration of their validity formed the cornerstones of male pleasure.

Finally, a woman's body was subjectively placed in such a position that it constantly ran the risk of being deprived of all autonomous significance. Everything was so arranged that every part of her body had no meaning except in terms of the private use to which it was destined by her dominator: an abode whose function it was to receive a liquid emission along with the sheath that carried the fluid. And one rediscovers in the culture of militarism all the characteristics of this sensualist economy and all the central elements of its relation to the object that subtends it.[13] It is from that source that this culture derives its referents, its terminology, and its practices. Today, this culture and this sensualist economy find their principal point of articulation in the—relatively novel—conjunction of the gun and the phallus.

---

[13] Here we are only dealing with the ebullitions of masculinity. For an attempt at a feminist interpretation, see Mama (1999), and other writings by the same author.

This displacement can be explained. In effect, during the last quarter of the twentieth century the phallus considered as the central symbol of power and appanage of male domination was very seriously called into question. This calling into question took various different forms. In some cases the form assumed was that of marital instability and relatively frequent changes of partners among women (Cohen 1971). In other cases it was that of urban panics at the heart of which lay the fear of castration (Sackey 1997). In yet others, it took the route of affecting the imagination, so that for the image of the erection there came to be substituted the danger of a vaginalization of the phallus and its being definitively swallowed up, or at least being permanently fixed in a state of irremediable detumescence. In the cultural cartography of the end of the twentieth century in Africa, therefore, one finds oneself confronted with a phallic dynamic that is, more than ever before, capable of moving in a variety of directions. Certainly, the phallus continues to represent a symbol of a character that is essentially differentiatory. However, its primordial functions are shrouded in confusion, to the extent that we are now imperceptibly returning to an age characterized by the demasculinization of men, under the impulsion of various forces of which some are of an economic order, whereas others relate to different factors.

But far from leading to any reduction in conflicts between the sexes, the crisis relating to the centrality of the phallus in the workings of masculinization and in the workings of power has brought with it an increase in incidents of brutality in everyday relations. Little by little, there is hardly any violence that does not leave its imprint on the bodies of its victims, just as there is no longer any sexual enjoyment, however brief, that does not lead to a further rigidification of the dichotomy between the sexes. There are emerging somehow or other, if not in the public sphere, then at least in the collective unconscious, forms of sexuality hitherto repressed, such as [male] homosexuality and lesbianism.[14] In the face of the sense—widespread among men—of menacing feminization, rites of proving or demonstrating one's virility are multiplying. With the assistance of a context dominated by wars, the tension between what is threatened with extinction and what both formerly has been and now is suppressed is exacerbated, and relations of substitutability between the phallus and the gun are instituted.

On the one hand, and for a number of child-soldiers who now make up the greater part of the armed bands, the demonstration of one's virility is achieved by means of the gun. The possession of a gun acts, in its turn, as the equivalent of the possession of a phallus on one's pas-

---

[14] On homosexuality, see McLean and Ngcobo (1995); Murray and Will (1998); Epprecht (1998); and Donham (1998).

sage out of the age of virginity. But the mediation of the gun for the phallus is only imaginary. Putting to death by means of the gun takes place almost simultaneously with being put to the test through the act of sex—in this case, generally speaking, by group rape. On the other hand, to possess a gun is to enjoy a position of almost unrestricted access to sexual goods; it is, above all, to have access in a very concrete manner to a certain form of abundance at the heart of which woman is constituted as a superfluity, as what one can dispense with without concern for whether one will be able to replace it with a similar provision at a later date. Finally, the sexual act itself manages to become an element, not merely of rape, but of violence as such. Rape, to the extent that access to the inwardness of woman is achieved by breaking and entering; violence, to the extent that one uses force to possess and to dominate someone else's will as one would in combat. And so enjoyment through the gun and through the phallus are conjoined, the one ending in a corporeality that is inert and emptied of all life, death; and the other by a discharge as violent as it is brief, the orgasmic satisfaction by the means of which the power of enjoyment is converted into a power of radically objectifying the Other, whose body one bores into, digs into, excavates, and empties in the very act of rape.

Without necessarily taking on the lineaments of a generalized war or a dynamic of a truly phallic nature, social violence tends to crystallize around currently crucial questions such as the constitution of identities, the modalities of citizenship, the management of mobility, and the capture of free-floating resources. The emergence of one-party states has in effect relaunched struggles for identity on a scale that is now more visible than it formerly was. From the fact of the informalization of the state and of the fragmentation of society mentioned earlier, collective mobilization with a view to access to resources is effected more and more through registers of identities (Pérouse de Montclos 1999). In these new forms of social struggle three sets of themes stand out: that of the community of origin (territoriality), that of race, and that of religion. On the basis of the theme of the origins, new social actors put their efforts into establishing differences between their communities and others with which they are in competition.

And so, in the course of the last quarter of the twentieth century, at least two different conceptions of citizenship have impressed themselves upon the public consciousness. On the one hand, there prevails the official idea whereby the citizen of a country is whoever the state recognizes as possessing the necessary attributes. On the other, there is a dominant idea that citizenship derives not from the place where the individual lives, but from that of his birth and from his genealogy. Genealogy in effect allows one to set up and ground a distinction between the "indigenous" and the "foreign," between "natives" ("aborigines") and "strangers" (Geshiere and Nyamjoh 2000). This project of identity-creation has fostered, over the past twenty years, the reemergence of ancient kingdoms and chieftaincies and the creation of new ethnic groupings, either by hiving off from the old ones or by their amalgamation into larger groups; it has also precipitated violent conflicts that have resulted in numerous forced mass migrations, and has also, finally, given sustenance to outbreaks of irredentism, notably in countries where minorities have had the feeling of being excluded from the exercise of power and its material rewards (Eyoh 1998).

All these developments show that, far from being of a linear nature, political transformation in Africa has proceeded along various trajectories. The paths followed in different countries undoubtedly exhibit significant differences. But they also bear witness to profound convergences. In every country can be found, more and more, a concatenation and entanglement of the configurations discussed earlier. The political imagination, too, takes on various forms. They relate to paradoxical logics that defy, by that very fact, the dichotomies generally laid down in the traditional analyses of politics and of cultural production in Africa. Moreover, the material conditions of the maintenance of life have been profoundly transformed in the course of the last quarter of the twentieth century. These transformations have been accompanied by a decisive change in the paradigms and the imaginaries of power, politics, and conflict. There have appeared, simultaneously, in large parts of Africa, a gamut of new arrangements whose articulation, distribution, and dissemination have transformed the relations that it was customary to establish between life, power, and death.

BODY, LOCALITY, AND INFORMAL SOVEREIGNTY

an irreducible core of the practices of modern states—for example, in their capacity to take and exterminate life through its ethical neutralization and desymbolization. Linking sovereignty not merely to the formal right over life and death but to the actual disregard of life, Agamben affords us to think further and to disentangle sovereignty from its conventional moorings in territory and state power.

Georges Bataille's idea that the source of sovereign power resides in life itself—in the body—and in the will to disregard it, to take life at will and with impunity, may be helpful here. Let me make three preliminary propositions about the character of sovereign power.

First, sovereign power is essentially an unstable and precarious form of power whose efficacy as a social authority capable of disciplining and creating subjects is dependent on its constant public reiteration and performance, or the rumors thereof.

Second, sovereign power originates in acts of violence characterized by excess—not merely in their brutality but also in their apparent lack of intention and moderation. Sovereign violence—whether committed in the name of an individual, a community or a state—is essentially self-referential as it asserts itself through terror and disregard of life (Bataille 1991, 220–34).

Third, insofar as sovereignty is constituted by the capacity for excessive violence, abstaining from violence, or acts of generosity toward subjects, become perceived as equally excessive and lacking in rationality. This only adds to the mystical aura of sovereign power that also underpins the actions of the modern state. This couplet, terror and generosity, is at the heart of the inherent ambivalence of any form of public authority that in turn depends on what I, in a different context, have termed its profane as well as its sublime dimensions (Hansen 2001a).

Drawing on Dumezil's work on Indo-European myths, Marshall Sahlins argues that the notion of the king as a "stranger," an usurper who gradually gets acculturated through marrying a woman "of the soil," is at the heart of a large number of myths of origin of royalty across the world. This amounts to an ontology of the political, or kingship, argues Sahlins, as something that is not entirely reducible to society itself, because "usurpation itself is the principle of legitimacy" (Sahlins 1985, 80–81). The enduring magicality of sovereignty arises from this ineradicable element of something "foreign" (78)—that is, something which cannot be understood in terms of a society's everyday function. Sovereign power grows out of the combination and tensions between the violent and creative "war function" (*celeritas*) and the judicious, venerable and productive "peace function" (*gravitas*), the combination of "king and priest, will and law" (90). Understood in a more generalized sense, violence or terror remains the "foreign" and disruptive dimension, which the productive and generous dimensions of sovereign power always seek to domesticate.

Understood as fundamental in the ontology of political life, we can begin to understand sovereignty as existing in many overlapping and competing forms at many levels within the same territory and temporal frame: from the family and clan, to larger communities, to the nation-state. Local forms of adjudication of disputes, community elders meting out punishments, revenge killings, blood feuds, shadow economies or control of territories and people by gangster syndicates, or political organizations defying the state, are all examples that illustrate how fragile and incomplete the sovereignty of the state is in many parts of the world. The Hobbesian idea of sovereignty—the power to make final and incontestable decisions within a territory and its population—must, in other words, be seen as a tentative and never completed endeavor that constantly struggles to halt its own fragmentation.

Such an understanding of sovereignty as multiple, provisional, and always contested, and of the state as an unfinished and continuous project of control and subordination resonates meaningfully with the trajectory of colonial and post colonial state formation in South Asia.

The conceptual history of sovereignty in India has not yet been fully written but there exists a rich literature on both colonial and precolonial state formation. The debate on precolonial state formation especially in South India demonstrated the emergence of "segmentary forms of state" (Frykenberg 1977; Stein 1980). Here, the central state received tribute but served primarily as an arena for exemplary performance of power and privilege that subsequently were replicated and copied at relatively independent subcenters, or "little kingdoms" (Cohn 1987, 320–42), where much of the actual taxation and adjudication over life and death took place. This system accorded considerable room for independence and change of loyalties at lower levels while the sovereignty of the central state was often of a less tangible nature. Sovereignty was performed to maintain a moral-religious authority or "ritual sovereignty" (Inden 1978), that often revolved around performance of religious rituals and sponsorship of central religious institutions and pilgrimage sites (Appadurai and Breckenridge 1976).

This conception of sovereignty depended on what Dumont, in a reading of classical texts and inspired by Dumezil and Hocart, calls the "unity of the two forces," *brahman* and *ksatra,* the spiritual and the material, the priest and the king (Dumont 1970, 63). This unity was, however, always contested and fragile, and the moral superiority of either of the poles never settled. Dumont concludes, nonetheless, that the realm of politics and the state—guided by *dandaniti* (lit. "the conduct of punishment") and the principle of *artha* (interested action)—was only "relatively autonomous with regard to the all-embracing domain of religion and absolute values" (86–87).

Dumont's perspective is textual, classical and Hindu and cannot incorporate the types of sovereignty that developed over the nine centuries when Muslim political elites dominated northern and central India. This so-called Muslim period has often been interpreted as the introduction of an entire Muslim civilization and the imposition of a specific form of political organization on the subjected peoples.[2] It often has been assumed that the "foreignness" of Muslim rulers was a liability, and that legitimacy only could be established during periods of "indigenized" or "tolerant" rule. With notable exceptions,[3] this perspective—which originates in efforts to portray British rule as saving India from the despotism of a corrupt and decadent Muslim elite (see Sen 2002, 41–56)—has inhibited the inquiry into the actual configurations of sovereignty and legitimacy of precolonial forms of state and rule. For our purposes it suffices to conclude, however, that precolonial India had a longstanding tradition of segmented, overlapping and stratified forms of sovereignty.

The East India Company governed large parts of the Indian subcontinent for almost 150 years. It acquired statelike features and its policies, military campaigns, and establishment of sovereign power on behalf of the Crown were hotly debated in Britain throughout the period. India became in many respects the laboratory for the development of technologies and ideologies of modern colonial rule, and, indeed, a central field of experience that shaped British ideas of race, culture, domesticity and domination. It was the encounter with India that consolidated the idea that British "forcefulness" and ability to establish its sovereignty throughout the world originated in the "natural liberty" of English men, a liberty founded on ownership of property and on patriarchal domination of domestic life (Sen 2002, 1–17).

The configuration of overlapping and parallel sovereign powers in the emerging colony was complex. It involved local landholding *jagirdars* and little kings retaining substantial rights of taxation and adjudication, local courts and *panchayats* (councils) deciding local disputes and offences, and religious authorities adjudicating matters considered exclusive to Muslims or to various Hindu castes or religious communities, and administering land and property. The military dominance

---

[2] This is evident even in scholarship of a materialist orientation, for example, Habib (1963).

[3] Studies by Andre Wink on the character of Mughal sovereignty and land administration, Gordon's study of the Maratha Empire, and Eaton's studies of state formation in medieval Bengal all try to escape the civilizational perspective on so-called Muslim rule in India (Eaton 1996; Gordon 1994; Wink 1986).

won by the Company armies in the early nineteenth century and the economic resources at the disposal of the Company were not employed to create anything resembling the indivisible territorial sovereignty that was the ideal in Europe. This form of state was deemed unfeasible for India where reliance on the legitimacy of loyal local princes and allies was seen as the only means to maintain political stability. The Company experimented with a range of legal-political arrangements to maintain the formal and symbolic sovereignty of the Mughal empire and various notables across the subcontinent. Indian subjects were generally deemed "barbaric" and unfit for freedom and self-determination because of the absence of unalienable private property and stable domestic discipline. Company officials warned in the 1770s that if such conditions were created, the quest for freedom would also arise (Sen 2002, 17).

In 1790 it was decided to create a more uniform system of law in British-controlled India and to promote a professionalization of the legal profession (Cohn 1987, 463–82). Under the influence of Christian missionaries and in the interest of rationalization, it was decided to promulgate a uniform criminal legislation, and to create a native "colonial public" through Western education and selective incorporation of elite groups into the structures of what was to become a modern colonial society. The Penal Code promulgated in 1833 was, as Radhika Singha notes in her study, an important step in a process aimed at "civil pacification" and "disarming of Indian society" (Singha 1998, ix). The Code tried to establish a monopoly of violence and qua its representation of sovereignty as indivisible and the Company state as both universal and "neutral" vis-à-vis particular communities it also introduced a novel construct in Indian history: the universal legal subject. Moreover, the colonial state began to define the notion of a "public interest," a term that obviously made very limited sense in a society structured by deep segmentation of morality, justice and economy along lines of caste, locality, and religious community. The construction of the public interest was driven by a desire to limit the power of obligations toward local notables and heads of households and thus produce freely available labor and more pliable subjects. Moral concerns in the name of universal standards of humanity, and the desire to create proper domesticity in India, also played a role in justifying bans on a range of practices within the family—*sati*, slavery, infanticide, adultery, and so on (121–62). Similarly, the application of uniform rules of taxation aimed at substituting local whimsical despotism with what was seen as rational law encouraged industriousness (xv). These types of legislation aimed at reforming Indian society, of exercising authority without consulting local communities and at establishing by decrees an "enlightened" sphere of life, interest and opinion in the name of universal norms.

This imposition of the sovereignty of the colonial state through procedures of legality, taxation and the spectacles of the courtroom was based upon the use of systematic and often excessive violence and the assertion of the right of the local *faujdar* (military commander) to have the ultimate right to decide to take life. The Company's courts used capital punishment much more often that any of the native courts, permanent gallows were erected on public places, prisons constructed and a great deal of effort went into modifying Islamic law into a stricter form that used capital punishment with more frequency (xi–xii). Punishment was institutionalized in a growing range of penal colonies and prisons. Although these institutions were explicitly modeled on European forms, the bodies of the convicts were nonetheless differentiated along lines of caste and religious communities and notions of pollution and appropriate food for the convicts remained highly contentious issues, often involving the local population around the penal colonies (Yang 2004).[4]

The body also was the site of various forms of resistance to the colonial assertion of sovereignty. Brahmin communities across North India refused in the eighteenth century to pay taxes as it violated the privileges of their ritual authority that exempted them from taxation and most punishments. Causing harm to a brahmin body was considered a grave sin. Brahmins would stage hunger strikes (*dharna*), sitting naked at the door step of the British collector, disrupting the household, refusing to get up and blaming the tax collector for the harm or death, caused. In other cases, brahmins would put old women on top of funeral pyres, or even behead their old mothers, in front of the colonial administration offices, thus inflicting "blood-guilt" and causing the restless spirit of the woman put to death to haunt the colonial officer (86–91). In an attempt to subject brahmins to its penal regime, the Company courts decided to turn the traditional tattooing, *godna,* into a penal instrument. Refraining from executing brahmins, their convictions were tattooed on their foreheads before being sentenced to prison terms and thus literally writing the sovereignty of the colonial state upon the bodies of the ritual specialists of the Hindu social order (Singha 2000, 166–67; Anderson 2000).

Even when draconian measures were taken, the Company insisted on presenting its governance and forms of justice as indigenized and in keeping with traditions of rule and sovereignty in the subcontinent. The revolt across North India in 1857 was a watershed that inaugurated

---

[4] Anand Yang has pioneered a string of studies of colonial penal systems. See Yang (1985); Sen (2000); Mills (2000); Anderson (2000); and Mills and Sen (2004).

an era of direct rule and more intensive and biopolitical rationalities of governance.[5] In the latter half of the nineteenth century scientific racism became a dominant paradigm in starkly paternalist forms of governance of colonial people, as well as the laboring populations of Europe and North America.[6]

Although racial distinctions kept Indians out of high offices until the last decades of the Raj, the more important distinctions were those of class and social hierarchies. The reproduction of a distinction between respectable and nonrespectable subjects became the bedrock of everyday governance and the incipient forms of native representation from the end of the nineteenth century. The political elites of the princely states, and the *zamindari* landlords dominating the countryside, were incorporated through a traditionalizing register. The *durbar*, the Mughal imperial court where the lesser lords paid their respect and tribute to the overlord, was reenacted at local levels and was also adapted to the lavish coronation of English royalty as Emperors of India up to 1911 (Cohn 1987, 632–79). Another register, decidedly modernizing, was employed in the efforts to create a modern, educated middle class as the backbone of the modern urban economy and bureaucracy.

Beyond these relatively small groups, the vast number of ordinary people encountered sovereign power in much harsher and more violent forms. The state's administration of justice was divided into criminal offences falling under the Penal Code, and other types of offences or disputes that fell within communitarian forms of justice, either as Personal Law applying to family, religion and inheritance, or as disputes adjudicated by caste *panchayats*, local notables or local headmen of villages. In many cases, members of the so-called criminal tribes—the traditional form of "bare life" and often itinerant and nomadic communities as the *banjaris* in western India—were punished for offences after the most superficial court procedures. The overriding problem was to gather information about criminal activities and as in other fields the colonial officers encountered multiple problems of classification and categorization. The campaigns against the *thuggees* in central India in the 1830s and 1840s and the passage of the Thuggee Act in 1836 created an important precedent in criminal law in India in terms of its attempts to know, classify, police, and ultimately eradicate what was called a "great pollution." The unequivocal identification of individuals for the purposes of recruitment of labor, soldiers, and "coolies" in the large,

[5] This is reflected in the academic literature on the period (see, e.g., Bayly 1998, 238–75; Washbrook 1978).

[6] Many of the studies that are highly critical of colonial governance focus on this period (see Cohn 1987; Chatterjee 1993; Dirks 2001; Pandey 1990).

floating, and largely illiterate population was especially difficult. Despairing in the face of what appeared as "dishonest" and changing forms of self-identification, police officials began in the 1890s to apply fingerprinting techniques. The method proved extremely popular and soon the fingerprints became a ubiquitous means of identification used in a range of routine bureaucratic operations from exams to job and pension applications. Respectable Europeans, princes and gazetted officials and others "well-known by other means" were, however, exempted (Singha 2000).

In spite of this obvious fragmentation and lack of a monopoly of violence, the colonial officers were determined to assert and perform the paramountcy of colonial power. Although many of the colonial policies on crime, health and population resembled the policies pursued in Europe, "colonial biopolitics" seemed always be mediated by principles of indirect rule and segmentation. Except for the relatively small sections with western education who were believed to be able to behave like responsible quasi-citizens, ordinary Indians were not seen as individuals, or single subjects. The elementary unit of governance was communities, *jatis*, religious categories or sects whose inner affairs, practices, and beliefs were governed by passion and irrational impulses and therefore to be left to adjudication by authorities within those communities. The problem of public order, especially in urban areas, where supply of disciplined labor was a persistent concern, remained the main concern of the colonial police.

Among police officers in the urban centers, a doctrine of the specific requirements of colonial policing emphasized that the use of force had to be more resolute and excessive than in Europe because of the religious passions among the masses and the tradition of strong authority in the Orient (Chandavarkar 1998, 174–94). These notions of the necessity of visiting excessive violence on the bodies of the ordinary and impoverished groups in Indian society to maintain order and stability is still in vogue among police officers in contemporary India (Hansen 2001b, 121–59).

In spite of these efforts, the worlds of the colonial subjects remained somewhat opaque and impenetrable and were in most cases approached through what was assumed to be local informers and "natural leaders" of communities and localities. Colonial biopolitics shared many rationalities and modes of intervention with similar policies in Europe but the methods of disciplining, of persuasion and negotiation did not aim at creating responsible and self-governing individuals as Cruikshank points out in the context of the early-twentieth-century United States (Cruikshank 1999). The paramount aims of colonial bio-politics were to maintain stability and order, whereas the grooming of colonial quasi-citizens was highly selective and always circumscribed by both class and race.

Sovereignty and the Nation

These configurations of authority and sovereignty in colonial India make it evident why the incipient Indian nationalism saw the nation as lodged in what Chatterjee has called "the inside," family, language and community. In spite of multiple transformations and legal interventions, this was regarded as the uncolonized heart of Indian society, while the colonial state was seen to make its presence felt in only the "outer" and public domains (Chatterjee 1993, 1–14). This figure of thought, inspired by European ideas of popular sovereignty, resonated well with a lived reality of segmentation and fragmented sovereignties in India. In almost perfect inversion of colonial inability and reluctance to interfere in the moral life of communities, nationalists could now construct the community (samaj, qaum) in opposition to the "cold monster" of the state and the corrupted world of politics.[7]

The idea of the sovereignty of the nation and its constituent communities as separate from, and independent of, the state became more problematic as the state moved from being "outside" and alien to become the very heart of the national imagination. The new state and its constituent assembly set out to reform the enormously diverse society through constitutional and legal means. The unprecedented number of Directive Principles in the Indian constitution obliging the government to pursue social and cultural reforms on a large number of issues bears witness to the enduring power of legalistic thought. Sudarshan notes this continuity between the colonial and postcolonial state: "[the framers of the constitution] were more inclined to trust the judiciary and the civil service because these institutions were expected to remain aloof from politics and insulate the state from the consequences of partisan pursuit of narrow interests" (Sudarshan 1999, 108–09).

The era of Nehruvian reformism saw an unprecedented intensity of governance, of regulation in intimate matters of faith and family life,[8]

[7] Ayesha Jalal's recent work on sovereignty and selfhood among Muslims in South Asia (1999) attempts to straddle, unsuccessfully in my view, both an argument of the Muslim community as reified/constructed by the colonial state (e.g., pp. 570–76), and, at the same time, internally cohesive and meaningful on the basis of shared notions of qaum, attachment to watan (the territorial homeland) (13), and even the existence of a shared "Muslim psyche" (14).

[8] Such as the Hindu Code Bill that standardized and legislated Hindu family law. For a critical discussion of this intervention, see Chatterjee (1995).

of interventions in the name of economic development, the use of law to uplift communities and ameliorate the effects of caste discrimination (see Galanter 1989). The constitution granted formal and equal rights to all citizens and unequivocally defined the individual as a legal subject. Yet, colonial assumptions regarding the constitutive differences between the educated who were fit for responsible citizenship, and the uneducated who should be dealt with as communities, persisted.

Marc Galanter's analysis of Supreme Court cases adjudicating the legitimacy and validity of conversions from one religion to another is a case in point. Galanter highlights the practice according to which the validity of conversion among the "lower strata" of society is made to depend on evidence of actually changed ritual practices. This is partly because rituals are assumed to be "of utmost importance for people of this class," as one judgment states, and, one should add, because the utterances and self-descriptions from "this class" supposedly cannot be trusted. In the case of educated people the required evidence is merely an unequivocal enunciation of intent, for example, "I am a Muslim and no longer a Hindu." It is noteworthy, however, that in both cases it is not enough to say, for instance, "I am not a Hindu," or to renounce all Hindu practices. One remains a Hindu, Muslim, etc. until one has proved in practice, or said unequivocally, that one is something else (Galanter 1989, 237–58). In practice, the secular state left no room for secularity and little space outside communities.

In spite of a concerted effort among leading bureaucrats, planners and political leaders to curtail the structures of indirect rule and community sovereignty in post colonial India, many decisions, also on life and death, were never taken to the state or the legal system. The everyday administration in localities, political mobilization, the implementation of laws and government decrees, as well as court proceedings and policing, remained firmly mediated, if not controlled, by local notables and hierarchies of "big men" who exercised *de facto* sovereignty in most everyday matters. I shall return to this below.

The disjunction between these discrete repertoires of authority widened as state interventionism intensified in the early 1970s. Emergency rule from 1975 to 1977 demonstrated how deep-seated and entrenched this configuration of authority was. Indira Gandhi sought to create a biopolitical dictatorship by administrative decree. The regime intruded deeply into intimate matters of the body and reproduction when it embarked on the infamous program of forced sterilization and extensive slum clearances. The regime also tried to enforce a conservative public morality and to discipline the working class and the poor— supposedly to safeguard the nation and further its economic development, while also aiming to curtail the power of informal sovereigns, local middlemen and brokers. Even this grand experiment in authoritarian centralization ultimately had to rely on the very structures of informal sovereignty in slums and neighborhoods it sought to curtail. The functioning of the state at the level of localities had always depended on such figures. Soon, the draconian policies of the Emergency turned into a randomly brutal and dispersed despotism (Tarlo 2000).

Opposed to this biopolitical authoritarianism stood a coalition of disparate forces, among them the Hindu nationalist movement, rallying around Jayaprakash Narayanan's Gandhian call for "total revolution" of the outlook and ethos of the political world, the state and the economy. At one level, this was a protest against corruption and highhandedness appealing to the idea of the nation as a moral and sovereign entity beyond, and in opposition to, the state and the political world. At another level, it was a struggle over how far and deep the state and its sovereign prerogative should be allowed to enter into issues of family, morality and reproduction that conventionally had been regulated in the name of community norms.

ASSERTING THE SOVEREIGNTY OF THE HINDU COMMUNITY

Organizations and movements aiming at social transformation through moral reform and self-making beyond the realm of politics, the law, or the state, have proliferated in postcolonial India. They base their arguments on the historical reification of "communities" as the natural repositories of morality and ethical life in India, separated from, and conceptually opposed to, the state. The *locus classicus* of this reification of community was disputes over family matters and the control of female sexuality as in the protracted debates over the age of consent— from the 1860s to 1929—and the Special Marriage Act of 1872 that made assertions of religious and social barriers to marriage unlawful. The defense of the right of various communities to define their own sexual practices invoked a wealth of arguments: how climatic differences between East and West impinged on maturity and sexual desire, the impossibility of regarding an Indian woman as an individual in the Western sense, etc. (Gupta 2001, 121–40; Sarkar 2001, 191–262). These debates—premised on the rights of men to control, discipline, and punish members of their family, and to define the domain of worship and belief—were crucial in the formation of communities as more clearly bounded entities endowed with rights and public representation. In North India, colonial legislation and female education were widely portrayed as emasculating Hindu men and corrupting weak and gullible women. Ostensibly concerned with matters of religion and morality, the formation of a Hindu community in the late colonial period revolved, in other words, vitally around notions of virility, pride, and potency vis-à-vis Muslims and the government, and a reduction of the feminine to the function of the reproductive mother made national icon (Gupta 2001, 120–222).

The Hindu nationalist movement has, with considerable success, exploited and redefined these deeply rooted historical definitions of the Hindu community as defined by a perpetual defense of Hindu bodies—male and female—against the state and the law. Hindu nationalists claim to organize Hindus in a parallel civil society of its own—a Hindu nation beyond the state with the *Rashtriya Swayamsevak Sangh* (RSS) as its chief executive, protector and purifier; with specialized mass organizations such as the *Vishwa Hindu Parishad* (VHP) and the *Bharatiya Janata Party* (BJP) intervening into families and exercising strict discipline over the bodies and minds of their members.

The so-called religious parliament, *Dharma Sansad,* organized by the VHP is supposedly adjudicating religious matters of importance to Hindus. This rather chaotic body of *sadhus* from all over India, is also passing resolutions on nuclear armament, international trade, Kashmir, globalization, and so on. According to the VHP, which seeks to control the *Sansad,* these issues cannot be fully adjudicated by courts or the state as they all concern faith, national feelings and other higher causes. These were also the arguments used when the VHP refused to respect High Court verdicts on the disputed Babri Masjid in Ayodhya in the early 1990s. The systematic violence against Muslims in the 1980s and 1990s organized by the VHP and other Hindu nationalist organizations has consistently been portrayed as expressions of "spontaneous anger" felt by "Hindus" as such, supposedly when their religious or national feelings were hurt. The burning and killing of Muslims by Hindu crowds were, in other words, nothing but expressions of the inert sovereignty of the Hindu community-nation, an entirely natural and inevitable violence that cannot—and should not—be controlled by the state.

The ambivalence regarding state power in the Hindu nationalist movement indicates the protracted attempt to straddle the tension between the sovereignty of the community-nation and an equally strong desire for a powerful state capable of maintaining order (Jaffrelot 1996, 169–71). This contradiction has been eased over the last decade. The Indian state has expanded its armed forces and promoted rapid capitalist development and the Hindu nationalist movement has been able to move the dominant national discourse toward a majoritarian-ethnic notion of Hindus constituting the core of the nation.

The recent pogrom in Gujarat in February–March 2002 was a chilling demonstration of how the RSS and BJP combine these repertoires. The pogrom which lasted for weeks and in which thousands of Muslims perished, was justified as a "natural" reaction of the Hindu *samaj* as such to revenge the deaths of dozens of Hindu *kar sevaks* (temple volunteers) killed in the arson of a train in the town of Godhra. As so often before, the Hindu nationalist movement sought to become and embody the "community" by killing its imagined enemies in its name. The BJP government in Gujarat also provided crucial conditions for the pogroms by withdrawing the local police force and administration. Soon after, the government banned the direct reporting of the riots by privately owned TV channels. Similarly, the central government—also dominated by the BJP—refrained from effective measures for several days, allowing the local units of the RSS and VHP and their many local supporters to wreak deadly revenge on Muslims all over the state.

Although an official inquiry has been ordered into the riots, BJP asserted its *de facto* right to kill with impunity in the name of the Hindu community and its disregard for legal procedures and ideas of accountability by staging a large *yatra* (procession) in the state in August–September. The *yatra* was led by the state's BJP chief minister—who on this occasion claimed to lead the procession in his capacity as a "Hindu leader." The procession went through hundreds of towns in the state, many of which had been the scene of arson and slaughter of Muslims a few months before. To the BJP, the control of state power meant the capacity to prevent the assertion of state's formal monopoly of legitimate violence, to suspend the law and legal procedures, to transfer what was seen as overly diligent police officers, and to openly celebrate that the Hindu community had taken revenge, and that "natural justice" had been exercised.

While the exoneration of crowd violence in Gujarat is part of a well-organized political strategy, it draws on a longstanding tradition in South Asia of regarding crowds as legitimate expressions of grievances of communities, and as spontaneous outbursts of anger and emotion. Police investigations and official inquiries characterize crowds as faceless entities and—in the tradition of the colonial police—the cause of riots are attributed to imprecise factors such as incitement of hatred, inexplicable "tensions" (*tanav*), rumors, and so on.

Crowds are regarded as sovereign entities in that they may be dispersed and controlled by the police as crowds, but individuals are never held accountable for violence or destruction in the course of crowd action. To kill in a crowd is, in other words, to kill with impunity. To enter the crowd is also to enter a momentary space of exception where normal rules of behavior and conduct are suspended for a time and other rules and norms prevail in the moment of effervescence . The other is not merely an enemy but is turned into "bare life"—simple life upon which the sovereignty of the crowd and the community it claims to represent can inscribe itself. Crowds are driven by a search for "enemies" and their property that they can destroy and devour "in an almost cannibalistic fusion of self and other" (Tambiah 1996, 275). What Tambiah in passing calls the "substantialization" that evolves in a crowd (219) is obviously linked to a visceral economy of the physicality of the crowd: the sense of loss of bodily autonomy and the experience of a cosubstantiality that lead crowds to become "spaces of exception"—not with a single mind, but unified by a momentary sense of bodily authenticity, certainty, and exhilaration—driven by what Elias Canetti calls a crowd's "love of density," and therefore an entity without doubts or fear.

Although the Hindu nationalist movement has extended the logic and justification of crowd violence to become an index of community sovereignty, the use of the crowd and its violence as a legitimate political expression of anger and sovereignty is extensive across the political spectrum in contemporary India. As a repertoire of authority and moral argument, "community" is very powerful indeed *qua* its historical connotations of delineating a measure of "collective intimacy," that is, its incorporation of issues of honor, family, bodies, and reproduction. It remains unclear if the Hindu nationalist movement harbors any larger project aimed at reconstructing the state into an expression of the Hindu community, resembling the merging of state, society, and nation into an organic whole that characterized European fascism.

Hindu nationalism is premised on an assertion of the sovereignty of (upper caste) Hindu communities, which makes any Jacobin project of reform and intrusion into the family rather improbable. Hindu nationalists are not opposed to authoritarian and violent methods, but their vision seems to be to *control* the state and the legal process rather than *becoming* the state and hence through the use of state power and the sovereignty of the law, to assert a Hindu nationalist worldview. There are, indeed, real apprehensions among Hindu nationalists regarding the legal system, the courts and the expanding culture of protest and litigation in India. There is also a desire to take strong action that hammers through the sovereignty of the state—but it is a rather selective authoritarian desire pertaining only to curtailment of the rights of minorities or the perceived danger of illegal immigrants or "antinational elements." Most of the demands formulated in VHP's document *The Hindu Agenda* from 1998 concern banning of cow slaughter, ousting of foreign missionaries, repealing the official recognition of Urdu, rewriting of history books, state support for Hindu charities and pilgrimage, strict censorship against criticism of "Hindu culture and tradition," and so on (VHP 1998). In this document, VHP seeks to construct itself as the very embodiment of the nation elevated above political divisions. In spite of its apprehensions regarding state power, it urges all political parties to adopt the appropriate legislation "to protect Hindus" and to enforce these laws by use of the full powers of the state.

For all its pride in organization and capacity for action, the Hindu nationalist movement has resigned itself to a rather limited and conservative set of goals that never impinges on the social world of the middle class it emerges from. Yet public violence, or the threat of such violence, is at the heart of the movement: the uniforms and display of masculine values of the RSS volunteers, their militant marches through cities, the emphasis on physical training and the strong male body, the violent rhetoric, and so on. The RSS has successfully made itself into the armed wing of the "Hindu community," the war principle of *celeritas*, both disruptive, alien and fascinating, that neither the state, nor minority communities in India, dare to challenge anymore.[9]

"Big Men," Reputations, and Rumors of Violence

The local "big man" is ubiquitous in everyday life and central to most relationships between authorities and ordinary people in urban India. For those without education, such figures are vital in approaching authorities and formal institutions. In one of the few studies of its kind, Mattison Mines's explores the making of "big men" in the city of Madras. Contrary to Dumontian ideas of the marginality of individuality in South Asia, Mines argues that individuality in South Asia is a quality that can be achieved within spatially and socially defined networks of knowledge, reputation, and trust. Individuality is accorded to those who are known as men of eminence, those who are respected and known as big men (*periyar*)[10] by virtue of their generosity, their modest behavior, trustworthiness, and command of resources and networks. This earns respect as an individual capable of qualified judgments and as someone whose advice can be sought on a wide range of matters. Such men have what Mines calls "civic individuality" (Mines 1994, 18–23) and enjoy considerable autonomy. The maintenance of this status depends on one's reputation which in Mines's ethnography is constituted by three elements all conveyed by stories and rumors about the person: his good character (*kunam*), his generosity (*vallanmai*) and his efficacy, that is, his ability to prosper and make things happen according to his will within institutions, or in civic life more generally (42–43, 56–58).

---

[9] The RSS and affiliated organizations were banned three times in independent India: in 1948–1950, in 1975–1977, and parts of the movement in 1992–1993.

[10] In Hindi, such a figure is often simply known as *bare* admi, a big/important man.

Yet, generosity and power are surrounded by permanent suspicions of excessive self interest and public display of opulent wealth (60–65).

Mines's figures represent the *gravitas* of responsible and ostensibly law-abiding civic leadership. Other figures wield equal influence and have big reputations for both efficacy and generosity, but these are founded on reputations of violence, or connections with political parties or the underworld. These are men who represent the war-principle of *celeritas*. They are not necessarily respected but always feared, and even admired for their ruthlessness and their ability to "get things done."[11]

Networks of strongmen, brokers, and fixers can be found in any neighborhood, slum and chawl in Indian cities. Most of the activities of these men defy conventional distinctions between legality and illegality: they assist in getting water connections, jobs, housing, school admission; they adjudicate in disputes between neighbors; they provide protection for those who are loyal and dependent on them, and so on. But some of them also service debt, extort money, beat up opponents, and threaten those who defy or betray them. However morally ambiguous these men and their activities are in the eyes of local residents, they are, nonetheless, the elementary units of local politics, of social work, and of cultural organization.

In western parts of India, many of these men have found a political home—and some respectability, visibility, and eminence in their locality—within the chauvinist organization and political party Shiv Sena (Shivaji's Army), taking its name from a seventeenth-century warrior king. Shiv Sena styles itself as the embodiment of the sovereignty of the Hindu *samaj*. Through its network of local branches (*shakhas*) in Mumbai and other urban areas in Maharashtra, Shiv Sena has for three decades provided symbolic centers of localities, structures of informal governance and everyday assistance to local people by assuming a role as defiant, angry, and self-made men who will confront the state, or other communities without fear. The organization has asserted its power through a systematic use of violence against opponents and its "enemies"—from South Indians, left wing trade unions to Muslims. Yet, Shiv Sena never aimed at creating a "shadow state" or alternative forms of governance. On the contrary, Shiv Sena's vague program revolves around the state as the provider of jobs and benefits, recognition, rights, order, etc. The organization has been a dominant political force in Bombay for several decades, and became the ruling party in the state of Maharashtra in the latter half of the 1990s.[12]

[11] Kakar (1996), Hansen (2001b), and Eckert (2000) have recently attempted to cover some of this ground, in Hyderabad and Mumbai, respectively.

[12] The establishment and early history of Shiv Sena is analyzed in Katzenstein (1981) and Gupta (1982).

Shiv Sena's maverick leader, Bal Thackeray, style himself as "a law onto himself." He strives to be the incarnation of the obstinate *sainik* style of masculinity that is so central to his authority in the organization and his popularity throughout Maharashtra. This style was succinctly articulated by a longstanding member of Shiv Sena: "A Shiv Sainik is not a man that if someone comes up to him and slaps him, then he will not simply show the other cheek. We are not that type. My hands work out and he will get the slap, not me. I will not be slapped and allow him to slap." Although Shiv Sena relied on long-standing practices of brokerage and local strongmen in urban neighborhoods, the organization systematized the use of violence against opponents and added a new spectacular and public dimension to violence. Protests in the streets, brutal enforcement of *bandhs*[13] called by Shiv Sena, and generous sponsorship of spectacular popular festivals, now became ritual performances of the power of the organization and the popular world of the ordinary Hindus it claimed to express. Shiv Sena was essentially action, a young man told me: "With action we can at least achieve something [. . .] we always retaliate and react directly to any issue. We always react in mobs. We have the attitude of attack rather than tolerance. [. . .] In fact, the weapon is the most powerful. If you are armed you can get things done. They (the Muslims) have taught us that attitude and therefore we took up weapons." Thackeray asserts sovereignty as a person and a leader when he claimed that he had every right to defend Hindus by killing Muslims during the 1993 riots. This widely accepted discourse of retributive justice paints a picture of two sovereign communities locked in conflict onto death. Shiv Sena and other militant Hindus cherish the myth of the Mumbai gangster king Dawood Ibrahim as the secret leader and avenger of the Muslim community—its "monstrous double" so to speak. The Hindu community also needs protectors and avengers, and Shiv Sena performs this part, as men relieved from the burden of moral injunctions or the law, only faced with the fundamental task of defending the honor of Hindus in what they see as a state of permanent war.

Violence may be justified in various ways but the terror and surplus of meaning contained in violence, or the threat thereof, can never be fully contained or explained because it has no other cause than itself. Hence the attribution of sublime qualities and sovereignty to those who assert their own law, their seemingly archaic claim to sovereignty. After having been considered bad taste in the city's elite circles for decades, the Thackeray family became object of the most admiring writing and syco-

---

[13] The closure of shops and public services in protest against the government, or in reaction to political events or riots.

phancy as Shiv Sena assumed political power in the state (see Hansen 2001b, 200–05). The basis of this admiration was not only that Thackeray had demonstrated his will to break the law and create his own whimsical rules. It also was that he commanded the loyalty of thousands of men who had proved themselves to be willing to, and capable of, mimicking his style, creating havoc in the city they claimed to own.

Two biographical sketches may illustrate how the making of informal sovereign power combines both the reputation of violent ruthlessness— the self-interested and unpredictable—and acts of generosity and efficacy of the big man. Both these men were at various points connected with political parties and their careers and styles bear witness to a broader trend in the culture of politics in India.

Shashikant Sutar is a legend in the city of Pune. Sutar comes from a poor family and a lower caste community. He started his career as a tiffin-carrier in the industrial area in western Pune in the sixties. Through Shiv Sena he launched a career as a city councilor in the suburb of Kothrud, and was able to emerge as the primary political broker enabling the astonishing growth of the Kothrud area, which today is a residential middle-class area with more than two hundred thousand people. His political career was crowned by a period as minister in the Shiv Sena cabinet in the late 1990s. As a young man he was drawn to Thackeray's depiction of South Indians as the source of all the alienation and evils of city life. He liked Shiv Sena, "because it was so attacking": "In those days the South Indians were everywhere. [. . .] They had so much clout that it became increasingly difficult for the common man even to walk the roads [. . .] because of their business and their strong unity, they were very powerful [. . .] they were all over in the restaurant-business and they had small joints, also."

Sutar and some of his friends were active in Hindu-Muslim riots in the city in 1969 and the early 1970s and soon acquired a reputation as courageous and daring street fighters. Sutar recalled the period as exhilarating and formative: "We were rebels and several of us were nearly thrown out of our families because of our work in Shiv Sena. We were seen as hoodlums and criminals and only later did my family see that Thackeray was right. [. . .] I grew with Shiv Sena, it molded my political career and I will always remain loyal to Balasaheb."

Sutar and his group gradually established themselves as efficient and unorthodox in solving civic problems in the emerging suburbs where local landowners squeezed tenants into provisional slums while attempting to get permissions for the construction of houses. Sutar proved to be not only an effective protector of local residents but also an inordinately efficient operator in the politico-administrative structure in the civic administration. Deftly employing his personal charm, his autodidactic knowledge of the law and the reputation of his *sainiks* as violent and ruthless, Sutar became the central access point for builders who wished to invest in housing schemes.

Within a decade, Kothrud emerged as one of the largest residential areas in Pune and Sutar became known as the "King of Kothrud." Today he owns several big houses, has close connections with the municipal and state bureaucracy, most political parties, and enjoys an immense popularity among the residents of Kothrud. His house is open every morning and in the evening. Hundreds of people come every week to seek advice or help regarding civic amenities, tenancy-problems, or financial assistance. Sutar has established a dense network of contacts and a patronage power that enables him to solve most problems with a few phone calls. Sutar's flamboyant lifestyle with several large houses, a fleet of cars, several semi-official mistresses, and his careful nurturing of his constituency has made him a living legend in Pune. His generosity, cunning, and efficacy are widely admired qualities. He donates money to charities, temples, to the Shiv Sena party and to local causes. "You never return from Sutar's house with empty hands" as local residents would put it. Persistent rumors of corruption, extortion and *goonda* (criminal) methods have accompanied him throughout his career and even cost him the post as minister of state. Yet, none of this has affected his personal standing in the western parts of Pune where he is said to control four to six seats in the Municipal Corporation and one or two seats in the State Legislature (*Vidhan Sabha*). Sutar's status as a big man with financial power, political clout, and a capacity for violence has given him considerable autonomy and a personal, territorially defined basis of power to the extent that his person almost expresses the ownership and identity of Kothrud. He adjudicates local conflicts, several political parties have tried to win him over, and bureaucrats know that Sutar can stall their careers, or have them demoted or transferred, at his will. Sutar is a force to reckon with, a local sovereign because his trajectory has created a reputation of generosity combined with a capacity for ruthless violence if his path is crossed.

The importance of the local strongman and his reliance on violence and *celeritas* is not a phenomenon specific to Shiv Sena, as my story of Javeed, a Muslim "big man" in Mumbai testifies to. Javeed came to Bombay with his parents from an impoverished village in Uttar Pradesh. He grew up in a chawl in the old mill district in Bombay. Javeed had to leave school early to help his father run the small flour-mill he had set up. Javeed learned traditional wrestling at the local *gymkhana* and soon emerged as the best *pehlwan* in the neighborhood. He acquired a reputation as a strong and short-tempered man who one only challenged at one's own peril and who was involved with a range of dubious and illegal activities in the area. Javeed had become one of the hard men, colloquially known as a *bhai* (brother) aspiring to become a *dada* (literally grandfather) used colloquially as "elder brother" for a gangster/*bhai* of some standing.

Almost inevitably, he clashed with the local *dada* in his street and killed him in a street fight. He served time in prison but does not seem to regret anything. The murder, and his sentencing, were questions of *izzat* (honor) and self respect. "If I had not done it, he would have killed me or humiliated me—I had no choice." After his release, Javeed started a business in scrap metal that over the years has made him a relatively wealthy man with two cars and two of his sons studying in college. He has also turned to Islam and donates money to a local *madrasah* and to a local college attended by his sons. He is known to most residents in the neighborhood and respected for what he is—a warrior who can defend the neighborhood in times of crisis as it happened during the Bombay riots in 1992–1993. During those tense weeks Javeed was in the streets with his men and his sons, fighting the Hindu crowds (led by Shiv Sena) that attacked Muslim neighborhoods all over the city.

Most respectable and educated middle class families in the area despise Javeed and what he stands for. But many poorer residents, and particularly those who belong to the same kinship network (*biraderi*) as Javeed, will seek his help in the modest office with a telephone, a table, and a few chairs. Most evenings, Javeed receives visitors who ask for assistance in getting a job, help with getting a telephone connection, donations for poor families, or protection against abusive employers or landlords. Often a few phone calls from Javeed solves the problem, as his reputation in itself makes a difference. In other cases some of Javeed's men pay a "visit" to those concerned. These acts, in turn, only confirm the efficacy of his power and perpetuate his reputation. Like many Muslims, Javeed's family had supported the Congress party for decades but after the riots in 1992–1993, they turned toward the North Indian based lower caste Samajwadi Party for protection and representation. Javeed is now the chairman of their local branch and ran for office, unsuccessfully, at the latest municipal elections in Mumbai. He hopes to expand his reputation as a political leader in the future but is well aware that his reputation as a *dada* may be one of the obstacles: "Because I have been in prison people think that I am still a criminal. But one mistake when you are young should not follow you throughout life. I have changed and many people know that I will put myself at risk to protect our *mohalla*. They understand that and will elect me the next time."

Unlike Sutar and other Shiv Sena men, Javeed does not enjoy the protection and support of the police. As a Muslim with a criminal record he can be singled out as a threat although the police hardly interferes in the everyday life of Muslim *mohallas*. Like other low-income areas and slums these areas are governed and policed at a distance and always through ubiquitous local informers and leaders. To assist the police is another route to some local standing and power but not to respectability, or a good reputation. Javeed clearly hopes that a political career can enhance his autonomy and make him a more effective informal sovereign than he already is.

The reputations and autonomy of local big men are always contested and need to be maintained and reiterated. They have all established their reputations, their autonomy and their sovereignty through the killing of external enemies or internal rivals. Their reputations and power are circumscribed by other local forms of authority—the police force, political parties, the bureaucracy, and so on. They are also competing with men whose reputations are founded on money, education and prudence, the principles of *gravitas*, and whose claims to represent locality also carry much weight. While the local big man may challenge the authority of the bureaucracy at some junctures by bending the law, he may also be a useful partner in maintaining order and in creating legibility.

One key to understanding how the repertoire of informal authority operates alongside those of the community and that of legality lies to my mind in the concept of *mardangi*—manliness/virility—a Persian term found in Urdu, Hindi, and other Indian languages. As we saw styles of masculinity are at the heart of local registers of respect and eminence. It is the performance of a certain style of public authority—generous but also with a capacity for ruthless violence—that determines who can define and represent the community, defend neighborhoods, punish, and discipline. Adelkhah's work on the ethic of *jawanmardi* (literally "young man") in Iran suggests that *mard* is linked with a broader, and older model of playful and defiant masculine sovereignty. *Jawanmardi* refers to a code of ethics that combines generosity and courage and refers historically to the young, mobile, unattached men who are morally ambiguous, at the edge of respectable society, but also heroic and in the forefront of rebellions against injustice (Adelkhah 1999, 33). Adelkhah describes a number of popular and well known men in Tehran—entrepreneurs and political figures—who lived by this ethos that "is above all about building and assertion of the self" but also marked by moral ambiguity and contradictions, so that "while arousing recognition and admiration (the *jawanmard*) also provokes perplexity by his unpredictable, rash and sublime sides" (45).

This describes quite accurately the styles of masculinity and self-assertion of many local political figures in India, the warriors, the dark side of the community esteem described by Mines (1999). India's political modernity have accorded an ever more prominent place to such ambiguous figures who through assertion of *mardangi* negotiate their own autonomy, the representation of community in the streets and at the ballot box, and the meanings and efficacy of legal regulation in most urban localities.

THE HOUSE OF MANY MASTERS

The material presented above suggests that the right and the capacity to make decisions, to adjudicate, to govern, and even to kill and punish, historically has been distributed between a range of authorities and institutions in India. The three repertoires of authority I have tried to outline operate in an intertwined and simultaneous way. Some acts of sovereign power are taken outside the state and the legal framework, as in the so-called underworld, whereas others, such as policing, operate within a legal framework—at least in theory. Political parties and social movements like the Shiv Sena often operate both within the framework of state institutions as well as outside where they are based in local and informal structures of authority and violence. This inordinately dispersed structure of governance and sovereignty indicates the limits of state authority in India.

To control the government, the state and the powers of legislation are important dimensions of the exercise of power in India. These forms of authority are also easily subverted and negotiated, and can be challenged in multiple ways because their efficacy depends on the informal sovereigns depicted earlier. The fragmentation of both governance and sovereignty in contemporary India—the historical roots of which I tried to indicate—should be borne in mind both when discussing the dangers of right-wing authoritarianism, and the possibilities of social reform and accountability through legislation. Given the antidemocratic impulses that many Hindu nationalists share with parts of the Indian elite and middle class, it is maybe a blessing in disguise that the Indian state in its present form offers little potential for imposition of authoritarian control throughout society.

The Sovereign Outsourced: Local Justice and Violence in Port Elizabeth

Lars Buur

INTRODUCTION

Vigilantism is one of the most contentious issues in the new South Africa because it exposes the limits of the new state's capacity to secure justice for all. The new democratic state faces a triple legitimation crisis: it has to legitimate the new government as the incumbent of the independent state; it has to legitimate the state itself as the overriding locus of political authority in society; and, finally, it has to cope with extremely high levels of crime. The problem is that the political sensibility of major sections of the population has been forged in antagonism to the state, and/or that the state does not reach large sections of the population. The wider field of local justice enforcement systems has become an arena for state formation, both organizationally and with regard to the values underpinning the new state (see Buur 2001). Here the state has attempted to integrate local justice structures—like the *Amadlozi*[1] from New Brighton township on the outskirts of Port Elizabeth, Eastern Cape, who presumably work independently of the state—into state structures like the Community Policing Forum (CPF). This chapter examines the problems and strategies the new state encounters when integration is attempted.

First, the inclusion of formerly excluded sections of the population exposes the limits of the constitutional rewriting process from 1993 to 1996. The aim here was to undo former injustices by legislative means and to bring everybody under the same sovereign rule of law: "One *law* for One *nation*" as it is stated on the first page of the new Constitution. But the constitutional process by and large postponed or *suspended* settling the issue of customary and/or township justice enforcement by referring it to future legislative processes, which at best can be de-

---

[1] Amadlozi is a Zulu word meaning "ancestors." The term is popularly understood as "the ones we can trust when there is nobody else." I have nonetheless heard people who dislike Amadlozi state that it means "sperm." In the semiotic universe of powerful ancestors the two meanings of the term—ancestors and sperm—are not necessarily in contradiction with each other.

scribed as an "uncomfortable accommodation" (Currie 1996). In the legislative void, the CPF emerges as the only state-initiated, nationwide strategy competing with informal justice structures in the South African townships (see the next section).[2]

Second, the process of integrating local justice initiatives under the ambit of the state highlights the difference between the new state's adherence to human rights and due process on the one hand, and the values and practices used locally in dealing with crime on the other. Although the Bill of Rights disallows the use of force and corporal punishment, it is widely accepted by structures like the Amadlozi and its constituency as a necessary and justified form of discipline, as a legitimate way to restate and internalize the core moral values of the community, and as a way to extract information about alleged crimes. In order to counter the levels of crime, violence, and vigilantism in South Africa, the state, NGOs, and other bodies embarked on a massive educational campaign, through which they sought to change the behavior of the police, CPF, and local communities by means of human rights sensitization workshops. Because of the attention this gave to education and change in sections of the population, it was concerned with the "conduct of conduct"—that is, the innumerable forms of biopolitics through which human conduct is directed by calculated means (Foucault 1976; Dean 1996). The education strategy thus provides us with an example of the state's approach when confronted with local perceptions of crime, discipline (in the form of corporal punishment) and moral community adopted by marginalized justice structures.

Theoretically, the process of integrating the Amadlozi as an extension of the state is interesting because it provides us with an example of how the state locally—as the sovereign—manages its formal monopoly on legitimate violence, be it through the use of force, as emphasized by Weber, or symbolic forms of violence (Bourdieu and Wacquant 1992, 112). The state's integration of the Amadlozi furthermore opens a window on the forms of resistance or rather forms of "conviviality" (Mbembe 2001, 110) that integration generates in the encounter between the state's approach and local justice structures. I hesitate to use the concepts of subordination or resistance in these encounters because there is not necessarily either open or silent disjunction. Instead struc-

---

[2] There does not seem to be a coherent plan in place with regard to control and authorisation besides the CPF that is not directly formed to attend to the problem of "the other law" (Schärf and Nina 2001). Some NGOs and academic institutions have assisted in writing up appropriate legislation for the formalization of "traditional" and "community" courts (see, for example, Schärf 1997a), but the government appears to be dragging its feet.

tures are characterized by "the dynamics of domesticity and familiarity, inscribing the dominant and the dominated within the same *episteme*" (110). I suggest that if we explore the new Constitutional *credo* of liberal individual rights and how, in everyday encounters, it meets and merges with other ideas about what constitutes a moral community, we will be exposed to how the integration engenders its own modes of conviviality. Although the problem of corporal punishment and vigilantism has been removed from the public eye (and ear), it is nonetheless left thriving in the twilight of its own rejection. My argument is that physical violence does not disappear with the development of the modern state and its different forms of biopower but instead continues to exist in a parallel and partially invisible domain. In other words, routine violence continues to exist as a subtext in the township because it is through violence that people are turned into human beings, and it is through the constant performance and embodiment of violence that the moral community is performed, despite the official adherence to constitutional democracy.

The first section gives a brief account of the history of township justice in South Africa mainly from the perspective of the 1980s and through the lenses of recent developments in Port Elizabeth, hereunder the formation of the Amadlozi. Sections two, three and four introduce the main characteristics of the Amadlozi and present the *modus operandi* of its public quasi-court sessions through two case studies. Here attention is given to the values and practices manifest in its work, as well as how issues related to exclusion, inclusion and violence, as a means of creating order, are played out. Finally, in the last sections I outline the CPF's attempts to integrate the Amadlozi as part of the state. I consider the consequences that the constitutional *credo* of avoiding violence has for how the sovereign—as holder of legitimate physical violence—seems to operate in poor townships like New Brighton.

FROM STRUGGLE POLITICS TO CRIME CONTROL

Forms of self-regulation and community discipline have long been a feature of rural and urban communities in South Africa (Schärf and Nina 2001; Seekings 2001). These forms of informal justice, however, evolved after 1984 from a general concern with *social regulation* to focus primarily on *political regulation*. This development paralleled an upsurge of political mobilization that took place mainly within the framework of the United Democratic Front (UDF).[3] Two of the key mobilizing slogans adopted by

[3] The UDF was an organization that was formed in the early 1980s to wage liberation struggle internally in South Africa. It became the main organization involved in the liberation struggle and was affiliated to ANC (see Seekings 2000 for an elaborate analysis of UDF).

the African National Congress (ANC) and the UDF were "people's power" and making the country "ungovernable." These slogans referred to attempts to dismantle the apartheid government and security forces, and seize control of policing, administrative, welfare, judicial, and other functions in the townships, thus creating an alternative sovereign. This included, among other things, establishing forums to administer civil and criminal justice through "people's courts." At a more organized level, police estimates suggest that there were roughly four hundred people's courts in operation in the 1980s, organized mainly around street committees (Seekings 2000; see also Schärf and Nina 2001).

People's courts were a way of enforcing resistance strategies in the township, and as such they were used to instill discipline and produce particular political communities. This often resulted in a recasting of gendered and generational hierarchies, for example the young, ANC-aligned "comrades" challenging the authority of elder men. Thus, the closing of political ranks within organizations and communities often had the result of splitting communities according to political allegiance, leading to some of the most violent political conflicts in the country's liberation history. An example of this is the conflict between the militant left wing organization Azapo (Azanian People's Organization) and ANC-aligned groups in Port Elizabeth during the 1980s.[4] Although the redress of criminal and social problems remained a focus of the people's courts, the nature of the transgression broadened to include the crime of collaboration. Two main targets were identified: first, persons employed by the state (including councilors, police and employees of local state structures), and, second, persons identified as traitors for a range of reasons. These included people suspected of giving information to police, people who were state witnesses in political trials, girlfriends of state employees—or those with other types of relationships with them—and people who defied local campaigns such as strikes and consumer boycotts (not to forget personal enemies). With this shift in the concept of what violated the community, people's courts became strongly associated with physical punishment and execution during this era. The introduction of collaborators as a target for popular justice signaled the sanction of killing. Whereas execution had rarely been seen in the longer history of popular justice in South Africa, it became in many ways an icon for the people's courts, particularly the infamous "necklace" for those who were construed as political enemies within communities.[5]

[4] In fact, such conflicts often were fueled by the apartheid regime (TRC Final Report 1998).

[5] Necklacing, or burning somebody alive with a car tire around the body, is widely associated with people's justice. Police statistics indicate that seven hundred to eight hundred people were necklaced or burned to death between 1985 and 1989 (see TRC Final Report 1998). Women were not exempted but formed a large portion of the victims, particularly those seen as girlfriends of policemen.

After 1990—and particularly after the first democratic general election in 1994—township life became less politicized in the name of development (see Jensen 2001), or, more precisely, it became politicized in a different manner. Politics increasingly revolved around power struggles between civic movements like the South African National Civic Organisation (SANCO, an umbrella body for the various civic, street, and area committees of the 1980s) and the ANC over who should represent particular areas in government, who should decide on which township localities should be developmentally "upgraded" and how decision making should be conducted. During this time, most street and area committees, the most prevalent forms of local court systems, ceased to function (Buur 2003a; Jensen 2001; Seekings 1996). In the early 1990s SANCO tried to organize and monopolize street committees in order to carry on the work of the people's courts under the name of "anticrime" structures. However, after SANCO fell out with the ANC in 1996, this initiative largely broke down, leaving township citizens/subjects with little access to more organized forms of local justice.

It is in this perceived and real void that many new, local township structures emerged to deal with crime after the 1994 election, when it became one of the main public and political preoccupations. The new emphasis and public preoccupation with crime (instead of political violence) after 1994 was obsessive. As one commentator wrote, "Crime is seen to be so pervasive that we make jaundiced claims of being the world's most crime-ridden society" (Mistry 1997, 3). In 1996, the government approved a National Crime Prevention Strategy (NCPS) that tried to come up with a novel conceptualization and management of the "crime problem" (see Singh (1997) for an analysis of the NCPS). The same year the Community Policing Forums (CPFs) program was launched, through the Police Act, with the purpose of improving and rearranging the highly conflictual relationship (because of the role the police had played in enforcing the apartheid regime) between police and the communities in the townships. On the one hand, it was aimed at making police more sensitive and accountable to local policing priorities through, for example, assisting in defining crime priorities, running community campaigns and so on. On the other hand, the establishment of CPFs was to facilitate community involvement in policing by building trust or partnerships between the police and local communities so that new (formerly excluded) citizens felt encouraged to report crime, and engage with and assist the police, for example by pointing out culprits in the community. Furthermore, it was stipulated that CPFs could when necessary establish Safety and Security structures (S&S) at ward level (the lowest local government administrative level) to cater for "petty crime." But these strategies did not seem to have much impact as crime rates continued to rise over the following years.

In the township of New Brighton at the outskirts of Port Elizabeth, the local government-sponsored CPF had not managed to establish any local Safety and Security structures due to political infighting. The police station was in disarray, with the white, Afrikaans station commander embroiled in conflicts with black police officers and residents marching to the station to demand that a black (i.e., more responsive) commander be installed. At the same time, registered crime had risen to the highest levels ever. It was in this context that the local justice structure, the Amadlozi, was born. It emerged as a force during 2000, but seems to have operated in a less coordinated manner as early as 1999. It consists of a mixture of former protagonists in the localized political conflict during the 1980s and early 1990s between Azapo and UDF/ANC-aligned members. The group also includes active members of two other political forces in the region, namely the Pan Africanist Congress (PAC) and United Democratic Movement (UDM). Although many Amadlozi members are former enemies from the extremely violent political conflicts of the 1980s, they are now working together in "fighting crime." The group was formed when "crime became intolerable" in New Brighton to such an extent that, according to their own recollections, they spontaneously organized themselves in order to "chase criminals and bring justice to the community." As a leader of the Amadlozi explained to me: "When enough is enough and you are fed up with the passivity of the police, we decided to do what we have done before" (clearly referring to the "people's courts" of the 1980s). The *founding myth* that they claim brought people to the point of organizing, refers to an incident in which a group of young men dressed in traffic police uniforms hijacked delivery trucks bringing goods such as furniture and refrigerators to both private homes and shops in New Brighton and the neighboring township, Kwazakele, to steal the goods. Nobody did anything about it, so some of the residents in one of the areas worst affected by crime decided to take matters into their own hands.

Their first meetings took place on a street corner under the streetlight, but in 2000 they managed—after pressure from some of the most active leaders—to get access to four classrooms at the Molefe Primary School in New Brighton. The group came into being under the name "Abahlali Concerned Residents Against Crime" (CRAC), which later became known as the Amadlozi. As a concerned residents' group, it operates with a loose leadership structure and is based on what can best be described as "charismatic leadership," to use Max Weber's famous conceptualization. The leaders are all well-known personalities from New Brighton, and the three main public figures all have good rhetorical skills: one as a lay priest, and the others from years of political organizational work. None of the public faces have high-profile positions in established community or political structures, with the single exception that one is the leader of the local MK Veterans' organization (ANC's military wing during the war of liberation, Mkonto we Sizwe—The Spear of the Nation) in New Brighton. The CRAC/Amadlozi (hereafter Amadlozi) organization nonetheless had support from a range of relatively prominent local ANC members, including the director of the New Brighton Community Hall, who would use its members as security guards for public functions in the hall and make the venue available for public meetings. This group of well-known ANC members acted as "backstage" brokers between the police and Amadlozi members, facilitating the intervention of high-profile regional police so that New Brighton police officers—particularly the white station commander—were forced to cooperate with the Amadlozi.

The CPF saw the cooperation as illegitimate because Amadlozi members had not been formally elected according to the established protocol. They therefore refused to cooperate. According to CRAC's 2000 progress report, compiled by backstage members, the agreement reached gave CRAC members the "authority to arrest the suspects and further investigate other cases," to work as an "intelligence unit" for the police, to participate in patrols with the police, and to participate in "Management and Crime Meetings that discuss anticrime strategies" (CRAC 2000, 3–4). The New Brighton station commander initially refused to cooperate with CRAC, maintaining that the CPF was the only official local partner. However, pressure from high-ranking (mainly black) regional police officers forced his acceptance of Amadlozi's approach to crime prevention. He was also pressured to open the regular Management and Crime Meetings, formerly only for white and Indian/colored police officers, to black police officers and Amadlozi members. In addition, Amadlozi held meetings with officers of the "Magistrate's Office" to discuss bail conditions for criminals.[6]

Amadlozi operated without membership cards, a written constitution or a political manifesto, except if we accept that "combating crime in the community" constitutes a political manifesto—which I think we should, in spite of the apolitical language applied by the Amadlozi. It claims not to be accountable to any civic groups or political organizations. Accountability is articulated solely in relation to the diffuse and ambivalent category of "the community." This is not only because of the trivial

---

[6] These meetings continued over the following year, this time primarily revolving around bail conditions for Amadlozi members arrested on a variety of charges.

fact that most claims to having a mandate from "a community" or working for "the community" rest on the reified and tautological notion that the community is a stable, unproblematic entity where the identity of the community explains the community's identity. Often communities first come into being through being named by somebody—that is, as concrete, empirical identities that are socially constructed. In other words, as Bourdieu in his analysis of political representation asserts, a given political community does not exist as a political entity prior to representation, meaning that political representation both precedes and produces the represented as a political entity (Bourdieu 1991, 214; see also Jensen 2001). In South Africa, the apartheid state tried for many years to set the rules for what counts as "a group" and "a community" based on the grammar of race and culture.

Today one of the most important changes in the rules of the game relating to township politics comes from the new state. Whereas communities under apartheid were governmentalized through race and culture, the new governmental regime is based on democratic ideals of participation (Jensen 2001, 249), which clashes with the Amadlozi's notion of community participation. According to the Amadlozi leadership, members of the community "elect," often *ad hoc,* at more or less spontaneous gatherings, the people they want to represent them. As it was explained to me: "We are chosen by *the community*, therefore we cannot be accountable to anybody else than the community. They chose us because we work for them and if they are not satisfied they will tell us what they do not like. There is no fuss there, no agendas, no politics. We are not like the politicians . . . like the CPF" (Interview with Amadlozi leadership 2001). In this sense the leadership of the Amadlozi draws on, or is modeled after, the "direct democracy" or "radical or popular democracy" formations of the "people's courts" of the 1980s, which is based an understanding of community that is identical with the ANC's popular political jargon and national discourse. This discourse springs directly from the ANC's past as an antistate movement, when it was identified and legitimized as the representative of the moral community—the subject of popular sovereignty. This notion of community stands in stark opposition to the political tradition that the state-initiated CPF referred to, which can be termed "constitutionally democratic." By this I mean that the executive body of the CPF is elected by representatives coming from different known and accepted constituencies like political organizations (most notably the ANC, which has successfully monopolized political life in New Brighton), church groups, and civic, business and sport associations. Accountability here means to be accountable to the representatives electing them, who presumably represent the will of the people.

Ambivalence is also caused by the empirical reality that "the community," in the name of which the Amadlozi work, is impossible to demarcate territorially. The Amadlozi operate all over the Nelson Mandela Metropole, New Brighton, Kwazakele, Zwide, Soweto at Sea, Kwamagxaki, Kwadwesi, Motherwell and further—and, in addition, people from other areas come to them. Although it started out as a local structure around the Molefe Primary School in New Brighton, the Amadlozi developed relatively rapidly into a translocal justice structure unlike any of the other structures in Port Elizabeth's adjacent townships. This, of course, creates problems with other justice structures under the CPF, which is territorially bound by ward demarcations, because they compete over turf. Nonetheless, the Amadlozi, because of its proximity to the New Brighton police station, continues to serve "the local community of law-abiding people," as they phrase it. In other words, although the community can be defined in terms of locality, *in casu* New Brighton, the *modus operandi* of the Amadlozi exceeds the proper name of the locality to which it belongs.

In general, the Amadlozi deals with a range of inchoate moral concerns related to the well-being of the individual and the community. It places itself somewhere between what is formally known as criminal justice, on the one hand, and civil justice, on the other, and it deals with different kinds of disputes and crimes, not all of which correspond to those dealt with by the judiciary. These include *petty crimes* such as family-related disputes (gender, matrimonial, inheritance), generational conflicts (sexuality, schooling, use of respectful language), theft by known relatives or neighbors, disputes around money-lending and between neighbors, and conflicts related to distribution of scarce resources such as jobs, land, cattle, and so on. A list of *serious crimes* might include witchcraft, murder, rape (of both women and children), burglary, and so on. However on a daily level, petty and serious crimes are usually spoken about interchangeably, and they are often dealt with in ways that can contravene the rights of the individual, at least from the perspective of the rights outlined in the Constitution. Furthermore, crimes are often articulated as communal disturbances, which hinder "the community" from accessing development, investments and employment initiatives, that is, reaching and realizing its full potential (Buur 2003a).

The Space of the Amadlozi

The Amadlozi meet three times a week for public, quasi-court sessions at the local government school, Molefe Primary. Two to three hundred (and at times up to four hundred) people from different sections of New Brighton and neighboring townships gather to present and deal with cases brought to the attention of the Amadlozi. Separate from, but still integrated into the public meetings, "working groups" conduct "raids." These working groups, operated by the Amadlozi, formally investigate the cases brought to their attention in the public sessions, held most of the time in the evening. They consist of groups of residents, usually one or two older members and five to eight younger members. If necessary, they will drive out and conduct raids that resemble ordinary police investigations or operations. At times they will gather a group of residents to work as protection when they approach suspected criminals, conduct investigations, "hunt down criminals," arrange rallies, summon people, or enter premises for investigative purposes. Working groups can also deal with cases brought to the personal attention of one of the Amadlozi members or try to settle cases outside the public eye if they consider it necessary.

Besides these public tasks, the Amadlozi also have a type of work they call "in-camera" sessions. These are cases that have been judged "too sensitive" for the open sessions, or those emerging from working groups that have not yet been brought to the open group's attention. Sensitive cases include those related to cattle theft, rape, disputes between older members of families, certain instances of money-lending disputes, and disputes between neighbors. In-camera sessions are usually steered by a trusted male member of the Amadlozi who works together with a younger member (male or female) with specific knowledge about the subject up for settlement. But in-camera sessions are also used for other purposes, most notably interrogations where physical punishment is applied. The fact that these interrogations take place outside the immediate public eye protects the Amadlozi members inflicting the pain against complaints to the police (as it minimizes the number of eyewitnesses).

I will detail two cases where the Amadlozi make use of a particular space in the classroom where public court sessions take place. The space is located to the left of the chairperson but is not marked out in any particular manner. I call this place a "space of transformation" because persons who pass through the space usually find their status as a person, family, or community member severely altered. While the space is used in similar ways in both cases, the consequences for the persons placed there are highly divergent, even though their treatments show common characteristics.

In the first case study, I will consider an incident in which "social relations expressed in practices of identification" (van Beek 2001, 527) become reordered. From a general point of communitarian order, each person may simultaneously have several distinct identities when considered in relation to the different ritual pretexts in which they are engaged (family, clan, political affiliation, and so on). These forms of identification can all, so to speak, be remade or reshaped to various degrees in the Amadlozi court sessions.

Case 1: Untying and Exclusion

Two young brothers in their early twenties had been summoned to appear in court because their father had complained about the lack of respect they showed him in his house, where they stayed together. The old father, sitting to the left in the room on a school-chair and surrounded by several family members, was the first person to speak. He stood, took off his hat and told how his sons had stopped respecting him: they used rude words, they complained about the income he brought to the household (he received only a monthly pension of R580), they ate the food he bought without themselves contributing, stole money from him and, worst of all, they brought their girlfriends home and slept with them there even though he had forbidden them to do so.

The chairperson then asked the two young men to rise. They were sitting to the right in the room on tables along the wall. They, too, were surrounded by people, in this case young friends and a few middle-aged women who were presented as aunts. They were asked by the chairperson to give their side of the story. They acknowledged that the situation was tense in the house, and complained about their father not understanding their needs as "young initiated men." "We do not want to be treated as boys, we are men now and we can do as we wish." Furthermore, they complained about their father being unable to support the family properly. This made the chairperson visibly angry, and he told them to shut up. When they sat down, the chairperson immediately told them to stand, which they were forced to do by younger members of the Amadlozi. The chairperson then turned towards the audience and asked for advice. He pointed out that this was a "family matter," which should be dealt with more discreetly, but the situation required that the community did not play "hide and seek." "We have to take responsibility," he said. Many different age groups in turn commented on what they had heard—some suggesting that the sons be taken out for punishment, others that they both be punished and sent away from home, whereas a few elderly women opted for further counseling.

The chairperson then turned to the father and asked him what he wanted the Amadlozi to do. The father responded that he did not know what to do, but maybe it was time for his sons to leave the house—something he had suggested to them on several occasions, to no avail. The chairperson then gathered a group of Amadlozi youths by pointing them out in the room, and asked the two sons to accompany them, together with one older member of the Amadlozi, to the house, which was close by. Half an hour later they came back. The two sons came into the room with their heads bowed. They were directed to the space I have denominated "space of transformation." They looked as though they had been beaten up. Two Amadlozi youths were holding two plastic bags.

The chairperson then ordered the two sons to leave the house and not come back. If they did, the Amadlozi would take charge and severely punish them. The two sons were then given the plastic bags and told to leave the room. On their way out, several community members rose from their seats at the front to lash out physically at the two sons, and many people shouted at them. The father stayed behind for some time. When he left the room he was smiling and surrounded by people, including the aunts. When I asked my research assistant what would happen to the sons now that they did not have any shelter or access to money or food, he partly laughed and partly looked concerned. He said that they would have to go to another "location" (townships are often called this) and try to set up a shack there, get a job and start taking responsibility. But when I pushed the issue, he acknowledged that the chances of their becoming "real criminals" were high, because they were now without access to any of the networks that "help you when life is tough." What happened "is the worst that can happen to a person living in the township—to be alone."

The conceptualization of the "space of transformation" is not *emic;* it is my own conceptualization. The Amadlozi do not, as such, mark out the space, just as they do not use this phrase or any wording at all for this space. But changes in the status of persons nearly always involve their being placed there, or at least passing through this area of the classroom. It is generally used after complaints have been raised and the accused have had the opportunity to defend themselves, or when they are brought into the court. When people are placed there, it usually has consequences for their status as members of the community and the values associated with being part of the community: family membership, access to the Amadlozi, living in the area, and so on. In most cases, people do not enter this loosely defined space, in that most complaints and the further negotiations concerning them—sanctions, fines, compensation and so on—do not cause people to leave the places they occupy as community members. In other words, they remain with the family members and friends they arrived with while decisions are being made.

Whereas a courtroom modeled after the Western judicial system would ritually affirm the ontological, already established identity and his/her constitutional and civic rights—thus securing due process irrespective of what a person may have done—personhood seems to fluctuate in the Amadlozi quasi-court (see Buur 2003b). These fluctuations happen according to the conjunction of ritual positions participants engage in. From a rights perspective, this does not seem to subordinate the indigenous amalgam of allegiances, commitments and law to the constitutional values of citizen-rights.

Identity in this sense is defined in terms of relations and is subordinated to the values that order the community (which themselves are constantly redefined, even if this is not necessarily generally recognized).[7] The speech-acts and instruments of discipline performed in the Amadlozi quasi-court have the power to radically *change* the status of the subjects as part of relationally constituted forms of identity so that the subjects become either human beings or outlaws—part of the community or outside of it. They may, by passing through the "space of transformation," be relegated to the status of "bare-beings"—that is, beings whom one can treat as one wishes with impunity and without regard for their psychological and physical well-being (Agamben 1998).

In this sense, the community and its relational identities—kinship, family, clan, political affiliation, and so on—are "founded not as an expression of a social tie but as an untying that prohibits" (Badiou quoted in Agamben 1998, 90). Following Agamben's perspective on how the juridical-political community is produced, the untying of social relations should be understood here not so much as the untying of pre-existing ties (often understood as contracts or pacts), but instead as the original form where social ties come into being by exclusion of some identities. It is through untying by the unconditional sovereign power—here exemplified by the Amadlozi, which can abandon one to an extent that causes, if not actual death, then social death—that human life is politicized. What is produced through sovereign untying is the commu-

---

[7] The attention I give to identity as relations does not mean that reified *emic* notions of "Xhosa culture" do not exist. They do, but I will suggest that "Xhosa culture," when it is articulated as such, should, following Herzfeld (1996, 141), be understood as stereotypical images of fluctuating and compound practices of social identification (see also van Beek 2001, 527).

being firm before everything becomes chaos "so even our children do not respect us any longer."

After the discussion, the grandmother, the young girl, and a group of young Amadlozi girls (none of them older than twenty) leave the room. I thought that they had gone to another room for further talk, but when I heard the sound of lashes and weeping I left the classroom and went to the courtyard. There is no doubt that the girl was being punished in one of the closed classrooms. Standing next to what turned out to be a twenty-five-year-old woman, I asked: "Is this just?" She replied "No," and then added: "No it is not just, because it should be the old woman who punishes her, not the young girls, so it is not just." I asked her how they were punishing the girl and she told me: "Here, it is the belt (and she points at my black leather belt) who rules. . . . She needs to learn what is right and wrong. You cannot know right from wrong without punishment." Then suddenly the door of the classroom opened, and out came a smiling girl—with her head stoutly lifted—hand in hand with her grandmother and a group of young Amadlozi women, all chatting, greeting people in the schoolyard as if nothing in particular had happened. There was no sadness, no sulking, no resentment, no tears and no harsh words as they left the school. The harmony seemed to have been restored.

When force or corporal discipline are utilized, it does not happen only when people are in extreme circumstances, acting out of passion, despair, exhaustion of other options, or irrational mob behavior. The use of force and corporal punishment are also used to deal with crime, where crime as a generic category covers a range of disturbances or what is often referred to as the "breakdown of the social fabric" of the community or society. The two cases presented speak volumes about how generational and gendered relations—involving young men/boys/women/girls and the older generations—are settled. Where young men can be forced out of the household more readily after initiation, this seldom seems to be the case for young women/girls. Instead, every attempt is made to reintegrate them and teach them "the right way" through discipline.[8] The routinization of daily violence presents a paradox because it is usually asserted that violence will disappear when modern states are governed not by violence and force, but by biopower relations.

---

[8] The explanations I was given for this difference by people participating in the sessions range from "the need to protect the girls from pregnancy" to preventing them from "ending up as prostitutes." Young men, by contrast, are expected to leave the household at a certain point and take responsibility for themselves, which often involves building a shack in the backyard or moving in with relatives.

In Michel Foucault's (1976) well-known argument concerning bio-power, "a society's 'threshold of modernity' has been reached when the life of the species is wagered on its own political strategies" (143). That is, when the "action of the norm" (144) has taken precedence over the law enforced by the sword, the ultimate consequence of which is death. According to Foucault, the development of biopower—in which subjects are inscribed in a range of governmental techniques for "the good life" that becomes self-regulative—transforms how "the law operates" so that it works more and more as a norm, where "the judicial institution is increasingly incorporated into a continuum of apparatuses (medical, administrative, and so on) the function of which are for the most part regulative" (144).

There can be no doubt that there is a long history of governmental techniques (not only enforced by the [colonial] state but also by NGOs and others) working on the domain of the body, values, and norms in South Africa. But this does not by any means imply that corporal punishment and associated techniques for societal regulation and production of subjectivities do not have any foundation in South Africa. Rather, corporal punishment does not disappear and become substituted by the rule of norm/biopower but continues to live in the twilight of its rejection, more precisely in an invisible and parallel domain, partly outside the public eye. The use of force and physical discipline cannot therefore be assigned only to the exceptionally high levels of crime, which in turn necessitate exceptional measures. Rather, the prevalence of corporal punishment resonates and merges with everyday practices and strongly held ideas concerning the production of human beings, that is beings that can distinguish between "right and wrong" that in turn have an increasing importance for production of authority (where the great irony is that new legislative measures prohibiting the use of corporal discipline are seen as one of the causes of the breakdown of the social fabric).

The wider sociocultural universe giving legitimacy to the use of corporal punishment is intimately related to how socialization is perceived—the essence of which, as it has been articulated to me time and again, is: "How can you know what is right or wrong if you have not been beaten?" There is a profound sense that "If you put the iron to the fire the iron will be strong"—and the saying applies to the psyche. The need for feeling pain is a recurring explanation when one asks parents about physical discipline and teaching proper behavior. Discipline is nearly always directed at the future in the form of "prevention," "change of behavior," and "learning the right way." It is within this wider domain of socialization, asserting authority, and painful socioeconomic transformations that parents who can no longer physically discipline youngsters come to structures like the Amadlozi. It is not that physical discipline is uncontested—it would be wrong to assert that. After the new legislation prohibiting corporal punishment had been implemented and knowledge about children's rights disseminated, fear of being framed or made accountable to the police made the Amadlozi and CPF-aligned structures more wary.

If one circulates among leaders in academic, government, and NGO circuits there is a profound uneasiness about what is going on in the townships but, when one moves to the townships, the emerging picture is very different. As I have illustrated, the use of force in the form of corporal punishment seemed to be accepted among the people in the quasi-courtroom. People from all walks of life were present in the court: NGO staff working for recognized human rights organizations in Port Elizabeth, off-duty police officers, teachers and unemployed people, as well as known ANC members and members of other political parties. None of them seemed to react negatively to what was going on. The Amadlozi is therefore not unique in this regard.

PUBLIC DISCOURSE AND POPULAR SOVEREIGNTY

It has been a feature common to the Amadlozi and other similar structures that the "blessing" to take the law into their own hands can be traced back to, on the one hand, a perceived (and real) incapacity by the police and the judiciary to deal with crime, and a series of calls by prominent government ministers to local communities to take action, on the other. Perhaps one of the most important reasons that the Amadlozi has been so successful in New Brighton is the fact that it can react to "crime" instantaneously and in a manner that suits the needs of vast groups of South African citizen/subjects. As one of the leaders of the Amadlozi phrased it: "We act here and now, we do not, as the police do, drag our feet." A comment like this captures a recurrent theme. Since the political transition to democracy, the police have had to change their *modus operandi* from beating confessions out of suspects to working within the law, accepting due process and human rights as their foundational order. This is proving a difficult transformation, with a police force badly equipped to conduct basic investigations (Schärf 2001). The perception is that the police is "incompetent" and "corrupt," that they "protect the criminals" with the new Constitution in their hands and therefore are "nonresponsive" to the needs of the South African townships.[9] Although

[9] These were some of the common reactions I got from a survey of one hundred households on experiences of crime, which, with two research assistants, I conducted in Ward 14 of New Brighton in July and August 2001.

I agree that the police generally have a serious capacity problem, I am not sure that the story ends there.

Proper police work and adherence to the human rights *credo* cannot in itself do the trick, as I have described elsewhere (see Buur 2003a). Even the best police work can hardly deal with the fact that people in the township are not insured and therefore need the goods back; that justice is seldom related to seeing people placed behind bars, mutilated beyond recognition, raped, or whatever else takes place in the over-crowded cells; not to forget the marginalization of vast population groups on the outskirts of the postindustrial cities. It is not that good policing, security and human rights are not—seen from the outskirts—admired, wanted, or even considered a common good. But when it comes to reconstructing the moral community, theft and the disciplin-ing of thieves it has very little to offer. This is also what makes such structures and the control over them pertinent for the new state. Popu-lar justice enforcement is not restricted by the Constitution in the same way as the police and in many cases the police use the Amadlozi's (and similar structures') capacity to put "their ear to the ground," and to conduct the on-the-ground police work.

There is an interesting convergence between popular demands re-garding how to deal with crime on the one hand, and the wider frame-work of public speeches made by politicians on the other. All the local justice structures I have worked with refer to a series of speeches and statements made by, for example, the late minister of Safety and Secu-rity Steve Tshwete or President Thabo Mbeki, whose calls for local communities to take action have been directly linked to the formation of such structures. They are seldom correctly quoted, but the quotes al-ways capture sentiments like: "criminals are animals [and] we must show them no mercy" (expressed by Steve Tshwete during 1999) or, on how the police should deal with criminals: "When we visit criminals we will not treat them with kid gloves. We are going to make them feel like cowboys [. . .] those who raise the dust must not complain that they cannot see. We will unleash the police force on them." When structures like the Amadlozi see their work as a defense of the Constitution it res-onates with Tshwete's words in September 2000, when he spoke about the relation between the Constitution and how criminals should be dealt with: "Criminals must know the South African state possesses the authority, moral and political, to ensure by all means, constitutional or unconstitutional, that the people of this country are not deprived of their human rights" (Tshwete 1999 and 2000, all quoted from *Electronic Mail and Guardian*, November 10, 2000).[10]

[10] See <http://www.mg.co.za>.

In essence, Steve Tshwete had informally declared a state of emergency that suspended the validity of the law (Schmitt 1985) and given the police *carte blanche* to do what they considered necessary to get crime under control. Rather than undermining the Constitution, one could say that Tshwete's words seek to stabilize the rule of law. There was criticism of this informally declared state of emergency in many quarters of South African society, but in many townships (not to forget the middle-class, gated communities, which of course applauded Tshwete for different reasons), there was a profound resonance with local ideas of exception and sovereignty. It is interesting how the official ANC discourse—exemplified by Tshwete's words—in many ways can be said to resurrect the discourse of the struggle of the 1980s, with the ANC as the sole representative of the community and popular sovereignty. Here the state and the community's interests are identical, and are aimed at undoing the same injustices due to the present elective power of the ANC. It is this identity between the interests of the state and the community that makes it possible for Tshwete (with such profound resonance in the townships) by implication to outsource sovereignty to the community in the name of moral superiority and historical rightness (this, I suggest, has involved—in a place like New Brighton—a *de facto* outsourcing of sovereignty by the police). Just as it happened during the struggle, one can argue that the ANC and the state as such try to claim, or maybe more precisely capture, a sociocultural domain which it has never before controlled. But through incorporation (here outsourcing of popular sovereignty can be seen as a form of incorporation) of this domain into the state's structures, it can claim to control and govern.

I suggest that for structures like the Amadlozi to emerge, the normal rule of law has first to be suspended in certain spaces. The difficult issue here is to apprehend that apparently nobody took this decision. Instead it came into being by the neglect of the "other law" in the constitution, public statements by politicians, locally administered outsourcing by the police and a deep resonance between popular ideas about crime and national preoccupations or imaginings. Whether acts of violence are committed in this ambivalent state of suspension does not depend on "One *law* for One *nation*" as such. Rather, it depends on the civility and ethical discretion of local justice structures—and by implication the police—who stand in for the clearest instantiation of the sovereign in present-day South Africa (and most other societies, I suggest). The question is whether what at first seemed a temporary suspension of the law has not, in fact, become more the rule than the exception, making the erstwhile exception a pertinent and constant feature of township life. This is the issue I will deal with in the final section of this chapter, in which I will consider how incorporation takes place and the effects thereof.

THE EFFECTS OF DEMOCRATIC ORDER AND CONTROL

Even before serious talks about converting the Amadlozi into a CPF-aligned S&S had begun, the police had raised the issue of force on several occasions, especially when charges had been laid against Amadlozi members for individual cases of beating, torture or excessive violence. In response to the problem of individual responsibility, the Amadlozi developed a tactical approach to the subject: "we developed a strategy, because it must not be seen as if they are being beaten, so we take them by their arms and legs and throw them up to the Almighty. How are we to decide? So we simply throw them up and they come down. Then Mother Nature knocks them out [laughter]. And they talk." This particular way of appropriating and living with the new Constitutional *credo* became the legendary trademark of the Amadlozi. The crux of the matter is that knowledge about rights is constantly present. In order not to be held accountable, corporal punishment becomes enforced in such a way that nobody can be called to account for it.

The methods of the Amadlozi have been extreme, but New Brighton has also been an extreme place to be during the 1990s and early 2000. The police—after the initial reservations from the station commander that were mentioned at the beginning of this chapter—saw the emergence of the Amadlozi as positive, particularly once the effects of the Amadlozi were felt on their workload. The crime statistics showed a reduction of 90 percent (this was always quoted in meetings with police officers and the station commander). This did not mean that the Amadlozi was above criticism, because issues of accountability to known structures, representation and constituency continued to surface from the CPF and some concerned ANC leaders. But the pragmatism about crime seemed to have gained the upper hand, and one of the female secretaries of the Amadlozi was placed in the CPF office at the police station so that the caseload could be "properly" distributed among the Amadlozi, the CPF, and the police. When there were new developments in the relationship between the CPF and the Amadlozi, they always took place immediately after the police had arrested Amadlozi members, because complaints had been made concerning excessive violence. After each of these encounters, the Amadlozi would promise to elect a ten-person committee and become an official structure as well as scale down the use of force.

But force continued to be used by the Amadlozi; they just became more cautious after each round of arrests. When a person was taken into the classrooms next to the public venue for in-camera sessions, often as many as seven or eight Amadlozi members would enter (before, only a few would participate in the sessions); also, during interrogation, either the light would be turned off or the culprit would be blindfolded so that he could not see who was beating him. Such measures were developed to protect Amadlozi members from being charged for the use of force.

Nothing really happened before high-ranking police officers reacted to the alarming statistics of vigilantism—of which nearly all were associated with or related to the work of the Amadlozi. As the chairperson of the CPF phrased it: "Currently we are having a problem, we have been called by the Area Office [the Commissioner], we have also been called by the Provincial Office, to account for mob justice." The problem was that "people that have been victims of the actions of Amadlozi predominantly [were] all in all 19 cases, and the police have done nothing" (Interview with Chairperson of CPF August).

It seems to have been a national trend at the time that the police should clamp down on vigilantism, because it also happened in other parts of the country. After the call from the Area Commissioner, a sequence of events finally brought the Amadlozi on board with the CPF. First, a group of six Amadlozi members were arrested one Friday in a coordinated police action backed by CPF members. Simultaneously, members of the CPF forced the principal of the Molefe Primary School to close the school as a venue for the Amadlozi. The closing of the school for the Amadlozi was legitimized with reference to the fact that schoolteachers had on several occasions found bloodstains on the classroom walls. This was considered "too much for the school children" (Interview with Amadlozi leadership 2001).

The Amadlozi did not give up without a fight. They tried to secure another venue, but the CPF board had done their homework, and all possible venue holders refused the Amadlozi permission to operate from their premises. In the end they gave in and accepted that an election would be held in the name of the CPF. Thereafter the Amadlozi was once again allowed to use the school premises—on the assurance that blood strains would no longer be found in the classrooms. According to the Amadlozi leadership, they had been told by the CPF and the police to do their business outside the classrooms at the back of the school. There was an understanding of the need for force, but they had plainly been told to be more discreet, because the Area Commissioner would not tolerate any more cases of vigilantism. When I came back to Port Elizabeth in December 2001, the venue for the in-camera information extraction and disciplining sessions had been moved to the backyards of the premises of some of the Amadlozi members, or to the open field behind the school. The nineteen cases implicating the Amadlozi for vigilantism had been put aside, and now functioned as a permanent reminder for the structure to "clean up our act," as it was phrased by one of the public leaders of the Amadlozi. This had clearly happened, because "We have not had any cases against us since," I was told.

This removal from the public eye and ear to the private backyard and open fields behind state institutions is not new—and neither is it exceptional for the Amadlozi. As far as I can assess, it follows a wider pattern of how state integration of local justice structures took place in Port Elizabeth. To be a good structure in the eyes of the CPF is a question of numbers and statistics, not what really goes on. As the Chairperson of the New Brighton CPF in August 2001 stated "you never see that Safety and Security committees have [. . .] been charged—there is not a single charge that has been laid against them. Whatever method that they have used to try and take information from a particular culprit, there is no way that a person can go and say, 'I will go and lay a charge against them' [. . .] that is something that we want to achieve in all the Safety and Security. Yes, we understand there is this moral fiber that we need to build." In other words, for the Amadlozi to be accepted as a formal structure is not to have any charges laid against its members. It is not to stop using force but merely to use force in an acceptable manner—that is, use of force that is invisible in the statistics of the police. The CPF has managed this by applying what they call "minimal force."

In different S&S structures I have seen minimal force techniques like: playing "good cop-bad cop"; by forcing "criminals" to stand on their heads for up to a hour at a time and when they fall down on the concrete floor, raising them and letting the session continue; giving slaps and punches on body parts where it does not leave marks; or letting criminals beat each other up. For example, placed facing each other, one criminal is asked to stand with his hands down the side and the other is asked to hit the other person over the shoulder area with a *sjambok*, so that half of the *sjambok* reaches down over the person's back. After ten lashes, they change places and the session continues until one of them breaks down (this method can also be applied with open-handed slaps in the face, kicks, and so on). As it was explained to me by a member of an S&S structure in Kwazakele after a full-day workshop on human rights arranged by the CPF, the good thing about extracting information in this manner is: "You see it is better in this way. If they go to the police and lay a charge they will ask them. 'Okay who beat you?' [. . .] Nobody can blame us. It is not that we like doing it, but it is necessary." Sessions like these take place behind closed doors, but this does not mean that they are "secret" as such. Family members and girlfriends would pass by the Amadlozi office making arrangements for supper or exchanging keys; community members would come around to lay new charges and policemen would pass the office to exchange information on cases, or just to take a break from patrolling. They would leave the offices with comments like: "Oh, we can see you are working, good luck!" and laugh. "Secrecy" here takes on a different notion than what we usually think secrets are about. Here it is related to invisibility in the official statistics.

Concluding Remarks

The sessions behind closed doors resemble what Taussig (1999) calls "public secrets": something we all know but do not speak about. The danger when speaking about such "secrets" is that the use of force becomes disembodied from the social context, and enters the realm of a real exception: outrageous (which it certainly is—I do not condone the use of force, but there is more to it than that), and the work of a few men only. The closer structures like the Amadlozi and the CPF-aligned S&S structures come to the state, and officially take on state duties, the more invisible becomes the use of force. However, this does not by any means imply that the use of force has disappeared.

My point is that the Amadlozi and most S&S structures work as a locally accepted exception from the Constitution. Thus, they are not outside the law and the state as such, but act as the "extra" element in policing that makes it possible to combat crime, a neat and nice way of outsourcing the sovereign power of the state. Somebody once said that a crisis is a productive condition—one just has to remove the taint of the misfortune. This is, I think, what is currently taking place with the removal of the use of force and corporal punishment from the public gaze and the creation of conditions for a new form of "conviviality" (Mbembe 2001). It challenges the widespread tendency to posit a sharp dualism—with regard to both values and concrete *modus operandi*—between state agencies and vigilante formations.

With the disappearance of apartheid came rapid changes in urban demography, class, gender, generational composition and political relations. Along with these came a perceived decay in the morality of township life, exemplified by the high crime levels—but no unifying mechanism for control has been put in place to regulate township life. The transition to democracy seems to have had the effect of leaving a power vacuum in which, almost by default, the Amadlozi and CPF-aligned structures emerged as a local sovereign instance of control, regulation and production of social ties. There are two reasons for this. First, these structures are sensitive to the complex network of relationally constituted identities characterizing township life with all the perceived and real problems related to gender, generation and morality. Second, they deal with crime in a manner that is both locally acceptable and accessible.

One cannot overestimate the constitutive relation between the state-of-emergency kind of hype around the crime rate during the 1990s, on the one hand, and the emergence of local justice structures, on the other, for a correct understanding of the nature of local justice structures like the Amadlozi. The call for action was made when crime levels were not only threatening the safety of communities, but also bringing the security of the state into question, causing problems with attracting investments, slowing the tourism industry down and so on. It seems as if the decision to nurture informal local justice structures was a last-ditch effort to protect the individual rights enshrined in the Constitution by avoiding the re-introduction of laws that characterize a "real" state of emergency.

The new and intriguing development is that local justice structures—as discrete and independent entities—have been rendered invisible by the kind of state of exception that brought them into being as legitimate counterparts—in other words, their status as exceptions to the Constitution. Nonetheless, they continue to accomplish what they were doing all along, under relatively "normal" circumstances (with crime rates brought down), only further removed from the public eye and ear. In this sense—as long as they do not enter public statistics—local justice structures occupy the intriguing space that opens up when the state of exception starts to become the rule.

Situations like these remind us of those that Taussig (1992, 2) calls "ordered disorder, the exception and *the* rule" (emphasis in original). Taussig analyzes terror in Columbia and elsewhere in Latin America, focusing particularly on how state-controlled death-patrols have operated through fear, and how the state of siege became the norm. The special conditions of this situation were that the state declared the exception. It tried to control its reach, which, according to Taussig, was impossible because it became appropriated and turned against the sovereign itself and therewith attempted to ensure the sovereign's special effects. Here, the arbitrariness of power has implications for the legitimation of authority, since reason is suspended and replaced with force and violence. But when the ordered condition is produced, disorder nonetheless continues to boil beneath the surface, retracted from the public gaze. If similar mechanisms can be seen to characterize both democratic and some of the least democratic regimes, then maybe we are touching upon some of the inherent paradoxes in constitutional democracy and its blindness toward sovereign power. The fact is that somebody always already has the right (and duty in the national interest) to declare the exception, and as we have seen, to produce particular territories where the "other law" can thrive in its own productive ways of being as local instances of sovereign power. The question is, of course, how "other" is the "other law," compared with real sovereign power? There are differences, but the mechanisms seem to be the same— or at least that is up for a test.

What started out as a paraphrase of Agamben (2000, 38.2)—as a temporal suspension of the state of law—seems to have become a permanent spatial arrangement (not without order but ruled by the "other law") that, as such, remains constantly outside the normal state of law. As such it is still confined, just as it always has been, to the outskirts of the cities and the gated communities ruled by citizenship. In South Africa this is synonymous with the townships on the margins of the new state—outside the normal judicial order and yet still included by virtue of their very exclusion.

Above the Law: Practices of Sovereignty in Surrey Estate, Cape Town

Steffen Jensen

During the latter part of the 1990s, Cape Town saw the emergence of a number of anti-crime organizations. Most prominent was the vigilante group Pagad (People Against Gangsterism and Crime) whose war first with drug dealers and later with the state engulfed the city in violence from 1996. But Pagad was far from the only anti-crime organization. All over the city, local neighborhood watches emerged to police the townships.[1] Most commentators, along with anti-crime organizations, agree that the combination of inept and corrupt policing and the crime level in the city makes for the emergence of nonstate forms of policing (Nina and Schärf 2001). Commentators also draw attention to a strong Muslim element in the organizations (e.g., Dixon and Johns 2001; Tayob 1996). Tayob, for instance, argues that because many drug dealers were Muslim, there was a need within the Muslim community to assert a morally righteous Islam. Although these explanations carry weight, I argue that we must take cognizance of the fact that most of those participating in the organizations were classified as colored during the apartheid regime. The central thrust of this essay is therefore how the apartheid regime's objectification of colored and interventions in colored areas impacted upon the upsurge of Muslim anti-crime organizations in the 1990s.

Historically, coloreds as a group came into existence during the early part of the twentieth century, and with the Population Registration Act of 1950 "colored" became a legal category. This legal status affirmed and reproduced the notion that coloreds were different as a matter of nature. Whereas whites were viewed as inherently civilized and Africans were constructed according to a notion that they could prosper only in rural areas, apartheid interventions towards coloreds were informed by racial stereotypes revolving around a colored hooligan, the *kaapse skollie*. These constructions cast colored men as prone to drink, criminal, happy-go-lucky, inherently violent, weak, and untrustworthy.

---

[1] In this essay, I consider only colored townships. For elaboration of anti-crime organizations in African townships, see, for example, Schärf (1997b) and Nina (1995).

Although the embodiment of this problematic abstraction, according to the knowledge informing governmental interventions, was to be found only in certain classes and spaces, the interventions impacted on the ways in which colored Muslims—and colored men in general—could assert a positive masculine identity.

So how are Muslim anticrime practices related to apartheid's production of coloreds? As argued by de Certeau (1984), groups appropriate identities to surprising effects. By redeploying and relocating in space the official apartheid stereotypes of the *kaapse skollie* through the practices of patrolling—and subsequently turning poor colored men into what Agamben (1998) has termed "bare life" (see the Introduction to this volume)—Muslim neighborhood watches can produce moral communities that are above the state as well as the individual. This is important in two ways. On the one hand, the practice reproduces the demonization of colored men from the townships. On the other hand, the performance of the moral community taps into a repertoire of bodily disciplines or practices defining the Muslim masculine community—dress code, habits of temperance, strength, solidarity, fearlessness, and commitment. These practices and values all negate the *kaapse skollie*.

Anti-crime organizations also draw on anti-apartheid notions that the real and true sovereignty is located in the community rather than in the state. However, sovereignty cannot be reduced to institutions; it should rather be seen as a practice that needs to be performed on a continual basis. In Surrey Estate, which provides the empirical basis for this essay, this takes place through the active policing of boundaries. The sovereign practices inherent in the maintenance of boundaries range from relatively benevolent development projects to violence—all of which are authorized in a moral community where the rules are different from—and above—constitutional law.

The essay begins by tracing the objectification of coloreds as different from Africans, whites and Indians. The essay then explores the strategies of becoming a moral person in Surrey Estate in the face of racialized, gendered and social stereotypes and marginalization. It does so by tracing and examining the practices and discourses of a group of middle-aged, well-to-do Muslim men in Surrey Estate. Surrey Estate is the home of some six thousand people, where approximately 90 percent are Muslim middle-class families living in relatively stable socioeconomic conditions. It is located some fifteen kilometers outside Cape Town city center on the vast flatland area known as the Cape Flats, to where most of the city's nonwhite population was relocated during apartheid. Although Surrey Estate is different from the townships surrounding it, it still bears the mark of apartheid interventions.

Part 1: Apartheid and the Governmentalization of the Coloreds

From the 1920s the global depression engulfed South Africa aggravated by extended periods of drought. People of all races turned towards the cities, whose numbers swelled considerably. This restructuring of society upset social and racial hierarchies of South Africa, and urban problems became critical (Dubow 1995; Norval 1996; Sparks 1990). After 1930, a number of Commissions of Inquiry were created in order to provide the necessary (scientific) information to deal with the consequences of the dislocation. Elsewhere I have analyzed the commission reports in more detail (Jensen 2001). For now, suffice it to say that they were instrumental in producing coloreds as separate from whites, Africans, and Indians (Lewis 1987, 151). Furthermore, they differentiated coloreds along lines of class and gender. In terms of class, the reports operated with three categories of coloreds. The first was "the undesirable class, comprising the "skolly boys," [. . .] the habitual convict, the ex-convict, the drunkards, and the habitual loafers." The second class comprised "the farm and the unskilled laborers, the factory workers, and the household servants in rural and urban areas." The last category comprised "the relatively well-to-do and educated colored people" (Union of South Africa 1938, par. 48–50). Finally, as is also evident in the class categories, the Commissions operated with sharp gender divisions. Women were the potential homemakers, always struggling in an uphill battle against poverty and social disintegration, whereas men often constituted a disrupting force within the families at the lower end of the class spectrum. On a similar note but in a different report, the Liquor Commission had the following to say about the colored man: "He degenerates into a 'won't-work,' the squatter in and near bars. [. . . H]e may remain a lazy, harmless, good-for-nothing, but it is also possible that his activities may develop criminal tendencies in him and turn him into a skolly" (Union of South Africa 1945, par. 16). This colored man was incarnated in the notion of the *kaapse skollie* that would come to inform, either directly or indirectly, most government actions in the years ahead, as well as the ways in which coloreds began to self-identify.

DCA Practices: Making the Population Healthy

One of the most important institutions charged with intervention in relation to the coloreds was the Department of Coloured Affairs (DCA). The DCA began operating under apartheid logic from 1952 where it employed a total staff of twenty-one and grew incrementally to employ more than fifty thousand when it was disbanded in 1992. The mission of the DCA, from its first Annual Report, was to uplift the colored submerged classes and employ colored elites to do it under the appropriate guidance of whites. Thus the DCA increasingly regulated, supervised, assisted, and, when all else failed, imprisoned the submerged classes. The most significant expansions took place from 1958 to 1964 after what Evans (1997) calls the "winning formula" was extended to the rest of the state from the Department of Native Affairs, where Hendrick Verwoerd, the prime apartheid architect, had developed the notion of separate development. After 1985 there was further development as a result of a new constitution, which made provision for a Tricameral parliament. Each of these expansions naturally increased the funds available to the DCA, as well as the staff. Expansion always took place within the parameters of separate or parallel development, and was informed by biopolitical attempts to make the population healthy: psychological, dental, and professional welfare services. These practices produced and confirmed the existence of three categories of people: the middle class, and poor women and poor men as two separate groups.

In relation to the colored elite, the DCA actively advocated particular routes of employment to produce and promote a middle class. The bulk of this middle class would be hired to work in government agencies concerned with coloreds, either as teachers or as social workers. In 1970, approximately 84 percent of all colored professionals were employed in state agencies, notably the DCA (Goldin 1989, 150). The colored and white middle classes did not share the same life conditions. The colored middle class faced a host of problems that would prompt them to resist the regime in the end: impediments to social mobility; limits of housing to certain racially designated areas; limited access to cultural amenities; a general sense of humiliation because of white prejudice; material losses because of job reservation; wage differentiation; inadequate economic prospects; symbolic lack of status and inadequate political powers (Republic of South Africa 1976, 470–71). All these impediments prevented the colored middle class from taking up the kind of life worthy of "educated and civilised people whose needs are typical of civilised human beings" (470).

In contrast with its approval of the colored middle-class, the DCA and the various commissions—including later ones—viewed the "submerged classes" with considerable pessimism, as the poor coloreds had been "crippled in body or in spirit by their poverty" (Republic of South Africa 1976, 479). Apart from structural poverty, hopes of colored advancement were often thwarted by special problems, which were inherently gendered. Whereas women fought an uphill battle to make ends meet, the destructive actions of the men—their irresponsibility as providers, their alcohol habits, criminal tendencies and inherent violence—persistently countered women's attempts to become "potential homemakers." Many social workers, often coloreds themselves, lamented the situation (266). However, the solution lay in elaborate governmental intervention from private welfare institutions and the DCA, through which it would be possible to address the problems of the colored "submerged classes." Consequently, with increasing force, the DCA entered into colored working class families on the side of women, who became the most important ally of the welfare state.[2] Whereas colored men suffered incarceration to an extent that made them the most imprisoned group in South Africa,[3] colored women received increasingly substantial welfare benefits and elaborate guidance on how to become a true homemaker (Jensen 2001, 74–81).[4]

In this sense, the DCA's actions were instrumental in gendering, classing and racializing the coloreds. They worked from the premise that there were inescapable differences between the different racial groups, and ended up reproducing the differences. The DCA was terminated in 1994 when the ANC took over the reins of government and began to deracialize the state bureaucracy. Its exit was peaceful and virtually unnoticed.[5] But although disbanded, most of its practices continued in other institutions, like the Cape Town City Council that took over housing and the Provincial Department of Welfare, which took over probational services and the maintenance grant. Often lodged in the same buildings, staff, and recipients persisted in calling it "Colored Affairs."[6]

---

[2] This is similar to Donzelot's analysis of the way in which the French state entered into the lives of lower-class families in the latter part of the nineteenth century (Donzelot 1979, xxii, 90–95).

[3] Coloreds were imprisoned four times as often as Africans in spite of them not being subject to the same pass law regulations (Pinnock 1984, 74).

[4] The so-called State maintenance grant provides a vivid illustration of the gendered and gendering governmental interventions. In principle this was non-racial, and before 1960 it was paid primarily to poor white Afrikaner women. The maintenance grant increasingly became a colored grant to the extent that by the beginning of the 1990s colored women received around 50 percent of the total amount spent on maintenance. The criteria for reception of the grant matched perfectly with the stereotype of the colored man as irresponsible, criminal, violent, and weak, and it became close to inevitable that the grant would be implemented in a racialized as well as in a gendered manner.

[5] The last Director-General, P.D. McEnery, reported all was well in the Annual Report of 1992, and promised that the DCA would continue its important work "in enabling South Africa to face the future with confidence" (House of Representatives 1992, 1).

[6] As an experiment, I used the term "Colored Affairs" in some interviews with staff and recipients when asking about present state institutions such as housing and welfare. Nobody took offense or even noted my use of the term.

The Group Areas Act: The Production of Surrey Estate

If the activities of the DCA went largely unnoticed the opposite holds true for the Group Areas Act, which came to incarnate the evil to which the apartheid regime exposed the coloreds. Without going into detail—that has been done in great detail elsewhere[7]—suffice it to say that implementation of the Group Areas Act had profound repercussions for the production of coloreds as a separate group. Together with the Population Registration Act, which categorized the diverse South African population into four unambiguous racial groups, the Act provided the legislative framework for residential segregation. Extremely unequal spaces in terms of access to resources and possibilities were marked out for each group (Western 1996). The Group Areas Act was also instrumental in reproducing the class differences pointed out by the commission reports and institutionalized in the practices of the DCA. The Cape Flats, to where the bulk of the coloreds were removed, was divided up into homeowner areas and public housing areas. Some of the latter were class differentiated in terms of quality and price. These differentiations were not haphazard; they were the result of careful planning within the National Housing Commission, the Department of Community Development, the Cape Town City Council and the Demarcation Board. The Group Areas Act had profound gendering effects. State-provided residences were based on nuclear families (Pinnock 1989, 167). The nuclear family structure often ran counter to networks and social ties that were in existence before the Group Areas Act—with the result, as Pinnock asserts, that social support structures broke down, as extended families were scattered around the Cape Flats (Pinnock 1984, 18–30).

These racialized, classed, and gendered practices and discourses all went into the production of separate colored spaces like Surrey Estate. The squatter camp there was demarcated as a colored, middle-class, homeowner area in the beginning of the 1960s. Together with the few Africans in the area, those coloreds who could not afford to live there, moved out. Those who could afford it stayed on and built their own homes, often spanning a period of some thirty years, extending their houses little by little. Others moved to Surrey Estate as they were forced out of middle-class areas closer to town, or after amassing enough money to leave public housing areas. By 1950 its residents had begun constructing a mosque, and as a result Surrey Estate became a place where Muslims, a minority among the coloreds, wished to stay. Today Surrey Estate comprises some 90 percent Muslims.

---

[7] See, for instance, Maylam (1995); Mabin (1992); Mabin and Parnell (1995); Pinnock (1984, 1989); Jensen (2001); Western (1996); and Goldin (1989).

As in other residential areas, it is modeled after what Pinnock terms the Garrison City. By this he means it has few access roads, and the streets often double back or end in cul-de-sacs. The few access roads made it easy for police to seal off the area in case of riots (Pinnock 1989). But that security function is still in use today. The limited thoroughfare makes it easy for the neighborhood watch to control the streets, as strangers found there seldom have what the patrols consider legitimate purposes. In contrast to the townships, the streets are quiet and empty. The plots and houses are quite large and give the impression of relative wealth. The houses I visited often had new furniture, and the walls were adorned with Islamic images like pictures of the Qua'ba and Arabic writings in gold. Most families I knew had extended family households with several generations living under the same roof. Socioeconomically, most who wanted to work—many women preferred to stay home, thereby conforming to the notion of a respectable homemaker—held relatively well-paid jobs in construction, or public administration, or had their own business. This thumbnail sketch of Surrey Estate should indicate that although the area is different from the rowdy, busy, and often overcrowded council areas, it still incarnates a specific embodiment of apartheid's objectification of coloreds in Cape Town.

The Production of Political Subjects

Apartheid and separate development did not remain stable throughout the period from the Nationalist takeover, but developed haphazardly, in nooks and crannies. The apartheid project also met with significant resistance on an increasing number of fronts. For coloreds, one rallying point was the demolition of the old working class area of District Six (see, e.g., Jensen and Turner 1996; Pinnock 1984, 1989; Western 1996), but the regime's constant encroachments of colored voting rights also prompted increasing resistance (Goldin 1989; Lewis 1987).[8] When the regime adopted a constitutional change in 1983 to introduce the Tricameral parliament—whereby coloreds and Indians were to vote for segregated parliaments—a major wave of resistance arose, as anti-apartheid activists used the reform to mobilize coloreds and Indians (Seekings 2000). On a popular level, the disillusionment with the regime translated into a refusal of the categorization as "coloreds," and people began referring to themselves as "so-called coloreds." Being colored became synonymous with less than full-blown citizenship, which was reserved for "whites only." The distinction between being a full citizen or something less

[8] Coloreds were taken off the common voters' roll in 1951 and they lost their municipal vote in 1971.

echoes the Tocquevillean distinction between citizens and subjects. Whereas citizens are self-governing participants in politics, subjects are restrained by some external force (Cruikshank 1999, 19). Seen in this perspective, coloreds and other nonwhites were, in Tocquevillean terms, subjects and not citizens. Without disputing the subjugation, my analysis highlights the apartheid regime's attempts to create *colored* citizenship. Welfare reforms, construction of houses, even the creation of particular colored political institutions with less power than those of the whites, were aimed at producing colored citizens reaching their fullest potential.

Importantly, both opposition to apartheid and the regime itself operated through the Tocquevillean distinction, and although with radically different readings, they both reproduced the dichotomy between citizen and subject. But as Cruikshank points out, "the democratic citizen is not a species apart from the subject" (1999, 20). She argues that people, including citizens "are not born; they are made" (3). Following this line of thought, it would be a mistake to assert, as the anti-apartheid activists did, that subjugation would end with the end of apartheid. Instead of the dichotomy between subject and citizen, Cruikshank suggests the hyphenated form of citizen-subjects to indicate that both are subjugated to power. However, by dissolving the dichotomy Cruikshank ignores that both the dichotomy and the citizen are reproduced because they are powerful imaginative and symbolic ideas. The ideology of the citizen, flawed as it is by its enmeshment in governmental power relations, is what keeps politics at the center of the social. Cruikshank's Foucauldian analysis helps us understand how racialized, gendered, and social taxonomies were generated, institutionalized and spatialized, and the regime's techniques were remarkably efficient doing just this. Coloreds are coloreds because this group of people has been subjected to very specific forms of power. But even the most hegemonic constructions are negotiated, if not overtly then in everyday encounters between representatives of the dominant structures and the dominated (de Certeau 1984). The outcome of these contestations aimed at stabilizing identities are always dependent on local specificities and histories, and often produce very surprising results. It is one such local variation of coping with racialization, gendering and classing that we shall follow in the next section.

PART 2: INTO SURREY ESTATE

Apartheid also impacted on coloreds in more subtle ways than the physical manifestations of state intervention. The majority of coloreds I spoke to on the Cape Flats accept the stereotype of the colored as untrustworthy, weak, work-shy, alcoholic, and criminal. Coloreds do not accept these stereotypes as images of themselves but accept the existence of the abstract problematic colored. This ambiguous relationship is captured in words like *gam*.[9] The question then becomes how individual coloreds exorcize this problematic coloredness. Clearly, strategies to defer the stereotypes depend on the social position of individuals or groups of coloreds, but there is a structure to the narratives that revolves around the construction of social and spatial boundaries. Problematic coloredness is deferred to "the other side" of immorality and contrasted with the decency and basic humanity of "this side." The social and symbolic boundary becomes the basic element in drawing lines of exclusion around a moral community. At a township level, these boundaries might be between homeowner and rental areas, or between different parts of townships or between home and street (Jensen 2001, 99–141). In the case of the people in Surrey Estate two basic principles of exclusion are at work. First, Surrey Estate is contrasted with—and draws its basic morality from—*not* being like the surrounding townships. Second, Surrey Estate is constructed as a Muslim space, apart from the Christian majority at its doorstep. It is from the rental areas that drugs, gangs and violence emanate, and although people recognize that Muslims also engage in violence and drug peddling, it is only with religious and moral commitment that the problem of drugs and gangs can be fought.

The stereotypes of coloreds cannot, the story goes, apply to true Muslims. In contrast with being weak and appendages to the whites, as one of the stereotypes would have it, Islam is the strongest religion on the planet and one of the few institutions challenging the hegemony of the West (interview with member of Muslim *ullema*). True Muslims do not drink or use drugs; they are not disorganized and lacking in moral fiber—they live regimented moral lives. Although these assertions are ideological constructions aimed at exorcizing *gamheid*, they have consequences that go further than mere discourse. First, the constructions translate into particular bodily practices and disciplines, including dress code and so-called civilized manners. These manners are related to racial categories in complex ways through the concept of *gam maniere*, or *gam* manners, which the abstract colored engages in. When asked what *gam maniere* mean a young woman recounts a seemingly innocuous occurrence at work, where a colleague had taken more than

[9] The following is from a conversation with a young colored couple. They reply to the question of what *gam* means: "*Gam* means the colored people." "Oh really? All colored people are *gam*, *gam* is just another word for colored?" "No," the couple replies, "it is a word that colored people use about other coloreds if you are doing certain things, you know, something *gam*."

his share of the cake in order to take it home to his wife. The woman had said, "No, you typical *gam;* typical colored *maniere!*" Thus, in order to avoid being interpellated as "typical colored," people have to engage in a strict disciplinary regime. Secondly, the ideological constructions that translate into the spatial deference of violence and crime to outside Surrey Estate—to Christians and township people—provide the impetus for exerting rather severe practices of spatial and social control in the territory of Surrey Estate. To explain the discourses and practices associated with the constructions of this moral community, I need to situate Surrey Estate neighborhood watch in the larger framework of collective nonstate action in Cape Town after the fall of apartheid.

The Rise of Collective Action on the Cape Flats

The importance of crime and violence in the everyday experience of people in African and colored townships has been an issue as far back as the 1930s and 1940s when the first attempts to deal with the *"skollie menace"* in District Six had been made (Pinnock 1984, 21–30).[10] After relocation to the Cape Flats, successive attempts through the 1970s and 1980s at establishing neighborhood watches failed, and often turned into criminal structures. Thus, crime and violence was an everyday concern long before it became the perennial political issue of the 1990s.

Another kind of response in Cape Town to crime and violence were civic organizations that began to organize around the issue of drugs and related violence. One of the first of these organizations was the Salt River Anti-Drug Committee that was launched in the inner-city suburb of Salt River in 1986 (Omar 1996). Four years later in April 1990, the Committee organized what was to become the first anti-drug march in Cape Town. The march was tear-gassed by a police force fearful of disruptions to the fragile transition and still trained in apartheid methods of crowd control (Omar 1996, 45). In the late 1980s and early 1990s crime, like most other social issues, was subsumed under the meta-narrative of resistance to the apartheid regime. The assumption was that apartheid was to blame for the crime and violence, and once the regime disbanded, crime and violence would cease to be a problem. Thus, most civic organizations concentrated their efforts on fighting the regime, regardless of their initial focus on crime control, education, welfare, or housing.

The transition to democracy heralded a change in the conditions under which civic organizations worked. Civic organizations lost the position as champions of political rights; donors cast their lot with state

[10] See Glaser (2000) for a similar perspective on Johannesburg's African townships, first Sophia Town and later Soweto.

and ANC structures rather than NGOs, and finally the ANC became the dominant force in township political life. These developments led to a drastic decline in the influence of the civics and ANC-affiliated civic life was fundamentally disrupted, divided, and incapacitated between 1994 and 1996 (Seekings 1996). When civic life reemerged after 1996, it was with a clear focus on crime and violence. Indicative of the change, one of the leading figures in Cape Town's civic life said in an interview in 1997: "I used to be involved in politics and development, but these days it is all about security and crime. I nearly don't do anything with development."

There were at least three causes for the shift in civic concern from political rights to crime prevention. First, the state wanted to change its *modus operandi* in relation to the police, and Community Policing Fora were established at most police stations. Second, state structures were increasingly preoccupied with crime, which influenced civic organizations to engage in the state's priority area. Finally, the pattern of violence changed, not least with the emergence of Pagad, forcing the state and civics alike to focus on crime and violence.

Many commentators (e.g., Dixon and Johns 2001; Mattes et al. 1998; Omar 1996; Tayob 1996) have discussed reasons for the rise in collective action against drug dealers and gangsters on the Cape Flats. Although they differ on several counts, they all agree that Pagad and collective action were responses to a need on the Cape Flats to confront gangs. Sometimes the need was borne of personal experiences, sometimes of a more general fear for personal security or that children might become involved with drugs. Pagad developed into a mass organization only after the killing of a notorious drug dealer in August 1996. In the following months, the organization was able to field huge demonstrations at stadiums, mosques, and in front of known drug dealers' houses, where warnings to stop the drug trade were issued to drug dealers. The implicit message of these marches was that the dead drug dealer's fate would befall all who refused to stop peddling drugs.

Interviews conducted on the Cape Flats indicate that Pagad initially gave many residents on the Cape Flats a sense of power vis-à-vis drug dealers and gangsters, who had hitherto been untouchable. Although not all drug dealers heeded Pagad's warnings, some did. The state's response to Pagad was ambiguous. Shortly after the execution the then Minister of Justice, Dullah Omar, asserted that although he vehemently opposed residents taking the law into their own hands, "[Pagad] has awakened the soul of the community. [. . .] We should use the atmosphere that has been created to good effect" (Dullah Omar quoted in Manjra 1996, 39). The initial successes caused a groundswell of support in the general population, if not for Pagad then at least for collective, extrastate action.[11]

According to my interviews, the people that dominated Pagad in the initial months of 1996 came from Surrey Estate. They comprised a group of men who, following the kidnap and torture of one of the men's sons, went on a rampage at night in the streets of Surrey Estate and the neighboring townships. The man whose son was tortured explains: "This whole effort of Pagad didn't just blossom out of the sky. It started by us here because me and him [a friend] went out at night. We used to bring the guys [the gangsters] up here and fuck them up. [. . .] We used to pick up the guys—they were carrying firearms and drugs—and we would *donner* them before we took them to the police." As time went by, more and more people latched on to the new method of addressing the gangsters' rule. When the men decided to march on drug dealers' houses, the name of Pagad came up. Although the Surrey Estate men were attached to the mosque and the neighborhood watch, their nightly excursions took place outside the ambit of the neighborhood watch. As Pagad took off, these men as well as most of the people in the neighborhood watch participated in the mass demonstrations. There was, however, one significant exception: the Imam Sheikh Irfaan, the Imam of the Surrey Estate mosque.

Irfaan had been suspicious from mid-1996 of what he saw as an emerging leadership of Pagad with other, political, agendas than those of fighting crime and violence. When the main Muslim body, the MJC (the Muslim Judiciary Council) aligned themselves with Pagad in the hope of generating more support among Muslims (Jeenah 1996, 20), Irfaan discontinued his membership of the MJC. He stated in 1999, "I still believe that we need an organization like Pagad, if the intention is sincerely against drugs and gangsterism. Unfortunately the guys that were involved in Pagad, I knew them, they were Qibla guys [radical Islamist movement] and I knew what they were up to." During 1996 and into 1997 antagonisms between the two factions of Pagad increased, resulting in several incidents of arson, drive-by shootings, and harass-

---

[11] Idasa (Institute for a Democratic Alternative in South Africa), a South African NGO doing research and intervention to promote democracy and transformation, found that people on the Cape Flats overwhelmingly supported some kind of collective action against the gangs. Thus, the figures for 1996 showed that around 90 percent would sign petitions, 85 percent would attend rallies and boycott businesses dealing with gangsters, 80 percent would march on police stations to demand action, 70 percent would march to known drug dealers' houses, and as many as 60 percent would themselves use violence to target criminals. The figures for 1997 tend to be higher than the year before (Mattes et al. 1998, 22). Although support for Pagad was lower, around one third of the respondents supported Pagad, another third was neutral, and the final third was against (24).

ment. After these incidents most support from Surrey Estate, state authorities and Muslim organizations was withdrawn, and Pagad became increasingly violent and marginalized (Dixon and Johns 2001).

But Pagad's impact was greater than its organizational or numerical strength in 2000 would indicate, as it brought collective, violent action to the fore as a necessary means to fight gangs and drugs. Although very few people interviewed expressed any support for Pagad in its present guise, many would still say, "I supported the first Pagad. Not the second Pagad [that is, the one dominated by Qibla]." The political establishment, although fiercely prosecuting Pagad members, endorsed the primacy of security on the political agenda. Pagad thus initiated a process in which the merging of political concerns and everyday experiences with crime and violence with collective action as the solution.

Surrey Estate and Collective Action

In Surrey Estate, a neighborhood watch began operating around 1990. Tracing its emergence illustrates localized, specific actions of Muslims against crime and drugs. This account is based on interviews with a number of high-profile residents, organized around the central figure of the local Imam and his mosque, and observations from neighboring Heideveld, where I did most of my fieldwork. Although there were dissenting voices present in Surrey Estate, most residents supported this group, at least in its actions against drug dealers, large-scale welfare services and in terms of education.

In the first interview session, a leading figure in the congregational life of the mosque stressed the importance of leadership. He referred to the local Imam, Sheikh Irfaan. Irfaan was born in Surrey Estate when it was still a squatter camp. But by then a mosque had been built to service the small farming and squatter communities. Irfaan spent most of the 1980s in Saudi Arabia studying to become an Imam. He returned in 1987 after graduation and came back to Surrey Estate. When the old Imam died, he took over the responsibilities of the mosque.

Irfaan gradually became aware of the problem of drugs and crime in Surrey Estate, and by 1990 he and a friend were patrolling the streets around their houses. Other people picked up the idea and a neighborhood watch was formed with the mosque as its organizational center. In the beginning the members performed the patrols themselves, but five years down the line the watch was reorganized and each household in Surrey Estate paid a monthly fee to hire people to patrol the streets. Today, Surrey Estate has a twenty-four-hour neighborhood watch that is considerably faster at responding than the police. Compared to other areas on the Cape Flats, crime is very low. There are no longer any drug dealers operating within Surrey Estate, and the police, with whom the neighborhood watch has developed relatively cordial relations, have for all purposes stopped patrolling in the suburb. This was far from the picture during the first half of the 1990s. Up to ten drug dealers operated in the area and relations with police were hostile.

The relationship with the police began changing in 1994 when the ANC took over government. Police became obliged to work closely with the communities they policed, as the principle of community policing was adopted and given a legislative framework in the Police Act of 1996. But the neighborhood watch soon realized that although the police had formally transformed to become an accountable police service, collusion with drug dealers had changed very little.[12] As a first step against the corruption, people in the watch began monitoring drug dealers' houses on a twenty-four-hour basis. They noted car registration plates, checked them for police registration and subsequently reported to provincial police, the number of police cars outside the different dealers' houses, demanding reasons and that police leadership put a stop to the corrupt practices. After an extended period, the tactics worked, at least to the extent that police were less direct in their corruption.

Simultaneously, the neighborhood watch began targeting drug dealers. At first, this happened through targeting customers, who were threatened with violence if they entered drug dealers' houses. This harassment worked to some extent, but it also seriously antagonized the drug dealers. In a number of incidents between Irfaan, the neighborhood watch and drug dealers, the former two slowly got the upper hand. Irfaan tells about one confrontation:

> I remember one day, it was on the corner of Durr and Taurus Road, this guy was selling drugs like sweets on the road and it seemed to me you could just never get these guys. Now this guy was a main operator there, he was known as a gangster, and one night I saw him selling drugs to people, he would sell it, take the money, run into the bush, take out the drugs. [. . . T]his evening I remember I was just sick and fed up of him and I went there myself I said "Right you sell the drugs now, sell the drugs. I want you to sell the drugs." So I told him, "Sell the drugs now." Right, I warned him, "Right you touch me, you'll see what I do to you, I'm not afraid of you, I'm not afraid of that merchant."

In part because of the pressure from collective action, the drug dealer ceased to trade in drugs, as did most of the other dealers. In 1998, only

[12] See also Jensen (2000).

one dealer remained in Surrey Estate. His drug dealing days ended when about one hundred neighborhood watch members with the Imam demolished his house in Comet Road.

> The best we could do was hassle him. We used to hassle his customers coming there, we used to hassle him, regular fights there and so on, until we got to a stage where we said to the community "Look, we have done legally everything that we can do. No one can touch this guy." Because he was standing on the streets saying you can't do anything to me, I am a gangster and I sell drugs and you can't do anything to me. The week before that he actually stood face to face with the Imam of the mosque, saying you can't do anything to me. So, the people went after mosque, and they said that's it. I have never seen a wall fall down like I saw a wall fall down that night. It physically fell over, okay, with people pushing against it, whatever. They just threw the walls down. They carried the roof away and threw it one side—that was the anger of the people. The police was there yes; fortunately they didn't take action because it was the whole community. We said to them "Don't talk to us, we are not the leaders, this is the community taking action."

Today, the ruin stands as a monument to the success of driving the drug dealers out of Surrey Estate. Moreover, it is arguable that this form of collective action—demolishing a house, physical harassments and fights, even shoot-outs—fed on and drew particular strength from Pagad's methods.

But we cannot reduce the demolition of the house or the activities of the neighborhood watch to the effects of Pagad. The way in which the watch functioned and crime was fought also relates to what we might term "Muslim politics" of the Cape Flats. At the risk of oversimplifying the complex congregational field among colored Muslims, it is fair to say that there are historically three strains within Islam: A modernist, cosmopolitan strain; a traditionalist, radical strain, and a political Islamic strain. The modernist strain is currently located in Claremont Main Road mosque. The Main Road mosque draws its congregation from colored Malays who work in business, administration and education. They advocate women's rights, oppose the death penalty and have been highly vocal in their defense of the government. The second strain encompasses the majority of mosques on the Cape Flats, also Surrey Estate. This strain is more traditional in its interpretation of Islam, focusing on family values and moral issues. It is in staunch opposition to the ANC anti-death penalty and pro-abortion discourse. Its most prominent feature is the congregation's loyalty to the local Imam, whom, according to my interviews, they will defend at all costs. This would indicate that we are dealing with a localist strain of Islam. How-ever despite its local perspective it draws on notions of Islamic univer-salism and Sharia-informed morality, and thus forms part of the Islamic revival that has taken place throughout the Muslim world. The last strain—political Islam—has in recent years been located mainly at the Habibia mosque in Rylands and the Gatesville Mosque under Imam Sadulah. Historically, this strain has always been the most politicized, and Muslim opposition to apartheid began with this strain at the Stegman Road mosque under Imam Sep, and incorporated people like Achmat Cassiem, a Robben Island convict, later to become the leader of Qibla. This strain had a much more radical interpretation of politics, where Islam became the signifier through which a general opposition to the dominant white society could be articulated. Consequently, it was not possible to isolate oneself in a particular locality. This was con-tinued in Pagad, and the fights between different groups over the dis-course of anti-crime and drugs also must be read as a struggle for the heart and mind of the Muslim population. Whereas the politicized strain dominated for a few months in 1996 in Surrey Estate, the second strain of Muslim politics regained its strength during 1997.

In summary, collective action in Surrey Estate has been informed by three related processes: the relationship between police and the com-munity, including police corruption and transformation; the commu-nity's relationship to drug dealers and gangsters operating in the area, and Muslim politics on the Cape Flats, where a traditional faction, re-volving around defense of the mosque, Imam and neighborhood held sway.

The Production of Legitimate Rule

The immediate consequence of the collective action that, through the neighborhood watch, controls the streets of Surrey Estate is that crime and drug peddling levels have fallen to some of the lowest on the Cape Flats, and that the police are hardly ever present. But there have also been other, less obvious consequences of the collective action: a *de facto* replacement of state sovereignty in Surrey Estate, which has been su-perceded by local institutions emanating from the mosque. With this appropriation of state authority, new criteria for who has the moral right to stay in Surrey Estate have been introduced, and the boundary between moral and immoral groups is policed vigorously.

The creation of local institutions in Surrey Estate took off from the neighborhood watch but, because of the perceived immorality of the public school system—sexual profligacy, rape, academic laziness, drunken teachers, lack of discipline, and the gang wars haunting the township schools—in 1995 people around the mosque founded a Muslim high school. It began with twenty-five students but now has about six hundred. Because of the immorality of the universities, as Sheikh Irfaan asserts, they are contemplating a private Muslim university as well. But the institutional building extends further than security and education. After a confrontation between a group of prostitutes and the Sheikh, the welfare fund of the mosque, the so-called *Zaka* fund, was extended to give food and other necessities to those in need in order for them not to have to resort to crime (in this case, prostitution). The Sheikh explains:

> I said [to the prostitute], "What are you doing here on the road? What do you plan to do here? Get out of our sight otherwise I'll kick you away from here!" Then she told me, "Are you going to give me a piece of bread?" So I said, "Yes, I will give you, what's your problem?" She said she's got children and this and that and I said, "Fine, come with me." Then I got information how she operates and where she operates and all these things. I said, "Okay fine, I'm going to give you food for your children and I'm going to see to all your problems, whatever you have, I came to the mosque, I took some meat, I gave her groceries, took her home."

The *Zaka* fund also helps out with school fees, rent and other necessities. The same logic of trying to rid Surrey Estate from crime—or, rather, immorality—was behind another initiative from the mosque and Sheikh Irfaan. A vacant building in the middle of Surrey Estate was to reopen as a video game shop. Irfaan and people close to him suspected that it would be a front for a drug dealing enterprise and went to the owner with their suspicion. He, concerned about the missed income opportunity, refused to accommodate the Sheikh's worries. Irfaan consequently offered to take the lease and the committee of the mosque opened a workshop making school clothes. The employees of the workshop are all single mothers, and the income they earn becomes "a means of them earning an income instead of taking hand-outs" (interview with Irfaan). In sum, the people around the mosque and around Irfaan have created a situation where functions attributed to the South African state have been taken over by people in Surrey Estate. As Irfaan asserts: "So now you see—what we have is a make-up of so many things, we have the mosque, it's a central thing, a center for guidance, of education, of teaching people how to live and commitment towards the community, and the high school and the *Zaka* Fund shop where they make clothes for so many schools and we have the patrols. So it's a makeup of lots of components that makes a success of a community." Needless to say, the mosque, "the center of guidance" is firmly controlled by a specific group of people who claim to represent the community of Surrey Estate. However, they "precede and produce" what they claim is there from the beginning, as Bourdieu has it in his analysis of political representation (Bourdieu 1991, 214). These very people are in a position to define what is right and wrong, what the community needs, how to achieve that end, and crucially who belongs to the moral community. The critical point here is that what is legal and what is considered a crime does not refer only to legal or constitutional norms as defined in the new democratic dispensation of the country, but to moral norms set down and acted out in the practice of patrolling. Clearly, drug dealing is illegal under all dispensations, but the boundary already blurs in relation to the actions taken against prostitutes. The neighborhood watch and the Sheikh also take action against people who under the present dispensation are not impeaching any laws other than the moral codes at work on the streets of Surrey Estate.

A first example of this is homosexuals. Although specifically protected by the Constitution, according to Irfaan they are in breach of every conceivable moral code, and are to be ostracized. Irfaan explains about one incident:

> Then these gays were just standing on the road here and I got out of the car and I just chased them with stones, you know "you're causing corruption in the society!" [. . .] "Go somewhere else, don't come in our area." So that I did on a few occasions because I feel that we also have a democratic right to protect our children of our community. Then what they do, they go into communities that allow it. We don't allow it here. I'm not prepared to . . . we're prepared to go to prison.

Irfaan's use of the term "democratic" along with his insistence that he will go to jail for his right to bash gays indicates that another, moral principle is at work in the assertion of democracy.

Other people, considered with suspicion and sometimes treated with downright aggression, are those who move at the wrong times and in the wrong ways. The neighborhood watch's leader asserts that they had had a specific problem with lovers attempting to find a "private" space and club-goers who passed through at night from the nearby club, the Galaxy, to their homes in the townships. They would choose Surrey Estate because it was the safest route, but that caused trouble and anxiety in Surrey Estate. Sometimes the passersby would commit crimes on their way through, as the people around the mosque assert. Hence this movement had to be controlled. Earlier on the problem of movement was linked to drug customers, but this was extended to all forms of movement not sanctioned by the moral authority of Surrey Estate.

Although all non-sanctioned movement (that is, going somewhere other than work, the mosque or shopping) is problematic,[13] one group's movements are more problematic than all others': that of young colored men, embodying the townships that encroach on Surrey Estate from all sides. They embody the gendered, racialized, aged, and classed threat to respectable society. It matters little what they do—no more than their presence is enough to warrant immediate action on behalf of the moral community. During my fieldwork, I recorded several stories from both sides, that is, from the neighborhood watch as well as from young, colored men who had been harassed as they passed through Surrey Estate. Faizel's story is then quite representative: "I was on my way home from the Gala [the Galaxy] with some friends. We weren't acting badly or anything—just walking along, laughing. Suddenly out of nowhere came these *ouens* (guys). They pushed us to the ground and screamed they were gonna *moere* us (beat us up). One of them even had a gun pointed at one of my friends. You have to be really careful walking through there on that side." Other young men tell of how they were dragged from their cars, or how they were slapped around and verbally abused as they passed through Surrey Estate.[14] The way in which space is controlled in Surrey Estate, especially aimed at the young men from the townships incarnating the *kaapse skollie*, indicates that policing is not always related to criminal deeds but more often to local interpretations of moral spaces and the demarcation of boundaries between what is moral and immoral, safe and dangerous. This has prompted accusations that those in charge of morally policing the streets of Surrey Estate suffer from what is known in South Africa as the *laager*-mentality,[15] that is, they band together, women and children inside the circle, men facing outward, to protect themselves from a perceived outside threat. The central persons around the mosque deny that this is the case. However, other residents in Surrey Estate are substantially more critical towards the circle around the mosque and Irfaan. One example is a well-educated man in his thirties who works in a central position in local

[13] This was brought home to me one night when I looked for the house of a friend. I looked around for perhaps thirty seconds before deciding which house it was and entering the house. Less than two minutes later, the neighborhood watch paid a visit because they had been notified that a suspicious-looking stranger had appeared.

[14] Most young colored men from the townships experience violent encounters on multiple occasions in their dealings with other young men, police, and community. In that sense, the violence incurred on the streets of Surrey Estate is not of a different intensity, and most of the young men shrugged the experiences off as yet another incident among many others.

[15] This concept is derived from Afrikaner history and denotes the practice of *voortrekkers* to build a circle out of ox wagons to protect against the encroaching African continent.

government. Like many others of his social position and political observation, he attends the mosque in Claremont Main Road, and follows the highly intellectual Iman Rachied Omar. The man intensely dislikes the autocratic and intolerant style of Sheikh Irfaan. He also challenges Irfaan's assertion that he and the people around the mosque represent the community of Surrey Estate in any substantial way. However—and this seems indicative for most of those opposing Irfaan—pushed by the very real threat of drug dealers, gangs and violence, he still pays the neighborhood watch its monthly subscriptions, and thereby de facto supports the particular mode of moral policing of Surrey Estate's streets.

CONCLUSION

Among the conclusions that might be drawn from this short case study of Surrey Estate, two related points stand out: first, the appropriation of sovereignty by a section of the community, and, second, the construction of a moral community. Surrey Estate as a physical, social and historical space was the product of the racialized, gendered and classed interventions of the apartheid regime. The regime was remarkably efficient in producing separate social spaces in terms of race, class, and gender. Yet the tactical appropriations, to invoke de Certeau, in the end fundamentally recast the social space according to the same racialized, classed and gendered structures that interpellated (Hall 1996; Althusser 1971) the colored man as the incarnation of moral decay. By cleansing the streets, the middle-aged Muslim men in Surrey Estate deferred evil to the nearby townships. The colored township men came to play two distinct roles. On the one hand, they were incarnated in the drug dealers operating from Surrey Estate, drawing their clientele from the townships and representing a real and concrete threat to people in Surrey Estate. On the other, they became the vehicle through which a particular group in Surrey Estate could come to terms with the fears of their own coloredness by redeploying stereotypes of the *kaapse skollie*. By invoking age and religion as the important identity markers, race, class, and gender could be dispelled and a positive masculinity could be asserted. This was confirmed each time a patrol targeted young colored township men. Through the extra-state practices of sovereignty, the men of Surrey Estate became moral beings with control over their own lives. In this way, the patrols and other practices of the men around the mosque become a means through which to become principled men in a situation where colored masculinity is seen as inherently and almost irredeemably problematic.

In the process of asserting their moral position, the people around the mosque and Sheikh Irfaan to a large extent, supplanted many of the institutions in which sovereign power is most often located. In other words they displaced the structures of the emerging democratic state as they carried out state functions like welfare, policing, criminal justice, education and the exercise of local authority. Although my analysis is locally specific, a similar process seems to be replicated across the South African territory (Nina and Schärf 2001), indeed across the postcolony (Comaroff and Comaroff 2000). This, as this essay has illustrated, does not lead to a return to a Hobbesian state of nature, as some scholars on the collapsing African state have argued (e.g., Zartmann 1994; Thomson 1999). Although sovereignty has been identified historically as the privilege of the state, sovereignty should be viewed as a figure rather than as always already institutionalized within the nation-state.

This approach to sovereignty is inspired by Carl Schmidt (1934 [1985]) and further developed by Giorgio Agamben (1998—see Introduction to this volume). In this approach, sovereign power is defined as the ability to name somebody as a threat to the moral community. However, as argued by Ernesto Laclau (1994, 34–35), no polity has a reality apart from the attempts to make it exist. It has to be performed on a perpetual basis. This means that the process of cleansing and exclusion is what constitutes the moral community.

The people in Surrey Estate are well aware that through instituting and exercising non-state forms of sovereign power they are contravening state law. Irfaan says, "People say yes we were breaking the laws of the country. But what they [the ANC-government] were putting up here weren't laws. All they were putting up was corruption. And we are cleaning up the area" (interview with Irfaan). Thus, the production of a moral community, referring to a law above the laws of the country, have led to the introduction of new categories of citizenship and rights of belonging that defer the problem of coloredness to the locus of evil— the ever-present, ever-threatening colored townships just across the road.

POSTCOLONIAL CITIZENSHIP IN THE EMPIRE

Citizenship and Empire

Barry Hindess

"Empire is materializing before our very eyes" (Hardt and Negri 2000, xi). The opening line of Michael Hardt and Antonio Negri's *Empire*, like the title itself, points to a glaring asymmetry in the contemporary global order, an asymmetry that "globalization," the more usual term for the condition they address, fails to properly apprehend. Empire, in their view, is the emerging global form of sovereignty. It "establishes no territorial center of power and does not rely on fixed boundaries or barriers. It is a *decentered* and *deterritorializing* apparatus of rule that progressively incorporates the entire global realm within its open, expanding frontiers." In this respect, empire is quite unlike the earlier European imperialism, which rested on the territorial boundaries "defined by the modern system of nation-states" (xii).

Like Edward Said's *Orientalism*, *Empire* seems likely to both establish the importance of the fundamental issues which it aims to address and, having done so, to frustrate those who would explore these issues further.[1] The sources of this frustration are many and various, as one might expect of such a deliberately provocative work, but the two I wish to address in this paper have already been flagged in my opening paragraph: the assertion, on the one hand, that Empire does not rely on territorial boundaries and the insistence, on the other, that there is a radical discontinuity between our present condition and the earlier imperial world order. There is something to be said for both propositions, of course, and Hardt and Negri are able to cite striking empirical examples in their support. My point is not that these propositions are

A much earlier version of this essay was presented at the "Sovereign Bodies: Citizenship, Community and the State in the Post-Colonial World" Workshop, Sandbjerg Manor, Denmark, December 2000. This version draws heavily on Hindess (2002). It has been written as part of a collaborative project (with Bruce Buchan and Christine Helliwell) supported by the Australian Research Council. I am grateful to many individuals for their criticism and advice, most especially to the editors of this volume and to Brett Bowden, Bruce Buchan, Christine Helliwell, Engin Isin, Jane Kelsey, Robyn Lui, and Sanjay Seth.

[1] I draw the parallel between *Orientalism* and *Empire* from Rob Walker's (2002, p. 345) contribution to a discussion of *Empire* in *Millennium*, 31(2). See also contributions by Barkawi and Laffey, and Callinicos and Shaw.

entirely false but, rather, that they are one-sided: territorial boundaries may have been displaced in some respects but they nevertheless remain at the heart of the emerging global order and, although there is an obvious and fundamental difference between the direct subordination of imperial rule and self-governing independence, there is an equally fundamental continuity between the two conditions.

The character of postcolonial citizenship exemplifies both of these claims. First, citizenship plays a central part in the government of modern populations, whether as a matter of internal relations between a state and its citizens and between the citizens themselves, or as a marker of difference, advising various state and nonstate agencies of the particular state to which an individual belongs. In both respects, the workings of citizenship are predicated on the maintenance of territorial boundaries between states. My second claim is more complex. Many critics of the contemporary international order have argued that the work of the World Bank, IMF, and the major international development agencies really amounts to a colonization or recolonization of much of the non-Western world (e.g., Bello 1994). The fundamental perception here is one that would be difficult to dispute but it goes against Empire's equally compelling perception of radical discontinuity. My claim is that both perceptions are correct, and thus that it would be misleading to rely on either of them alone. The perception that we are in an era of colonization and recolonization misses precisely what is most distinctive about the promotion of citizenship and representative government by international development agencies and financial institutions. Indeed, where the liberal government of non-Western populations was once predicated on a denial of citizenship, contemporary liberal attempts to govern the people of the non-Western world are increasingly channeled through the institution of citizenship itself. The perception of radical discontinuity, by contrast, misses the liberalism of both governmental regimes. If "empire" is, with some qualifications, a good way to characterize the emerging global regime, then "liberal world order" is another. The two descriptions have more in common than it might seem (Ikenberry 1999).

To establish these points I begin by noting that the view of citizenship as a matter of internal relations within a state is seriously incomplete. Citizenship should also be seen as part of a supranational governmental regime in which the system of states, international agencies and multinational corporations all play a fundamental role. This leads, first, to a brief history of the modern system of states and, second, to an account of liberalism as a project of government that focuses not just on the populations of particular states but also on states themselves and the larger population which they collectively encompass. I turn, finally, to an examination of how the move from imperial subjection to independent statehood has impacted on this liberal project. This last discussion brings us to the condition of citizenship in the contemporary world order.

CITIZENSHIP IN THE SYSTEM OF STATES

Although citizenship is most commonly regarded as a matter of relations between individuals and the state to which they belong—that is, of relations that are internal to the state in question[2]—it is also one of the markers used by states in their attempts to regulate the movement of people across borders. These two aspects of citizenship are usually treated separately but there is much to be said for bringing them together. To do so, in fact, is to highlight the role of citizenship in a supranational regime of population management that operates first, by dividing humanity into discrete subpopulations, each consisting of the citizens of some particular state, and, second, by assigning to each state both the right and the obligation to manage its own internal affairs, including, of course, the regulation of entry and exit (Hindess 2000a, 2001a). If to govern is, as Michel Foucault suggests, "to structure the possible field of action of others" (2001, 341), then the organization of citizenship within the international system of states should itself be seen as an apparatus of government.

Perhaps the most disturbing effect of the first element of this regime, the division of humanity into the populations of particular states, is that each state is expected to look after its own citizens. The other side of this expectation is the view that states should be correspondingly less concerned about the condition of those who belong to other states or to no state at all. Thus, while the U.N. Declaration of Human Rights claims to be "universal" in scope, it nevertheless places responsibility for the realization of the rights it proclaims on the state to which the individuals in question belong, leaving other states with only limited responsibilities in this respect. As for this regime's second element, concerning each state's management of its own internal affairs, it is clear that states which fail to satisfy their obligations in this respect are likely to be seen as posing a threat to other states and therefore as legitimate objects of intervention by the international community.

To understand the role of citizenship within this regime, it is useful to

[2] This perspective is nicely captured in Aristotle's definition: "He who has the power to take part in the deliberative or judicial administration of any state is said by us to be a citizen of the state; and, speaking generally, a state is a body of citizens sufficing for the purposes of life" (Aristotle 1988, 1275b, 19–22).

begin with a brief history of the modern states system. There have been many systems of states—for example, in the Americas, China, Europe, South Asia, the Malay Archipelago, and Western classical antiquity—but the system dominated by the modern West is the first to have become truly global in scope. This system has its origins in seventeenth-century European attempts to bring destructive religious conflict under some kind of control. In the history of international relations, the 1648 Treaty of Westphalia and other agreements which brought the Thirty Years' War to an end are conventionally taken to mark the emergence of a new European order of independent sovereign states. These agreements sought to contain the political problems resulting from the existence of powerful religious differences between Catholics, Lutherans, and Calvinists by granting territorial rulers supreme political authority within their domains, leaving it to rulers and their subjects to reach some accommodation in matters of religion. The principle of noninterference in the internal affairs of a sovereign state, which aimed to prevent states from intervening in the religious affairs of other participating states, played a fundamental part in this regime of pacification. Political arrangements designed to pacify warring populations effectively transformed the condition of the Western part of Europe: populations that had been subject to a variety of overlapping and conflicting sources of authority were assigned to sovereign rulers who were themselves acknowledged as having the primary responsibility for the government of the populations within their territories.[3]

We shall see that its emergence within the system of states established by the Westphalian agreements has fundamental consequences for the role of citizenship in the world today. Before proceeding to that discussion, however, we should note the implications of the modern system of states for our understanding of contemporary states themselves. First, where the familiar image of the social contract presents the state as constituted internally, by real or imaginary agreements between its members, this focus on the system of states suggests that the sovereignty of a state is also a function of its recognition as a state by other members of the system (Weber 1995). Thus, government of the state, in the broad sense noted earlier, is not restricted to the activities of the state itself: it certainly takes place within states but it also appears in the interactions between them. The rights of states to manage their own affairs have always been heavily qualified (as rights commonly are) by a corresponding set of responsibilities to what is often called the "international community"—that is, to the overarching system of states to

<hr>

[3] There is an extensive literature on the emergence of the Westphalian system and its geopolitical effects. See, for example, Held (1995); Hirst (1998); Schmitt (1950); Spruyt (1994); Walker (1993).

which they belong. The existence of a system of states also provides conditions in which international systems of regulation could be further refined and developed.

If the sovereignty of a state requires that it be recognized by other states (and sometimes by agencies of other kinds) this suggests that the order secured within the more successful states depends in part on the order which prevails in the relations between states. It also suggests, of course, that much of the disorder within less successful states also may be a product of this latter order.[4] Thus, a second implication is that effective government within the member states of the Westphalian system is predicated on political conditions secured by the system itself— it depends, in other words, on conditions that operate above the level of the individual states themselves. The European system of states and the sovereignty which that system secured for participating states provided conditions which made possible the internal development of citizenship that Marshall (1950) so influentially—and so misleadingly— outlined in the British case. Following his pioneering discussion of English developments, sociologists have routinely described the history of modern citizenship as involving the emergence, in roughly this order, of three sets of rights: the *civil* right to liberty and equality before the law; the *political* right to vote and to participate in the political process; and the *social* right to participate fully in a way of life that is shared by the citizens as a whole. Recent commentators have disputed many aspects of Marshall's argument but their criticisms have rarely focused on the intrastate character of his analysis. They have been concerned, rather, with its anglocentrism (Mann 1987; Turner 1990), its evolutionism (Giddens 1982; Mann 1987), and its relatively undeveloped account of the state and of the internal political conditions required for the emergence and maintenance of citizenship (Barbalet 1988; Roche 1987; Turner 1986, 1990).[5]

Third, at least in its early stages, the Westphalian states system was specifically European, covering territories and populations in parts of Europe by means of treaties and understandings between participating states. It imposed few constraints on the conduct of these states towards those who inhabited territories, European or otherwise, not cov-

[4] During the Cold War, powerful states on both sides intervened to destabilize states within their opponent's sphere of influence. More generally, states tend to recognize those who hold effective power within a state as its legitimate government, however that power has been obtained or is currently exercised. Thomas Pogge (2003) points out that this itself can be a powerful source of internal disorder, securing conditions in which rulers with little popular support are able sell off state assets and enrich themselves at the state's expense.

[5] The impact of Marshall's analysis of citizenship is discussed in Bulmer and Rees (1996).

ered by these agreements and who were thought to possess no sovereign states of the European kind (Schmitt 1950, 1996).

Thus, whereas European states were consolidating their rule over their own populations—in part through the development of the civil and political rights of citizenship—several of them also were engaged in imperial adventures elsewhere. Perhaps the most striking result of these adventures was to bring a substantial portion of humanity into the remit of the modern system of states through direct imperial rule. Much of the remainder was brought into this system indirectly through the deployment by European states of a "standard of civilization" in their dealings with independent states elsewhere (Gong 1984). Elaborate systems of capitulations, which acknowledged the extraterritorial jurisdiction of Western states, were imposed on states that were judged not to meet this standard (Fidler 2000). Indirect domination was also exercised, of course, through "the imperialism of free trade" (Gallagher and Robinson 1953). This phrase derives from Gallagher and Robinson's controversial (Louis 1976) interpretation of nineteenth-century British policies, but it has an obvious relevance for us all today. To describe European imperialism simply as "an extension of the sovereignty of European nation-states beyond their own boundaries" (Hardt and Negri 2000, xii) is to miss the impact of the European imperial order on the peoples of, say, China, Thailand, and the Ottoman Empire who were not subjected to direct imperial rule by European powers.

The subordination of substantial non-European populations to rule by European states was clearly a central feature of European imperialism, but so, too, was the incorporation of those populations and the territories they inhabited into the European system of states. Most accounts of imperialism focuses on the first of these features—and Hardt and Negri's discussion is no exception. However, the second feature has been the more enduring, and it has played a central role in the development of the modern system of states. Direct or indirect imperial domination was the form in which the European system of states first became global in scope. The imperialism of Western states and the development of citizenship within them had the effect of dividing the world into distinct kinds of populations: the citizen populations of Western states; noncitizen populations governed by these states; and populations of states that were neither subject to direct rule nor recognized as full members of the states' system.

This process of incorporating non-European populations into the European system of states was followed, more or less rapidly, by the second stage in the globalisation of the European states system. The achievement of independence throughout much of the Americas in the first half of the nineteenth century and its achievement or imposition elsewhere around the middle of the twentieth, dismantled one aspect of imperial rule while leaving the other firmly in place: the state, as Michael Hardt and Antonio Negri put it, "is the poisoned gift of national liberation" (2000, 135). To be an independent state is not to be subject to the rule of another state, but it is, nevertheless, subject to the regulatory regimes that operate within the system of states. Thus, political independence in the modern sense both expanded the membership of the system of states and set in place a radically new way of bringing non-Western populations under the rule of that system (Seth 2000). As a result, these populations found themselves governed both by modern states of their own and by the overarching system of states within which their own states had been incorporated. The second, twentieth-century wave of independence marks the point at which citizenship became a universal human condition.

The citizenship that was attained through the transition from imperial rule to independent statehood emerged from a radically different trajectory than that traced by Marshall and other sociologists for modern Western states. I turn to the implications of this difference in a moment, but first it is necessary to consider aspects of the regulatory regime which operates in the recently expanded system of states. We can begin by noting that, as with other regimes of government that possess no controlling center—the workings of an established market or of civil society, for example—some members of the modern system of states are clearly more equal than others. Not only is the overarching system hierarchically structured, containing stronger and weaker states and more or less exclusive inner circles, but also many of the recently established states are highly dependent on outside assistance, having inherited poorly developed infrastructures and governmental practices designed to serve an inexpensive system of rule by outsiders. Moreover, like the modern states established in non-European territories that were never in fact colonized, they are recognized as members of the international system of states without, in most cases, being admitted to its more exclusive inner circles. As a result, they are subject to regulation by international financial agencies that are clearly dominated by Western concerns and, in particular, by an updated version of the standard of civilization noted earlier (Donnelly 1998). This modern "standard of civilization" requires states to demonstrate their fitness to participate in various international arrangements (OECD, GATT, and its successor, WTO, providing the most obvious examples) and it clearly informs the rhetoric of humanitarian intervention by the "international community" (e.g., Cooper 1996; Kaplan 2000).

There is little that is new in this last set of points, but they do provide an important background to our examination of liberalism as a regime of government developing within and operating over the modern states' system.

LIBERALISM AS A GOVERNMENTAL PROJECT

Standard academic accounts of liberalism usually present it as a normative political doctrine or ideology organized around a commitment to the protection of individual liberty, especially against the state—and here, too, Hardt and Negri's discussion is no exception. This view is not entirely false but, like the view of citizenship as a matter of internal relations within a state, it is certainly incomplete. Throughout the nineteenth and much of the twentieth centuries, many of those ruled by liberal states were subject peoples of European imperial possessions and it is clear that, for these peoples, liberal government was a kind of authoritarian rule—as it is now in the independent states of Central and South America[6] and in parts of Asia. This observation suggests one important respect in which standard accounts of liberalism have to be corrected. The liberal ideal may be for the state to rule over, and to rule through, the free activities of autonomous individuals but liberals have traditionally taken the view that substantial parts of humanity do not, as a matter of fact, possess the minimal capacities for autonomous action that would enable them to be governed in this way (Helliwell and Hindess 2002). That they have taken this view is a matter less of liberal hypocrisy, as some commentators have suggested (Guha 1997; Said 1992), than of liberal attempts to deal with a perceived reality that fails to satisfy the conditions required for the operation of their preferred form of liberal government.

Such apparent disjunctions between ideal and practical reality, in turn, suggested to liberal political reason both that the settings in which government takes place may be ranked in an hierarchical order and that many of these settings are in need of a corresponding project of reform. John Stuart Mill (1977) argued that, unlike the inhabitants of European states, the people of British India were not yet ready to govern themselves. It was therefore in their own interests for them to be governed by outsiders. The hierarchical order suggested by this perception is one in which some people, the more cultivated inhabitants of civilized states, are seen as being relatively close to the condition of individual autonomy while others are seen as being at a greater or lesser distance from that condition. The corresponding project of reform is that of the civilizing mission of government, a project of gradually im-

---

[6] See the discussion of Colombian liberalism in Rojas (2002).

proving subject populations. While the civilizing mission did not appear as a distinct budget item in imperial administration, it nevertheless served as a major organizing principle of imperial rule (see, for example, Conklin 1997). Together with closely related imperial practices of divide and rule, it generated systematic patterns of discrimination between populations and subpopulations within them on the basis of what seemed to be their existing level of civilization or "improvement."

Now, the shift noted earlier from direct imperial rule to independence left the liberal perception of a hierarchy of social arrangements more or less in place, but it radically transformed the conditions under which the corresponding liberal project of improvement could be pursued. However, before turning to the consequences of that change, we need to consider a second important respect in which standard accounts of liberalism must be corrected. I began this section by suggesting that liberalism is commonly understood as a normative political doctrine or ideology, but it also can be seen as a positive project of government—a project concerned not only with establishing normative criteria in terms of which the actions of states may be judged and sometimes found wanting, but also and, more importantly, with addressing the practical problems involved in governing states and their populations.[7]

Many observers have noted that the image of the market as an exemplary form of free interaction plays a fundamental role in liberal political thought, where it is seen as demonstrating how the activities of numerous individuals may be regulated and coordinated without direction from a single controlling centre. In this respect, the market is seen as a decentralized mechanism of government operating at two rather different levels. At the first and most immediate level, the perception is that individuals are governed, at least in part, by the reactions of others with whom they interact and that, at least among more civilized peoples, their interactions will normally take a peaceful form— the market itself providing the most obvious example. This view suggests that, although the promotion of suitable forms of free interaction may be an effective way of dealing with the government of civilized populations, it is likely to be less successful in other cases. Second, over the longer term, interaction with others is thought to influence the internal standards that individuals use to regulate their own behavior— by affecting, for example, their sense of good and bad conduct, of what

[7] The productive character of liberalism as a project of government operating within states has been of particular concern to the "governmentality" school of social analysis, and its work has resulted in many valuable explorations of the diverse ways in which individual choice and self-regulation have been deployed as instruments of liberal government. See, for example, Burchell et al. (1991); Barry et al. (1996); Dean and Hindess (1998); Dean (1999); Rose (1999).

is acceptable or unacceptable in particular contexts, and so on. At this level, market interaction itself is seen as a powerful instrument of civilization, inculcating such virtues as prudence, diligence, punctuality, self-control, and so on (Hirschman 1977; Holmes 1995). This view suggests that, if only suitable forms of property can be set securely in place and nonmarket forms of economic activity reduced to a minimum, then market interaction itself may function as a means of improving the character of less civilized peoples. In this case, authoritarian state intervention to reform property relations and impose conditions that would enable widespread market interaction to take off, may be seen as a liberal move toward a situation in which individuals could in fact be governed through their free interactions.

The ideal image of the market, in effect, provides liberal political reason with a model of the governmental uses of freedom. In this spirit, for example, Foucault observes that the market plays "the role of a 'test,' a locus of privileged experience where one can identify the effects of excessive governmentality" (Foucault 1997, 76). Foucault's own account of liberalism and the governmentality accounts which have followed his lead have focused on the rationality of the government of the state—that is, on the government of state agencies and of the population and territory over which the state claims authority—and they have accordingly pitched their analysis of the governmental usage of markets at this level. However, as other commentators have argued, this liberal perception of the governmental utility of markets has been seen as relating as much to the conduct of states (and other organizations) as to the conduct of human individuals (Burchell and Linklater 1996; Howard 1978). International trade in goods and services, in other words, has been seen by liberals not only as a means of promoting the wealth of nations but also, and perhaps more important, as a means of regulating the conduct of states. The same applies, of course, to trade in financial instruments. It is well known that the freedom of action of national governments is often severely constrained by international financial markets but it is not sufficiently recognized that these markets have been constructed, as a matter of deliberate policy, by a number of powerful states and supranational agencies (Helleiner 1994).

This last point brings us back to my earlier observation that liberalism should be seen as a governmental project that developed initially within the conditions provided by the European system of states. If the Westphalian system addressed the problem of pacifying warring populations by assigning those populations to the exclusive rule of discrete sovereign states, this did not entirely resolve and in some respects it exacerbated, the related problem of pacifying states and their rulers. Indeed, the problem of civilizing states was a major concern of liberal political thought in the eighteenth century and it has since remained a central theme in liberal discussions of international order. It may, in fact, be misleading to follow mainstream political theory in regarding liberalism as concerned primarily with governing the particular populations of individual states and thus to treat the liberal discussion of international order, if its presence is acknowledged at all, as a derivative, secondary development. John MacMillan (1998), for example, argues that early liberal thinkers saw absolutist and feudal relations within states and the Westphalian system of relations between states as mutually supportive components of an overarching illiberal order, with the result that their critiques tended to focus on both the domestic and the international aspects of this overarching order. Thus, considered as a positive project of government, liberalism should rather be seen as concerned with the problem of governing the larger human population. It addresses this problem at two levels: first, by incorporating humanity within the modern system of states, as the regimes of modern imperialism and post-colonial independence have each done in their own way; and, second, by using market interactions and other devices to civilize and to regulate the conduct both of states themselves and of those within the particular populations under their authority.

THE CONDITION OF POSTCOLONIAL CITIZENSHIP

How does this sketch of the liberal project of government relate to the contemporary condition of citizenship? I have suggested that, in order to understand the character of citizenship in the modern world, it is necessary to locate it as part of a supranational governmental regime in which the international system of states plays a fundamental role. I went on to argue that the sovereignty of states should be seen as an artifact of the system of states to which they belong and that it is therefore misleading to regard states as constituted essentially on the basis of formal or informal agreements among their citizens. There are important structural or systemic limitations on the role of citizens in the government of contemporary states, however internally democratic they might appear to be.

This point gives a very different twist to the Aristotelian view of the citizen as both ruler and ruled. Not only are there now, as there always have been, important respects in which citizens are not the rulers of the state to which they belong but, to the extent that they are, this serves to reinforce their subordination to agencies and forces over which they have little real control. There are many other reasons for this condition too, of course. Indeed, the institutions of representative government—which provide the predominant modern understanding of democracy—

are clearly designed to ensure that citizens play a strictly circumscribed role in the government of the state to which they belong (Hindess 2000b). This is the substantive empirical foundation of the "realist" theory of democracy, one of the most influential doctrines in twentieth-century political science.[8] Modern democracies, realism tells us, are governed by a combination of elected officials and professional state bureaucracies, and the people decide who is elected to rule them, not the substantive policies which their government is to pursue. The significance of this view for the liberal project of government lies in its suggestion that modern democracy brings together three different sources of political legitimacy:

- the charismatic element of leadership;
- participation in the appointment of elected officials that, as with other forms of participation, promotes among participants a sense of responsibility for the decisions that result, even if their influence on those decisions is actually very small;
- and the rationality of professional bureaucracy that ensures that state agencies are administered by suitably qualified personnel and their practices are governed by the relevant expertise.

The anticipated effects of this combination are nicely captured in Talcott Parsons's account of the evolutionary advantage, as he saw it, of democracy over other forms of government. What is most distinctive about democracy, he argues, is not so much the general sense of legitimacy that it promotes, as this feature can also be found in a number of other political regimes. Rather, it is that democracy alone is most able to "mediate consensus in [the exercise of power] by particular persons and groups, and in the formation of particular binding policy decisions" (1967, 516).

Democracy, on this view, secures a degree of legitimacy for the practical activities of the state and its various agencies which other regimes are simply unable to match. It is this perception that particularly appeals to the development agencies and financial institutions involved in promoting "good governance" in the developing world—as it does, of course, to those engaged in the government of Western states themselves. In both cases, it seems, democracy is the most effective means of ensuring that the people will "own,"[9] or at least that they not actively

[8] The classic statement is Schumpeter (1976). Sartori (1987) presents a forceful recent statement of the realist position.

[9] The language of "ownership" now plays an important part in development discourse. Joseph Stiglitz, then vice president of the World Bank described the bank's proposed Comprehensive Development Framework as involving "a new set of relationships, not only between the Bank and the country, but within the country itself. . . . Central is the notion that the country (*not just the government*) must be in the driver's seat" (Stiglitz 1999, pp. 22–23—emphasis added; see also Wolfensohn 1999).

resist, the package of political and economic reforms which their governments are required to implement.

The fact that the behavior of contemporary states is subject to significant external constraints is not in itself a cause for concern—quite the contrary, in fact. What should concern us, rather, is the grossly unequal character of the international order from which these constraints derive. All contemporary states, even the most powerful, are subject to the general supervisory mechanisms of the enlarged system of states—to a variety of international conventions, treaties and a developing framework of international law on the one hand and the "civilizing" effects of international trade on the other. But a clear majority of the new states that emerged from the twentieth-century end of empire, along with many non-Western states that had never been colonized, also found themselves subject to supervisory mechanisms of a different kind: those of the more specific international regime of development. Some of these states (with more than a little help from their friends) have played the development game with a notable degree of success, whereas others have tried to play by radically different rules, usually with unhappy results, but most have fallen somewhere between these extremes.

The condition of citizenship in postcolonial states is also seriously constrained by the governmental institutions and practices inherited from the colonial period, most of which were predicated on a view of the subject population as considerably less civilized than their rulers. In practice, of course, some such view of the subject population is held by the political/administrative class in all modern states but it was more pronounced, and far more freely expressed, in the case of populations subject to modern imperial rule. Colonial rule by Western states involved a clear distinction between citizens and subjects and a systematic development of what eventually became known, in the case of Britain's African possessions, as indirect rule: that is, of a practice of government which worked through institutions that relied on what were thought to be indigenous customs and structures of authority.[10] Precisely because they were, at least in intention, based on indigenous practices, the detailed character of these ersatz governmental arrangements varied from one population to another. But their overall effect was to institutionalize a differentiated pattern of relations between the colonial state and sections of the subject population which promoted localized authoritarian rule—a regime that Mamdani (1996) aptly describes as "decentralized despotism"—and reinforced, or even created, divisions between them

[10] The most influential British statement of the case for indirect rule is Lugard (1923). However, the practice of working through what were believed to be indigenous institutions was a pervasive feature of Western imperial administration (Malinowski 1929; Mamdani 1996).

(Appadurai 1993). Thus, Mamdani argues, while independence displaces the colonial distinction between citizen and subject, the laws and administrative practices inherited from the period of indirect rule continue to subvert many of the civil and political rights of citizenship.

I noted earlier that the attainment of citizenship through political independence involves a radically different trajectory than the successive development of civil, political, and social rights traced by T. H. Marshall (1950) and other sociologists for contemporary Western states. One implication of this difference has just been noted. Another, relating to social rights in particular, concerns the argument of Marshall and many social policy analysts that the role of the state's social policy was to ensure that citizens were not in fact excluded from participation in the life of their society by reason of poverty, ill-health or lack of education. While this sociological literature focuses on the prosperous (and predominantly Western) states of the OECD, it is worth noting here since its insistence on the role of the state in securing the social rights of citizenship serves to mark another significant difference between citizenship in the West and citizenship elsewhere. These social rights are comparatively well-developed in most Western states, although they are now under considerable neo-liberal pressure, but in the majority of other states they have barely had a chance to develop. Thirdly, the imperial legacy of communal division suggests that the challenge to citizenship posed by ethnic, linguistic, religious, and other group memberships within the state or cutting across its boundaries, should not be seen simply as a product of late twentieth century developments. On the contrary, there is an important sense in which this challenge has been a condition of postcolonial states from the beginnings of citizenship itself.

An imperial legacy of a different kind concerns the liberal perception, noted earlier, of a hierarchy of social conditions and of a corresponding need for a civilizing mission to bring about the improvement of the less advanced. While many of its practices have been adapted by postcolonial successor states, this is a mission that can no longer be pursued in its familiar imperial guise. Instead, the liberal project of improvement is now pursued by two very different parties, with both overlapping and competing visions of what it might involve. It is pursued first, as it was of course in the colonial period, by significant minorities in the ex-imperial domains themselves, many of whom are also concerned to reaffirm (and thus to reinvent) elements of their own cultural heritage.[11]

[11] The formation of such liberal minorities was one of the intended effects of imperial rule but, as Bhabha (1994) observes, the mimicry that it involves invariably cuts both ways: although it serves the purposes of the colonial power in some respects, it works against them in others. The affirmation of their own tradition—of Asian values, for example—by such minorities is also a kind of mimicry, and one that can be no less ambiguous in its effects.

Like Western colonial officials before them, members of such liberal minorities can be expected to combine a civilized distaste for the dirty work of governing their less advanced compatriots with a reluctant acknowledgment of its necessity. Yet, because they also have taken over governmental functions that would once have been performed by officers of the imperial state, they do so under radically different circumstances. On the one hand, because of their local connections, the rulers and public officials of the successor states tend to be seen, and perhaps to see each other, as more vulnerable to corruption even than Western officials had been during the colonial period.[12] On the other, the positive affirmation of non-Western values provides them with a local, culturally specific variant of the patronizing liberal view that the people of these domains cannot yet be trusted to govern themselves.

The liberal project of improvement is also pursued, rather more remotely, by Western states themselves working through a more distant set of indirect means. They operate, in effect, through national and international aid programs that assist, advise, and constrain the conduct of postcolonial states, through international financial institutions and also, of course, through that fundamental liberal instrument of civilization, the market—including the internal markets of multinational corporations. In fact, the use of markets in regulating the conduct of states and in the conduct of government within them has become increasingly prominent as we move further away from the decolonization of the mid-twentieth century. In liberal eyes, as noted earlier, the market appears to perform a variety of desirable functions: not only does it promote prosperity overall, but also it regulates the conduct of states and fosters civilized attitudes and patterns of conduct among their rulers and inhabitants.

Where it could once rely on the decentralized despotism of indirect rule over the subjects of Western imperial possessions, liberal political reason now has no alternative but to treat those who it sees as most in need of improvement as if they were in fact autonomous agents. The old imperial divisions between citizens, subjects and non-citizen others has been displaced by the postimperial globalization of citizenship, while indirect rule within imperial possessions has been superceded by an even less direct form of decentralized rule, in which the inhabitants of postcolonial successor states are governed through sovereign states of their own. This is not to suggest that this new form of indirect rule is likely to be any more successful than its imperial predecessors in imposing its will on target populations. My point, rather, is that this new form of indirect rule provides a global political context in which to locate the activities of international development agencies and financial

---

[12] Rose-Ackerman (1999) offers a particularly clear example of this perspective.

institutions in promoting "good governance," a practice that is usually associated with a package of political and economic reforms, including the implementation of democracy and basic human rights. Good governance within states is now seen as involving the civil and political rights of citizenship—at least in the sense that the governments of states are expected to be minimally responsive to the wishes of their citizens. I noted earlier that the citizens in turn are expected to own, or at least to go along with, the policies of their government. But good governance is also seen as ensuring that the freedom of action of these governments, and therefore the ability of their citizens to determine what those actions will be, is severely constrained by both internal and international markets.

These last points bring us, finally, to the issues concerning the characterization of the contemporary global order with which I began. I have argued that the globalization of citizenship through the achievement or imposition of independence marked a radical break with the order of European imperialism, and that citizenship now serves as a fundamental instrument both of the government of populations within states and of the regulation of movement between them. In this respect, far from promoting a deterritorialized apparatus of rule, as Hardt and Negri suggest, the emerging global order in fact relies upon the capacities of territorial states to govern their own populations. The promotion of democracy, good governance, and human rights by international development agencies and financial institutions is designed to further reinforce these capacities.

Nevertheless, for all the striking differences between the order of European imperialism and our contemporary global order, there is an equally striking continuity between them. It resides in the liberal project of managing the larger human population first, by incorporating it within the modern system of states and secondly, by using market interactions and other devices to regulate the conduct of states and the populations within them. The governmental project so clearly expressed in the European imperialism of the nineteenth and twentieth centuries appears again in what Hardt and Negri call "Empire": they are the two fundamental forms of liberal world order.

Splintering Cosmopolitanism: Asian Immigrants and Zones of Autonomy in the American West

Aihwa Ong

INTRODUCTION

Every fall, wealthy Chinese resident-aliens of Vancouver leave for Hong Kong, like Canadian geese departing for warmer waters. Even more frequently, Taiwanese engineers shuttle across the Pacific, transferring knowledge, expertise and capital from the Silicon Valley to science parks in Taiwan. Yet other flows include thousands of Indian technomigrants who are contracted to work in Silicon Valley firms. Return flows of U.S.-trained Indian engineers set up high tech businesses in Bangalore and Hyderabad. Meanwhile, less well-heeled migrants—Chinese waiters, Hispanic janitors, and Southeast Asian electronic workers—supply the open labor markets that feed the feverish high tech centers driving the American West. What can these mobile Asian figures tell us about citizenship, its cosmopolitan and local dimensions? What are the political implications of such networks and circulations for America's corporate empire, and the diverse zones of neoliberal governance linked to postcolonial immigration?

Neoliberalism

I think it is useful to consider "liberalism" less as a philosophy than as the rationalization of government, as embodied in an array of programs and practices, that have varied effects on the constitution of citizen-subjects and the spaces that they inhabit (Foucault, 2000, 201–22). The philosophical view of liberalism suggests hostility to or the reduction of regulation. But on the contrary, liberal rationality has fostered conditions for the emergence of an array of regulatory techniques that foster liberal market conditions and the self-governing of free modern subjects. Following Foucault, Nikolas Rose argues that *neoliberalism* is best considered as a certain rationality of government that involves "the various deployments of the notion of entrepreneurship" (1999, 27). In the postwelfare era, government increasingly shaped by a neoliberal logic promotes enterprise and entrepreneurial conduct in all areas including economic regulations, education, professional activities, immigration policies, residential zoning, and so on. As the political rationality embraces neoliberal calculations, one can expect dramatic effects on the constitution of citizen-subjects and the governing of sovereign spaces. For instance, neoliberal calculations generalizing "'the enterprise form' to all kinds of conduct" (Burchell 1996, 29) not only come to privilege calculative, self-enterprising subjects regardless of citizenship, but also policies that free up borders, as evidenced by a variety of regulations that ease capital flows, business immigration and labor circulations. Such technologies of governing create circulations of entrepreneurial subjects and the emergence of technological fields that challenge older concepts of the sovereign subject and national sovereignty. Indeed, neoliberal calculations by governments and individuals alike have contributed to the reconfiguring of sovereignty in territory and in bodies. The interactions of regulations, technologies, and foreign subjects, I suggest, do not respect given national borders; these interrelations redirect flows of migrant bodies and reterritorialize sovereignty in new zones of governance.

Global Space or Global Assemblage?

In considering how markets and migrations have affected national sovereignty and citizenship, social theorists have identified two kinds of globalizing trends: the rise of city-networks and of managerial spaces of flows. Saskia Sassen (1991) argues that global cities, as sites of international financial activity and specialized services are the nodes in a "new geography of centrality." Manuel Castells maintains that the emerging "space(s) of flows" have enabled dominant managerial and entrepreneurial elites to create segregating spaces spanning cities and continents, giving rise to a network society (Castells 1999, 416). Scholars combining the insights of Sassen and Castells have suggested that we think of "the world city network" as the new metageography (Taylor 2000). But this focus on city-networks and managerial flows has not taken into account the variety of sites shaped by the contingent interactions among different migrant streams—investor, expertise, and labor. Furthermore, we do not know how different categories of migrant subjects are regulated at the site of articulation, and how territorialization make spaces governable in different ways. Indeed, this inattention to the specific regulatory politics of embedded governance is reflected in assertions that the spatial logic of flows in the new economy dominates "the space of places" (Castells 1999, 416).

My analytical starting point is not the logic of space, but rather the

Deleuzian notion of the assemblage, as a contingent and loosely linked set of technology, population, territory, discourse, and so on (Deleuze and Guattari, 1987, 504–05). Elsewhere, Stephen J. Collier and I use the term "global assemblage" to identify the problem-space constituted by "an ensemble of heterogeneous elements in contingent and provisional interrelationships.[1] The "global" refers not primarily to space (although the resulting field of interaction tends to be transnational), but to the intersections and interactions that have a "global" quality. Particular global assemblages of technical, political, social and ethical relationships extract and give intelligibility to new spaces. For example, global assemblages of high tech firms, venture capital, and knowledge workers can be found in different contexts, and are not simply predetermined by given geography. Particular articulation of diverse elements (re)territorialize new material, social, and discursive relationships, investing emergent sites with globality, and not the other way around. Thus, the assemblage of technology, politics, and elite migrants territorialize and give global form to technocitadels in the Silicon Valley. Other alignments of technology, expertise and capital shape science parks in Europe and Asia, often on the periphery of big cities, and centered on small towns, universities, and suburbs. Silicon Valley may be ground zero of what Ulrich Beck (1994) calls "reflexive modernization," a second modernization in which the old structures are superseded, and the new ones are highly provisional, risky, and unpredictable.[2] As I will argue below, the contingent alignment of neoliberal policies, flexible Asian entrepreneurs, and networks have created zones of governance in the American West.

My work in Southeast Asia informs this perspectivist view of instability in citizenship and sovereignty resulting from new alignments among government, capital, and ideal citizen-subjects. Neoliberal calculations invest in particular kinds of subjects and mobilize them in relation to capital accumulation. Flexible strategies of governing increasingly align social rights with market calculations, and coordinate the regulation of populations in relation to zones of "graduated sovereignty" (Ong 2000). Citizenship is not conceptualized as simply a legal relationship between citizens and government, but as the effect of flexible strategies of governing that unevenly invests in different kinds of

[1] For a discussion of the concept of "global assemblages" of technology, politics, and ethics as a problem space that is potentially independent of a nation, society, or culture, see Collier and Ong (2004).

[2] There is a single ethnographic study of the effects of the upheavals wrought by Silicon Valley culture on family forms and gender relations (Stacey 1990). Other aspects of the societal transformation represented by the open-ended network industrial system have not been seriously examined.

bodies, privileging rational, market-driven subjects over others. Flexible citizenship refers to the transnational practices of self-governing, managerial migrants who seek to circumvent as well as capitalize on different contexts of sovereignty (Ong 1999). More recently, I have explored the lines of immigrant flows and networks that etch "latitudes of citizenship" linking North America and Asia (Ong 2003; 2004a). This essay will focus on how layers of Asian immigrants shape the emergent landscapes of variegated governance in the Silicon Valley.[3]

I will first describe how administrative practice, the high tech industry, and migratory regimes have assembled an array of mobile Asian bodies—astronauts, body-shoppers, technomigrants, and sweated labor—in the American West. Second, I note that neoliberal regimes promote investment flows and business talents, while penalizing and controlling low-skilled and illegal migrants. Third, the varied regulation of migrant subjects, and the zones of governance that they inhabit—ethnic enclaves and communities of security—contribute to the fragmentation of sovereignty in the American West. Splintering cosmopolitanism is the outcome of intensified competition for entitlement among migrants, long-term residents, and workers, and transforms people's experience of citizenship.

Mobile Bodies, Flexible Practices

Zygmont Bauman (1998) reminds us, there is a polarization between those free to move and those forced to move, that is, between tourists and vagabonds, or travelers and refugees.[4] Such a "global hierarchy of mobility" is part of a worldwide and local redistribution of privileges and deprivations; a restratification of humanity (1998, 70). In other words, whereas a huge portion of the world appears to be on the move, some migrants can take advantage of flexible citizenship more than others, and different circuits of migration are differently encouraged, managed, and controlled. This situation of differently regulated mobile bodies and flexible subjects is striking in the American West, as a mix of immigrant policies, high tech growth and demand for foreign expertise and labor have gathered a variety of Asian subjects in strategic sites from Canada to California.

[3] A related concept of "variegated sovereignty" in Greater China, is explored in Ong (2004a).

[4] Bauman seems to locate the tension between the mobile and the localized outside this hierarchy of mobility. For ethnographic renderings of this other dimension of polarity and power imbalance among ethnic Chinese migrants and their families, see Ong and Nonini (1995).

Asian images of the good life in North America have shaped the aspirations of more and more people who are convinced that their destinies must unfold in the transnational conditions of possibility. After decades of rejecting and discouraging migrants from Asia, North America since the 1980s has sought to capitalize on the growing middle classes in the Asia-Pacific region. The growth of trade with Asia, and the demands of a new knowledge economy have stimulated Canada and the United States governments to actively attract Pacific Rim investors and professionals. The United States, Canada and Australia have introduced new visa categories in order to re-regulate the influx of people, increasingly from Asian countries. Such immigrant instruments are directed at attracting "Pacific rim capital" and professional talent. But while Asian managerial and professional elites can arrive with legal papers, many poor and unskilled rural folk who cannot qualify for the same, are not dissuaded from taking more arduous and risky routes. In spaces newly configured by the influx of diverse migrant populations, what balance can be struck between the rational goals of the market and cosmopolitan privileges of business migrants, on the one hand, and the substantive needs of laboring populations, on the other? I will focus on three kinds of interactions between Asian managerial immigrants and low-skilled or indentured laborers who have been assembled in the affluent and high tech sites on the West Coast.

Good and Bad Quality Arrivals

On a per capital basis, Canada receives more immigrants than any other country in the world. In the early 1980s, the Canadian Business Immigration Program sought to attract business migrants from Hong Kong and Taiwan, specifying categories such as "self-employed," "entrepreneurial," and "investor." Most of the flows of Asian capital and business migrants have been to Vancouver, where the state government has established a minimum of C$150,000 for entrepreneurial migrant businesses (which are expected to employ some workers), whereas investor migrants must invest at least C$350,000 in a business in British Columbia (Business Immigration Office, 1998). During the 1980s and 1990s, Hong Kong Chinese bought over two billion worth of real estate in Vancouver, and effectively transformed a sleepy British port into a Pacific Rim megalopolis, complete with Chinese Macmansions (Mitchell 1997). The city of almost two million is one third Asian, with ethnic Chinese making up 20 percent of the total. A joke about the city's Pacific Rim character goes like this: The Japanese want to buy Vancouver, but the Chinese won't sell it." The accelerating family and business networks linking both Vancouver and Hong Kong are producing a new globalized space in which Vancouver is more linked to Asia-Pacific sites, than it is to British Columbia or to other parts of the Canadian nation.

The use of the visa as an instrument to admit Asia business people and students has worked to keep out the poor and the unskilled. But Canadian laws has a loophole for the uninvited, in the generous programs for granting asylum status to refugees, and in the provision of generous welfare services to the poor. Thus thousands of unskilled Chinese migrants have managed to enter the country without visas. It is estimated that each year, about five thousand people flying into Canada tear up their papers and seek asylum. Others take a less direct route. In April 1999, two boatload of undocumented Chinese from Fujian were deposited near Vancouver. When apprehended by coast guards, these migrants pleaded refugee status (citing China's one-child policy or religious persecution, as many Fujianese are Christian) and sought asylum. More recent arrivals have been equally dramatic. Some Chinese migrants from the same province paid U.S.$30,000 to $50,000 to be smuggled in container ships—called "floating coffins," because some do not survive the trip. In January this year, another floating coffin containing eighteen survivors docked in Seattle. There is strong cross-border traffic with Vancouver, and the refugees· probably hope to escape into Vancouver since stowaways arriving in the United States are more likely to be deported.[5] Altogether, in the final two years of the last century, more than two hundred people have been caught while being smuggled into container ships bound for Canadian and U.S. ports.[6] Other illegal migrants who manage to escape detention slip underground, bound for indentured servitude to pay off their debts to their "snakeheads" or smuggling syndicates.

The waves of illegal Chinese migrants arriving in Vancouver introduce an unwelcome specter, an unexpected status risk for the jet-setting business migrants. For the affluent Hong Kongers, who had helped develop the former world trade fair site into a center of commercial and residential skyscrapers, their image as the new entrepreneurs of Canada is being undermined by impoverished Chinese migrants, many of whom do not come from the same place in Asia, and represent the backwardness that the former wish to be disassociated from. This tension between legal and illegal migrants, and welcome business investors and unwelcome illegal laborers, fans fears of an anti-Chinese

[5] Stowaways must be able to establish well-grounded fears of persecution if returned to their home country. In January 2000, the United States deported some 250 stowaways back to China. See the *New York Times*, "Deadly Choice of Stowaways: Ship Containers," January 12, 2000.

[6] *San Francisco Chronicle*, "Three Weeks in a Floating Coffin," January 12, 2000.

backlash. In a public debate, a Chinese Canadian activist remarked: "These are working class, peasant farmers. We have well-heeled Hong Kong Chinese, Canadian-Chinese and Taiwan Chinese looking down their noses at them. They feel these people water down their community."[7] A lawyer from Taiwan notes that the government has raised the cash amount required for business immigrants to obtain a visa. He continued: "There is a feeling we are kicking out the business people and taking in the boat people. The immigration system is not smart. We are pushing out the good quality people who can help Canada—and we are taking in the freeloaders." Although Hong Kong business elites have taken seminars on British Colombian social and esthetic mores regarding neighborliness and multiculturalism, and abided by the regulation of commercial and property markets (Mitchell 1997; Mitchell and Olds 2000), they feel that the illegal Chinese newcomers must submit to the regulation of the welfare state. Thus the clash between the two sets of governing rationalities—the neoliberal regime that prizes business opportunity and talent, on the one hand, and the liberal democratic values of human rights, on the other—highlight the new instability in Canadian notions of deserving citizenship.

The insistence that "good quality" ethnic Chinese should properly represent Canadian citizenship is somewhat undercut by their long absences for much of the winter. Hong Kongers remigrate to Asia in the fall, emptying out the apartment towers lining the Vancouver shoreline. Curtains uniformly drawn across hundreds of apartment windows present a blind visage to the harborscape. Such "resident expatriates" have come to symbolize the new cosmopolitan citizenship fueled by globalizing processes, but one that is mediated by ethnicity and lifestyle. Thus while citizenship has always been based on legal status and property-ownership, today the element of hypermobile cosmopolitanism has gained as much currency. Citizenship as embodied by this business elite has become not a relationship to the nation-state, but a relationship to oneself, a self-project on the global stage. As possessors of economic, social, and cultural capital, there is a new fusion between ethnicity and class which qualifies them as more worthy Canadian subjects than poor coethnics. The outcome seems to be a kind of reverse Hongkongization, a Chinese-Anglo cosmopolitanism that is a reimagining and recreation of Hong Kong through trans-Pacific entrepreneurial dynamism, but dragged down a bit by the undertow of illegal entries so reminiscent of colonial days on both sides of the Pacific.

[7] The following account of conflicts among different categories of Chinese immigrants is drawn from James Brooke, "Vancouver is Astir over Chinese Abuse of Immigrant Law," *New York Times*, Aug. 29, 1999, A6.

Chinese Astronauts

Whereas British Columbia is rebounding through the realignment of administrative practices, investor capital and business migrants, the Silicon Valley is a slice of high-tech globalization that is experimenting, at a feverish rate, novel combinations of peoples, industries, and urban planning.

The high tech borderland is the opposite of the old-line industrial insularity (Saxenian 1996). It is a site of extremely liberal conditions for entrepreneurialism, networking, and flexibility, and thus a rich source of opportunities for new regulatory activities that distribute benefits unevenly. Astronauts and body-shoppers are two kinds of Asian migratory figures that converge in high-tech industries, and giving new meanings to citizenship in California.

The astronaut family phenomenon is a late modern set of transnational practices that—through the acquisition of multiple passports—both utilizes and subverts the rationalities of the politic-spatiality of governmentality. As I have argued elsewhere, Hong Kong émigrés have excelled at what started off as a need to balance the risks of communist rule with the opportunities to make money in China's booming economy, but then became a normalized part of trans-Pacific commuting. From the perspective of Hong Kong, they are astronauts shuttling between livelihood and family on opposite sides of the Pacific. From the view of North America, they are resident-expatriates who bring Pacific Rim investments, and sometimes the butt of resentment for American minorities worried about opportunities in the changing economy. While some have misread my image of astronauts as simply agents of market rationality, I consider them more as reflexive elite subjects for whom the rational management of security is an individual project, one that takes them across national spaces. Thus the family and business networks linking between Hong Kong and California allow the manipulation of immigration rules by a dexterity informed by the dialectic of risk and insurance.

The unintended effects of such flexible citizenship maneuvers include the proliferation of divided loyalties—to the family in California, to the company in China, to the ethnic nationality (localized Chineseness), and to the new locality (multicultural California). The dispersal of family, and the fragmenting of domestic and work activities across many sites have engendered a sense of cultural dislocation. Hong Kong women who live with children in fancy suburbs, acquiring educational capital and gaining time for residency rights, are often unable to identify with Chinese Americans who are descended from earlier migrations into California. Some have thrown themselves into fighting

American educational systems in order to ensure that their children acquire the mix of cultural capital—high scholastic norms, music and sports activities, but also Mandarin classes and Chinese cuisine in the cafeteria—that will continue to ethnicize and index their cosmopolitan citizenship. Others have been motivated to create mini–Hong Kong cultures in upscale restaurants, old-boy's school clubs, tennis courts, and mahjong parties. Business migrants and families frequently return to Hong Kong where life is considered more exciting and sophisticated, and takes on a more real quality than life in a complacent Californian suburb. The managerial elite experience Hong Kong and California in real time, and yet as places with different temporal qualities, differently weighted in terms of cultural resonance and belonging. Shuttling across the Pacific is never merely for business reasons; such circulations have become an imperative to activate the dialectic of dissolution and reintegration of ethnic identity between the two poles of their existence. The flexible family regime, interacting with the rationality of market flexibility, steadily whittles away a notion of citizenship defined by membership in a nation-state. Instead, different juridical status and the possession of social and cultural capitals enable these well-heeled migrants to construct an ethnicized cosmopolitanism as a self-project of disembedded citizenship.

Indian Body-Shops

Other Asian expatriates have become a significant sociocultural force because of their centrality to the growth of the computer industry that has come to dominate Northern California's economy. In the early years of the high-tech industry, circa 1980s, companies hired Taiwanese and Indian citizens already in the country and trained at American universities. Many U.S.-trained foreign Asia engineers, programmers, and venture capitalists have contributed to the growth of the industry as a whole. But as the demand for professionals grew to keep pace with the booming economy, the computer industry put pressure on the federal government to increase the intake of skilled foreign workers to sixty-five thousand. Under the H-1B visa program, elite skilled workers were admitted to the country for six years, but they were now free to pursue permanent residency, or "the green card," while working for an American company. Many of the computer migrants came from Asian and European countries and China, but in most technology firms such as Hewlett Packard and Intel, one third of the engineering workforce is composed of skilled immigrants from Taiwan and India (Saxenian 1999). Furthermore, foreign-born entrepreneurs also have started up dozens of public technology companies. Taiwanese immigrants are focused on manufacturing computer and electronic hardware, while Indian immigrants specialize in software and business products (Saxenian 1999). Many Taiwanese-owned companies form partnerships with firms in the Hsinchu Industrial Park in Taiwan, creating a process of reciprocal industrial upgrading across the Pacific. Unlike the astronaut shuttles of the Taiwanese entrepreneurs, Indian migrant circulations are mainly operated by labor-contracting companies called body-shops.

As the Silicon Valley has grown by leaps and bounds, high tech firms have annually lobbied the U.S. government to raise the numbers for contract skilled migrants, especially from Asia. Companies claim that American universities are not producing enough qualified engineers to keep up with the numbers needed to sustain the growth of the technology industry. An Asian-American maker of circuit chips protests that if the visa for contract high tech workers was not readily available, businesses like his would fail. "We have been hiring people from Canada, from France and from Yugoslavia. We have engineers from Taiwan, and Vietnam. It's like a small United Nations."[8] But most of the foreign software workers (of different ranks) are brought over by body-shops from Bangalore, Mumbai and other cybersites in India. Indian computer workers are currently preferred over say equally qualified ones from China because of the former's command of English. By the end of the 1990s, more than half of the contract (H-1B) visas issued to foreign employees in the high tech industry were to professionals from India.[9] Huge Indian companies such as HCL Infosystems dominate the global supply of software workers, but in the Silicon Valley, hundreds of body-shops are operated by Indian resident expatriates and their partners in India. One estimate notes that almost 80 percent of Indian high tech professionals in the United States are from Kerala, about 10 percent each from New Delhi and Mumbai, and a tiny number from the Punjab.

Body-shops operate as agencies for admitting a secondary skilled labor relying on recruiters in India to find technical workers. Some body-shops have been suspected of exploiting these foreign workers from the moment of recruitment to the possible outcome of eventual expulsion from the United States. Recruitment practices may include receiving bribes from would-be contract workers in India, who may be able to buy false papers and qualifications. Once contract workers arrive in the United States, many are vulnerable to exploitation by the body shops and corporate firms. Body shops hold their visas and find them employment, often taking a cut of their salaries (from 25 to 50 percent). Furthermore, by keeping the workers' visas and holding out the

[8] "A New California," *San Francisco Examiner,* Feb. 20, 2000.
[9] "Ambiguity Remains Despite Changes in H-1 Program," *San Francisco Chronicle,* Sept. 21, 2000.

promise of eventually getting them a green card, the body-shop makes it risky for the migrant worker to change employers, complain about illegal conditions, or to undertake unionizing activities without jeopardizing his green card prospects.[10] Constrained by their fear of losing jobs and also their immigrant status, technomigrants are thus reduced to a kind of glamorized transnational coolies. An Indian engineer complains that a body-shop "threatened to send some [workers] back to India if they did not get contracts [to work with high tech firms]. These workers were in tears. They were nervous wrecks, ashamed to ask for money or help from their families back home."[11] The prospect of getting citizenship is used as a weapon to deny these migrant workers citizenship rights.

For the technomigrant, body-shops accrue mounting costs—documents, fees, passage, living costs, and so on—while holding out the promise of a green card. The route to the Silicon Valley thus involves many steps, agents, and hazards. I interviewed a twentysomething software worker I will call Satajit from Amritsar, Punjab, who received his degree from the Guru Nanak Engineering Technology Institute.[12] A few months into his first job in India, Satajit applied to Aviance, a body-shop, to be sent to the United States. Aviance obtained his ticket and visa permit, and found him a job in a software company in Houston. When this particular project was completed, Satajit joined the body-shop Novetel Network that operates mainly in California. He claims that Novetel paid him U.S.$1,200 a month for six months while locating a job for him in the Silicon Valley. While waiting for the job to materialize, Satajit was driving a cab, in an industry that is dominated by his countrymen. It is a flexible way for technomigrants to pick up some money during the dry spell, but "hard for an educated man" to take the abuse he has received from some passengers. Satajit was feeling a bit depressed. In order to save money, he shared a small apartment with three other body-shop workers. They were all waiting for the economy to pick up again, or they may have to return to India soon. Meanwhile, he dreams of the day he will be free of the body-shop and can find work on his own, with the expectation of making up to $75,000 a year if he gets a green card and can free himself from the body-shop machine.

Thousands of Indian technicians like Satajit are kept in a semi-indentured position by body-shops, required to be flexible to respond

[10] "Question of Fraud: Silicon Valley Pushes for More Foreign Workers Despite Federal Probes," *San Francisco Chronicle*, Sept. 21, 2000.

[11] David Bacon and Judy Goff, "Law Shouldn't Allow High-Tech Industry to Indenture Immigrants," *San Francisco Chronicle*, Sept. 9, 2000.

[12] Interview was conducted in the San Francisco Bay Area on September 18, 2002.

to fluctuating market conditions in the United States. They must be flexible enough to do high tech jobs on short notice, but also to switch to low-prestige jobs such as taxi-driving. Their daily existence, landing a job, and the opportunity to obtain legal citizenship depend on the body-shop regime that keeps them in a state of suspension as a circulating techno-migrants whose labor benefit Indian and American managers alike. Despite their travails, the Indian high tech migrant's dream burns bright. Indeed, Satajit was looking forward to a reunion of the hundreds of alumni of the Guru Nanak institute in the Bay Area! American labor organizers have a less sanguine view of these circulating software workers, and would like to end body-shopping altogether. They urge the high-tech industry to invest in training Americans, especially minorities. Companies like Cysco Systems have set up small classes for inner-city children, but it is doubtful that this tiny effort makes any different to the huge demand for skilled, foreign and cheap workers. Others argue that the first step in controlling the exploitation of migrant workers would be to allow them to work for different employers. Currently, a technomigrant who changes employer or loses his job forfeits the chance of gaining immigrant status. By removing this control, contract workers can fight for their rights without fear of losing their entitlement to citizenship.[13] But technomigrants are at the upper end of an ethnicized high tech hierarchy, and for many long resident workers, they seem an "unfair" competition. Especially since September 11, 2001, Indian migrants have on occasioned been misidentified as terrorists, and the economic recession has actually scaled back body-shop operations, forcing many technomigrants to return home.

Nicholas Rose (1999) uses the term "the capitalization of citizenship," to describe the ways neoliberal criteria have come to dominate our norms of citizenship. American visa instruments have directly and indirectly regulated the status of business and professional resident expatriates, as well as of legal and illegal uneducated labor. We have the ethnic Chinese astronaut who relies on multiple passports to manage family life and economic holdings located on opposite sides of the Pacific. Their networks facilitate capital and commercial flows. Taiwanese immigrant entrepreneurs in Silicon Valley represent another kind of astronauts who forge transnational technological-industrial-business networks with Taiwan. The high tech industry also benefits from temporary contract workers whose status as a temporary secondary skilled labor market is vulnerable to exploitation and unprotected by citizenship entitlements. Indian software migrants do not quite make it as a

[13] Before he stepped down as president of the United States, Bill Clinton signed a law allowing contract workers to change jobs without risk of damaging their chances for acquiring citizenship.

cosmopolitan class of neoliberal subjects; in fact the very body-shop regime and its contingent reliance on market conditions make the project of self-fashioning across national space, for many Indian software workers, a highly chancy one. This is especially the case for the migrants working in the belly of the affluent California society who are not regarded as being bearers of any forms of capital.

ETHNIC ENCLAVES, COMMUNITIES OF SECURITY

The interplay of immigration laws, high-tech industries, and migration also gives intelligibility to new zones of governance, domains that are increasingly maintained not by the state on behalf of citizens, but regulated by local strategies of containment and of securitization. The new landscapes of autonomous governance are most striking in California, a state characterized by political and regional factions, with an international cast of migrants rubbing up against long-resident farmers, workers, and urbanites. This potent mix is exacerbated by rapid technological growth and integration with Asia Pacific countries. Much has been written about the fragmentation of the greater Los Angeles metropolitan region (e.g., Davis 1990), but there is still a widespread lack of awareness about the Asian presence—in gigantic malls, upscale neighborhoods, high-tech back-offices and labor demimonde—that is shaping islands of relative autonomy. Different migrant figures use different techniques of risk management: we have labor bosses who cut costs by running high tech sweatshops on the one hand, and well-heeled managers striving to create risk-free suburbs on the other.

Demimonde of Immigrant Labor

Fables about techno-industrialists and immigrant superheroes in the Silicon Valley have overshadowed the plight of poor or illegal workers who are employed in a multiplicity of low-paid jobs—as electronics factory labor, garment workers, office-cleaners, hotel maids and janitors, restaurant and supermarket workers, farm hands and nannies—all critical to sustaining "the quality of life in California." In the restructured flexible economy, the exclusions of African-American inner-city populations from information and communication structures may well doom the ghetto young to downward mobility from the working class (Lash 1994, 132–33). Few African-American workers, for instance, realize that there are good jobs in Internet companies that do not require a college degree. Indeed, less-skilled jobs in the high-tech industries are almost overwhelmingly controlled by immigrant ethnic networks that show a talent for taking risks, keeping costs down, and responding rapidly to fluctuations in the markets. Such techniques are possible because there is an expanding pool of poor immigrant workers that ethnic power brokers can recruit and discipline as a cheap and highly exploitable labor force. After years of sending labor-intensive manufacturing jobs overseas,[14] post-Fordist strategies include having consumer items produced relatively cheaply on American soil. American businesses now turn to smaller U.S.-based firms—electronics assembly plants, garment sweatshops, food-processing centers—that are mainly operated by immigrant bosses to manufacture goods for the domestic market. These operations respond flexibly to the gyrations of the market because they employ mainly unregulated workers. Tapping into ethnic networks, Asian-owned companies take taken advantage of the ignorance, isolation, and poverty of unskilled immigrants.

For instance, ethnic Chinese garment sweatshops have been exposed for hiring illegal immigrants (Asians and Latinos) at the prize of a cup of *latte* (approximately $3) per hour, for hours on end, sewing designer clothes. In an infamous case uncovered in 1995, an El Monte sweatshop forced Thai and Latino immigrants to work for 70¢ per hour. The Department of Labor estimates that at least 60 percent of the approximately 150,000 garment workers in the Los Angeles area are routinely underpaid, but language barriers between the workers have obstructed union organizing.[15] Labor violations akin to those in the garment sweatshops have emerged in Silicon Valley. An Asian American owned electronics factory and its subcontractor have been charged with underpaying Southeast Asian immigrants who work in the factories as well as take work home. The high demand for computer parts have spurred many computer firms to outsource work to poor Southeast Asian immigrants at home, where women were paid by the piece rate. This practice violates state laws on two counts: the home workers' total earnings did not meet the state minimum wage, and electronic assembly was not permitted as industrial home work in California.[16] Altogether, an estimated 45,000 of Silicon Valley's 120,000 Vietnamese-American immigrants are employed to work at their kitchen table assembling printed wire boards, with no legal protection (see Ong, 2003, 262–72). Although immigration agents have on occasion raided garment sweatshops, electronic homework remains an area unpenetrably by the American labor inspectors and mainstream unions.

In these sweated demimonde, immigrant bosses can exert over-

[14] For an ethnographic account of "runaway factories," see Ong (1987).
[15] "BCBG Names in Sweatshop Suit," *Asianweek*, August 1999.
[16] "High Tech's Low Wages: Two Silicon Valley Forms Sued over Alleged Labor Violations," *Asianweek*, December 23, 1999.

whelming power over coethnics desperate for jobs in familiar situations where good command of English is not a necessity.

Peter Kwong has described New York Chinatown enclaves that exploit undocumented immigrants from Fujian, who, burdened with debts to the snakeheads, must work punishing hours in substandard jobs for years on end just to repay the snakeheads. Kwong goes on to note: "The ethnic enclave . . . is a trap. Not only are the immigrants doomed to perpetual subcontracted employment, but the social and political control of these enclaves is also sub-contracted to ethnic elites, who are free to set their own legal and labor standards for the entire community without ever coming under the scrutiny US authorities" (Kwong 1997, 10–11). In other words, the ethnic enclave system has allowed rich immigrants to create conditions of indentured servitude for poor coethnics. American immigration history is studded with stories about ethnic enclaves as a stepping-stone for earlier generations of immigrants towards the middle class. What is perhaps different about current ethnic enclaves is their degree of isolation in small towns and hidden neighborhoods, and their role as vital supports for the risk-taking, neoliberal subject. The path toward social mobility is highly uncertain, since uncertain, piecemeal work does not allow savings and long-term planning.

Many unskilled workers are easily exploited by coethnic bosses, hampered by language barriers, and fearing deportation, have difficulty breaking into the wider, unskilled secondary labor markets. Ethnic subcontracted domains are thus in a world of self-governance, under cultural norms of patriarchal discipline, coercion, and secrecy, at odds with liberal workplace standards in the larger society. The most vivid kinds of ethnic enclave exploitation in California are in the restaurant and supermarket trade that have greatly expanded to serve an affluent Asian expatriate community. Mega-supermarket chains have used kinship, language , and cultural authority to control and exploit Asian immigrant workers. The United Food and Commercial Workers Union's effort to organize underpaid workers in ethnicized supermarket chains have been unsuccessful because the owners employ relatives and friends, and invoke kinship as a way to inculcate worker loyalty. A Cantonese-speaking union organizer said, "In Chinese culture, employers have the same kind of authority as teachers and parents. If that's the case, you can't get workers to challenge them. And I think, partly, confrontation and conflict are not highly valued. I talked to one worker who said, 'We're in a new country. We don't want to start problems.' "[17] The interweaving of personal relationships and formulaic invoking of tradition,

---

[17] "When Unions Attempt to Organize Silicon Valley's Growing Vietnamese Workforce, They Find Custom, Language and History Stand in the Way," *Metro, Silicon Valley's Weekly Newspaper*, Sept. 16–22, 1999.

disguise the diversity of Asian migrant subjects who are not bound by the same set of ethnic norms or collective memory.

Nevertheless, as the above example of abused Thai workers shows, migrants illegal status and ignorance of American society makes them extremely vulnerable to immigrant bosses who treat them like indentured servants hidden in plain sight.

Habitat of Securitization

The hour-glass shape of the immigrant labor markets—with investors, managers and knowledge workers at the top, and a whole array of unskilled migrants at the bottom—has renaturalized and resegmented labor markets, giving a strong ethnic cast to occupational zones and residential communities. In California, Asian-dominated communities outside Chinatowns are emerging, forming distinctive suburbs of privilege where the main concerns are the controls of an exclusive lifestyle and risk management. Immigrant managers, engineers and workers achieve a kind of citizenship through investments or employment with an American company, or purchasing homes in the stratospheric real estate market. For example, Taiwanese venture capitalists and professionals now form a major presence in Silicon Valley communities like Sunnyvale, which boasts a Taiwanese Cultural Center funded by the Taipei government. Indian engineers and programmers have also spread across middle-class and upper-middle-class suburban cities such as Fremont that are served by Hindu temples, Indian shops and entertainment centers. High tech firms help newcomers to settle into the suburbs where a major attraction are excellent schools for immigrant children. An upbeat report commissioned by a pro-immigration advocacy group note that new immigrants mainly from Asia, Latin America and the Caribbean are embracing American lifestyle, according to four indexes: mastering English, home-ownership, becoming citizenship, and, especially in California, marrying across ethnic lines.[18] The individualization of citizenship thus manifests itself in single-issue "lifestyle" concerns such as "good education, good environment, and political stability."

Like many well-off Americans, upscale newcomers believe that security is no longer considered something that can be left to the state. Nikolas Rose uses the term "the securitization of habitat" to describe contemporary thinking about risk management as a matter of individual self-management and collective responsibility (1999, 246–47). The

---

[18] "Immigrants Quickly Becoming Assimilated, Report Concludes," *San Francisco Chronicle*, July 7, 1999.

widespread perception of risks, and the need to anticipate and plan for risks (Beck 1994), now take the form of pervasive anxiety concerning personal safety and home property. Techniques of risk-management include continuously monitoring for risks in the home turf (e.g., surveillance cameras outside the house). The "community of security" is more that a geographical space; it is an "intersubjective zone" (Rose 1999, 247), where like-minded, self-propelling individuals get together to instrumentalize and even take preemptive actions against outside threats to home security of their neighborhoods. Home ownership associations have sprung up as a mechanism of community sovereignty, where residents exercise a kind of freedom that includes zoning codes, controls over noise levels, and the maintenance of road signs that often confuse rather than guide outsiders. The parent-teacher association is another institution that regulates local quality of life issues. A Chinese American mother, the president of such an institution, said, "I think the voters are willing to pay a bit more for a quality education system and good quality roads." Demands for the maintenance and accumulation of high quality social capital are a form of risk management of the real estate values of the habitat of securitization. The fierce entrepreneurship of the Silicon Valley spills over into a competition for entitlement, especially the entitlement of well-endowed and highly educated people for protection against threats to business, personal property, and the body. Techniques of exclusion—for example, gated communities, difficulty of access from the freeway, vetting new residents, and so on—shape the ethical community of high achievers, and guard against more diverse outsiders.

Outside these secure habitats, ordinary working people, many of them new migrants as well, have to contend with a situation of reduced public support and increased uncertainty. There is an acute housing shortage in San Jose, the heart of Silicon Valley. Millions have been spent on civic renovations and redevelopment projects to lure middle-class professionals and high-tech business to the city, while the growing plight of the working-class people has been overlooked.[19] Thousands of ordinary workers have to take long commutes because they cannot afford housing in the Valley. There is an urban folklore about people making $45,000 having to sleep in their cars. An increasing number of working-class people are homeless, and some spend the night in buses or local shelters. The intensified gap between affluent young professionals

[19] A new report estimates a housing shortage of about forty-six thousand homes in Silicion Valley by the year 2010. San Jose authorities are planning to built affordable housing for low-waged workers and the homeless, and to double the number of shelter beds in the city. "San Jose Mayor Forms Housing Crisis Group," *San Francisco Chronicle,* Sept. 14, 2000.

(both migrants and citizens) and working-class families has rippled across Northern California. Thus, families in long-term immigrant neighborhoods in San Francisco are being displaced by skyrocketing real estate prices, and the city itself has become "a combination bedroom, office and den for Silicon Valley."[20] The situation has eased somewhat in the current economic minirecession, but working families still cannot afford to live in the suburbs of security where they may work as construction workers, gardeners, and maids.

Ethnic enclaves and suburbs of security are different types of self-governing zones given new life by the influx of diverse migrant streams from Asia. Some articulate with preexisting communities, but the current milieus have coevolved with the nexus of corporate policies, intensified migration, and discourse of Asian high tech talent. The outcome is a terrain fragmented by competing entitlements, dominated by capital-bearing migrants who instrumentalize their personal and corporate security, protecting islands of security in the midst of demographic, social, and economic upheavals and even disenfranchisement for ordinary working people and poor migrants.

Splintering Cosmopolitanism

Clearly, the archipelago of self-regulating zones emerging in the California landscape attests to the fact that some migrants and residents are more sovereign than others. Asian newcomers—investors, managers, professionals, and of low-skilled or illegal workers—come to embody rights and privileges that are weighed rather differently, and their powers of freedom and control are differently exercised in the creation of governable spaces.

Mobile high tech figures are cosmopolitan in more than a couple of ways: they possess the human capital in demand regardless of borders between rich and poor countries, and they also enjoy the perks that come with being first-class corporate figures, regardless of their technical status as citizens of the United States. In addition to such cosmopolitan capital and privileges, the practices of these newcomers incorporate a form of citizenship that is primarily in relation to consumption and controls over place, time, and circuits of communication. Practical citizenship for low-skilled migrant workers is also not based on relation to the state or to the wider public sphere but depends on linking up with ethnic networks that enforce work discipline and social -isolation.

The splintering of cosmopolitan privilege in neoliberal America chal-

[20] "Misson District Fights Case of Dot-com Fever," *New York Times*, Nov. 5, 2000.

lenges the uncritical acceptance of a cosmopolitan project some consider a positive answer to globalization and its discontents. Scholars such as David Held are guardedly optimistic about the proliferation of democratic forms that can come with the stretching and deepening of connections across spaces, and the growing awareness of "communities of fate" (Held et al. 1999). Proponents of a positive cosmopolitanism have not looked at the layering of governance and the splintering of cosmopolitanism below the global or national levels. There is as yet no systematic empirical evidence that the criss-crossing webs of multilateral agencies or the fostering of civic education will bring about a more effective accountability from governments or business.

There is a variety of communities that have come about through particular alignments of politics, technology and ethics. Thus, contrary to claims about the mobile multitude leading the battle for cosmopolitan liberation against the Empire (Hardt and Negri 2000, 293), this essay has shown that the migrant, the nonwhite, and the female refugee cannot be represented by a single or imposed language of political power. Indeed, very few of our Internet-enabled academics have ever noticed the multitude of invisible workers in America's cyber front yard.

This ethnographic exploration of diverse effects of technologies of migration and labor in the American empire instead pinpoints the permutations of citizenship and cosmopolitan advantage for different streams of migrants. Sovereign will is enjoyed by privileged and well-educated migrants, whereas it is not clear that one can refer to many poor and exploited migrants as sovereign subjects. It is clear that citizenship is less and less a relationship to the state, and more a relationship to the self, as in the self-actualization of the flexible, neoliberal entrepreneur who can engage in an array of private, corporate and social practices in cosmopolitan situations. It raises the question whether the advantages of citizenship enjoyed by mobile corporate subjects can be linked to the obligations of substantive citizenship for poor migrants. The shifting alignment of neoliberal logic, migration regimes, and political ethics is constantly evolving, but for now, the effects in the American West are splintering cosmopolitanism, giving rise to new spaces and practices of government for a variety of mobile bodies.

Virtual India: Indian IT Labor and the Nation-State

Peter van der Veer

INTRODUCTION

One of the most successful television shows in India over the last few years is the quiz "Who Will Become a Millionaire?" presented by the charismatic aging movie-star Amitabh Bacchan. The quiz has a transnational format taken over from British television and in its combination of sudden wealth, quick intelligence in Hindi, and nationalist knowledge (since many of the questions are about national history, religion, and achievement) it is a wonderful vignette of the glamorous real-life story, widely covered in the Indian media, of Indian IT entrepreneurs, such as Azim Premji of Wipro and Sabir Bhatia of Hotmail who indeed have become multimillionaires overnight. The entrepreneurial story is a well-known part of the image of the IT industry for especially younger Indians. It is the American middle-class dream of self-made men, constantly reinforced by the Indian media. But it is also a dream wonderfully lampooned in the recent movie *Guru*, in which the hero goes to the United States to meet his friend who he thinks is rich and drives a Mercedes, but in fact is poor and drives a taxi. This is the world of technocoolies. They participate in the hype of dot-com mania, but in fact live a quite limited existence at the margin of the IT industry. It is the connections between transnational high-skilled labor, dreams of sudden wealth, and nationalism as well as their inherent contradictions that are worth exploring in the context of this book's discussion of sovereignty in an era of renewed global mobility and flexible citizenship. It is a fact that the Indian IT sector has shown a phenomenal growth over the last decade. From 1990 to 2002 its output has doubled roughly every two years. The IT output has grown from 0.38 percent of GDP in 1990 to 3 percent. This growth has been based on expansion of exports of services and labor for the global market. Such growth has occurred in a policy environment of liberalisation, privatisation and globalisation. Culturally and politically IT is seen as the success-story of individual entrepreneurship, set free from the shackles of state intervention, of the "license raj" that had characterized the rule of the Congress Party. More than being just a successful industry, however, the Indian IT sector has also become an icon of a new form of development, of bringing India into the twenty-first century. This is brought out in the extraordinary attention to IT in the Indian media. Especially the gurus (mentors) of the industry, such as N. R. Narayana Murthy of Infosys, are seen as the heroes of today's India. Narayana Murthy, today a billionaire, often refers to his humble background as one of eight children in a lower-middle-class family as part of what one can call his signature image, promoted by leading marketers like Gurcharan Das (2002). It is not only their quick financial successes as self-made millionaires, but their attitudes, beliefs, and the image of the IT industry itself that make the IT entrepreneurs exemplars in middle-class dreams of endless global opportunities and of a new, revitalized Modern India. The Indian dream is not only particularistic but feeds on global imagery. Globally, the development of modern information technology has been welcomed as a revolution, resembling the Industrial Revolution. That revolutionary image has led to visions of a New Economy, guiding huge investments in dot-com startups and bringing citizens all over the world to invest their wealth and dreams in the new industry. The simultaneous production of these hopes and hypes all over the world points at a global modern culture that is integral to the nexus of capital and labor and to that of production and consumption.

The IT industry, the new economy, and the information revolution depend on hypes of various kinds. In Auguste Comte's foundational perspective the function of the social sciences is to get rid of society's myths. In the field of IT there are many myths, such as the idea that internet promotes democratization, that the new economy is based on entirely different principles than the old economy, that the IT industry will allow developing economies, such as India's, to leap-frog into the twenty-first century without going through all kinds of reforms that were necessary in other societies. Each of these ideas need reflection, discussion, and often rebuttal, but at the same time it is perhaps good to remind ourselves that hype and optimism are not only cultural reflections on "progress" but also are instrumental in furthering this field of activity. The extent to which Indians of all sections of the population "believe" in the IT industry and in its possibilities for individual and collective advancement is incredible. It appears that religious belief and belief in IT are the two dominant topics in newspapers and general discussion, just as there are software training centres and temples in every small town. The government, national and regional, fully participates in this culture of magical belief and even the big slump in the new economy does not seem to affect it greatly. It may be that India is particularly in need of hope and hype. India's development is quite dismal. In terms of size of population and geographical location it makes sense to compare India and China. In 1950 India was better off than China, but today the average Chinese citizen earns $890 a year, compared with $460 a year for the average Indian. The Chinese economy has grown at 8 to 10 percent a year for two decades, whereas the Indian economy has grown at 8 percent over only the last decade; the Indian population growth is twice that of China. Comparing China's development with that of India is a depressing activity for Indians and has been avoided as much as possible until recently. To rationalize this differential development out of the way by pointing at "the success of India's democracy" (Kohli 2001) may convince political scientists but no one else, and certainly not in India. The success story of the IT sector is a welcome antidote to cynicism about India's development and the corruption of state institutions.

For many young Indians the IT industry is seen as a means of social and spatial mobility, just as the Internet is seen as a means of personal emancipation. They think that careers in this industry are based on individual skills and professional achievement rather than on ascription, based on caste and class. The internal organization of the workplace is viewed as demanding but equal and unhierarchical. The American ideal of the self-made man, the pioneering hero, is one that is constantly invoked in the IT industry globally, but in India it is specifically contrasted with the Homo Hierarchicus of traditional Indian industry. There are two other related aspects to working in this industry that are particularly appealing. The comparatively high salaries as well as the opportunity to go abroad are attractive. This is related to the global organization of IT work. In the IT industry Indians get a chance to go abroad, earn an income that is in Indian rupee terms phenomenal, and get an opportunity to stay abroad as Non-Resident Indians. To be an NRI especially in the United States is a dream for many young people in India. If one cannot get into the United States, other options are taken, such as going to Australia. This dream is immediately connected to one's position in that other market of upward mobility and perhaps desire, marriage. Green card holders are the most eligible of marriage candidates and IT professionals in possession of this coveted document beat even Indian Administrative Service officers and medical doctors in the amount of dowry that they are able to obtain. Dowry prices have gone up all over India but especially steep in the IT sector.

In this contribution I want to address the arrangements of legality and illegality that are intrinsic to the concept of sovereignty and enable the transnational organization of IT labor. Second, I want to draw attention to the role of the nation-state and especially to some of the ideological or cultural aspects of globalization that are crucial to the understanding of India's IT industry.

BODY-SHOPPING

The IT industry in India is not fully integrated in the information revolution, but follows an old pattern of providing cheap Indian labor and services to a global market. Much of the media attention goes to high-skilled engineers, trained in top institutions, who have made it in the United States. The stories about their success also are retailed in business magazines like Silicon India. Although they are not untrue, they are only a small part of a complex reality. It has been observed that Graduate Schools of Engineering in the United States in the 1970s would have had to close because of too little interest in engineering careers in the U.S. population, if not for the influx of Chinese and Indian students. Between 1985 and 1996, 62 percent of all the doctorates in science and engineering granted to foreigners in the US were given to Chinese and Indians. This coincided with the Immigration Act of 1965 in the United States that allowed for a much larger quota for immigration for highly trained and educated professionals. The Immigration and Nationality Act of 1990 tripled the number of visas granted on the basis of occupational skills and thus further enhanced the immigration of engineers. These new laws also made it possible for Indian students to stay on in the United States. The earlier preference for going to the United Kingdom was replaced with a craze for "green cards." Nehru's vision of an Indian modernity which would be created by Indian engineers and scientists and would allow India to be fully self-sufficient ironically laid the basis for the emergence of a transnational cadre of Indian engineers who would be instrumental in creating wealth in the West (van der Veer 2003). The very top of the education pyramid in India is formed by the Indian Institutes of Technology (IIT) that have a competitive selection that can only be compared to the top echelon of American institutions such as MIT and CalTech. Only 2 percent of the more than two hundred thousand applicants that sit for the Joint Entry Exam are accepted. Their graduates head McKinsey & Co, United Airlines, Bell Laboratories, and, of course, a host of IT companies. These alumni have taken over some ideas from American private education and now also put money back into their old schools. Below the IITs one finds a whole range of engineering colleges of varying quality in all parts of India. This system of higher education depends on a huge system of pre-college education in which math and science are emphasized.

Although much attention is always given to the IT focus of the state governements of Andhra Pradesh and Karnataka (Hyderabad and Bangalore, respectively), also other states such as Uttar Pradesh produce a large workforce of IT graduates. It is the elite among these workers that has become entrepreneurial in the sense that they are crossing boundaries between engineering and entrepreneurship, between old economy and new economy, and, of course, by being transnational. Combined with the extraordinary emphasis in this field on innovation, breaking away from traditional hierarchies, on youth and on labor flexibility, this kind of person is the exact dream of the "new man" (*homo novus*), celebrated in European thought.

An important feature of the high-tech industry is that more than any other industry it is based on rapid innovation. Engineers have been able to gain so much wealth through their innovations that they also have become entrepreneurs. The information revolution in the United States is largely created by engineers who also took control over capital investments. And a large number of these engineers are born in China or India. There is a recent study of Chinese and Indian entrepreneurs in Silicon Valley by Saxenian (1999) that shows that between 1975 and 1990 the foreign-born population of the region doubled to almost 350,000. According to the 1990 census, more than half of Asian-born engineers in the region were of Chinese or Indian descent. By the end of the 1990s, half of the H-1B visas issued to foreign employees in the high tech industry were given to professionals from India. In 1998, 24 percent of the high-tech firms started in Silicon Valley were run by a Chinese or an Indian CEO. Together they employed more than fifty-eight thousand workers. A difference between Chinese-run and Indian-run firms is that the former are more concentrated in computer and electronic hardware manufacturing and trade, while the latter are concentrated in software and business services. Saxenian relates that to the superior English language skills of Indian immigrants.

The transnational migration of what sometimes are called "knowledge workers" has economic effects on both the country of immigration and on the country of origin. Saxenian (1999) demonstrates clearly that the politically motivated fears in California about Asian immigrants who take jobs away from native workers are false, because these Asians have massively created new jobs. There is a clear awareness in the American IT business community that the arrival of Asian engineers and scientists has been a great blessing for the American economy. The industry has been lobbying constantly for making more visa available for this category. The effects of the departure of these professionals on the Indian economy have generally been captured under the negative term "brain-drain." Clearly many more Indian professionals stay in the

United States after having benefited from Indian education than return. In short, India's brain-drain is the U.S.'s brain-gain. The effects of this can be partly calculated in terms of investments in education versus remittances.

Binod Khadria (1999) distinguishes financial resource flows, technological resource flows, and human resource flows back to India and comes to a very sceptical assessment of the benefits for India thus far. However, one has to realize that transnational connections are fundamental to India's position in the IT industry. Some members of this cadre invest "back home" in Bangalore, Mumbai or Hyderabad and it is in the transnational nature of their business activities that they become the cutting edge. Those who lead a life- and business-style of shuttling between country of origin and the United States are called "astronauts." They are nodes in technological-industrial-business networks that facilitate flows of capital, labor, and products. Saxenian (2002) interprets this as at least a partial reversal of the earlier brain drain and calls it "brain-circulation." She reports that the majority of Silicon Valley's Indian (76 percent) and Chinese immigrants (73 percent) respond that they would consider starting a business in their country of birth in the future.

However, more important than either brain-drain or brain-circulation is the fact that these IIT trained engineers have been the brokers for making flexible Indian labor available for the IT industry. One of the essential activities in this industry is called "body-shopping." Contrary to what the focus on IIT-trained engineer-entrepreneurs leads us to believe software engineering does only partly require high skills. New software development tools like Visual Basic make it possible for laborers with low programming skills to create usable software. One can discern in the software industry a huge labor force of relatively unskilled programmers. The organization of this labor force is in the hands of a number of body-shopping companies that also provide training in new software packages. India has been very quick in providing private education for training programmers who need only basic skills and can be easily reeducated to handle new software packages. The National Institute for Information Technology (NIIT), established in the early 1980s, has developed into international educational franchise that has a presence in thirty countries, including fifteen centers of excellence in China. Tata Consultancy Services with sixty-seven offices spanning eighteen countries and a team of ten thousand consultants also trains software workers for particular applications. This form of education has been instrumental in creating the body shopping phenomenon, about which we will speak later. The United States is the largest market for software development and H1-B visa are used to bring in software programmers for limited periods. The ethnographic accounts we have of body shopping suggest a strong dependence of workers on the firm sometimes to the extent of illegal exploitation. In the U.S. press, one finds with some regularity reports about raids of the police to find undocumented IT workers. By controlling visa and passports as well as housing, finances, and actual jobs the firms can exert a power over workers reminiscent of conditions of indentured labor in the nineteenth century. The term "technocoolies" is therefore perhaps not entirely inappropriate for at least part of this labor force.

Technocoolies participate in the hype of dot-com mania but in fact live a quite limited existence at the margin of the IT industry. The clients make use of body shopping companies to get cheap, flexible labor, and pay for that to the company. The company farms the worker out for a particular project, takes a large fee for that (something like half of the salary), and prevents the technocoolie to be hired on a permanent basis. Even contract workers who have worked for a company for years continue to be "owned" by the recruitment agent. The Y2K crisis especially put an enormous pressure on the market for temporary labor during a couple of years at the end of the 1990s. The coolies often live together in a house owned by the company. An important practice is "sitting on the bench," that is, waiting for a client, a period in which one does not earn anything but gets more and more indebted to the company. This kind of practice is central in the body shopping practice, because it creates a large reserve of workers that can be used at any time in a fluctuating market. Mir, Mathew, and Mir (2000) report about a "company apartment" in New York where some of the IT workers were working at minimum wage jobs to buttress a falling income. Although flexibility is a key word in the neoliberal organization of the IT industry, mobility is the key word in describing labor in this context. However, that mobility is very much circumscribed by visa regulations, contracts, and debts. In the story of debts one should also include the investments on education and in obtaining visas. Workers also are willing to pay substantial sums to start with a body shop. All this based on an optimistic scenario of becoming rich overnight, since one does not hear much about the failures, caused by individual collapse or by structural change, such as the decline of the dot.com industry. Finally, at the far end of the spectrum, we find South Asian workers at the assembly line as "low-wage temporary workers" without job security or health insurance. Every computer, printer or electronic device is assembled at production lines. Seventy percent of the two hundred thousand laborers working in manufacture in Silicon Valley are of Asian descent (Jayadev 2001).

Like nineteenth-century indentured labor, body-shopping also operates under a legal system that encourages transnational migration. The

Indian government is clearly encouraging this sector of activity by pro-viding education to create a labor force and by supporting the jobbers. The system puts people again under limiting legal conditions that are perhaps the more glaring because one is not living in the empire but in the postcolony. Exploitation of laborers is eminently possible under a system in which they enjoy few rights and can be easily deported. Also reminiscent of the conditions of nineteenth century indentured labor are the effects of this kind of transnational labor on sexual relations and the position of women. Some of these women are workers on H-1B visa themselves, but most are dependents of male workers and come on H-4 spousal visa. They live in apartment complexes that are expatriate compounds full of Indian co-workers. The H-4 spousal visa, which does not allow them to work in the United States, forces women to leave the United States immediately when their marriage ends. If di-vorced, such women are deportable. That situation gives husbands great power over their wives and wife battering appears to have in-creased under these conditions (Devi 2002). Because their family lives far away and they are not allowed to earn an independent income, such women are immobilized in various ways.

Contrary to the imagery of independent entrepreneurial success in a free market society the IT industry needs lower levels of labor and higher and lower levels are interconnected. The negative effects on Indian econ-omy and society from the emigration of scientists and engineers as well as the limiting conditions of body shopping could, in principle, be re-versed by the "death of distance" inherent in the new ICTs, which makes it possible that the work done by Indian ICT specialists in the United States (and elsewhere in the developed world) is also done in India itself (Aneesh in press). The rise of high-tech sites in Bangalore and Hyder-abad, as well as in a number of other cities in India, initiated mainly by U.S.-based or U.S.-returned Indian entrepreneurs may bear that possibil-ity out. This development has great potential which is already clear in the effects of this industry on the Indian economy, but the real issue is whether this industry which is still by-and-large providing low-grade, low-wage, low value-added services to the global market can develop into a more upgraded software industry. Transnational networks of NRIs and their India-based counterparts would be essential for such a devel-opment. The social field created by transnational migration would then really grow into a decentered economic field, enabled by ICTs.

THE NATION-STATE

The system of nation-states with its immigration laws and visa systems forms a central structuring feature of this transnational labor force.

Class differences turn out to be crucial not only for the flexibility of labor but also for the flexibility of citizenship under neo-liberal conditions. The idea of a self-regulatory market is an ideological notion that in fact allows all kinds of economic activities, including labor, to be ruled and regulated. Karl Polanyi has argued in his classic, *The Great Transformation: The Political and Economic Origins of Our Time* (1944), that "the congenital weakness of nineteenth century society was not that it was industrial but that it was a market society. Industrial civilization will continue to exist when the utopian experiment of a self-regulatory market will be no more than a memory" (250). Polanyi's view in the forties that the economy had to be under social control was realized in European welfare states, but has been increasingly contradicted by global policies, inspired by neoliberal criticism of such social control. However, notions of freedom and control, deeply rooted in European political philosophy, have to be understood in relation to policies that create freedom for some, constraints for others and are otherwise tied to the intricate economic nature of society. Under what kind of rules then does the system of body-shopping operate? Immigration laws and regulations in the United States and elsewhere remain under constant pressure from the IT industry that demands the raising of the limits. The temporality of contracts and visa is the key to this form of labor migration. By supplying software professionals in time and for the length of time needed, the body shopping firms assist companies to reduce the costs of keeping a permanent labor force (Xiang 2001). Although this is true for all forms of contract labor, organized by recruitment agencies for temporary work, the transnational character of the labor in this case adds the element of temporary immigration to it. This is called flexible labor, but it raises the question of flexible citizenship (Ong 1999, and Ong in this volume).

Migrant "legality" and "illegality" is an epistemological, methodological, and political problem (de Genova 2002). In the wealthiest nation-states in Europe and America, migration has emerged as the central political issue over the last few years. This has even worsened because of security anxieties in the network society following 9/11. One cannot separate Indian labor migration entirely from the more general story of mass migration. Despite the fact that liberalism and the IT industry itself promise freedom and creativity, the global market in fact produces at the same time great inequalities and incommensurable interdependencies. In the United States, Immigration and Naturalization Service (INS) raids on workplaces have to be announced three days in advance to enable employers to prepare the hiring records. This, obviously, also allows them to fire or temporarily discharge them and to gain complete control over them. Similarly, body-shopping firms participate in "revolving door" policies of keeping migrant labor flexible through a visa system that denies them citizenship entitlements. Policies of citizenship both in the sending and receiving countries play a major role in the regulation of migrant labor.

The policies concerning entry visa create huge differences among laborers who are in demand at different levels of the labor market. The highest strata of this system of stratification arrive with legal papers that give in time access to permanent residency and/or full citizenship. The transnational cadre of IIT-trained Indian engineers is firmly middle class. Nevertheless, despite their secure class position, when they want to play a role as "astronauts" they depend on multiple passports, on green cards, and on special fiscal policies for NRIs as well as on connections with cheap labor. Their entrepreneurial playing field is largely determined by national, international, and global arrangements of fiscality and security. Moreover, their activities both in the United States and in India depend on the mobilization and immobilization of cheap labor that is depended on other legal regimes.

India has seen the emergence of a special kind of hyphenated identity: the nonresident Indian (NRI). The Foreign Exchange Regulations Act of 1973 includes in this category: (1) citizens of India living abroad for the purpose of carrying on a business or career, but declaring their intention to stay in India for an indefinite period; (2) Persons of Indian origin holding a passport of another country. One is of Indian origin if one has held an Indian passport, or if either of the parents or grandparents was Indian. The wife of a person of Indian origin is held to be of Indian origin, too. Citizenship nor residence are thus the criteria for deciding who belongs to this category, but "origin" is and in that sense it has much in common with the German genealogical definition according to which migrant communities in Eastern Europe belong to the German nation and have the right to return to Germany. One reason for the Indian state to create this category is to raise foreign exchange, as NRIs are allowed to deposit money in Indian banks with competitive, guaranteed rates of interest. However, I would suggest that the main reason is not economic, but political. It is striking that it is not the lower-class migrant laborers in the Gulf region who are the primary targets of this policy, although they are among the migrants by far the most important economic actors in terms of remittances and other effects on the Indian economy. It is also not the older migrant communities of former indentured laborers and their descendants or even the older merchant communities that form the target of this policy. Rather, it is the new Hindu middle-class professional and entrepreneurial migrant especially in the United States that forms an important focus for Indian politics.

In 1998 the Hindu nationalist Bharatiya Janata Party (BJP) proposed further changes, such as the introduction of a PIO (Person of Indian Origin) card with a number of benefits attached to it. In 2001 the Indian Government, led by the BJP, announced the appointment of an ambassador at large for NRIs and PIOs at the embassy in Washington. The Ministry of External Affairs has also appointed an Additional Secretary in charge of NRIs and has convened a government-level diaspora committee. In 2003 the Indian Prime Minister announced dual-citizenship rights for nationals of the United States, the United Kingdom, Canada, and Australia at the first Annual Pravasi Bharatiya Divas (Indian Transnational Day). It is ironic that a party that derives so much of its political gains from a campaign which stigmatizes the indigenous Muslim community as "foreign" is so interested in Indians who actually live in foreign lands. Such Indians are primarily perceived as Hindus and Hindu nationalism mobilizes large groups of Hindu migrants all over the world. "Achievements" like the nuclear explosions of 1998, for example, enhanced enthusiasm under the NRIs in the United States. The announcement of international sanctions against India led to successful fund-raising by the Indian government under NRIs in the United States. Recent research has also shown how the BJP's mother organization, the Rashtriya Swayamsevak Sangh (RSS) and affiliated organizations raise money from the Hindus in the United States under the aegis of a purportedly secular charity, the India Relief and Development Fund which channels its money to a wide variety of Hindutva-related projects. Even the money raised by this Fund for the victims of the Gujarat Earthquake was discriminately distributed only to Hindus (see http://www.stopfundinghate.org). Transnational investment, global politics and the cultural capital of "belonging" go hand in hand here (Kurien 2002).

As I have argued elsewhere (van der Veer 1995, 2002), the articulation of nation and migration forms an important, structural feature within the politics of space produced by the South Asian diaspora. This articulation has been strongly reinforced by religious movements ranging from Arya Samaj missionaries to the Caribbean in the early twentieth century to Sai Baba missions to Fiji in the 1980s and to the Vishwa Hindu Parishad activities today. A striking element of nineteenth-century coolie migration was the importance of religious nationalism in it. Under colonial conditions imperial law distinguished between citizens and subjects. It is precisely these legal conditions that were challenged by those who were subjected to them. The treatment of indentured laborers—and especially of the women among them—was taken up as the first nationalist cause by the Indian National Congress under the leadership of Mahatma Gandhi. In 1919 the Congress forced the British to stop recruiting Indian laborers for indentured labor in other colonies. Gandhi's stay in South Africa had opened his eyes to the nationalist cause. He not only acquainted himself firsthand with the discriminatory treatment of Indians as "British subjects" under South African racial laws but also learned to see Indians as an ethnic group, and as a "nation." The marginal position of a migrant like even the well-educated Gandhi, and the special qualities of group formation among migrants, seem in general to play a significant role in the formation of nationalist discourse.

The question is whether we find a similar pattern in the current migration of knowledge workers under postcolonial conditions. In his impressive work on the network society, Manuel Castells (1997) argues that while the legitimizing identities of the state are declining in the information age, resistance identities and project identities (aiming at total societal transformation) are on the rise. In his view, these identities are produced by social movements which react against three fundamental threats: "globalization, which dissolves the autonomy of institutions, organizations and communication systems where people live. Reaction against networking and flexibility which blur the boundaries of membership and involvement, individualize social relationships of production, and induce the structural instability of work, space, and time. And reaction against the crisis of the patriarchal family at the roots of the transformation of mechanisms of security building, socialization, sexuality, and therefore of personality systems. When the world becomes too large to be controlled, social actors aim at shrinking it back to their size and reach" (Castells 1997, 66). Castells's observations are useful, but, at the same time, things look somewhat different when one examines a Hindu movement like the Vishva Hindu Parishad, the ally of the Hindu nationalist party BJP.

Rather than confirming the general analysis of Castells the VHP shows contradictory faces. On the one hand, the VHP is clearly a movement that promotes Hindu nationalism with an antisecular and anti-Muslim slant, and as such it is a movement that continues much of the religious nationalist rhetoric and methods of such movements since the late nineteenth century. It resists Westernization and globalization in so far as they are portrayed as "foreign" threats to the basic Hindu values of the Indian nation. Muslims as a community signify the "foreign" as "the enemy within." Ideologically, they are portrayed as "converts," with their allegiance outside of India. The VHP argues that they do not belong to India but to Pakistan or to Arabia, and have thus to be either religiously purified by reconversion to Hinduism or ethnically cleansed by forced emigration.

By contrast, the VHP is a movement that is very active globally and one of the prime agents for the globalization of Hinduism. In the United

States, it has been active since 1974, following sizeable immigration from India. The anti-Muslim politics central to its activities in India do not make much sense in the United States. Antiglobalization rhetoric that emphasizes restrictions on foreign capital flowing into Indian companies is conspicuously absent from the VHP propaganda in the United States, and rightly so, as its supporters there are strongly in favor of the liberalization and globalization of the economy. As NRIs, they also have direct personal advantage in the free flow of capital. The focus of the VHP in the United States is, as with many religious movements globally, on the family. The great fear of Indian migrants to the United States is perhaps not so much the threat to the patriarchal nature of the Hindu family, because many of these migrants are well-educated professionals and both men and women are income earners. Rather, it is the struggle to reproduce Hindu culture in a foreign environment in order to socialize their children into the hybridity of Indian Americans. The fear often is that the children will lose all touch with the culture of the parents and, thus, in some sense, be lost to them. Both Internet chatgroups and youth camps are organized by the VHP to keep Hinduism alive among young Indians in the USA. As Arvind Rajagopal (1997) rightly observes, the VHP needs different tactics, and different objectives in different places in order to be able to recruit members. In one VHP camp attended by Rajagopal, the 150 participants were mainly working in the IT sector (Rajagopal 2000). Instruction included Upanishadic management consultancy.

What is the connection between software engineering and the religious nationalist project of the VHP? First of all, it is important for religious nationalists to show that scientific progress is in tune with religious values. Hindu nationalism today continues the tradition of nineteenth-century rational religion. The BJP that now dominates the Indian government is very interested in combining the high-level education in technoscience in the Indian Institutes of Technology (IITs) with education in Hindu culture. This move to combine Hinduism with technoscience reminds one of similar moves that have taken place in Muslim countries, like Malaysia, where one finds a rise of technoscience education, backed by international corporations, coupled with the internationalisation of Islamic higher learning. Very important in this trend is the notion of authenticity (*asala* in Islam) that refers to an acceptance of technoscience, while resisting the Western cultural invasion (or Westoxification [*gharbzadegi*], as it is called in Iran).

Science and technology are central to conceptualisations of modernity, both in its secular and its religious variants. The enlightenment notion that there is an opposition between science and religion has been an important element in sociological and commonsense understandings of modernity and secularity, but many religious movements have not accepted such an opposition. It has been an ideological notion in particular secularist movements, especially in Western Europe, but has to be sociologically recognized as such. It is quite striking how provincial the sociological understanding of modernity often has been (van der Veer 2001). In societies as diverse as India and the United States "Enlightenment fundamentalism" (to use Ernest Gellner's term) has only played a very marginal role. There is no reason at all to expect Hindu engineers and scientists to "lose their religion" and become secular. Hindu modernity includes an ideological valuation of science and technology. The empirical question is rather to explore what religion does for them; what kind of specific needs it produces or addresses. The globalization of production and consumption, including the flexibility and mobility of labor, is addressed by movements like the Vishva Hindu Parishad and is a major element in their nationalist politics of "belonging." The idea that "symbolic analysts" (to use Robert Reich's term) are rootless because they are highly mobile misunderstands the imaginary nature of roots. To have roots requires a lot of work for the imagination (dreamwork). One element of that dreamwork is that pride in one's nation of origin is important in the construction of self-esteem in the place of immigration. It gives a different feeling to admit that one is from a country ravaged by famines and floods than to say with pride that one is from a superior civilization that is also very good in high-tech developments. The coherence of a Hindu modernity tied to the sovereignty of India's past and territory is gradually given way to a postmodern bricolage of deterritorialized and dehistoricized discourses on family values and cyberspirituality that is very hard to capture. Contrary to what their opponents think these movements are not "outside of modernity," they were very much part of it and are now moving beyond it.

Conclusion

In the nineteenth century, there was a connection among nation, migration, and religion that already complicated the notion of national sovereignty. Obviously, the diasporic communities of Indian indentured laborers and their descendants are quite different from the diasporic communities of middle class software engineers. To some extent this difference reflects a more general pattern in the global labor market, namely the marked growth of the professional-managerial class that is distinguished by its level of formal training and its position in the service economy. It is this class that is required to show full flexibility even to the extent that their members are required to go overseas to find jobs. This is a global phenomenon in which workers are asked to forget about career-long employment and to learn new skills every so many years. For Indian software workers the vagaries of transnational migration and changing regimes of visa regulation and citizenship add to this constant readiness for change. The uncertainties attached to this lifestyle and the required capacity for self-transformation is addressed by a variety of religious movements in Christianity, Islam, and Hinduism (Rouse 1995, 390). In all these religions such movements carry forward the heritage of nineteenth-century reformism that connected nationalism and religion and specifically addressed migrants in a missionary fashion. The new movements produce ideas of spiritual rebirth that are central to new versions of globalized spirituality and attuned to the production of flexible subjectivities. This is further connected to ideas of the nation. The hype found among many IT workers that they can and should play an important role in building the nation back home is a crucial part of the building of transnational networks through investments and circular travel (cf. English-Lueck and Saveri 2000). Nationalist politics of belonging is connected to transnational marriage politics and dowry at the level of the family, and to business and investment strategies at the level of the global nexus of capital and labor.

Inside Out: The Reorganization of National Identity in Norway

Oivind Fuglerud

INTRODUCTION

The aim of this chapter is to contextualize Norway's increasingly restrictive immigration practice by locating it within larger structures of discourse and meaning. The main point of reference, outside the field of immigration itself, is the way nationality is projected in the marketing of goods and values in the present era. The view put forward is that within both immigration and marketing the search for what may be called the "authentic product" reflects an increasing emphasis on culture, heritage, and local origin. This indicates a narrowing conception of national identity with implications in terms of racism and ethnic exclusion in Norwegian society. Briefly summarised, my argument revolves around the following points:

First, since the eighteenth century, the global scene has been dominated by what Malkki (1992) has termed the "national order of things"; the understanding that the world is, and should be, divided into sovereign geographical units containing groups of people with separate cultures and histories. Two dimensions of this order are of particular interest in the present context. One, the concept of sovereignty on which the nation-state as a political organization is based implies control over the geographical borders of the state, making transnational migration something to be brought under state control, for example, through visa regimes and identity documents (Torpey 2000). Two, the concept of the "nation" on which the nation-state rests has always been an ambiguous one, being understood partly as a category of people sharing the same rights because they live on a certain territory and partly as an organic unit into which you must be born. Whereas in Norway the importance of these different elements has varied in different periods (Fuglerud 2001, Gullestad 2002), biological ancestry now seems to become increasingly emphasized.

Second, although the nation-state model of the world is still with us—not the least because it is inscribed in national and international legal instruments—it is under pressure by forces normally discussed under the heading of "globalization." Although this term conceals a number of different processes, many of them are perceived by members of society to weaken the territorial control of the state and the cultural homogeneity of its people. In this situation national stereotyping of self and others become a means of dealing with an increasingly complex social environment.

Third, although such stereotyping may be a general phenomenon, the study of bureaucracy is of particular interest to the question of racism and ethnic discrimination. Basically, I agree with Sivanandan's viewpoint that racism as a social phenomenon is about power not about prejudice (Sivanandan 1983, 3, also 1985). This means that the racism involved in bureacratic decisions cannot be accounted for simply by invoking personal motives among decisionmakers. Rather, we must look into how state officials construe their own responsibilities and their own working situations within the wider world in which their activity is embedded. Government bureaucracies are particularly interesting organizations not only by the fact that they make descisions affecting large numbers of people but because they constitute arenas in which "the state" and "citizen" are imagined and discursively constructed (Gupta 1995). Although it is important to explore the ways in which bureaucratic organizations rationalise their own activity, and through this may come to develop a particular view of the world (Handelman and Leyton 1978; Handelman1981), it also is important to pay attention to the settings within which such outlooks develop. In the present case, this involves locating the immigration service and its activity within broader discourses on globalization and localization. In doing this I draw on material from the media as well as on my five and a half years of experience as an employee of the Norwegian Directorate of Immigration.

Brand-building and New Sovereignty

In a Norwegian television documentary on racism in 1996,[1] one of the immigrants interviewed expressed his frustration on meeting the slogan "Norwegian cucumbers are best!" every time he entered his local food store. He also commented on the need—from a lack of other options—to pour milk to his children every day from containers carrying the Norwegian national flag. What the man referred to was part of

---

[1] The program in question was "Brennpunkt," broadcast on national television on June 4, 1996.

a large campaign marketing Norwegian farm products under the brand name "Norwegian excellence" (*Godt norsk*).

This man's remarks capture something important with respect to the construction of national identity in Norway during the last decade of the last century. In particular the comment points to a connection between real or perceived ethnic discrimination, on the one hand, and the struggle for access to "the space of the visible" (Thompson 1995) through the use of national trademarks, on the other. Here this connection serves as a starting point for exploring certain aspects of what Aihwa Ong (1999, 217) has termed "zones of new sovereignty." She discusses the way states, to become or remain globally competitive, subject different sectors of the population to different regimes of validation and control, resulting in an uneven distribution of services, care, and protection. In Norway this graded sovereignty is found, for example, in administrative and legal measures within the field of immigration. For example, asylum seekers who are from conflict areas but who are seen by Norwegian immigration authorities not to fulfil the more detailed definitional criteria of "refugees" are provided temporary leave to remain without permission to work and without the right to family reunion.[2] New citizens of Norway under suspicion of having violated immigration regulations as part of their migration process sometimes have their passports marked in ways that make them invalid for travel to certain countries. Children of asylum seekers who have not been granted leave to remain but whom the government has not been able to deport are denied identity documents altogether.[3] Having violated no law, these children are allowed to stay in Norway but are denied one of the most fundamental citizenship rights: the right to territorial belonging.

Although measures such as these may seem relatively minor, they tie in with a more general tendency in Europe to accept increasingly larger social and legal differences between groups of people, especially when it comes to differences between people considered to be "native" and others. In most European countries, we find a growing number of people—illegal immigrants, asylum seekers whose applications have been rejected or not yet decided, refugees in transit—whose presence is more or less tolerated by the government but who are deprived of legal status (Noll 1999; Gibney 2001). The administrative and legal measures

[2] A notable example of this category is asylum seekers from northern Iraq. According to the newspaper *Aftenposten* (July 4, 2001), in July 2001 there were more than two thousand Kurds in Norway in this situation.

[3] *Aftenposten* (October 21, 2000). The article estimated that there were, at the time, approximately three hundred rejected but "unreturnable" asylum seekers in Norway, mainly from Ethiopia and Eritrea.

referred to above reflect a way of imagining the unit of the nation, the sovereign political body, which gives priority to its organic and ethnic dimensions at the expense of its civil and territorial aspects. I fully agree with Ong's argument (Ong 1999) that, rather than being obsolete, the concept of sovereignty, in this era of globalization, remains key to our understanding of the shifting relation between state, market, and society. Unlike Ong in her discussion of Malaysia, however, I am not convinced that the two sides to this response to globalization—the struggle for global visibility and the grading of rights—in Norway are the results of a coordinated state strategy. Rather, what we are dealing with are separate strands of thought and action converging into an altered image of self and other. Based on my years of experience as a civil servant in the Norwegian Directorate of Immigration, I am very comfortable with Philip Abrams's well-known understanding of the state (Abrams 1988). Abrams suggests that the state in the sense of a concrete political agency or structure, distinct from the social agencies and structures of the civil society, in which it operates, simply does not exist. What do exist, however, are two things. On the one hand, real power exists. That is, armies are real, and so are immigration departments, police officers, prisons, and deportation orders. On the other hand, the state does exist as an *idea*, as an ideological project. Abrams's conclusion, a conclusion that accords with my own experience, is that the idea of the state conceals the actual inconsistency and confusion in the exercise of state power. The state comes into being as a structuration *within* political and public practice; it starts its life as an implicit construct of action and then acquires a life of its own as a public reification. What we need to study is not the state as one abstract-formal entity but the coming together of *two* entities: on the one hand, ideas of the State, produced and transformed under specific historical conditions; on the other hand, public and political practices carried out in the name of the state. We should not be surprised, therefore, if different government institutions with overlapping responsibilities make different decisions on the same matter, nor by the fact that images of Norway projected by government institutions in the global arena are not coherent. For example, the Norwegian Foreign Ministry in its cultural campaigns abroad seems to emphasize the technological skills and economic expansiveness of present-day future-oriented Norway. The Norwegian Tourist Board, by contrast, in its posters and pamphlets, prefers to present an image of untouched natural resources and villages where little seems to have changed since the nineteenth century. However, both institutions work from the idea that there is, in fact, a Norwegian essence that can be displayed to an international audience. The Norwegian Tourist Board, which is a joint government and private venture, bases its marketing on a concept called "Trademark Norway." The presentation of this concept informs us that there are three main segments for this trademark in the global market, named, respectively "An active experience of nature," "At one with nature and culture," and "Quiet and re-energizing in nature."[4] In the summer campaign for 2002 the focus was on four so-called personal values of Trademark Norway: Authentic, Friendly, Well-shaped, Well-organized.

The use of Norwegian nationality as trademark is found not only in economic marketing but also in foreign policy and diplomatic relations. Norway is a small country with no more than four million people and situated at the periphery of the world. The ambitions of its politicians, however, have a touch of grandeur. Thoroughly disappointed by the people's vote not to enter the European Union in the 1994 referendum, Labour Party officials stated their ambition of establishing Norway as a "humanitarian superpower" (*humanitær stormakt*) as a way of gaining international recognition and attention.[5] Since then, Norway has been involved as mediators and facilitators in a series of conflicts and civil wars around the world—among them the Israeli-Palestinian, the Colombian, the Sudanese, and the Sri Lankan. Furthermore, it has played a significant role in the Balkans through its leadership of the KFOR military command in Kosovo, and recently managed to secure a position in the UN Security Council. Political ambitions go further than multilateral cooperation, however. Norway has put its oil-generated economic resources into active use for the purpose of strengthening democratic values on a worldwide basis. For example, some time ago it was revealed that the Norwegian government had paid large sums of money to the opposition against former President Milosevic in Yugoslavia, including $2 million in salaries to the police force in Montenegro asked for by President Djukanovic.[6] In fact, in international political science there is now said to exist the "Norwegian Model," implying the use of informal procedures, money transfers, and government financed NGOs to undermine regimes one does not agree with (Egeland 1994, 14). "Of course it is a political decision to intervene in another country's election campaign," the Norwegian Foreign Minister at the time, Thorbjorn Jagland, stated in an interview with reference to Norwegian financial activity in Yugoslavia, "but we made the decision because the regime had to be removed."[7]

---

[4] The presentation is found at the Norwegian Tourist Board Web page: <http://www.ntr.no>, unfortunately available only in Norwegian (translated by the author).

[5] Interview with Jan Egeland in *Aftenposten* (September 14, 1994), at the time political secretary in the Foreign Ministry in the Labour Party government.

[6] *Aftenposten* (October 12, 2000); *Dagbladet* (October 13, 2000).

[7] *Aftenposten* (October 12, 2000, p. 8).

OUTSIDE AND INSIDE

In the Foreign Minister's statement we see a downgrading of the territorial integrity of the nation-state that was unheard of during the Cold War era. The reason for bringing this up is not sympathy with former President Milosevic or rulers like him. Rather, I worry that the government's promotion of the "Norwegian Model" is comparable to the national flag on the milk containers, and may go together with an increasingly exclusionary understanding of national identity at home. During the recent period of aggressive foreign policy, there has been in Norway a tendency within the field of immigration toward increasingly strict border controls, a decreasing number of asylum applications granted, forced deportations to countries at war and so on. Characteristic of Norway's engagement with the world is that while conflicts like the Sri Lankan and the Palestinian are considered necessitating the contribution of time and money to their possible resolution, little mercy is shown to the victims of these conflicts asking for asylum on the Norwegian border. The main elements of this strict policy, legal and otherwise, were put in place in the late 1980s and early 1990s. For example, the rate of rejection of Sri Lankan asylum applications by the Directorate of Immigration rose from 1.7 percent to 56.25 percent between 1988 and 1993. The same tendency is reflected in the total numbers. The percentage of asylum seekers from all countries granted refugee status, which in 1987 was a modest 7.8 percent, reached an astonishing 0.5 percent in 1994. The percentage of total rejections, that is the refusal of both refugee status and residence permit on humanitarian grounds, during the same period increased from 24.2 percent to 90.9 percent (Fuglerud 1996). This trend has continued. In the year 2000 approximately fifty out of eight thousand asylum seekers were recognized as refugees.[8]

We need to put this policy into a broader perspective. In Norway, as in many other countries, global processes challenge—or are perceived to challenge—the power of the nation-state. The most visible results of global processes to most people are phenomena like tourism, immigration, and a reduced capability of traditional political and social institutions to protect the welfare of citizens. Recently, it has been pointed out

[8] Statistics within this field are a complex issue, because there are no separate accounts of decisions in cases in which applicants find their own way to Norway, as opposed to cases in which refugees are brought to the country under the quota program. The compilation of figures for the 1988–1994 period was done "manually" by the author as part of his doctoral project (Fuglerud 1996). The 2000 figure may be compiled from numbers found in the Web site of the Directorate of Immigration (<http://www.udi.no/>) by eliminating decisions in all organized acceptances of refugees from the total number.

that as a result of such external impact many people in Norway experience an increasing division between the home and the local community. This division works as a partially new grounding for the imagining of the inside and the outside of the nation, resulting in a cognitive and emotional revitalization of national identification (Gullestad 1997, 41). Under pressure of globalization traditional national themes are transformed by people with new experiences; "[w]hat it means to be Norwegian can no longer be taken for granted, and members of the majority population are thus constructing their national identifications in new ways" (Gullestad 1997, 41).

The late 1980s and the early 1990s was indeed a period when the presence of the outside world was increasingly felt in Norway. To the east, the Soviet Union was ridden by political instability. The controversy over Norway's relationship to the European Union was again heating up, a question that, before the referendum in 1972, had divided the country deeply. The fact that in 1994 for a second time in a referendum, a majority said no to a proposal for membership put forward by the country's largest political party reflects the insistent nationalist and protectionist feelings among sections of the public. In 1994 Norway also hosted the Winter Olympics, an economically costly event which in the preparatory phase met a great deal of criticism from the public. By those in favor the decision to host the games was explained with reference to increased global competition and the possibility of presenting Norway to a world audience. The cultural presentation of the games, like the opening ceremony, was mainly built around elements of natural mythology and folkloristic dress, dance, and music (Klausen 1995, 1996, 1999).[9] The event as a whole thus passed into history as a celebration of global economic liberalism, national competetiveness and cultural resurgence; the latter two—if not all three—summed up in the Prime Minister Gro Harlem Brundtland's infamous slogan coined for the event: "It is typically Norwegian to be good!"[10] This mixture of economic Tacherism, national hybris, and cultural revitalization can be traced within the field of immigration as well. The period when a more strict entrance policy was installed also saw a shift in public debate on the social integration of immigrants already settled in Norway

[9] A statement from the Minister of Education at the time, Gudmund Hernes, indicates the extent to which the organizers of the opening ceremony succeeded in locating a soft spot in the imagination of ethnic Norwegians. Describing his feelings while watching the ceremony, he explains: "The pride and the courage in our breasts were rising to a point where we in the end were overwhelmed by the fireworks, standing amid a sea of fire. Our hearts were pounding, the audience was steaming and we were spellbound, in the hearts of the volcano" (in Klausen 1999, 61).

[10] She presented this slogan during the prime minister's annual televised speech to the nation on January 1.

(Gullestad 2002). Whereas in the 1970s and 1980s refugees and guest-workers were mainly perceived as *victims*—victims of colonialism, of landlords, of government racism, and so on—the early 1990s saw a number of interventions in the public sphere by leading intellectuals arguing for a "greater realism" in Norway's immigration policy (31). Although some of these interventions argued that immigrants until now had been economically pampered and needed to be taught to support themselves (Gerhardsen 1991), others criticized the government for allowing the practice of foreign and repressive cultural traditions (Wikan 1995). Within the short span of a few years a new discursive construction of immigration and immigrants was established.

My interest here is to contextualize the interaction between these more general discursive formations and decision making within the field of immigration. Let it first be said that this interaction is not particular to Norway. The intertwining of nationalism, immigration policy, and projections of cultural difference has been an important theme in debates on the "new racism" (Barker 1981; Balibar 1991a, 1991b; Stolcke 1995; Wieviorka 1995). It has been pointed out that the concept of "culture" has come to replace "race" in public discourse and that rather than arguing for the existence of hierarchically ordered biological groups, current racist rhetoric emphasises unresolvable cultural differences among people.[11] These differences are more often than not assumed to be "national" in origin—"British culture," "Pakistani culture," and so on—and may therefore serve to justify a "politics of space" (Gupta and Ferguson 1992), of which a strict immigration control is a central element. From Australia, Pickering (2001) has described how in the media asylum seekers, because of their nonwhite appearance and their mostly Asian cultural background, are systematically portrayed not only as a problem but as a "deviant" problem (170). The notion of deviance is underpinned by a language of exclusion and a dichotomous construction of normality as being whatever refugees and asylum seekers are not. In this way race and ethnicity become shored up with a conception of inherent illegality.

This discursive construction of "illegality" is at the heart also of current immigration policy in Norway, and must be explored a bit further. In order to get a grip on the formation of such policies we need to focus

---

[11] At the same time, most authors on "new racism" do point to the fact that the cultural rhetoric still contains a biological subtext, in that it is often seen as "natural" to prefer to be with one's own, to fear unknown cultural traditions, or the like. As will become clear, I believe the biological element is very much present in the Norwegian discursive construction of foreigners. At present, foreigners are not normally considered to become "Norwegian" when they acquire Norwegian citizenship, neither by the immigration service nor by people in general.

our attention on the internal processes of bureaucracy (Fuglerud 2004) and on the relationship between these internal processes and the surrounding social environment. In my experience, Norwegian immigration officers see themselves as trying to protect the sovereignty of the state in a world, which, because of processes of globalization, has become disorderly. In particular, they seek to protect the sovereign agency of the state in a situation where this agency is perceived as being threatened both by nonstate actors, like organized traffickers, and by other states who increasingly bypass the rules for orderly interstate interaction—for example, by passing asylum seekers on to Norway. Rather than invoking law as the ultimate basis for judgement which is an image of the bureaucrat that is often projected, immigration officers look upon the law as an instrument in trying to recover a basis for government that is about to be lost. In the Directorate of Immigration, when facing some situation judged to be acute, I would often hear the question, "Where do we find a paragraph to deal with this?"—indicating that the need of the situation justified an instrumental use of the law. For example, the increasingly strict interpretation of the principle of "first country of asylum," under which asylum seekers may be sent back to a safe country traversed on the way to their destination, is regulated neither by Norwegian nor by international law. During my time in the immigration service, individual asylum seekers arriving in Norway by ferry from Germany were on several occasions kept "in orbit" on the boat, neither country accepting them on shore.[12] This kind of restrictive positioning, being the result of nonlegal decisions and entailing prolonged insecurity and suffering for the people in question, becomes difficult to comprehend unless it is construed as a symbolic demarcation of political sovereignty. Put differently: in order to explore the formation of immigration policies as an articulation of the idea of the state in Abrams's sense (Abrams 1988), we need to focus our attention on the nonlegal capacity of law.

THE ADMINISTRATION OF LEGAL CATEGORIES

In order to look at this in some more detail, it is important to realize that the legal categories administered by institutions like the Directorate of Immigration are not contingent facts or arbitrary frameworks imposed upon a preexisting social basis. The social basis of society is as much constituted by these categories as the other way around. As shown by Handelman (1981), Bauman (1991), and Herzfeld (1992), the paradig-

[12] This was before the Schengen agreement and the Dublin Convention, which today regulate this matter between the parties to the agreements.

matic form of organization in the modern nation state is that of bureaucracy, a bureaucracy whose basic function is to generate taxonomies in order to act upon them. To the Norwegian Directorate of Immigration, as to most other immigration authorities in the Western world, the main instrument in its taxonomic work pertaining to asylum seekers is the 1951 Convention Relating to the International Status of Refugees, by the United Nations High Commissioner for Refugees (UNHCR; 1995, 3) termed "the legal bible of refugee rights." In Norway the administration of this legal instrument is of particular interest, as its definition of refugees has been incorporated into national law, and thus helps to define the country's relationship to the international community in legal terms.

Without going into the finer points of interpretation, three characteristics of the 1951 Convention are particularly significant. The first is that a refugee is a person outside his or her country of origin. One cannot in a legal understanding be a refugee without crossing borders. The second is that what the Convention regulates is the signatories' right to *grant* asylum, not the refugee's right to obtain sanctuary in the form of residence permit. The legally binding principle of the convention, in other words, is framed in terms of a relationship between states, not in terms of a relationship between refugees and a particular government. The third characteristic of the Convention is that in contrast to the definitions of the 1920s and 1930s, the refugee definition found in the 1951 Convention is worded in terms of individuals.[13] The pre-1951 definitions, designed to deal with specific situations, normally demanded the fulfilment of only three criteria for refugee status to be granted: (1) a specific national or ethnic origin; (2) a lack of protection from the government of the person's home country; and (3) the nonacquiring of citizenship in another country (Vevstad 1993). As understood by most governments, the 1951 Convention demands an element of personal persecution from the person's own government for an individual to be recognized as a refugee.

The specific formulation of the refugee definition of the 1951 Convention, as part of an interstate agreement, may be understood to have a twofold function. On the one hand the definition articulates the official understanding of personhood in the era of the nation-state: the understanding of the individual constituted as a social person through his

---

[13] According to the 1951 Convention, a refugee is a person who: ". . . owing to well-founded fear of being persecuted for reasons of race, religion, nationality, membership of a particular social group or political opinion, is outside the country of his nationality and is unable to or, owing to such fear, is unwilling to avail himself of the protection of that country; or who, not having a nationality and being outside the country of his former habitual residence is unable or, owing to such fear, is unwilling to return to it."

or her direct relationship to a state—any state one may say. As often observed, it is in the nature of the nation-state to fight alternative sources of social order within its own area of jurisdiction (Gellner 1983; Schafer 1955). When a person—because of intolerable repression—strays outside the area controlled by one state, the solution to the problem inherent in this nongovernmental agency is to transfer the "responsibility" for him or her to another state. By contrast, portraying the refugee who does not fulfil this definition as "unacceptable" provides states the legitimate right to demonstrate their power to grant or reject entry. Through this, the taxonomy itself, and the capacity to uphold it, is manifested (Fuglerud 1997, 1999).

It is in this perspective the restrictive policies toward asylum seekers must be understood. The concept of "asylum seeker," to immigration officers, connotes *illegitimate* protection needs. Saying this implies that there may be a recognized protection need, but that this need is in some sense illegitimate. This illegitimacy has a double basis. The most obvious instance of this illegitimacy is that the need for protection is there for the wrong reasons. In 1985, already, the UNHCR concluded in its "Note on International Protection" that the majority of today's refugees and asylum seekers do not flee from personal persecution or from conflicts where they have been personally involved but from the effects of other people's violence. Thereby these refugees are considered by Immigration not to fulfil the definition provided in the 1951 Convention. This trend has continued since then. The other source of illegitimacy is more difficult to pinpoint precisely, but has to do with the way asylum seekers arrive and present their applications at the border. Under the present global visa regime, the presentation of asylum applications almost always involves the crossing of state borders without proper papers, something that provides the applications with a quality of "irregularity." Not only are such crossings formally illegal, but also they indicate the assistance from family members and/or professional agents; that is from causative agents other than the state itself.

These two elements, in fact, must be seen in conjunction. If a person is actually understood to be a refugee according to the 1951 Convention, it rarely matters much to the caseworker in charge by which means he or she arrived. In this case a forged passport will be fully justified as a *force majeur* measure to escape from a threatening situation. Also, immigration officers may feel sympathy for refugees of war as long as they are not present at the border. On many occasions persons, who would never have been granted residence permits if they had arrived as asylum seekers, have willingly been accepted as refugees to Norway on application from the UNHCR. I suggest that the reason for this paradox is that in these cases state representatives have been able to make decisions based on the state's own sovereign agency, without its representatives being put in "defensive modus." To immigration officers, asylum is understood to be an act of charity rather than a legal obligation (Pickering 2001). It is something to be offered on behalf of the state, not something to be claimed by individuals. As long as displaced people conform to the script of being passive and invited they may also be perceived as being persecuted by another state. What is the case with uninvited asylum seekers, by contrast, is that the perceived nonfulfilment of convention criteria and the irregularity of travel tend to collapse one into the other. Because applicants do not fulfil definitional criteria their travel tend to be perceived as "irregular"; because they arrive by irregular means their claimed need for protection are often understood to be "unfounded." This understanding is not limited to immigration officers as such. The irregularity of travel is a phenomenon whose definition as a problem is given official recognition not only by nation states and law enforcing agencies like INTERPOL and the FBI but also by organizations like the International Organization for Migration (IOM). IOM, for so long associated among refugees with assisting the freedom-travel from transit camps to resettlement countries, in one of the first issues of its newsletter, *Trafficking in Migrants,* stated a position that any Western government would find acceptable: "An important contribution to discouraging trafficking is the prompt return home of irregular migrants. In addition to thwarting the organisers of illegal migration, return deters those considering resorting to the services of traffickers by spreading the word—through returnees—that trafficking is a risky business" (IOM 1994, 1).

The fact that this view contradicts the UNHCR's position seems not to bother the IOM.[14]

THE TWO SIDES OF SOVEREIGNTY

There is little reason to be surprised by this situation. The 1951 Convention, written after the dissolution of the empires and before the oncoming of "globalization," reflects the fact that control over people's movement across borders is an inherent and essential component of the modern European idea of sovereign nation-states. It is, so to speak, the

[14] The executive Committee of the UNHCR, in its fifty-first session, recognized the importance of ensuring that, in the context of measures adopted to deal with irregular migration, trafficking, and smuggling of persons, the international protection and assistance needs of asylum seekers and refugees are fully met, consistent with international protection responsibilities, in particular the principle of nonrefoulement (Conclusion No. 89 {LI} of 2000. Preambular paragraph. A/AC.96/944 para. 23).

external demarcation of the states' internal control. As conceived by Grotius in his *De Jure Belli* from 1625, what gives the modern state such an extraordinary efficacy is exactly that its status as *suprema potestas* encompasses both territory and population. The philosopher Thomas Hobbes (1971 [1651]) saw the relation between ruler and subject as a social contract in which personal obedience was exchanged for territorial protection. In his advice to the Poles, Rousseau explicitly connects his viewpoints on nation-building to a need to construct a primary relationship between men and territory (in Connolly 1994). The apparent contradiction between the theory of universal rights, propagated by Rousseau (1978), and his advocacy of national sovereignty protected by borders, is only apparent because he sees universal values as deposited in the bounded community where all members have the same rights as citizens.

In the reasoning of these philosophers we find a concept of sovereignty somewhat different from the preceding and from the one emerging today. What becomes clear from the philosophers' arguments is that in discussing sovereignty under the nation-state we are dealing not with one but with two relationships that should be kept analytically separate.

On the one hand, we have a relationship between a government and its subjects couched in terms of territory. What is the subject of the state's authority is the "the people of . . . (e.g., Norway)." This dimension of sovereignty is ambiguous. As observed by Malkki (1992), botanical metaphores ("soil," "roots," etc.) have often been prominent in the formulation of this conception of territory *cum* people, suggesting that the national community be rooted in the soil which provides it with nourishment. Nevertheless, as proven by the history of almost any country, residence in the territory *has* until recently provided a possibility of incorporation within the nation (Anderson 1992), because the concept of territorial sovereignty has been understood to imply equality between citizens.

On the other hand, there is the question of relations between states. The noninterventionist principle played a major role in international politics in the twentieth century, and is the main reason why a person has not been considered a refugee before he or she is outside his or her country of origin. Until recently, the dominant understanding was that until the person had crossed the border, the individual was under the state's sovereign jurisdiction and no one could interfere by offering him or her protection. Governments' prerogative of admitting or not admitting foreigners is the corollary of this principle of nonintervention, a natural consequence of the nation state's claim for, and acknowledged right to, absolute control over its borders. This is the understanding behind the 1951 Convention where the purpose is to give legitimacy to states' rights to grant asylum, not the refugee's right to be granted.

During the last decade, we have seen a shift between these two components of sovereignty. As indicated by the "Norwegian model" of foreign policy discussed above, the noninterventionist principle is not as self-evident as it used to be. This is not the only indication. From the late 1980s, there has been an observable shift in preferred solutions to the world's refugee crises. While until this point the solutions given priority by the UNHCR were third country resettlement, first country integration, and voluntary repatriation, in that order, with the end of the Cold War "prevention" through outside intervention has become the main principle (Tjore 1998). Northern Iraq 1991, Bosnia 1993, Rwanda 1994, and Kosovo 1999 are some of the situations in which this policy has been implemented. Whether military or humanitarian, such interventions represent a breach with the principle of nonintervention as earlier understood. The most apparent consequence of this loosening up of the principle of territorial sovereignty is, somewhat paradoxically, an increased emphasis on local origin and through this on the state—subject aspect of sovereignty. In international refugee work we see this in the fact that although close to fifty million European refugees were resettled outside their country of origin between 1912 and 1969 (Marrus 1990, 54), this solution is today offered to less than one per cent of the world's refugees (Loescher 1993, 148). Refugees today are considered to "belong," in some fundamental sense, to the area where they are born in a different way from what was the situation a few decades back (Chimni 1998). The problem behind their displacement, the understanding now is, must be resolved by transforming the relationship between state and civilian population rather than through the offer of a new homeland.

Administering Nationhood

There is a close parallel here to the development in immigration policy described earlier. Within the field of refugee protection and the field of immigration alike the state—population dimension of the sovereignty issue seems to be perceived less in terms of "territory as people" and more in terms of a direct and graded relationship between governments and their subjects. The relationship between state and individual has been brought back into the discourse of sovereignty, as it was in the pre-Rousseauian concept of statehood (Dacyl 1996). Throughout the 1990s public debates on immigration in Norway have focused on the questionable loyalties of new members of society. For example, as a main propagandist of "realism" in debates on cultural integration Professor of Anthropology Unni Wikan argues that accepting a Norwegian passport while rejecting "fundamental Norwegian values" make immigrants "citizens of convenience" (*beleilighetsborgere*) (Wikan 1995, 177). In particular, the values of the thousands of Muslim immigrants who have arrived in the country since the 1960s and are now Norwegian citizens seem, in her view, to be less "fundamentally Norwegian" than those of the white majority society.

With the reorganization of the Norwegian immigration service in 1988, this public scepticism was incorporated into the Directorate of Immigration, the organization that administers nationality on a day-to-day basis. Instead of, say, caseworkers dealing only with asylum applications or only with visa questions, which would make sense in terms of legal categories, work in the Directorate was organized in offices deciding all different applications from one or a small number of countries. The reason for structuring work in this way was to build competence on specific nationalities of immigrants/cultural minorities and to allow caseworkers to make connections between different categories of applications. For example, the possibility of granting an application for tourist visa is seen as linked to the probability of the person "jumping ship" and applying for asylum while in the country. The understanding is that this probability can only be judged on the basis of previous experience with people from a certain family, region, or country. In deciding an application for family reunion with a former asylum seeker, the applicant's details will be checked against the information about his or her family that the former asylum seeker gave several years earlier. Since migration to Norway like to most other countries often does involve an element of chain migration, it is not uncommon for experienced caseworkers to "know" quite well a certain number of immigrant families or villages in countries of origin from material appearing in applications. Most caseworkers keep personal files in their desk drawers containing statements made by former applicants and judgements made earlier by themselves or their colleagues. On the basis of such "knowledge" applications are sometimes evaluated more or less offhand: "You can't give him a visa, his whole family is here," "This man doesn't need asylum, we sent his brother back last year," "There was no such organization in the Punjab at that time," and so on.

With respect to sovereignty, there is now a tendency for the interstate dimension of sovereignty to be dramatized and acted out by means of the control that the government has over people within its jurisdiction. One such situation involving refugees arriving from Germany has already been mentioned. When Tamil asylum seekers from Sri Lanka started coming to Norway through Sweden in relatively large numbers in 1994, it was decided to send them back across the border. Despite the fact that the Norwegian government during this period did not deport Tamils to their home country, and the fact that it was well known that the Swedish government did, a decision was made to regard Sweden as a safe first country of asylum. The general understanding in the Directorate of Immigration was that this might teach the Swedes to get their own control routines in order instead of passing people on to Norway. Interestingly this symbolic politics of sovereignty also has its beneficiaries. In 1995 regulations were enacted allowing Russian nationals of Norwegian ancestry to return to the country from where their parents and grandparents had emigrated. In the eighteenth century, whereas the borders between Norway and Russia were still open and fluid, a number of Norwegian families moved east to try their luck as fishermen along the coast of the Kola Peninsula. After the 1917 Revolution the border was closed, and the members of the Norwegian colonies were treated as traitors under the communist regime. Many were executed, while others were deported to distant parts of the Russian Empire. After more than seventy years without any contact, the Norwegian government decided to trace descendants of the migrants and offer them a more comfortable existence in their "fatherland." Because of their genes they are now seen to have inherent rights to move across the border from one of the poorest to one of the richest countries in Europe. The official justification for this intervention is interesting. "We have no time to lose," the Foreign Minister stated recently in an article in a local newspaper; "As a nation we cannot allow the fate of the Kola-Norwegians to become a burden for our reputation."[15] Although this conception of ethnic nationality is familiar to the situation of the *aussiedler* in Germany, the inscription of it in law is new to Norway. What emerges when comparing the case of Tamils and Russian-Norwegians is the use of graded ethnic categories for the demonstration of a form of sovereignty conceived more in terms of people than in terms of territory.

THE CHANGING METAPHOR OF THE BODY

In the reasoning of immigration authorities one is reminded of Emily Martin's discussion of the way war and police surveillance of illegal immigrants were used as metaphors in earlier media descriptions of the immune system of the human body (Martin 1994). What the areas of

[15] *Dagbladet* (October 28, 2000, p. 3). The original article by Foreign Minister Thorbjorn Jagland was published in the newspaper *Nordlys*.

immigration and immunology share is a preoccupation with outside versus inside, and the absorption, transformation, and possible danger of material passing from outside in. Vital to the understanding of the immune system, as to immigration, is the capacity to distinguish between self and nonself where the world of the nonself is conceived as foreign (or "alien") and hostile.

Martin's reason for analyzing medical literature is to point out how body functions and the social order are understood in terms of each other. Metaphors work both ways, and given the status of medical science in Western society there is little reason to doubt that images from this field of knowledge have been important in shaping our understanding of social and political relationships. The concrete physicality of the body provides a tremendous symbolic power, and allows arbitrary cultural categories to be invested with an aura of naturalness (Douglas 1973; Gutiérrez 1994). In Mary Douglas's words, "[t]he physical body can have universal meaning only as a system which responds to the social system, expressing it as a system" (Douglas 1973, 112). In our time "the immune system" as Haraway puts it, "is an elaborate icon for . . . systems of symbolic and material 'difference' in late capitalism" (Haraway 1989, 4).

I should make it clear that whereas immigration officers may certainly speak of "strengthening defences" and "removing parasites," I do not claim that the body works as an explicit and articulated model for their work. Nevertheless, immigration officers' understanding of their own function bears a certain resemblance to the image of the human immune system refered to earlier. To paraphrase Lakoff and Johnson (1980), it is a "metaphor they live by." It has shared with this image, the need to protect a closed unit faced by hostile causative agents. It also has shared the understanding of constant threat, of seemingly undramatic events representing a potential danger of encroachment. Openings in the protective shield must be tightened; individuals exploiting loopholes must be eliminated; and, security measures should be developed. For immigration officers, professionalism consists in the ability to spot irregularities and take appropriate action. This requires not only legal qualifications, but also knowledge of people's background, their migration patterns, their characteristic manner of fraud and deception, and so on.

Martin (1994, 8–9) points out that older and newer images of the immunity system exist side by side—as they do, I would argue, among immigration officers. In 1940s and 1950s, media descriptions focused the environment just outside the body as the most imminent threat to health. The most important defense against illness was strictly preventing germs from entering into the interior of the body. In the 1960s and

1970s, however, attention to the defenses *within* the body increased exponentially (32). From then on we find accounts of safeguards within the body that come into operation if the "outer fortifications" (the skin or mucous membranes) are breached. At the same time, concern with the cleanliness of the outside surfaces of the body diminishes: "It is as if, whatever is out there, and however deadly and dirty it is, the body's interior lines of defense will be able to handle it" (Ibid., 33).

While for a long period immigration work in Norway was based on the model of the naturally closed unit, with the reorganization of the immigration service in 1988 new elements were brought in, creating a resemblance to the new immunological understanding. In the early 1990s the Ministry of Justice, the ministry responsible for immigration control, initiated a policy of what was called "general foreigner control" (*generell utlendingskontrroll*) to be implemented by the immigration sector. This policy contained a number of elements, among them the establishing of a separate immigration police unit and the stationing of immigration officers at Norwegian embassies abroad. The task of these officers was not to hand out forms and issue visas; their work was and continues to be specifically tied to the investigation of claims made by asylum applicants in Norway (Fuglerud 1997). As indicated by the name and initiatives of the new policy, entrance control was no longer to be limited to the border itself—rather, what now came into focus was the connection between individuals and groups already in Norway and the outside world. For caseworkers in the Directorate of Immigration, one consequence of the new policy was that each country office was required to come up with suggestions for how the control of "their" nationalities could be strengthened. As a result, asylum cases were reopened and asylum applicants found to have lied about details in their background started having their settlement permits revoked. Individuals who were found to have traveled to Norway on illegal documents, or who had helped others to do so, were increasingly brought to court.

What emerges from this discussion is that the images of the human body and the nation-state alike are increasingly constructed as flexible, able to accomodate to changing environments.[16] As argued by Haraway almost a decade ago, "[n]either our personal bodies nor our social bodies may be seen as natural, in the sense of existing outside the self-creating process called human labour" (Haraway 1991, 10). In the clas-

[16] I am not able here to do justice to Martin's (1994) much broader discussion of the importance of flexibility in current popular understandings of the immune system in America. Partly this is because of the different natures of Norwegian and American societies. I would argue that Norway, with its strong state, its large public sector, and its long tradition of social democratic politics in general, has yet not reached the level of capitalist development that makes the concept of flexibility so important in the United States.

sical era of nation-states, now behind us, the discursive images of body and nation have shared two fundamental similarities relating them intimately to each other. One is the unmediated relationship between the individual (cell) and the composite unit, presupposing a cultural homogeneity between all individuals within the boundary of this unit; the other is the concept of body and nation-state as limited domains with clearly demarcated boundaries.[17] Today the human image is increasingly liberated from the constraints of the physical body through the possibility of surgical and reproductive techniques. Life-cycle categories have become blurred into a more fluid life course in which looks and feelings may conflict with one's biological age (Featherstone et al. 1991). The body is no longer perceived as a limited domain in the traditional sense. The question has even been posed of the "end of the body" as we have known it (Martin 1992).

With the present ongoing development within genetics and medical science it is too early to foretell in what form, if any, a new image of the body may stabilise. It may well be, however, that the "end of the body" translates into a split image of display and impression management, on the one hand (Featherstone et al. 1991), and biological essentialism, on the other (Gutiérrez 1994). This is what we may observe happening to the nation. On the one hand, politicians and businessmen strive to portray the body politic of the nation as a performing, marketable self; on the other, there is a tendency to conceptualize nationality, or, rather, national *authenticity*, in terms of biology. These dimensions may in fact go well together. In Norway, commercial interests are now striving to introduce a standard of brand names equivalent to the French system of "Appellation d'Origine Contrôlée" that we know from trademarks like Cognac and Roquefort, and that would imply a stronger protection of names indicative of local origin. In a recent newspaper interview, the Norwegian industrial attaché in Paris speaks warmly of this system.[18] "It means we have to treat people differently," he says, "We need to move away from the industrial product to the special character, to the original, to remain competitive. [. . .] For a product to defend its brand of origin, we must return to the soil and to the production methods of a product's home area. [. . .] It is a fact that origin is a major source of value," he adds.

---

[17] Compare the following two observations made by two of the most famous theorists of nationalism: "[Nation-states] are poorly endowed with rigid internal subgroupings; their populations are anonymous, fluid and mobile, and they are unmediated; the individual belongs to them directly. . . . Homogeneity, literacy, anonymity are the key traits" (Gellner 1983, 138). And, "[. . .] the nation is imagined as limited because even the largest of them, encompassing perhaps a billion living human beings, has finite, if elastic, boundaries, beyond which lie other nations. No nation imagines itself coterminus with mankind" (Anderson 1983, 16).

[18] *Verdens Gang* (December 3, 2000).

These ideas are recognizable in immigration policy as well. Here the question of authenticity has to do mainly with biologically grounded loyalty and trust. Whereas Russian nationals of Norwegian stock are assumed inherently to be covered by the trademark of nationality, this is not so with people of alternative origin. Their willingness to contribute added value to the Norwegian label cannot be judged by their own information. In their case, assessment of loyalty to their new nation takes the form of routine use of advanced medical examinations—X-raying, DNA-testing, dental examinations, and so on—used to test the truth, and thereby the loyalty, of new members of society. One way or the other credibility is in the genes.

By Way of Conclusion

Observed from a multicultural or human rights viewpoint, both the old and the new operational model of immunology at work in immigration has its obvious limitations. As pointed out by Pickering (2001), the discursive construction of irregular migrants as intruders establishes a binary model of illegality and legality. Because the original illegality resides with the other, all state responses are rendered legal. By way of conclusion, I believe it may be time to redeem the concept and practice of territorial sovereignty, understood as the protection by the state of a community of equal citizens. The alternative may well be the worst aspects of the pre- and post-Rousseauian versions of sovereignty: global restrictions on mobility and local "containment" of foreign elements. On the one hand, we have during the last decade seen strategies being designed to prevent refugees from reaching the borders. On the other hand, there has through the 1990s been an increasing tendency to limit the extent of integration of foreigners through administrative measures, including the limiting of residential visas in time, restricting the geographical validity of travel documents, assigning specific residential locations, and so on. These tendencies reflect the fact that the foreigner inside and the foreigner outside are subject to two different modalities of state power in a way so eminently described by Foucault (1977) with regard to discipline and punishment. The foreigner inside, the permanent resident and the naturalised citizen, is subject to the ordinary mechanisms of the modern state structure—only more so. Through photos, fingerprints, and the establishment of a separate file, he or she is, quite literally, inscribed into the disciplinary space of the nation state. The foreigner outside is in a different position. As an applicant awaiting decision, or, worse, as a nonperson caught in transit between different spheres of jurisdiction, he is subject to the old *"merum imperium,"* the ruler's absolute power over life and death. His position bears a strong resemblance to the person undergoing penal investigation in premodern Europe. Like this investigation, the asylum investigation is essentially not a judicial but a political process, and the possible outcome, the public execution or the deportation, not only a judicial but also a political ritual. Like criminal offence in the classical age, irregular migration represents an attack on sovereignty itself, and like public executions, deportations—made public through the media—"is a ceremonial by which a momentarily injured sovereignty is reconstituted. It restores that sovereignty by manifesting it at its most spectacular" (48). The connection to racism lies in the fact that both modalities of power—the internal and the external—represent ways of separating out dangerous substances from society; they reflect the vision of a pure product in a world of mixed blessings.

Suspended Spaces—Contesting Sovereignties in a Refugee Camp

Simon Turner

This essay takes its point of departure in Lukole refugee camp in North-western Tanzania, where close to one hundred thousand Burundian refugees kill time in a well-organized and clearly demarcated space. Based on ethnographic fieldwork, I explore the nature and limits of sovereign power in and around this exceptional space. That Lukole is exceptional is visible at first sight, sticking out as it does in the Tanzanian landscape with its order and bureaucratic efficiency. It is the kind of space that begs for questions about power, biopolitics, and sovereignty, pushing the limits of our received wisdoms on these issues.

The Tanzanian authorities take a number of measures to contain these refugees. Once they have been secluded in the camp where they are put under the authority of the camp commandant, they cannot leave a zone of four kilometers around the camp without special permission. He is the highest legal authority in the camp and is the local representative of the Ministry of Home Affairs (MHA) in Dar-es-Salaam. He does not answer to the district or regional commissioners, thus effectively placing the camp outside the normal jurisdiction of the Tanzanian state. The camp is at once in the grips of the state, trying to control and contain refugees through various harsh and restrictive measures, while simultaneously being placed outside the very same state as a kind of space of exception. Here, the words of the camp commandant are law.

It is tempting to see Lukole as an expression of Agamben's camp as the hidden matrix and *nomos* of modern political space (Agamben 1998, 166; Agamben 2000, 37). The camp for Agamben is related to the Schmittean state of exception—a temporary space that is related to the concept of a threat towards the stability of the political order. It is a temporary, exceptional space, created by a sovereign decision (Agamben 1998, 168–71). "[T]he camp is the structure in which the state of exception is permanently realised" (Agamben 2000, 40). Here, the Tanzanian state decides that the refugees are a threat to the nation-state and puts them in this exceptional space, that is at once inside and outside the law. In this case, the refugees are reduced to "bare life," outside the *polis* of national citizens. As Agamben argues, such disenfranchised bare life is at once outside the *polis*—the city of men—while being an "inclusive exclusion." That is to say that the political community of citizens depends upon the exclusion of certain human beings that are reduced to bare life.[1]

The main argument that I will propose in this paper is that this is only part of the story. Although the concepts of *bare life* and *the camp* are compelling, Burundian refugees in Lukole are not just any kind of bare life. For Agamben, the main point is that the camp is a space where the normal law is suspended, suggesting that anything from Auschwitz to the *zones d'attente* in French international airports count as camps. Whether atrocities take place or not does not depend on the law, he explains, but, rather, "on the civility and ethical sense of the police that act temporarily as sovereign" (Agamben 2000, 42). Although there are undoubtedly similarities between refugee camps, asylum centers, mining compounds, concentration camps, and slave plantations,[2] and a more systematic comparison could shed more empirical light on the subject, I suggest that we must also explore the particularities that often emerge if we change our perspective a little and explore the camp from within. In this paper, we explore the various sovereign spaces that emerge within and around the camp.

In the case of Lukole, it is important to acknowledge that the camp is being subjected to a strongly moralizing and ethical biopolitical project by humanitarian agencies. Whereas the camp commandant zealously controls who enters and who leaves the camp, guarding the perimeters of this island in Tanzanian territory, it is international relief agencies, led by UNHCR, that are in charge of the day-to-day "care and maintenance" of the camp. They exert a caring biopower, concerned with the life and health of the refugee population. This obviously poses questions about the character of power, authority and sovereignty in the camp.

Finally, the refugees themselves seek to maneuver in this temporary space, thus creating pockets of sovereign power outside the reach of either the camp commandant's restrictions or UNHCR's benevolent con-

---

[1] For further reading on Agamben's understanding of the camp see Agamben (1998, Part III) and Agamben (2000, 37–49). Along similar lines, it has been mentioned often in the literature that refugees appear to pollute the national fabric and are secluded in order to maintain what Malkki has called "the national order of things" (Malkki 1995b). By crossing borders, refugees and migrants challenge the naturalness of the citizen-nation-state nexus (Soguk 1999). By categorizing them as refugees and by problematizing them, they are transformed into objects of governmental intervention and can be managed, thus restabilizing the nation-state (Hyndman 2000; Soguk 1999).

[2] See also Mbembe (2003) for a comparison with slave plantations.

trol. Although they are positioned as bare life by the Tanzanian state, they are not paralyzed. And, likewise, as much as the biopolitics of UNHCR attempts to create moral apolitical beings, it never succeeds and history and politics strike back. Although the refugees themselves also conceive of the camp as an exceptional space—a temporary suspension of moral order—they are constantly working on constructing their own political subjectivities—their own sovereign decisions.

In other words, sovereignty is complex and multilayered in the camp as are the means of exercising it. In order to grasp this complexity I will approach the camp from three angles. First, we will explore the ways in which the Tanzanian authorities tackle issues of displacement and mobility. This will involve a brief historical overview of policies concerning refugees since independence linking it to Nyerere's *Ujamaa* and to the later economic and political liberalization policies. In the second part, we explore more carefully the governmental actions of the international humanitarian organizations that, for all means and purposes, are the most powerful actors in the camp and the surrounding border area. I will show how UNHCR, on the one hand, treats the refugees as bare life—as biological beings that simply need to be kept alive and healthy while they wait for the day they will return. On the other hand, UNHCR is in charge of an ethical project. The desire to help requires that the beings one is governing, are moral beings. I show how this leads to a kind of paternalistic experiment in turning the refugees into innocent victims without a political past and preparing them for real life after the camp, in this sense reconfirming the idea of the camp as a temporary exception. Finally, in the last section, we look at the camp from the inside. From the point of view of the refugees, the camp marks a temporary suspension of moral order where norms, hierarchies and status are constantly being renegotiated. I show how a certain class of "big men" make use of the amoral space to create localized spaces of sovereignty. Striving for political and social subjectivity, they use a mixture of political networks, contacts with relief agencies and brute force to create spaces of authority that are outside the governmental reach of either the camp commandant or the international organizations.

THE CAMP AS A SECLUSION SITE

Burundians have crossed the border to Tanzania in search for livelihoods and security in waves and trickles for decades. Many have settled in villages in the border region buying land from local Tanzanians or setting up business as masons and tailors. Others were gathered in reception centers and then moved to settlements or refugee camps—secluded from Tanzanian villages. Lukole refugee site was created in 1994 in response to the massive influx of refugees following the murder of Burundi's first democratically elected Hutu president by Tutsi officers and the violence that this event triggered in late 1993.[3]

Whereas Tanzania in the 1970s and 1980s was often commended by humanitarian agencies and academics for its hospitality towards refugees (Anthony 1990; Armstrong 1990, 1991), it is generally agreed that there has been a toughening of policies toward refugees in the 1990s.[4] In late 1997 and early 1998 the Tanzanian army tried to "flush out" anyone living in villages along the border with Burundi who was not in possession of the right resident papers.[5] Those who were considered to be Burundians were given the choice to return to Burundi or to go to the camp. According to testimonies that I collected from people who had been "rounded up," the army came without warning and rounded up whole villages asking everyone to present their documents. Those who failed to present Tanzanian documents were immediately sent to the camp, often splitting families, if some members had been out of the village at the time. Other families were split, if they were mixed Tanzanian-Burundian marriages.[6] People who had migrated to Tanzania in search of land twenty to thirty years ago now found themselves in a refugee camp, surrounded by Burundians who were there for very different reasons. With this operation, the Tanzanian army made sure that everyone who was not truly Tanzanian was classified as a refugee and was treated as such, thus trying to eliminate ambiguity along the border.

What goes on inside the camp is of less interest to the Tanzanian authorities who leave the everyday care and governing of the camp population to UNHCR. This division of labor is not that clear-cut, however, as Tanzanian authorities do meddle in internal issues in the camp if they are seen to affect Tanzanian security and diplomatic relations with Burundi. For instance, the Tanzanian authorities do their best to purge the camp of "rebels." Tanzania is continuously being accused, directly or indirectly, by the Burundian government of housing and feeding

[3] For accounts of these events, see Lemarchand (1996) and Reyntjens (1993).

[4] The most obvious sign of the tougher line on refugees and migrants can be seen in the forced expulsion of Rwandan refugees in December 1996 and January 1997. This operation was heavily criticized, as it is a breach of the U.N. convention on refugees' principle of nonrefoulement. For a more balanced analysis of the causes behind the repatriation, see Whitaker (2002).

[5] See Human Rights Watch (1999) for a critical account of the exercise.

[6] Tanzanian women had to follow their Burundian husbands (and Burundian children) to the camp or be separated from them, whereas Burundian women could remain in the villages with their Tanzanian husbands (and Tanzanian children).

Hutu rebels in the camps along Burundi's borders. It is therefore of the utmost importance for the Tanzanian authorities to show that they can control the camps and keep them free of rebels.

Another way in which the Tanzanian authorities interfere with the camp is to ban agricultural activities and to decrease plot sizes. Until 1997 the refugees were allowed to cultivate crops inside the 4 km zone, as long as they stuck to annual crops such as beans and sweet potatoes. Perennial crops such as bananas—a favored staple diet and essential for beer brewing—were not allowed, as this would signal that the refugee site was a permanent solution. Repatriation was the only "permanent solution" envisaged by the Tanzanian authorities. In 1997 this policy was tightened further as all agriculture was banned except on the ever-smaller plots that were allocated. This policy was adopted with the explicit aim of encouraging repatriation. In other words, the Tanzanian authorities are maintaining the exceptional character of the camp. As long as the camp remains exceptional, the law can be suspended, confirming the sovereign power of the Tanzanian state.

The hostility toward refugees is often described as a natural reaction to the massive influx of refugees that entered the country in the mid-1990s and the negative impact they were assumed to have had on the environment, security, and development. As several studies have shown, however, the impact of refugees on the border regions cannot be unanimously described as negative (Hoyweghen 2001; Landau 2001; Waters 1997; Whitaker 1999). Instead, the reasons should be found in the shifts in Tanzanian political reforms in the post-Nyerere era.

During the Nyerere period, the Tanzanian government perceived refugees as an economic asset. Resettlement villages, constructed in the mid-1960s for Tutsi refugees from Rwanda, functioned almost as a pilot project for the government's ambitious *villagization* program that was launched a few years later (Hoyweghen 2001, 16–17). Similarly, Hutu refugees who fled Burundi in 1972 were relocated in settlements in scarcely populated areas in the Tanzanian interior and given enough land to become self-sufficient. As Malkki, amongst others, comments this was a strategy of the government to exploit and develop these un-inhabited areas in line with the general agrodevelopmentalist spirit of the Nyerere period (Malkki 1995a). The sociopolitical context of the Nyerere period was agriculturally based developmentalism and general optimism and refugees were seen as an economic resource. In the 1980s they were even offered Tanzanian citizenship (Gasarasi 1990; Sommers 1993). Hoyweghen argues that with the collapse of the Tanzanian economy in the 1980s and the following liberalization of the economy and the political sphere, the post-Nyerere Tanzanian state has gradually shifted perceptions of the migrant from being an economic asset to being a security concern (Hoyweghen 2001, 3). We also should recall that Tanzania was a frontline state, actively supporting the anti-apartheid movement. South African, Zimbabwean and Namibian refugees were welcomed and encouraged to continue their political activities. With the end of apartheid, the ideological backing for refugees disappeared and in the name of peaceful cohabitation with neighboring states, the Tanzanian state led a stricter control with political activities among refugees (Chaulia 2003).

What happens then to the authority of the Tanzanian state when it is not able to deliver services to the Tanzanian population and large international relief organizations take care of building and rehabilitating roads, water, schools, and health clinics in the border region? Is there a sense that the Tanzanian state is de facto relegating sovereignty over its territory to "the international community" given the latter's obvious financial hegemony? Loren Landau finds that the Tanzanian state has surprisingly not lost its legitimacy among the population, and argues that this is because of a strong discourse in Tanzanian postcolonial historiography, depicting Tanzania as a virtuous victim of international actors. Although the restructuring of the Tanzanian economy in the 1990s has resulted in inflation throughout the country, Tanzanians living near the refugee camps attribute the rising cost of living exclusively to the presence of refugees and highly paid humanitarian staff (Landau 2001, 22).

In other words, local Tanzanian authorities are successful, not only in blaming the refugees for economic hardships that are a result of its own failed policies, but also in making it look as if the government of Tanzania has been altruistic and sacrificing. UNHCR and other relief agencies, by contrast, engage in "state spectacles" (Hansen and Stepputat 2001) that symbolically reify the Tanzanian state. Being financed primarily by donors such as the United States and the European Union (EU), one might expect that the organizations could put enough pressure on a poor aid-dependent country like Tanzania to make the latter simply follow suit. To a large degree this is also the case in Ngara district. As U.N. experts fly in on U.N. aircraft, having funded the maintenance of the runway, to put up parallel water and electricity supplies and means of communication for staff, they tend to forget the Tanzanian authorities. However, certain rituals of state sovereignty are still played out and respected. For example, a Tanzanian immigration officer is always driven (in a U.N. vehicle) to the airstrip to control the visa requirements of arriving and departing U.N. personnel. In this way the international organizations pay homage to the nation-state. In other words, all actors—the Tanzanian population, the Tanzanian authorities and international organizations—act as if the Tanzanian state were the sovereign power.

In this section, we have seen how the Tanzanian authorities at one level are impotent and in terms of delivering services rather irrelevant both in the camp and in the surrounding villages. However, the Tanzanian authorities have the right to decide who is to be included and who is to be excluded, thus making it possible to define the limits of the camp (the 4 km zone) and who can move in and out of it. Furthermore, we have seen how the Tanzanian attitude toward refugees has become increasingly "hostile." Refugees have gone from being an economic asset to being a security threat. Along with this shift, the Tanzanian state has shifted from being actively involved in integrating and governing refugees to merely leaving them in the hands of international agencies. In the prevailing security discourse, national sovereignty is assured by making the camp as temporary as possible, maintaining its exceptional character, keeping it outside the Tanzanian law and handing as much as possible of its daily management over to international organizations.

The Camp as a Biopolitical Experiment

In general UNHCR and other relief agencies were there in order to help the refugees. However, in order to do this in a manner that made any sense and made sure that everyone was treated as fairly as possible, a bureaucratic machinery was unavoidable. Upon arrival in the camp, every refugee was registered by UNHCR and each household was given a plot upon which to build a *blindé* (hut). There were rules on where and how to build one's *blindé*. Thus, they were not allowed to build fences around their plot—allegedly because of fire and health hazards. Similarly, for health reasons every household was obliged to build a pit latrine of a minimum depth and at a certain distance from their *blindé*.

In order better to govern the camp and deliver the services that were identified as needed in order to keep the population healthy, the camp population was divided into several subgroups depending on "vulnerability" and hence on how needy they were evaluated to be. In a preliminary registration and demography report based on a registration exercise conducted February 28–March 5, 1997 (UNHCR Memorandum 03.05.97), two pages are devoted to "vulnerability." Here, twenty categories of vulnerability are identified from relatively common groups such as "EA—Elderly Adult," "SP—Single Parents" and "UAMs—Unaccompanied Minors" to more complex categories such as "SP/MD—Single parent/mentally Disabled" and "FF/UAM—Foster Family/Unaccompanied Minor." In the report the latter categories are termed "double vulnerable" and defined as "individuals with more than one type of vulnerability" (9).[7] The UNHCR and implementing partners also operate with the term EVGs "Extremely Vulnerable Groups" in their attempt to target those most in need of help.

Apart from achieving low mortality and morbidity rates, the effect of this is to categorize the population according to certain scientific criteria, effectively producing a population that can be subjected to governmental practices.[8] In other words, in order to cater for the camp population, the agencies in charge need to count, categorize, and control the refugees through various routine bureaucratic practices that have been developed to perfection. This bureaucratization is a means of governing the camp, not through interdictions and restrictions—which were the main tools of the MHA—but through everyday practices of caring for the lives of the refugees.[9]

It was my clear impression that most ground staff were generally committed to helping the refugees but, due to the bureaucratic imperative to count and control, a true tug-of-war would often take place between relief staff and refugees. This may seem paradoxical and it certainly frustrated many on both sides. However, the logic for the staff involved was that they were helping the refugees in the best possible and most cost efficient way, considering the circumstances, and they were committed to getting the relief operation to run smoothly. Any refugee who disrupted the operation was working against the good of all. Thus, when a refugee cheated with food rations, he was taking food from other deserving refugees. When the street leaders at a meeting with agencies expressed that they wanted blankets from UNHCR as payment for their work, they had to realize that the extra blankets were for elderly refugees who needed them more. In other words, the relief agencies had found the winning formula that would ensure the optimal result for the population as a whole and they merely needed to convince the refugees of the sense in this. Behind these practices lies a will to help the victims of war and flight and hence an assumption that it is the agencies that know what is best for the refugees who must be controlled for their own sake.

Although the agencies assumed that they knew what was best for the

[7] The report gives the following illustration to clarify. *"Example: 'FF/SP, means foster family of single parent/ household head.'"* (UNHCR Memorandum, 9) I assume it helps to know the right "dev-speak" to grasp this "clarifying" example.

[8] For similar observations in a camp in Kenya, see Hyndman (2000). See also Rajaram (2002).

[9] This analysis is strongly inspired by the Foucauldian "governmentality school," although I attempt through concrete analysis to supersede this way of thinking. For examples of studies in governmentality, see Cruikshank (1999); Dean (1999); Foucault (1978, Part V); Burchell et al. (1991).

refugees, I found that several of them were concerned that their generous handouts and impressive planning would produce passive clients who suffered from a "dependency syndrome." Relief workers were troubled by the lack of initiative among the refugees. In private discussions, staff would often express fear of the dependency syndrome and speculate how to make the refugees take more responsibility for their own lives.

The dependency syndrome is assumed in part to be due to the services given, creating a "begging mentality." It is also assumed that old social and cultural values of displaced and uprooted people have broken down as the following quote from a UNHCR publication, "Guidelines on the Protection of Refugee Women," illustrates: "Prior to flight, women typically have opportunities to express their concerns and needs, sometimes through their husbands and other times through traditional support networks" (UNHCR 1991, 10).

The publication goes on to argue that such networks no longer exist in refugee situations and that it is the objective of participation programs in relief work to "build the values and sense of community." In an article, "The Liberal Government of Unfreedom," Barry Hindess argues that there are certain categories of populations—in particular among the colonized—who are not found suited to be governed as free citizens (Hindess 2001b). These are basically categorized as either those who are victims of circumstances or those whose moral capabilities are so primitive or degraded so as to not be able to handle self-government. What Hindess does not elaborate, but is mentioned by Mitchell Dean (Dean 1999), is the fact that there is a constant fear that individuals in the first category might slip into the latter; that is, that victims of circumstances might become morally corrupted. We see this logic come forth in relation to the dependency debate. Scholars in "refugee studies" are busy pointing out that refugees are not inherently lazy but that the top-down structure of relief aid creates a "relief mentality" (Harrell-Bond 1986; Hyndman 2000; Kaiser 2000; Kibreab 1993). Meanwhile, as the expression "relief mentality" insinuates and as we see in the UNHCR guidelines, there is a fear that it can become a trait. The solution is, then, to remedy this mentality among the refugees.

In Lukole, relief agencies attempted to mobilize the community in several ways. Educational programs and information campaigns sought to heighten the "awareness" on technical issues such as environment, hygiene, sexually transmitted diseases, and violence against women. It was not enough to tell the refugees what they were and were not allowed to do. They also had to be *convinced* of the value of these rules. They should incorporate them in such a manner that boiling water and sweeping the *blindé* would seem natural to them as a norm rather than a law. By learning to "love the law" they would feel responsibility toward the rules of the camp, not only making camp management easier but also making the refugees more content. This was certainly the intention. In other words, the refugees were not just reduced to bare life. The ethical humanitarian project demanded that they be more than that.

Relief agencies already had the answers ready when promoting refugee participation. The refugees needed educating in the art of self-management and even then, their possibilities of making decisions of any significance to their lives in the camp were heavily circumscribed. They had no choice in what or how much to eat. They had no choice to leave the camp. They could not even choose to build their houses in clusters or circles if they so should wish. Nevertheless, UNHCR made sure that every block and street/village had a leader, elected by the refugees.

In 1997–1998, UNHCR was in the process of arranging elections for leaders, partly because there had been problems between the leaders and the security guards (employed by UNHCR) because of political rivalry. This caused UNHCR to decide to employ new security guards and have new leaders elected. It was the intention of UNHCR to make sure that these elections were "free and fair" and not just a question of a few "big men" appointing someone. At a population meeting called by UNHCR and MHA in May 1997, in relation to the conflict between the camp chairman and the chief security guard, UNHCR's field officer expressed her concerns with politics. She advised the refugees to refrain from activities that disrupt security and endanger "harmonious social life" among the "great majority of the refugee community" who fled their country "in search of peace and security." She also advised the refugees to assess the political involvement of candidates so as to avoid electing individuals who would like to use the forum for furthering their political interest "at the expense of innocent people." According to her discourse, politicians are driven by selfish interests rather than the interests of the common good, and if they are given the chance, a few such selfish individuals will destroy the life of the great majority of refugees who are "innocent people." She went on to give advice to the leader candidates. They should be ready to serve the people who entrust them with the responsibility of representing them on any forum. They should be ready to put aside their individual interest and provide service to the people they lead.

In spite of encouraging refugee participation, all political activity in the refugee camps was strictly banned by the Tanzanian authorities and the UNHCR. For refugees to act as genuine victims, they are expected—in humanitarian discourse—to be helpless and passive.

Such helpless and passive victims can be helped and activated through special programs. They are not expected to be political or strategic of their own accord. In other words, apathy has to be combated, but not at any cost, as certain kinds of refugee activities and agency are perceived to be better than others. Being void of politics, participation is also void of power relations and is merely a question of finding the optimal solution to the "true interests" of the community.[10] Thus, finding a "true community" is about finding a moral community where the individuals involved share common goals and interests.

UNHCR had several practices through which it could nurture the community and formalize it into certain institutions.[11] What must be seen as the most successful program, seen from the perspective of promoting a sense of community and combating a relief mentality, was the use of foster families in the camps. When I was in Lukole, there was no orphanage in the camp, and the handful of street children present had been given *blindés* and put together in "families." All other unaccompanied minors had been placed in foster families. When hundreds of thousands of Rwandans arrived in the area within a short time in 1994 and thousands of children had lost their parents, a policy of supporting foster families rather than orphanages was actively pursued. Staff in "community services" (what used to be termed social services) in UNHCR and the implementing agencies at the time would pride themselves in the good results they had achieved in this innovative approach (NPA[12] staff member, November 1996). Orphanages were perceived to be alienating, destroying the social and moral fabric of the children who would lose their cultural moorings. It was therefore perceived to be culturally sustainable to have children in foster families. Not only did this system ensure the children a culturally proper environment, it also benefited the community as a whole. By taking responsibility for the children rather than leaving it to the NGOs, the refugees avoided the dependency syndrome, strengthening the social and moral fabric of the refugee community, it was assumed.

The case with the foster families illustrates how there is a sense that one has to sacrifice one's own interests for the community. The reward, by contrast, cannot be measured in individual wealth. It is the reward of dignity and community spirit. It must be noted here that these families did not merely take these children at their own initiative. It was all

[10] For a discussion of the concept of community, see Taylor (1994) and Frazer (1999).

[11] Nikolas Rose points out that the community is not merely something to be governed, it also is a means of government. Therefore, it needs to be "celebrated, encouraged, nurtured, shaped and instrumentalised" (Rose 1996, 335). However, for community to become functional as a governmental practice, it needs technocratizing (332).

[12] Norwegian People's Aid.

organized and systematized by UNHCR and implementing partners. In other words, the community needed "pushing" a little in order to come off the ground. However, this enforced solidarity is not merely a question of the refugees learning the art of governing; learning to become like "us." It is doubtful whether such unselfish acts of solidarity would be expected of citizens in other societies. Would British or French families be expected to sacrifice that much—except in times of war? It is as if, because the refugees are poor and have been through so much in terms of war and disruption, they cannot afford to be demanding. In such situations of extreme human distress, one is expected to be able to sacrifice oneself for one's fellow suffering human beings. And if the refugees do not volunteer on their own accord, they can be induced to volunteer (through campaigns and various material support for foster families) for the sake of the community spirit.

Obviously, the sense of community is opposed to, and posited as a cure against apathy and relief mentality. It is, ironically, also opposed to the kinds of behavior in the camp that are farthest from being apathetic and passive. One such type of behavior that is perceived to subvert the community is party politics. The other is cheating and misusing development projects. Both kinds of behavior express agency and refugees taking initiative, but they do so the "wrong way."

A consequence of this dichotomization between the community and a few individuals is that the agencies are able to maintain a belief in the sublime qualities of "the community" as an antidote to the dependency syndrome and ultimately a means of catering for the mental well-being of the camp population. By creating a category that is preventing the fulfillment of community—the politicians and the misusers—they can retain the illusion of the community. Simultaneously, by conferring "trouble" on this group, it is possible to maintain a strongly controlled government "from above" while promoting participation. If UNHCR did not control the process so tightly, troublemakers would misuse the system and promote self-interested politics.

The refugees are cast as bare life: being taken out of their (national) context, their culture is assumed to have crumbled, leaving them as loose atoms without any norms to guide them. UNHCR also encourages this state of affairs because it does not want to face up to the dubious political identities of these people. Particularly since the 1994 genocide in Rwanda, UNHCR has met critique from all sides for supporting the Hutu extremists in camps in Tanzania and Zaire. There is, therefore, a general mistrust toward Hutu and a desire to erase their past. They are better dealt with, as clients. On the other hand, such bare, biological life is dangerous. Like the life of *initiands* in *rites de passage,* it can lead to anything if it is not controlled. Therefore, the refugees need to be inserted into a new context. The moral community is central in this project of preparing the refugees for a normal life after the camp. In this perspective political rivalry is seen as the antithesis of the community, emerging from the divisive power struggles of these dislocated individuals; a symptom of a broken-down community. What UNHCR is doing is to try to create a moral community of innocent victims. In this way it can avoid the fact that politics is not just a symptom of social breakdown and alienation but is anchored in the Burundian past.

The Camp as Political Battlefield

When I was in the camp I was constantly confronted with what I have called "tales of decay."[13] There were numerous accounts of women no longer respecting their husbands because it is UNHCR that feeds her. There were stories about men beating their wives or spending their money on beer and prostitutes rather than clothes for their wives and children. There were tales about children no longer showing their parents respect and about peasants treating "big men," such as teachers and previous government officials, as equals "because we all receive the same food rations." The fact that everyone was treated equally by UNHCR made it difficult for the refugees to distinguish who was big and who was not. In the camp these categories and hierarchies had to be negotiated and fought over. In this section, we see how refugees, on the one hand, refer to the presumed norms that were lost while, on the other hand, making use of the liberating forces of the amoral space of the camp in their search for social and political subjectivities. I will show how politics becomes one of the fundamental structuring principles of the camp, in spite of (and perhaps because of) remaining clandestine. And I will show how a certain group of "big men" emerges, creating pockets of sovereignty outside the reach of UNHCR and MHA.

The narratives of loss express a sense of having lost the moral and social order that prevailed in Burundi. By contrast, such loss of old norms and hierarchies may have liberating effects as well. By virtue of being in the camp—outside the social control of Burundi—the refugees can in principle act "immorally," in the sense that they are not bound by norms and moral constraints. In practice, however, this freedom is not unlimited, just as morality is not totally absent, for several reasons. First, the camp is full of new rules, defined by the new rulers. Although MHA defines the limits of the camp and rules through the threat of ex-

---

[13] See also Turner (2001).

pelling refugees who do not behave, UNHCR controls and regulates daily life in detail. Second, the temporary character of the camp means that the refugees do not simply leave Burundi behind them and endorse a new set of norms. They are still bound by obligations to the country to which they wish to return some time in the indefinite future. That is to say that, although the norms and hierarchies of Burundi are not reproduced in the camp, they certainly are renegotiated.

In this exceptional space refugees constantly meander between the norms and memories of Burundi and the new rules that count in the biopolitical space of the camp. In this exceptional space I found that a group of young, semi-educated men had been successful in managing to adapt to the new situation and creating an important place for themselves as brokers.[14] Some of them would be street leaders, officially collaborating with UNHCR and MHA. Others would be employed by international relief agencies as "community mobilizers" (the new term for social workers), teachers, medical assistants, security guards, and so on. Common to these positions is the fact that they function as intermediaries between relief agencies—who provide the bulk of resources flowing into the camp—and the camp population. The self-made businessmen, trading in everything from surplus maize to video shows, are arguably also brokers and "big men" in the camp. They play a slightly different role, as they are less connected with the relief agencies and more connected with Tanzanians and Burundians outside the camp.

UNHCR does not contemplate that the posts that it can provide for refugees can be imbued with power or politics, as the lens of the humanitarian agencies only sees them as administrative positions. Like in an ideal-typical Weberian bureaucracy, the individual does not hold any power and only executes a function. That is not how refugees perceive these positions, however. Given their central position in controlling flows of resources and information, they are subject to intense power struggles and are highly politicized. Apart from the vertical relations that these brokers can tie to clients, they also are enmeshed in large networks based on horizontal relations with other like-minded big men. These networks of young male brokers were instrumental in the sense that they could assure the members access to jobs and other resources.

Mousa is an example of one of these influential young men. He has worked for an NGO as a coordinator for community mobilizers but stopped that and did some business for a while until he took up another job with an NGO. Meanwhile, he has a plot of land that he employs another refugee to till for him. He is thirty years old, married,

[14] See also Turner (1999).

with two small children. His wife works as a schoolteacher. He has passed his *humanité* exams from secondary school and used to work as an accountant in Burundi. He was a member of FRODEBU[15] in Burundi and was even *bourgmestre* for a short while from 1993, when the prior FRODEBU *bourgmestre* fled the country, to 1994 when he was compelled to flee himself. His fluent English and Swahili along with an easy-going and self-confident attitude means that he seems to be able to move wherever he wants in the camp. He can start up a friendly conversation with Tanzanian policemen in one of the more expensive bars in the camp. He can joke with an Irish relief worker or flirt with a Tanzanian nurse. With the right handshakes and smiles, he can wander into any NGO office and borrow a typewriter or just have a chat.

In spite of having no official position in the camp as either street leader or security guardian, he is still treated as a "big man" by fellow refugees and even by camp authorities.[16] His large network of friends in high places make him a figure to reckon with. It is him neighbors go to if they have problems with a ration card. He will go with them to the UNHCR office and explain (in English, French, or Swahili) their problem and make sure things are sorted out. He is also awakened at three in the morning to help sort out a robbery in his street, negotiating with the security guardians and the Tanzanian police. One day I found him at the security guards' office, negotiating the release of a suspect. He is, in other words, the archetype of the new "big man" in the camp. His activities show how "big men" can exercise public authority using links to the official camp authorities, but quite clearly on their own terms and also strongly linked to their involvement in political networks. Mousa has managed to carve out a space for himself in the camp, maneuvering within the new rules of UNHCR and MHA. His authority is founded in this ability and his ability to adapt. It is also founded in the fact that he is part of a political network, supporting one of the two political factions in Lukole. He is recognized as a "big man" by his neighbors and friends because of his benevolent practices. In the following, I show how the sovereignty of these political elites is not only practiced benevolently but also underpinned by the threat of violence.

When asking people in the poorer part of the camp, Lukole B, if they had any employment, they would reply: "No, we haven't got enough money." This really surprised me—assuming that the objective of employment was to earn money and not vice versa—until they explained

---

[15] *Front Démocratique du Burundi*, a moderate Hutu party. Most former FRODEBU supporters in the camp now supported its armed wing, the CNDD (Conseil National pour la Défense de la Democratie).

[16] Thus, he was invited to a meeting called by the camp commandant to deal with the security situation in June 1997. It appears that the camp commandant was aware of the de facto power-holders in the camp.

the bribes involved. "These people who came recently don't know where to find a job. *They don't know the mechanisms of the camp.* These people who have already got jobs in Lukole, charge them some taxes in order to get a job. And these people are very poor. They don't have shillings to pay. That's why they don't have jobs" (village leader, B3). Being employed by an NGO is so attractive that people will pay up to half their wages to the person who gets them a job. The quote reveals a perception that the NGO employees make up a close-knit and impenetrable network. That such networks are closely linked to and organized around political affiliations is illustrated in the following excerpt from a conversation with Joseph, a young man who claims to be politically neutral but who is known to support Palipehutu (*Parti pour la Libération du Peuple Hutu*), one of the two parties in the camp.

Joseph complains that virtually all the NGO staff are members of CNDD (*Conseil National pour la Défense de la Démocratie*) and that they make sure that nobody else gets a job. They tell lies to the Tanzanian staff about Palipehutu, so the Tanzanians believe that Palipehutistes are extremists and the ones causing the security problems in the camp, he says. In this way, Tanzanian staff is very reluctant to employ anyone who is not a CNDD sympathizer, he explains. It is very difficult to be apolitical when the NGOs are so biased and politicized. He complains that the medical assistants at the clinic openly wear Ndadaye badges. These badges with a picture of the assassinated president, although strictly speaking not connected to a political party and hence difficult for authorities to clamp down on, are political statements that signify CNDD support. Caps in CNDD colors, white, red and green, also express political loyalties in the camp. Joseph complains that if the Burundian hospital staff recognize a patient as CNDD, they give them good treatment. If they think that you are Palipehutu, they just tell you to leave. "Go and get treatment from Kosani"[17] they would say.

To support your local patron was also to support either CNDD or Palipehutu. To get a job with an NGO being a member of Palipehutu could be difficult if all the right people to know supported CNDD. Joseph's story no doubt expresses a paranoid vision of a great conspiracy, but he is not the only person in Lukole to see things this way. The more time I spent in the camp (I was there for more than a year), the more I came to realize that virtually everything was inserted into a dichotomous logic of either being Palipehutu or CNDD. Thus, everybody knew which party a certain candidate for a post as a street leader belonged to—although he would never say so openly.

[17] Kosani was the leader of the more radical Palipehutu wing, Palipehutu-FNL, at the time of field work. In the camp he was perceived to be the de facto leader of Palipehutu.

Similarly, the security guards were positioned according to the CNDD-Palipehutu dichotomy. UNHCR had become aware of this "problem" in mid-1997 when mutual accusations of political bias were put forward by the chief security guard, Palipehutu, and the camp chairman, CNDD. This had led UNHCR to dismiss all security guards and employ new ones after "screening" them in order to assure their political neutrality. Security guards were in principle the extended arm of UNHCR and the Tanzanian authorities in the camp, charged with keeping law and order and collaborating closely with the Tanzanian police. There was only one police post in the camp (which was empty during nighttime until June 1997) and patrolling the camp was left more or less to the security guards. They were allowed to imprison people for up to two days and would also fine people for minor offences. In practice, this gave them a substantial amount of discretionary power outside the control of MHA and UNHCR.

The binary political logic also was reflected spatially. Lukole is administratively divided into Lukole A and Lukole B. Lukole A housed refugees who fled shortly after the assassination of President Ndadaye in October 1993. Among them were many from the elite who fled because of their political activities. They appear to have established themselves and their political party, CNDD, in this part of the camp. The refugees in Lukole B arrived in Tanzania in 1995–96 and were mostly peasants who fled widespread fighting that had broken out between the Tutsi dominated army and Hutu rebels in the province bordering Tanzania. Here Palipehutu with its more radical and populist demands seemed to dominate.[18]

In April–June 1997, threats against people belonging to the "wrong" party were so strong that large numbers of refugees chose either to repatriate, in spite of the bad security situation in Burundi, or to move to another part of the camp, effectively "cleansing" each section of the camp of political opponents. Interviewing a group of community workers employed by AEF[19] and working in Lukole B in June 1997, they explain why most of them have moved to Lukole A and now commute between the two parts of the camp every day. They say that there are "men with long coats," hiding long knives who go around Lukole B claiming "taxes" from people. They dare not tell me that it is taxes for Palipehutu, but merely hint that it is for a "so-called party." If you do not pay these taxes, they will surely slash you with their knives. It became apparent towards the end of the interview that they actually did not like me making these inquiries. They were afraid that some of these

[18] For an analysis that is more nuanced than this crude depiction, see Turner (1998, 2001).
[19] African Education Foundation.

men with long coats might hear what we were talking about and then they would be in trouble.

In other words, the political rivalry is not just an innocent game of words, and the public authority of these "big men" is not merely secured through access to resources provided by UNHCR and NGOs. It is also underpinned by the threat of violence. This threat materialized regularly, like when at least ten people were killed in December 1996 in clashes between the two parties or in April 1998 when camp authorities discovered that CNDD supporters incarcerated and tortured political opponents in Lukole A.

Because of its clandestine nature, politics was shrouded in mystery, rumor, and hints. In relation to an upsurge in violence in April–May 1998, I talked to the chairman in Lukole A. He insinuates that the recent violence is politically motivated: "There are many kinds of crimes. Someone can come in with the purpose of killing you, but he will say that he was coming to steal from you. But he has another purpose" (Camp Chairman, Lukole A, May 1998).

This "other purpose" is apparently politically motivated. I ask him what these politicians do. "Do they go round collecting taxes?" "They are among those bandits who come in the night and kill them or cut them with *pangas* (machetes)" he claims. They attack people from the other party. He goes on to explain that "they" are also among those people who are against watchmen at night. I had heard from several people that some refugees—even wealthy ones—did not support the neighborhood watch teams that had been organized recently. Such people were assumed to be Palipehutu supporters, and were sure not to be targeted. In other words, every act of violence, whether politically motivated or not, is interpreted through a framework of political conspiracies.[20] Likewise, displays of conspicuous wealth might be interpreted as the result of dirty political connections. Finally, there are countless rumors about the other party influencing relief agencies and Tanzanian authorities in order to gain power, as we saw in Joseph's account.

The fact that politics is clandestine makes it all the more powerful—a kind of power that emerges from conspiracies and rumors.[21] Knowing that there might be some big political network behind these acts of violence rather than merely being robberies, conjures up an image of an opponent with access to hidden powers. This political rivalry illustrates

[20] Rumors about politics are rather ambiguous, however, as politicians from the rival party most often are depicted as being simple bandits who are in it for the money rather than pursuing a noble political cause. See also Turner (2001, Ch. 7).

[21] Parallels could be drawn with the occult power (Comaroff and Comaroff 1999b; Geschiere 1997) or with rumors and urban legend on politicians and large corporations (Fine 1986; Turner 1993). See also West and Sanders (2003).

how refugees are trying to negotiate the suspended, temporary space of the camp. Political rivalry is related to broader ideological struggles taking place in Burundi, thus bringing their own political past into the camp, where international relief agencies try to turn them into ahistorical bare life. As I have argued elsewhere (Turner 1998, 2001, 2002), the political changes among the refugees in Tanzania are closely linked to shifts in the political field in Burundi. In the camp the constant struggles, fights, and rumors are also attempts to make space meaningful. They operate within the secluded and depoliticized space that has been marked out for them by MHA and UNHCR. And in many ways they accept these conditions. It is, in other words, not a question of resistance to UNHCR and MHA. In fact they would often use these institutions in their struggles. Both factions were keen to present themselves as law-abiding and cooperative, accusing the other of subverting the laws of the country and UNHCR. They all play a double role of wresting a space of their own from UNHCR/MHA while finding recognition from the international community very important (cf. Turner 2002).

However much they try to gain recognition from MHA or UNHCR, and however much they use these as avenues for their own political projects, they do, however, manage to create pockets of sovereignty outside the reach of either UNHCR or MHA. Here, whoever it is that possesses the mystical power, has the control of life and death irrespective of the interdictions of MHA and the attempts by UNHCR to create a community of victims. The world of politics is at once frightening and fascinating. Because of its secrecy and clandestine nature, politics is all the more mystical and powerful. Thus, in a paradoxical manner, the attempts by UNHCR and MHA to void the camp of politics have created a sense of politics that is much more powerful.[22]

LAYERED SOVEREIGNTY: CONCLUDING REMARKS

This essay has shown how differently the camp is perceived from different angles and different roles it can play for the Tanzanian state, for international humanitarian organizations, and for refugees, respectively. This results in overlapping sovereignties and competing claims to public authority.

The Tanzanian state can only uphold its sovereignty over the national territory by declaring a small part of this territory an exceptional space—effectively outside the "normal" biopolitical space of the Tan-

[22] One might suspect that a long history of fear and intimidation has created a similar political culture in Burundi. René Lemarchand has pointed out to me that rumor-mongering and scheming have been prominent features of political life in Burundi since precolonial times.

zanian state. This exceptional space cannot be governed like the rest of the national space as its population is set apart from the true citizenry of the nation—the foundation of biopolitical sovereignty. Not being part of the national population that the state claims to represent and whose sovereignty it must defend, the refugees are set apart and contained by the Tanzanian state and handed over to others to govern. This is where UNHCR enters the picture.

The relation to UNHCR and other international relief agencies is ambiguous and precarious. On the one hand, it is necessary to have them govern the camp for the above-mentioned reasons. On the other hand, there is uneasiness about delegating power to these institutions. The immense scale of their economic and institutional capacity is visible in the landscape of the border area—thus challenging the sovereignty of the Tanzanian state. In this situation, it is important for the Tanzanian state to show that it has the power to decide which agencies may operate in the camp and to demonstrate that it can expel international staff at any time.

In spite of the camp being an exception from the *polis* of the Tanzanian nation, and the refugees treated as bare life, they are subjected to state-of-the-art biopolitical humanitarian interventions. This is reflected in the focus on objectifying knowledge of the refugees' bodies in terms of ration cards, vaccination programs, and hygiene education. However, relief agencies are not content with maintaining the bodies of refugees; they also are concerned with the well-being of "the community spirit" as they try to combat the dreaded dependency syndrome, assumed to emerge among aid dependent populations. There are here quite clear indications of attempting to improve the population—physically and morally/mentally.

But the camp remains an exception. Everyone agrees (and hopes) that it is a temporary condition. This obviously affects the ways in which relief agencies approach the project of improving the population. In some senses, it makes the benevolent humanitarian project so much more straightforward, as refugees are assumed to be *tabula rasa*. They have no past and they have lost all cultural and moral codes in the process of being "uprooted" from where they belonged. This makes helping them all the easier, as there are less unknown factors to create "noise" and confuse the benevolent project. Hence the ambitious projects of social engineering that relief agencies embark on in refugee camps. Apart from being a place of "no longer," the camp is also a place of "not yet." Although no longer being rooted in Burundi culture, refugees are not yet ready to be fully self-governing citizens either. The programs of moral uplifting and community development are not made for life in the camp but simply preparations for a life yet to come; real life after the pseudo life of the camp. Again, this in a sense simplifies the biopolitical humanitarian project.

However, as I have shown in the latter part of this essay, refugees are not blank slates when they enter the camp; they are not simply bare life and, although they also treat the camp as an exception, they still strive to inhabit it and give it social and political meaning. They bring politics and their history with them into the camp—not as it was in Burundi, but in new, constantly contested, and negotiated shapes.

Organizing politically is perhaps the most prominent means of defying the laws of UNHCR and the camp commandant and refusing to play the role of innocent victims. Their strategies are, however, not independent of the restrictive laws of the camp commandant or the benevolent programs of UNHCR and the "big men" strategically make use of both in their struggle to outdo their rivals and dominate the camp. Paradoxically, when seeking recognition from international relief agencies, they create pockets of sovereignty outside the reach of UNHCR/MHA where it is the "big men" who decide who belongs and who does not belong.

This forces UNHCR to do all in its might to void the camp of politics and try to establish a community of innocent, ahistorical, apolitical victims in need of help. This UNHCR does partially by appealing to "the community spirit" and pinpointing "trouble" to a few individual refugees who are thus blamed for obstructing the fulfillment of the true community. But it is also upheld by a paternalistic twist to the so-called empowerment projects. In spite of the good intentions, UNHCR decides, in the last instance, the size of the food rations, just as MHA decides who can leave the camp. But this need not be a contradiction for UNHCR, since the camp is still a temporary space and empowerment is more about preparing refugees to take care of themselves in the future than changing present power relations. In this way, paternalism can be defended as acting in the name of progress. Behind the benevolent biopolitical project lies an idea of "saving these wretched people from themselves." Therefore, they are their own worst enemy and harsh measures must be taken in order to save them.

We might argue with Agamben that the refugees are bare life. The kind of life that stands outside the *polis* of biopolitics, reduced to bodies without political rights attached. But they are not any kind of bare life. UNHCR has a humanitarian objective of helping victims of war. This is a strongly ethical project. For UNHCR, the camp becomes a kind of human laboratory—an experiment in some kind of decent despotism. As with other laboratory experiments, it might tell us something about processes that take place elsewhere outside the controlled environment of the laboratory. Thus, the paternalistic side of biopolitics that becomes so visible and obvious in Lukole, might be symptomatic of biopolitics elsewhere. Similarly, the constant subversion of this project by the "big men," illustrates the limits of the biopolitical dream and how politics strikes back.

Bibliography

Abercrombie, Thomas A. 1998. *Pathways of Memory and Power: Ethnography and History among an Andean People.* Madison and London: Wisconsin University Press.

Abrams, Philip. (1977) 1988. "Notes on the Difficulty of Studying the State." *Journal of Historical Sociology,* 1(1): 58–89.

Acocks, J. 1953. *Veld Types of South Africa.* Botanical Survey of South Africa, Memoir 28.

Adam, H., F. van Zyl Slabbert, and K. Moodley. 1998. *Comrades in Business: Post-Liberation Politics in South Africa.* Cape Town: Tafelberg.

Adamson, R. 1929. "Vegetation of the South-West Region." In *The Botanical Features of the South-Western Cape Province.* Cape Town: The Specialty Press of South Africa.

———. 1958. "The Cape as an Ancient African Flora." *The Advancement of Science,* XV, 58: 118–27.

Adelkhah, Fariba. 1999. *Being Modern in Iran.* London: Hurst and Co.

Adorno, Theodor W. 1998. "Freudian Theory and the Pattern of Fascist Propaganda." In *The Essential Frankfurt School Reader.* Edited by Andrew Arato and Eike Gebhardt. New York: Continuum.

Agamben, Giorgio. 1998. *Homo Sacer: Sovereign Power and Bare Life.* Stanford: Stanford University Press. (Translated by Daniel Heller-Roazen.)

———. 2000. *Means Without End: Notes on Politics, Vol. 20.* Minnesota: University of Minnesota Press.

Akkurt, Aydin. 2000. *Kutsal Kavgalarin Korkusuz Neferi Dr. Niyazi Manyera.* Lefkosa: Akdeniz Haber Ajansi Yayinlari.

Allen, T. 1991. "Understanding Alice: Uganda's Holy Spirit Movement in Context." *Africa,* 61: 370–99.

Alonso, Ana-Maria. 1995. *Threads of Blood: Colonialism, Revolution and Gender on Mexico's Northern Frontier.* Tucson: University of Arizona Press.

Althusser, Louis. 1971. *Lenin and Philosophy, and Other Essays.* London: New Left Books.

Anderson, Benedict. (1983) 1990. *Imagined Communities: Reflections on the Origin and Spread of Nationalism.* London: Verso.

———. 1992. *Long-Distance Nationalism: World Capitalism and the Rise of Identity Politics.* Amsterdam: Centre for Asian Studies Amsterdam (CASA).

———. 1994. "Exodus." *Critical Inquiry,* 20: 314–27.

Anderson, C. 2000. "Godna: Inscribing Indian Convicts in the Nineteenth Century." In *Written on the Body: The Tattoo in European and American History.* Edited by J. Caplan. London: Reaktion.

Aneesh, A. In press. *Virtual Migration: The Programming of Globalization.* Durham, N.C.: Duke University Press.

Anthony, A. C. 1990. "Rights and Obligations of Rural Refugees in Tanzania: A Case Study of Mpanda District." *The African Review,* 17(1/2): 21–39.

Appadurai, Arjun. 1990. "Disjuncture and Difference in the Global Cultural Economy." *Public Culture*, 2: 1–24.

————. 1993. "Number in the Colonial Imagination." In *Orientalism and the Postcolonial Predicament: Perspectives on South Asia*. Edited by C. A. Breckenridge and P. van der Veer. Philadelphia: University of Pennsylvania Press.

————. 1996. *Modernity at Large*. Minneapolis: University of Minnesota Press.

Appadurai, A., and C. Breckenridge. 1976. "The South Indian Temple: Authority, Honor and Redistribution." *Contributions to Indian Sociology* (n.s.), 10(2): 187–211.

Apter, Andrew. 1999a. "The Subvention of Tradition: A Genealogy of the Nigerian Durbar." In *State/Culture: State Formation after the Cultural Turn*. Edited by George Steinmetz. Ithaca, N.Y.: Cornell University Press.

————. 1999b. "IBB = 419: Nigerian Democracy and the Politics of Illusion." In *Civil Society and the Political Imagination in Africa*. Edited by John L. Comaroff and Jean Comaroff. Chicago: University of Chicago Press.

Arendt, Hannah. 1951. *Origins of Totalitarianism*. New York: Harcourt, Brace.

Aristotle. 1988. *The Politics*. Cambridge: Cambridge University Press.

Armstrong, Allen. 1990. "Evolving Approaches to Planning and Management of Refugee Settlements: The Tanzanian Experience." *Ekistics* (342/343): 195–204.

————. 1991. "Resource Frontiers and Regional Development: The Role of Refugee Settlement in Tanzania." *Habitat International*, 15(1/2): 69–85.

Asad, Talal (ed.). 1973. *Anthropology and the Colonial Encounter*. New York: Humanity Books.

Ashforth, A. 1999. "Weighing Manhood in Soweto." *CODESRIA Bulletin*, 3–4.

Bakhtin, M. M. 1981. *The Dialogic Imagination: Four Essays*. Austin: University of Texas Press.

Bales, K. 1999. *Disposable People: New Slavery in the Global Economy*. Berkeley: University of California Press.

Balibar, Etienne. 1991a. "Is there a 'Neo-Racism'?" In *Race, Nation and Class: Ambiguous Identities*. Edited by E. Balibar and I. Wallerstein. London: Verso.

————. 1991b. "Racism and Nationalism." In *Race, Nation and Class: Ambiguous Identities*. Edited by E. Balibar and I. Wallerstein. London: Verso.

Barbalet, Jack. 1988. *Citizenship*. Milton Keynes: Open University Press.

Barkawi, Tarak, and Mark Laffey. 2002. "Retrieving the Imperial: *Empire* and International Relations." *Millennium: Journal of International Studies*, 31(1):109–27.

Barker, Martin. 1981. *The New Racism*. London: Junction Books.

Barry, A., T. Osborne, et al. (eds.). 1996. *Foucault and Political Reason: Liberalism, Neo-Liberalism and Rationalities of Government*. Chicago: University of Chicago Press.

Bartelson, Jens. 1995. *Genealogies of Sovereignty*. Cambridge: Cambridge University Press.

Bataille, Georges. 1967. *La part maudite*, précédé de *La notion de dépense*. Paris: Minuit.

————. 1991. *The Accursed Share (Vol. II and III)*. New York: Zone Books. (Original in French in *La Souverainité*, Vol. 8, in *Oeuvres Completes* [Vols. 1–20]. Paris: Gallimard, 1970–88).

Bauman, Zygmunt. 1991. *Modernity and Ambivalence*. Ithaca, N.Y.: Cornell University Press.

———. 1998. *Globalization: The Human Consequence.* New York: Columbia University Press.

Bayart, Jean Francois. 1986. "Civil Society in Africa." In *Political Domination in Africa: Reflections on the Limits of Power.* Edited by P. Chabal. 109–25. Chicago: University of Chicago Press.

———. 1993. *The State in Africa: The Politics of the Belly.* London, New York: Longman.

Bayart, Jean Francois, Stephen Ellis, and Beatrice Hibou. 1999. *The Criminalization of the State in Africa.* London: James Currey.

Bayart, Jean Francois, Achille Mbembe, and C. Toulabor. 1993. *Le politique par le bas: Contribution à une problématique de la démocratie en Afrique noire.* Paris: Karthala.

Bayly, C. A. 1998. *The Origins of Nationality in South Asia: Patriotism and Ethical Government in the Making of Modern India.* Delhi: Oxford University Press.

Beck, Ulrich. 1994. "The Reinvention of Politics: Toward a Theory of Reflexive Modernization." In *Reflexive Modernization.* Edited by U. Beck, A. Giddens and S. Lash. Stanford: Stanford University Press.

Bello, Welden. 1994. *Dark Victory: The United States, Structural Adjustment and Global Poverty.* London: Pluto Press, and Amsterdam: TNI.

Benei, Veronique. 2000. "Teaching Nationalism in Maharashtra Schools." In *The Everyday State in India.* Edited by Chris Fuller and Veronique Benei. Delhi: Social Science Press.

Bennett, D. 1999. "Burghers, Burglars, and Masturbators: The Sovereign Spender in the Age of Consumerism." *New Literary History,* 30: 269–94.

Bennett, Tony. 1999. "The Exhibitionary Complex." In *Representing the Nation: A Reader.* Edited by David Boswell and Jessica Evans. New York: Routledge.

Berlant, L. 1991. *The Anatomy of National Fantasy: Hawthorne, Utopia and Everyday Life.* Chicago: University of Chicago Press.

Berry, Sara S. 1985. *Fathers Work for their Sons: Accumulation, Mobility and Class Formation in an Extended Yoruba Community.* Berkeley: University of California Press.

Bhabha, Homi K. 1994. *The Location of Culture.* London: Routledge.

Biaya, T. K. Forthcoming. "Eroticism in Senegal and the Art of Ousmane Dago." *Public Culture.*

Biersteker, Thomas, and Cynthia Weber, (eds.) 1996. *State Sovereignty as Social Construct.* Cambridge: Cambridge University Press.

Biolsi, Thomas. 1995. "The Birth of the Reservation: Making the Modern Individual among the Lakota." *American Ethnologist,* 42(1): 28–53.

Boahen, A. 1962. "The Caravan Trade in the Nineteenth Century." *Journal of African History,* 3: 349–59.

Bobbio, Noberto. 1996. *The Age of Rights.* Cambridge, Eng.: Polity Press.

Bodin, Jean. 1992. *On Sovereignty: Four Chapters from The Six Books on Commonwealth.* Cambridge: Cambridge University Press.

Bolus, H. 1886. "Sketch of the Flora of South Africa." In *The Official Handbook of the Cape of Good Hope.* Edited by J. Noble. Cape Town: The Columbian and Indian Exhibition Committee.

Bond, W. 1993. "What Important Questions Remain Unanswered in the Fynbos Biome." In *Monitoring Requirements for Fynbos Management: A Collaborative*

Report of the Fynbos Forum Group. Edited by C. Marais and D. Richardson. Foundation for Research Development Programme Report Series, No. 11.

Bonfil Batalla, Guillermo. 1987. *México Profundo. Una Civilización Negada.* Mexico, D.F.: CIESAS-SEP.

Bourdieu, Pierre. 1991. *Language and Symbolic Power.* London: Polity Press.

Bourdieu, Pierre, and Loïc Wacquant. 1992. *An Invitation to Reflexive Sociology.* Cambridge, Eng.: Polity Press.

Brace, L., and J. Hoffman. 1997. *Reclaiming Sovereignty.* London: Francis Pinter.

Brass, Paul. 1997. *Theft of an Idol: Text and Context in the Representation of Collective Violence.* Princeton, N.J.: Princeton University Press.

Brydon, L. 1999. "'With a Little Bit of Luck . . .': Coping with Adjustment in Urban Ghana, 1975–90." *Africa* 69(3): 366–85.

Bull, Hedley. 1977. *The Anarchical Society.* London: Macmillan.

Bulmer, Martin, and Anthony M. Rees (eds.). 1996. *Citizenship Today: The Contemporary Relevance of T. H. Marshall.* London: UCL Press.

Burchell, Graham. 1996. "Liberal Government and Techniques of the Self." In *Foucault and Political Reason.* Edited by A. Barry, T. Osborne, and Nikolas Rose. Chicago: University of Chicago Press.

Burchell, Graham, Colin Gordon, and Peter Miller (eds.). 1991. *The Foucault Effect: Studies in Governmentality.* Chicago: University of Chicago Press, and London: Harvester Wheatsheaf.

Burchell, Scott, and Andrew Linklater. 1996. *Theories of International Relations.* Basingstoke: Macmillan.

Business Immigration Office. 1998. *Entrepreneurial Immigration.* http//www/ei/gov.bc.ca/immigration.

Butler, Judith. 1997. *The Psychic Life of Power.* Stanford: Stanford University Press.

———. 1999. "Revisiting Bodies and Pleasures." *Theory, Culture & Society,* 16(2): 11–20.

Buur, Lars. 2001. "Reconciliation, Conflict Resolution and Non-State Forms of Justice." In *Conflict Prevention and Peace Building in Africa: Report from the Maputo Conference, 28–29 June, 2001.* Edited by Bjørn Møller and Finn Stepputat. Copenhagen: Danida, Ministry of Foreign Affairs.

———. 2003a. "Crime and Punishment on the Margins of the Post-Apartheid State." *Anthropology and Humanism,* 28(1): 23–42.

———. 2003b. "The Concept of the Person in two South African Quasi-courts." Paper presented at the research workshop on "Senses of Right and Wrong: Judicial Settlements, Truth Commissions, International Tribunals, and the Politics of Popular Justice in the Aftermath of Collective Violence." Danish Institute for International Studies, Copenhagen, December 15–16, 2003.

Callinicos, Alex. 2002. "The Actuality of Empire." *Millennium: Journal of International Studies,* 31(2): 319–26.

Carr, G., J. Robin, and R. Robinson. 1986. "Environmental Weed Invasion of Natural Ecosystems: Australia's Greatest Conservation Problem." In *Ecology of Biological Invasions: An Australian Perspective.* Edited by R. Groves and J. Burden. Canberra: Australian Academy of Science.

Castells, Manuel. 1997. *The Power of Identity.* Oxford: Blackwell.

————. 1999. *The Rise of Network Society*. Oxford: Blackwell.

Castoriadis, C. 2002. *Sujet et vérité dans le monde social-historique. Séminaires 1986–1987. La création humaine I*. Paris: Seuil.

Centeno, Miguel Angel. 2002. "The Centre Did Not Hold: War in Latin America and the Monopolization of Violence." In *Studies in the Formation of the Nation State in Latin America*. Edited by James Dunkerly. London: Institute of Latin American Studies.

Chandavarkar, R. 1998. *Imperial Power and Popular Politics*. Cambridge: Cambridge University Press.

Chatterjee, Partha. 1993. *The Nation and Its Fragments: Colonial and Postcolonial Histories*. Princeton, N.J.: Princeton University Press.

————. 1995. "Religious Minorities and the Secular State: Notes on an Indian Impasse." *Public Culture*, 8 (Fall): 11–39.

————. 1997. "Secularism and Toleration." In *A Possible India: Essays in Political Criticism*. Delhi: Oxford University Press.

————. 1998a. "Beyond the Nation? Or Within?" *Social Text*, 16(3): 57–69.

————. 1998b. "Community in the East." *Economic and Political Weekly*, 33(6): 277–82.

————. 1998c. "The Wages of Freedom." In *The Wages of Freedom: Fifty Years of the Indian Nation-State*. Edited by P. Chatterjee. Delhi: Oxford University Press.

————. 2000. "Two Poets and Death: On Civil and Political Society in the Non-Christian World." In *Questions of Modernity*. Edited by Tim Mitchell and Lila Abu-Lughod. Minneapolis: University of Minnesota Press.

————. 2004. *The Politics of the Governed: Popular Politics in Most of the World*. New York: Columbia University Press.

Chaulia, Sreeram Sundar. 2003. "The Politics of Refugee Hosting in Tanzania: From Open Door to Unsustainability, Insecurity and Receding Receptivity." *Journal of Refugee Studies*, 16(2): 147–66.

Chimni, B. S. 1998. "The Geopolitics of Refugee Studies: A View from the South." *Journal of Refugee Studies*, 11(4): 350–74.

Clapham, Christopher (ed.). 1982. *Private Patronage, Public Power*. London: Francis Pinter.

Cody, M., M. Mooney, and H. Mooney. 1978. "Convergence Versus Non-Convergence in Mediterranean-Climate Ecosystems." *Annual Review of Ecology and Systematics*, 9: 265–321.

Cohen, Jean L., and Andrew Arato. 1992. *Civil Society and Political Theory*. Cambridge, Mass.: MIT Press.

Cohen, R. 1971. *Dominance and Defiance: A Study of the Marital Instability in an Islamic African Society*. Washington, D.C.: American Anthropological Association.

Cohn, Bernard, S. 1987. *An Anthropologist among Historians*. Delhi: Oxford University Press.

Collier, Stephen J., and Aihwa Ong. 2004. "Global Assemblages, Anthropological Problems." In *Global Assemblages: Technology, Politics and Ethics as Anthropological Problems*. Edited by Aihwa Ong and Stephen J. Collier. Cambridge, Eng.: Blackwell.

Comaroff, John L., and Jean Comaroff. 1991. *Of Revelation and Revolution, Vol. I.* Chicago: University of Chicago Press.

———. 1997. *Of Revelation and Revolution: The Dialectics of Modernity at a South African Frontier.* Chicago: University of Chicago Press.

———. 1999a. *Civil Society and the Political Imagination in Africa: Critical Perspectives.* Chicago: University of Chicago Press.

———. 1999b. "Occult Economies and the Violence of Abstraction: Notes from the South African Postcolony." *American Ethnologist,* 26: 297–301.

———. 1999c. "Alien-nation: Zombies, Immigrants, and Millennial Capitalism." *Codesria Bulletin,* 3(4): 17–28.

———. 2000. "Millennial Capitalism: First Thoughts on a Second Coming." In *Millennial Capitalism and the Culture of Neoliberalism.* Edited by J. Comaroff and J. L. Comaroff. Special Edition of *Public Culture,* 12(2): 291–343.

Comaroff, Jean, and John L. Comaroff. 2000. *Millennial Capitalism and the Culture of Neo-Liberalism.* Durham, N.C.: Duke University Press.

Conklin, Alice L. 1997. *A Mission to Civilize: The Republican Idea of Empire in France and West Africa, 1895–1930.* Stanford: Stanford University Press.

Connolly, William. 1994. "Tocqueville, Territory and Violence." *Theory, Culture and Society,* 11: 19–40.

Coombe, R. 1998. *The Cultural Life of Intellectual Properties: Authorship, Appropriation and the Law.* Durham, N.C.: Duke University Press.

Cooper, Robert. 1996. *The Post-Modern State and the World Order.* London: Demos.

Coquery-Vidrovitch, C. 1972. *Le Congo au temps des compagnies concessionnaires 1898–1930.* Paris: Mouton.

Cowling, R., D. Le Maitre, B. McKenzie, R. Prys-Jones and B. van Wilgen (eds.). 1987. *Disturbance and the Dynamics of Fynbos Biome Communities: A Report of the Committee for Terrestrial Ecosystems.* Pretoria: Foundation for Research Development, Council for Scientific and Industrial Research. South African National Scientific Programmes, Report No. 135.

Cowling, Richard, and D. Richardson. 1995. *Fynbos: South Africa's Unique Floral Kingdom.* Cape Town: Fernwood Press.

CRAC. 2000. *Abahlali Concerned Residents Against Crime: Progress Report 2000.* New Brighton: Port Elizabeth.

Cronon, W. 1983. *Changes in the Land: Indians, Colonists, and the Ecology of New England.* New York: Hill and Wang.

Cruikshank, Barbara. 1999. *The Will to Empower: Democratic Citizens and Other Subjects.* Ithaca, N.Y.: Cornell University Press.

Crush, J., A. Jeeves, and D. Yudelman. 1991. *South Africa's Labour Empire: A History of Migrancy to the Gold Mines.* Cape Town: David Philip.

Currie, Iain. 1996. "Indigenous Law." In *Constitutional Law of South Africa: Revision Series 1, 1966.* Cape Town: Juta and Co.

Dacyl, Janina W. 1996. "Sovereignty versus Human Rights: From Past Discourses to Contemporary Dilemmas." *Journal of Refugee Studies,* 9(2): 136–65.

Darian-Smith, E. 1999. *Bridging Divides: The Channel Tunnel and English Legal Identity in the New Europe.* Berkeley: University of California Press.

Das, Gurcharan. 2002. *India Unbound: From Independence to the Global Information Age*. London: Profile.

Davidson, Basil. 1992. *The Black Man's Burden: Africa and the Curse of the Nation-State*. New York: Times Books.

Davis, Mike. 1990. *City of Quartz: Excavating the Future of Los Angeles*. London: Verso.

Dawson, Alexander S. 2000. "The Indian, the Nation, and Performances of Citizenship in Mexico's *Casa del Estudiante Indígena*, 1926–1932." Paper delivered to the 2000 meeting of the Latin American Studies Association.

Day, J., W. Siegfried, G. Louw, and M. Jarman (eds.). 1979. *Fynbos Ecology: A Preliminary Synthesis*. Pretoria: Foundation for Research Development, Council for Scientific and Industrial Research. South African National Scientific Programmes, Report No. 40.

Dean, Mitchell. 1996. "Putting the Technological into Government." *History of the Human Sciences*, 9(3): 47–68.

———. 1999. *Governmentality: Power and Rule in Modern Society*, London and Thousand Oaks, Calif.: Sage.

Dean, Mitchell, and Barry Hindess (eds.). 1998. *Governing Australia: Studies in Contemporary Rationalities of Government*. Melbourne: Cambridge University Press.

de Boek, P. 1998. "Domesticating Diamonds and Dollars: Identity, Expenditure and Sharing in Southwestern Zaire (1984–1997)." *Development and Change*, 29: 777–810.

de Certeau, Michel. 1984. *The Practice of Everyday Lives*. Berkeley: University of California Press.

de Genova, Nicholas P. 2002. "Migrant Illegality and Deportability in Everyday Life." *Annual Reviews in Anthropology*, 31: 419–47.

Degregori, Carlos Ivan, José Coronel, and Ponciano del Pino. 1998. "Government, Citizenship and Democracy: A Regional Perpective." In *Fujimori's Peru: The Political Economy*. Edited by John Crabtree and Jim Thomas. London: Institute for Latin American Studies.

de la Cadena, Marisol. 1998a. "Silent Racism and Intellectual Superiority in Peru." *Bulletin for Latin American Research*, 17(2): 143–64.

———. 1998b. "From Race to Class: Insurgent Intellectuals *de provincia* in Peru, 1910–1970." In *Shining and Other Paths: War and Society in Peru 1980–95*. Edited by Stephen J. Stern. Durham, N.C., and London: Duke University Press.

———. 2000. *Indigenous Mestizos: The Politics of Race and Culture in Cuzco, Peru, 1919–91*. Durham, N.C., and London: Duke University Press.

———. 2002. "Mestizos are not Hybrids: Genealogies, Dialogues, and Mestizajes in Peru." Unpublished manuscript.

de la Peña, Guillermo. 2000. "Mexican Anthropology and the Debate on Indigenous Rights." Paper prepared for the 2000 meeting of the American Association for Anthropology.

Deleuze, Giles, and Felix Guattari. 1987. *A Thousand Plateaus: Capitalism and Schizophrenia*. Minneapolis: University of Minnesota Press. (Translated by Brian Maasumi.)

Derrida, Jacques. 1992. "Force of Law: The 'Mystical Foundations of Authority.'" In *Deconstruction and the Possibility of Justice*. Edited by Drucilla Cornell, Michael Rosenfeld, and David Gray Carlson. New York: Routledge.

———. 1994. *Specters of Marx: The State of the Debt, the Work of Mourning, and the New International*. New York: Routledge. (Translated by Peggy Kamuf.)

Devi, S. Uma. 2002. "Globalisation, Information Technology and Asian Indian women in the US." *Economic and Political Weekly*, October 26.

Diop, B. Boris. 2000. *Le livre des ossements*. Paris: Présence africaine.

Diouf, M. 2000. "The Murid Trade Diaspora and the Making of a Vernacular Cosmopolitism." *Public Culture*. 12(3).

Dirks, Nicholas. 2001. *Castes of Mind: Colonialism and the Making of Modern India*. Princeton, N.J.: Princeton University Press.

Division of Colored Affairs. 1952–1958. *Annual Reports, 1952–1958*. Pretoria: Government Printer.

Dixon, Bill, and Lisa Johns. 2001. *Gangs, Pagad and the State: Vigilantism and Revenge Violence in the Western Cape*. Violence and Transition Series, Vol. 2. Johannesburg: Center for the Study of Violence and Reconciliation.

Donham, D. 1998. "Freeing South Africa: The 'Modernization' of Male-Male Sexuality in Soweto." *Cultural Anthropology*, 13(1): 3–21.

Donnelly, Jack. 1998. "Human Rights: A New Standard of Civilization." *International Affairs*, 74(1): 1–24.

Donzelot, Jacques. 1979. *The Policing of Families*. New York: Pantheon Books.

Douglas, Mary. 1973. *Natural Symbols*. New York: Vintage Books.

Dubow, Saul. 1995. *Scientific Racism in Modern South Africa*. Johannesburg: Witwatersrand University Press.

Dumont, Louis. 1970. *Religion/Politics and History in India*. Paris and The Hague: Mouton.

Eaton, Richard. 1996. *Rise of Islam and the Bengal Frontier: 1204–1760*. Berkeley: University of California Press.

Eckert, Julia, M. 2000. "Participation and the Politics of Violence: Towards the Sociology of an Anti-Democratic Movement." Berlin: Dissertation zur Verlage am Fachbereich Politik und Sozialwissenschaften an der Freien Universität Berlin.

Edkins, Jenny, Nalini Persram, and Veronique Pin-Fat (eds.). 1999. *Sovereignty and Subjectivity*. Boulder, Colo.: Lynne Rienner Publishers.

Egeland, Jan. 1994. "Norge som internasjonal fredsmegler." Paper given at Trondheim University, August 26, 1994.

Ellis, S. 1999. *The Mask of Anarchy: The Destruction of Liberia and the Religious Dimension of an African Civil War*. London: Hurst & Company.

English-Lueck, J. A., and A. Saveri. 2000. "Silicon Missionaries and Identity Evangelists." http://www.sjsu.edu/depts/anthropology/scvp/iden.html.

Epprecht, M. 1998. "The 'Unsaying' of Indigenous Homosexualities in Zimbabwe: Mapping a Blindspot in an African Masculinity." *Journal of Southern African Studies*, 24(4): 631–51.

Esposito, R. 2000. *Communitas: Origine et destin de la communauté*. Paris: Presses Universitaires de France.

Evans, Ivan. 1997. *Bureaucracy and Race: Native Administration in South Africa.* Berkeley: University of California Press.

Eyoh, D. 1998. "Conflicting Narratives of Anglophone Protest and the Politics of Identity in Cameroon." *Journal of Contemporary African Studies,* 16(2): 249–76.

Fabre, Henri. 1977. "The Dynamics of Indian Peasant Society and Migration to Coastal Plantations in Peru." In *Land and Labour in Latin America.* Edited by Kenneth Duncan and Ian Rutledge. London: Routledge.

Falk-Moore, Sally. 2001. *Law as Process.* London: James Currey. Second Edition.

Fall, A. S. 1998. "Migrants' Long Distance Relationships and Social Networks in Dakar." *Environment and Urbanization,* 10(1): 135–45.

Featherstone, Mike, Mike Hepworth, and Bryan S. Turner (eds.). 1991. *The Body: Social Process and Cultural Theory.* London: Sage.

Feldman, Allen. 1991. *Formations of Violence: The Narrative of the Body and Political Violence in Northern Ireland.* Chicago: University of Chicago Press.

Fidler, David P. 2000. "A Kinder, Gentler System of Capitulations? International Law, Structural Adjustment Policies, and the Standard of Liberal, Globalized Civilization." *Texas International Law Journal,* 35: 387–413.

Fine, Gary. 1986. "Redemption Rumors: Mercantile Legends and Corporate Beneficence." *Journal of American Folklore,* 99: 208–22.

Flores Galindo, Alberto. 1994. *Buscando un Inca: Identidad y utopia en los Andes.* Lima: Editorial Horizonte. Fourth Edition.

Foucault, Michel. 1976. *The History of Sexuality.* New York: Penguin Books.

———. 1977. *Discipline and Punish: The Birth of the Prison.* Harmondsworth: Penguin.

———. 1978. *The History of Sexuality: An Introduction, Vol. 1.* New York: Pantheon Books.

———. 1979. *Discipline and Punish: The Birth of the Prison.* New York: Vintage Books.

———. (1972) 1994. "Two Lectures." In *Culture/Power/History.* Edited by Nicholas Dirks. Princeton, N.J.: Princeton University Press.

———. 1997. *Ethics: Subjectivity and Truth.* Edited by Paul Rabinow. New York: New Press.

———. 2000. "Power." In *Power: Essential Works of Foucault 1954–1984.* Edited by James D. Faubion. New York: New Press.

———. 2001. "The Subject and Power." In *Power: Essential Works of Michel Foucault, 1954–1984. Vol. 3.* Edited by J. D. Faubion. London: Allen Lane, Penguin Press.

Franke, Pedro. 2000. *Políticas sociales y construcción de ciudadanía en zonas afectadas por violencia política.* Lima: Mesa Nacional sobre Desplazamiento y Afectados por Violencia Política and Coordinadora Nacional de Desplazados y Comunidades en Reconstrucción del Perú.

Fraser, M., and L. McMahon. 1988. *A Fynbos Year.* Cape Town: David Philip.

Frazer, Elizabeth. 1999. *The Problems of Communitarian Politics: Unity and Conflict.* Oxford and New York: Oxford University Press.

Frykenberg, R. E. 1977. "Company Circari in the Carnatic, c. 1799–1859: The Inner Logic of Political Systems in India." In *Realm and Region in Tradi-*

tional India. Edited by Richard G. Fox. Durham, N.C.: Duke University Press.

Fuglerud, Oivind. 1996. Between Nation and State: Aspects of Refugee-Migration from Sri Lanka to Norway. Unpublished Dr. polit. degree. University of Oslo: Department of Anthropology.

———. 1997. "Ambivalent Incorporation: Norwegian Policy towards Tamil Asylum-Seekers from Sri Lanka." *Journal of Refugee Studies*, 10(4): 443–61.

———. 1999. *Life on the Outside: The Tamil Diaspora and Long Distance Nationalism*. London: Pluto Press.

———. 2001. *Migrasjonsforståelse: Flytteprosesser, rasisme, globalisering*. Oslo: Universitetsforlaget.

———. 2004. "Constructing Exclusion: The Micro-Sociology of an Immigration Department." *Social Anthropology*, 12(1).

Galanter, Marc. 1989. *Law and Society in Modern India*. Delhi: Oxford University Press.

Gallagher, J., and R. Robinson. 1953. "The Imperialism of Free Trade." *The Economic History Review*, 6 (Second Series) (1): 1–15.

Gamio, Manuel. 1916. *Forjando Patria (Pro Nacionalismo)*. Mexico, D.F.: Librería de Porrúa Hermanos.

Gandhi, Mohandas. 1958. "Bihar and Untouchability." In *Collected Works*, 57. New Delhi: Publications Division.

García Canclini, Néstor. 1995. *Hybrid Cultures: Strategies for Entering and Leaving Modernity*. Minneapolis: University of Minnesota Press.

Gasarasi, Charles. 1990. "The Mass Naturalization and Further Integration of Rwandese Refugees in Tanzania: Process, Problems and Prospects." *Journal of Refugee Studies*, 3(2): 88–109.

Geffray, C. 1990. *La cause des armes au Mozambique: Anthropologie d'une guerre civile*. Paris: Karthala.

Gellner, Ernest. 1983. *Nations and Nationalism*. Oxford: Blackwell.

Gerhardsen, Rune. 1991. *Snillisme på norsk*. Oslo: Schibsted.

Geschiere, Peter. 1997. *The Modernity of Witchcraft: Politics and the Occult in Postcolonial Africa. Sorcellerie et politique en Afrique: La viande des autres*. Charlottesville: University Press of Virginia.

Geschiere, Peter, and Francis Nyamnjoh. 2000. "Capitalism and Autochthony: The Seesaw of Mobility and Belonging." In *Millennial Capitalism and the Culture of Neoliberalism*. Edited by J. Comaroff and J. L. Comaroff. Special Edition of *Public Culture*, 12(2): 423–52.

Gibney, Matthew. 1991. *Outside the Protection of the Law: The Situation of Irregular Migrants in Europe*. Oxford: Refugee Studies Centre.

Giddens, Anthony. 1982. *Profiles and Critiques in Social Theory*. London: Macmillan.

Girard, René. 1977. *Violence and the Sacred*. Baltimore, Md.: Johns Hopkins University Press.

Glaser, Clive. 2000. *Bo-Tsotsi: The Youth Gangs of Soweto, 1935–1976*. Cape Town: David Philips.

Glick Schiller, Nina. 1999. "Transmigrants and Nation-States: Something Old and Something New in the U.S. Immigrant Experience." In *The Handbook of*

International Migration. Edited by Charles Hirschman, Philip Kasinitz, and Josh DeWind. New York: Russell Sage Foundation.

Gluckman, Max. 1955. *The Ideas in Barotse Jurisprudence.* New Haven, Conn.: Yale University Press.

———. (ed.). 1969. *Idea and Procedures in African Customary Law.* London: Oxford University Press.

Goldin, Ian. 1989. *Making Race: The Politics and Economics of Colored Identity in South Africa.* London: Addison-Wesley.

Gong, Gerrit. W. 1984. *"The Standard of Civilization" in International Society.* Oxford: Oxford University Press.

Gootenberg, Paul. 1989. *Between Silver and Guano: Commercial Policy and the State in Postindependence Peru.* Princeton, N.J.: Princeton University Press.

Gordon, Stewart. 1994. *Marathas, Marauders and State Formation in Eighteenth Century India.* Delhi: Oxford University Press.

Gould, Jeffrey L. 1998. *To Die in This Way: Nicaraguan Indians and the Myth of Mestizaje, 1880–1965.* Durham, N.C.: Duke University Press.

Goux, J. J. 2000. *Frivolité de la valeur: Essai sur l'imaginaire du capitalisme.* Paris: Blusson.

Guha, Ranajit. 1997. "Not at Home in Empire." *Critical Inquiry,* 23 (Spring): 482–93.

———. 1998. *Dominance Without Hegemony.* Cambridge, Mass.: Harvard University Press.

Gullestad, Marianne. 1997. "Home, Local Community and Nation: Connections Between Everyday Life Practices and Constructions of National Identity." *Focaal,* 30/31: 39–60.

———. 2002. *Det norske sett med nye øyne: Kritisk analyse av norsk innvandringsdebatt.* Oslo: Universitetsforlaget.

Gupta, Akhil. 1995. "Blurred Boundaries: The Discourse of Corruption, the Culture of Politics, and the Imagined State." *American Ethnologist,* 22(2): 375–402.

Gupta, Akhil, and George Ferguson. 1992. "Beyond 'Culture': Space, Identity, and the Politics of Difference." *Cultural Anthropology,* 7(1): 6–23.

Gupta, Charu. 2001. *Sexuality, Obscenity, Community: Women, Muslims and the Hindu Public in Colonial India.* Delhi: Permanent Black.

Gupta, Dipankar. 1982. *Nativism in a Metropolis.* Delhi: Manohar Publishers.

Gutiérrez, Natividad. 1999. *Nationalist Myths and Ethnic Identities: Indigenous Intellectuals and the Mexican State.* Lincoln: University of Nebraska Press.

Gutiérrez, Ramon A. 1994. "Decolonizing the Body: Kinship and Nation." *American Archivist,* 57: 86–99.

Guyer, J. I. (ed.). 1994. *Money Matters: Instability, Values and Social Payments in the Modern History of West African Communities.* London: James Currey.

Guyer, J. I., L. Denzer, and A. Agbaje, (eds.). Forthcoming. *Money Struggles and City Life: Devaluation in the Popular Economy in Nigeria, 1986–96.*

Habib, Irfan. 1963. *The Agrarian System of Mughal India.* Delhi: Oxford University Press.

Hale, Charles R. 1996. "Introduction." Special Issue on Mestizaje in Latin America. *Journal of Latin American Anthropology,* 2(1): 2–3.

Hall, Anthony Vincent. 1979. "Invasive Weeds." In *Fynbos Ecology: A Preliminary*

Synthesis. Edited by J. Day, W. Siegfried, G. Louw and M. Jarman. Pretoria: Foundation for Research Development, Council for Scientific and Industrial Research. South African National Scientific Programmes, Report No. 40.

Hall, Stuart. 1996. *Questions of Cultural Identity.* London: Sage.

Handelman, Don. 1981. "Introduction: the Idea of Bureaucratic Organization." In *Administrative Frameworks and Clients.* Edited by J. Collman and D. Handelman. Special issue of *Social Analysis,* 9: 5–23.

Handelman, Don, and Elliot Leyton. 1978. *Bureaucracy and World View: Studies in the Logic of Official Interpretation.* Social and Economic Studies 22. St. John's: University of Newfoundland.

Hansen, Thomas, B. 2001a. "Governance and Myths of State in Mumbai." In *States of Imagination: Ethnographic Explorations of the Postcolonial State.* Edited by T. B. Hansen and F. Stepputat. Durham, N.C.: Duke University Press.

———. 2001b. *Wages of Violence: Naming and Identity in Postcolonial Bombay.* Princeton, N.J.: Princeton University Press.

———. 2002. "Between Diaspora and Autochthony: South African Indians after Apartheid." Paper presented at the conference "Regions in Globalization," Kyoto University, October 23–25, 2002.

Hansen, Thomas B., and Finn Stepputat (eds.). 2001. *States of Imagination: Ethnographic Explorations of the Postcolonial State.* Durham, N.C.: Duke University Press.

Haraway, Donna. 1989. "The Biopolitics of Postmodern Bodies: Determinations of Self in Immune System Discourse." *Differences,* 1(1): 3–43.

———. 1991. *Simians, Cyborgs, and Women: The Reinvention of Nature.* New York: Routledge.

Harbeson, J., D. Rothchild and N. Chazan (eds.). 1994. *Civil Society and the State in Africa.* Boulder, Colo.: Lynne Riemer.

Hardt, Michael, and Antonio Negri. 2000. *Empire.* Cambridge, Mass., and London: Harvard University Press.

Harrell-Bond, Barbara. 1986. *Imposing Aid: Emergency Assistance to Refugees.* Oxford and New York: Oxford University Press.

Harts-Broekhuis, A. 1997. "How to Sustain a Living: Urban Households and Poverty in a Sahelian Town of Mopti, Africa." *Africa,* 67(1): 106–31.

Harvey, David. 1990. *The Condition of Postmodernity: An Enquiry into the Origins of Cultural Change.* Oxford: Blackwell.

Harvey, W. 1859–65. *Flora Capensis: Being a Systematic Description of the Plants of the Cape Colony, Caffraria and Port Natal.* Dublin: Hodgess, Smith and Co.

Hasan, Khalid. 1987. "Introduction" to Saadat Hasan Manto, *Kingdom's End and Other Stories.* London: Verso. (Translated by Khalid Hasan.)

Hegel, G.W.F. (1821) 1991. *Elements of the Philosophy of Right.* Edited by Allen Wood. Cambridge: Cambridge University Press.

Hegeman, S. 1991. Shopping for Identities: A Nation of Nations and the Weak Ethnicity of Objects. *Public Culture,* 3(2): 71–92.

Held, David. 1995. *Democracy and the Global Order: From the Modern State to Cosmopolitan Governance.* Cambridge, Eng.: Polity Press.

———. 2000. *A Globalizing World: Culture, Economics and Politics.* London: Routledge.

Held, David, et al. 1999. *Global Transformations*. Oxford: Blackwell.

Helg, Aline. 1990. "Race in Argentina and Cuba, 1880–1930. Theory, Policies and Popular Reaction." In *The Idea of Race in Latin America, 1870–1940*. Edited by Richard Graham. Austin: University of Texas Press.

Helleiner, Eric. 1994. *States and the Reemergence of Global Finance: From Bretton Woods to the 1990s*. Ithaca, N.Y.: Cornell University Press.

Helliwell, Christine, and Barry Hindess. 2002. "The 'Empire of Uniformity' and the Government of Subject Peoples." *Cultural Values* 6(1): 137–50.

Herbst, Jeffrey. 2000. *States and Power in Africa: Comparative Lessons in Authority and Control*. Princeton, N.J.: Princeton University Press.

Herzfeld, Michael. 1992. *The Social Production of Indifference: Exploring the Symbolic Roots of Western Bureaucracy*. Chicago and London: University of Chicago Press.

———. 1996. *Cultural Intimacy: Social Poetics in the Nation-State*. London: Routledge.

Heusch, Luc de. 1982. *Drunken King, or The Origin of State in Africa*. Bloomington: Indiana University Press. (Translated by Roy Willis.)

Heyman, Josiah McC. 1995. "Putting Power in the Anthropology of Bureaucracy: The Immigration and Naturalization Service at the Mexico–United States Border." *Current Anthropology*, 36(2), (April): 261–87.

Hibou, B. (ed.) 1999. *La privatisation des États*. Paris: Karthala.

Hill, Jane 1991. "In Neca Gobierno de Puebla: Mexicano Penetrations of the Mexican State." *Nation-States and Indians in Latin America*. Edited by Greg Urban and Joel Sherzer. Austin: University of Texas Press.

Hindess, Barry. 2000a. "Divide and Govern: Governmental Aspects of the Modern States System." In *Governing Modern Societies*. Edited by R. Ericson and N. Stehr. Toronto: University of Toronto Press.

———. 2000b. "Representation Ingrafted upon Democracy." *Democratization*, 7(2): 1–18.

———. 2001a. "Citizenship in the International Management of Populations." In *Citizenship and Cultural Policy*. Edited by D. Meredyth and J. Minson. London, Sage.

———. 2001b. "The Liberal Government of Unfreedom." *Alternatives*, 26(2): 93–111.

———. 2002. "Neo-Liberal Citizenship." *Citizenship Studies*, 6(2): 127–43.

Hirschman, Albert O. 1977. *The Passions and the Interests*. Princeton, N.J.: Princeton University Press.

Hirst, Paul. 1998. "The International Origins of National Sovereignty." In *From Statism to Pluralism*. London: University College London Press.

Hobbes, Thomas. (1651) 1971. *Leviathan*. Harmondsworth: Penguin.

———. 1991. *Leviathan*. Cambridge: Cambridge University Press.

Hoffman, John. 1998. *Sovereignty*. Buckingham: Open University Press.

Holmes, Stephen. 1995. *Passions and Constraints: On the Theory of Liberal Democracy*. Chicago: University of Chicago Press.

House of Representatives. *Annual Reports, 1985–1992 (DCA)*. Pretoria: Government Printer.

Howard, Michael. 1978. *War and the Liberal Conscience*. London: Temple Smith.

Hoyweghen, Saskia van. 2001. "Mobility, Territoriality and Sovereignty in Post-Colonial Tanzania." *New Issues in Refugee Research* (Working Paper No. 49).

Human Rights Watch. 1999. *In The Name of Security: Forced Round-Ups of Refugees in Tanzania*. Human Rights Watch, Vol. 11. New York.

Hyndman, Jennifer. 2000. *Managing Displacement: Refugees and the Politics of Humanitarianism*. Minneapolis: University of Minnesota Press.

Ikenberry, G. John. 1999. "Liberal Hegemony and the Future of American Postwar Order." *International Order and the Future of World Politics*. Edited by T. V. Paul and J. A. Hall. Cambridge: Cambridge University Press.

Inden, Ronald. 1978. "Ritual, Authority, and Cyclic Time in Hindu Kingship." In *Kingship and Authority in South Asia*. Edited by John F. Richards. Madison: University of Wisconsin Press.

International Organization for Migration (IOM). 1994. "Discouraging Trafficking While Helping the Victims." *Trafficking in Migrants, IOM Newsletter* 3 (June).

Jackson, Robert. 1990. *Quasi-states: Sovereignty, International Relations and the Third World*. Cambridge: Cambridge University Press.

———. 1999. *Sovereignty at the Millennium*. Oxford: Blackwell.

Jacobsen, Nils. 1993. *Mirages of Transition: The Peruvian Andes, 1780–1930*. Berkeley: University of California Press.

Jaffrelot, Christophe. 1996. *The Hindu Nationalist Movement and Indian Politics*. London: Hurst.

Jalal, Ayesha. 1999. *Self and Sovereignty: Individual and Community in South Asian Islam since 1850*. London and New York: Routledge.

Jayadev, Raj. 2001. "IT Industry: USA." *Sarai Reader*, 1: 169–71.

Jeenah, Naeem. 1996. "Pagad: Aluta Continua." In *Drugs, Gangs and People's Power: Exploring the Pagad Phenomenon*. Edited by Rashad Galant and Faik Gamieldien. Cape Town: Claremont Main Road Masjid.

Jensen, Steffen. 2000. "Of Drug dealers and Street Gangsters: Power, Mobility and Violence on the Cape Flats." In *Focaal*, 36: 95–106.

———. 2001. "Claiming Community, Negotiating Crime: State Formation, Neighborhood and Gangs in a Capetonian Township." Roskilde University, Ph.D. Dissertation.

Jensen, Steffen, and Simon Turner. 1996. *A Place Called Heideveld: Strategies and Identities among Coloreds in Cape Town*. Roskilde: Institutes of Geography and International Development Studies, Roskilde University, Research Report No. 112.

Johnson, M. 1976. "Calico Caravans: The Tripoli—Kano Trade after 1880." *Journal of African History*, 17(1): 95–117.

Juenger, Ernst (1925) 1996. *The Storm of Steel: From a Diary of a German Stormtroop Officer on the Western Front*. New York: Howard Fertig.

Kaiser, Tania. 2000. "Promise and Practice: Participatory Evaluation of Humanitarian Assistance." *Forced Migration Review*, 8: 8–12.

Kakar, Sudhir. 1996. *The Colours of Violence*. New Delhi: Viking.

Kantorowicz, Ernst. 1957. *The King's Two Bodies: A Study in Medieval Political Theology*. Princeton, N.J.: Princeton University Press.

Kaplan, Flora. 1994. *Museums and the Making of "Ourselves:" The Role of Objects in National Identity*. London and New York: Leicester University Press.

Kaplan, Robert D. 2000. *The Coming Anarchy.* New York: Random House.

Karlstrom, Mikael. 1999. "Civil Society and its Presuppositions: Lessons from Uganda. In *Civil Society and the Political Imagination in Africa: Critical Perspectives.* Edited by John L. and Jean Comaroff. Chicago: University of Chicago Press.

Katzenstein, Mary, F. 1981. *Equality and Ethnicity: Shiv Sena Party and Preferential Policies in Bombay.* Ithaca, N.Y.: Cornell University Press.

Kaviraj, Sudipta. 1998. "The Culture of Representative Democracy." In *The Wages of Freedom: Fifty Years of the Indian Nation-State.* Edited by Partha Chatterjee. Delhi: Oxford University Press.

Khadria, Binod. 1999. *The Migration of Knowledge Workers.* New Delhi: Sage.

Kibreab, Gaim. 1993. "The Myth of Dependency Among Camp Refugees in Somalia 1979–1989." *Journal of Refugee Studies,* 6(4): 321–49.

Klausen, Arne Martin. 1995. "Traditional and Modern Elements in Norwegian Culture: Did the Winter Games Change Anything?" Paper presented at Conference at Lillehammer, April 18–19, 1995.

———. 1996. *Lillehammer-OL og olympismen: Et moderne rituale og en flertydig ideologi.* Oslo: Ad notam, Gyldendal.

——— (ed.) 1999. *Olympic Games as Performance and Public Event: The Case of the XVII Winter Olympic Games in Norway.* Oxford and New York: Berghahn Books.

Knight, Alan. 1990. "Racism, Revolution, and Indigenismo: Mexico, 1910–1940." In *The Idea of Race In Latin America, 1870–1940.* Edited by Richard Graham. Austin: University of Texas Press.

Kohli, Atul. 1991. *Democracy and Discontent: India's Growing Crisis of Governability.* Cambridge: Cambridge University Press.

———. 2001. *The Success of India's Democracy.* Cambridge: Cambridge University Press.

Korten, David C. 1996. *When Corporations Rule the World.* East Hartford: Kumarian Press.

Krasner, Stephen D. 1999. *Sovereignty: Organized Hypocracy.* Princeton, N.J.: Princeton University Press.

Kratochwill, Frederick. 1986. "Of Systems, Boundaries and Territoriality." *World Politics,* 34(1): 753-75.

Kruger, Frederick. 1977. "Ecology and Management of Cape Fynbos: Towards Conservation of a Unique Biome Type." Paper read to the South African Wild Life Management Association's Second International Symposium, Pretoria 1977.

———. 1979. "Fire." In *Fynbos Ecology: A Preliminary Synthesis.* Edited by J. Day, W. Siegfried, G. Louw and M. Jarman. Pretoria: Foundation for Research Development, Council for Scientific and Industrial Research. South African National Scientific Programmes, Report No. 40.

——— (ed.). 1978. *A Description of the Fynbos Biome Project: Report of the Committee for Terrestrial Ecosystems, National Programme for Environmental Sciences.* Pretoria: Cooperative Scientific Programmes, Council for Scientific and Industrial Research.

Kumar, Nita. 2001. "Children and the Partition." In *Partitions of Memory.* Edited by Suvir Kaul. Delhi: Permanent Black.

Kurien, Prema. 2002. *Kaleidoscopic Ethnicity: International Migration and the Reconstruction of Community Identities in India.* New Brunswick, N.J.: Rutgers University Press.

Kwong, Peter. 1997. *Forbidden Workers: Illegal Chinese Immigrants and American Labor.* New York: New Press.

Laclau, Ernesto. 1994. *The Making of Political Identities.* London: Verso.

Lakoff, G., and M. Johnson. 1980. *Metaphors We Live By.* Chicago and London: University of Chicago Press.

Lallemand, S. 1986. *La sexualité dans les contes africains.* Paris: L'Harmattan.

Landau, Loren. 2001. "The Humanitarian Hangover: Transnationalization of Governmental Practice in Tanzania's Refugee-Populated Areas." *New Issues in Refugee Research* (Working Paper No. 40).

Lash, Scott. 1994. "Replies and Critiques." In *Reflexive Modernization.* Edited by U. Beck, A. Giddens and S. Lash. Stanford: Stanford University Press.

Laski, Harold. 1950. *A Grammar of Politics.* London: George Allen and Unwin.

Law, R. 1985. "Human Sacrifice in Pre-colonial West Africa." *African Affairs,* 84: 53–87.

Lefort, Claude. 1988. *Democracy and Political Theory.* Cambridge, Eng.: Polity Press.

Lemarchand, René. 1996. *Burundi: Ethnic Conflict and Genocide.* Washington, D.C.: Woodrow Wilson Center Press, and Cambridge: Cambridge University Press.

Léon-Portilla, Miguel. 1990. *Endangered Cultures.* Dallas: Southern Methodist University Press.

Levyns, M. 1936. "The Flora of the Cape Mountains." *Journal of the Mountain Club of South Africa,* 39: 16–20.

Lewis, Gavin. 1987. *Between the Wire and the Wall: A History of South African "Colored" Politics.* Cape Town: David Philips.

Lloyd, I., and Susanne H. Rudolph. 1987. *In Pursuit of Lakshmi: The Political Economy of the Indian State.* Chicago: University of Chicago Press.

Loescher, G. 1993. *Beyond Charity: International Co-operation and the Global Refugee Crisis.* New York: Oxford University Press.

Lomnitz-Adler, Claudio. 1992. *Exits from the Labyrinth: Culture and Ideology in the Mexican National Space.* Berkeley: University of California Press.

Long, Norman, and Bryan Roberts (eds.). 1978. *Peasant Cooperation and Capitalist Expansion in Central Peru.* Austin: Texas University Press.

Louis, William R. (ed.). 1976. *Imperialism: The Robinson and Gallagher Controversy.* New York: New Viewpoints.

Lowell, W. George. 1990. *Conquista y Cambio Cultural: La sierra de los Cuchumatanes de Guatemala, 1500–1821.* Guatemala: CIRMA/PMS.

Lugalla, J. 1995. *Crisis, Urbanization, and Urban Poverty in Tanzania: A Study of Urban Poverty and Survival Politics.* London: University Presses of America.

Lugard, Frederick D. 1923. *The Dual Mandate in British Tropical Africa.* Edinburgh: W. Blackwood.

Mabin, Alan. 1992. "Comprehensive Segregation: The Origins of the Group Areas Act and its Planning Apparatuses." *Journal of Southern African Studies,* 18/1.

Mabin, Alan, and Susan Parnell. 1995. "Rethinking Urban South Africa." *Journal of Southern African Studies*, 21/1: 35–61.

MacLaren, Peter. 2000. *Che Guevara, Paolo Freire and the Pedagogy of Revolution*. Oxford: Rowman and Littlefield.

MacMillan, John. 1998. *On Liberal Peace: Democracy, War and the International Order*. London and New York: I. B. Tauris.

Malinowski, Bronislaw. 1929. "Practical Anthropology." *Africa*, 2: 22–39.

Malkki, Liisa. 1992. "National Geographic: The Rooting of Peoples and the Territorialization of National Identity Among Scholars and Refugees." *Cultural Anthropology*, 7(1): 24–44.

———. 1995a. *Purity and Exile: Violence, Memory, and National Cosmology among Hutu Refugees in Tanzania*. Chicago: University of Chicago Press.

———. 1995b. "Refugees and Exile: From Refugee Studies to the National Order of Things." *Annual Review of Anthropology*, 24: 495–523.

Mallon, Florencia E. 1995. *Peasant and Nation: The Making of Post-colonial Mexico and Peru*. Berkeley and Los Angeles: University of California Press.

———. 1996. "Constructing Mestizaje in Latin America: Authenticity, Marginality and Gender in the Claiming of Ethnic Identities." Special Issue on Mestizaje in Latin America. *Journal of Latin American Anthropology*, 2(1): 170–81.

———. 1998. "Local Intellectuals, Regional Mythologies, and the Mexican State, 1850–1994: The Many Faces of Zapatismo." *Polygraph*, 10: 39–78.

———. 2002. "Decoding the Parchments of the Latin American Nation-State: Peru, Mexico and Chile in Comparative Perspective." In *Studies in the Formation of the Nation-State in Latin America*. Edited by James Dunkerley. London: Institute of Latin American Studies.

Mama, A. 1999. "Dissenting Daughters? Gender Politics and Civil Society in a Militarized State." *CODESRIA Bulletin*, 3–4: 29–36.

Mamdani, Mahmood. 1996. *Citizen and Subject: Contemporary Africa and the Legacy of Late Colonialism*. Princeton, N.J.: Princeton University Press.

———. 1998. "When Does a Settler Become a Native? Reflections on the Colonial Roots of Citizenship in Equatorial and South Africa." Inaugural Lecture, May 13. University of Cape Town, New Series 208.

———. 2001. *When Victims Become Killers: Colonialism, Nativism, and the Genocide in Rwanda*. Princeton, N.J.: Princeton University Press.

Manders, P., D. Richardson, and P. Masson. 1992. "Is Fynbos a Stage in Succession to Forest? Analysis of the Perceived Ecological Distinction Between Two Communities." In *Fire in South African Mountain Fynbos*. Edited by B. Van Wilgen, D. Richardson, F. Kruger and H. van Hensbergen. *Ecological Studies*, 93: 81–107. Berlin: Springer-Verlag.

Manjra, Shuaaid. 1996. "Battle Plans in the Pagad Struggle: Political Fascism vs. Democracy." In *Drugs, Gangs and People's Power: Exploring the Pagad Phenomenon*. Edited by Rashad Galant and Faik Gamieldien. Cape Town: Claremont Main Road Masjid.

Mann, Michael. 1987. "Ruling Class Strategies and Citizenship." *Sociology*, 21(3): 339–54.

Manrique, Nelson. 1987. *Mercado interno y region: La sierra central 1820–1930*. Lima: DESCO.

Manto, Saadat Hasan. 1987. "Toba Tek Singh." In *Kingdom's End and Other Stories*. Edited by Saadat Hasan Manto. London and New York: Verso.

Mare, Gerhard. 1992. *Brothers Born of Warrior Blood: Politics and Ethnicity in South Africa*. Johannesburg: Ravan Press.

Marie, A. "'Y a pas l'argent': L'endetté insolvable et le créancier floué, deux figures complémentaires de la pauvreté abidjanaise." *Revue Tiers Monde*, 36.

Maritain, Jacques. 1969. "The Concept of Sovereignty." In *In Defense of Sovereignty*. Edited by W.J. Stankiewicz. London: Oxford University Press.

Marloth, R. 1924. "Notes on the Question of Veld-Burning." *South African Journal of Science*, 21: 342–45.

Marrus, M. R. 1990. "The Uprooted: An Historical Perspective." *The Uprooted: Forced Migration as an International Problem in the Post-War Era*. Edited by G. Rystad. Lund: Lund University Press.

Marshall, T. H. 1950. *Citizenship and Social Class*. Cambridge: Cambridge University Press.

———. 1977. *Class, Citizenship and Social Development*. Chicago: University of Chicago Press.

Martin, Emily. 1992. "The End of the Body?" *American Ethnologist* 19: 121–40.

———. 1994. *Flexible Bodies: The Role of Immunity in American Culture from the Days of Polio to the Age of AIDS*. Boston: Beacon Press.

Martínez, Oscar J. 2001. *Mexican-Origin People in the United Status: A Topical History*. Tucson: University of Arizona Press.

Mattes, Bob, et al. 1998. "Crime and Community Action on the Cape Flats 1996–97." *POS* 4. Cape Town: Idasa.

Maylam, Paul. 1995. "Explaining the Apartheid City: 20 Years of South African Urban Historiography." *Journal of Southern African Studies*, 21(1): 19–39.

Mbembe, Achille. 1992. "Provisional Notes on the Postcolony." *Africa*, 62(1): 3–37.

———. 1997. "The 'Thing' and its Double in Cameroonian Cartoons." In *Readings in African Popular Culture*. Edited by K. Barber. London: James Currey.

———. 1999. *Du gouvernement privé indirect*. Dakar: CODESRIA.

———. 2000. "At the Edge of the World: Boundaries, Territoriality and Sovereignty in Africa." *Public Culture* 12(1): 259–84.

———. 2001. *On the Postcolony*. Berkeley: University of California Press.

———. 2003. "Necropolitics." *Public Culture*, 15(1): 11–40.

Mburu, N. 1999. "Contemporary Banditry in the Horn of Africa: Causes, History and Political Implications." *Nordic Journal of African Studies*, 8(2): 89–107.

McLean, H., and L. Ngcobo. 1995. "'Abangibhamayo bathi ngimnandi' ('Those Who Fuck Me Say I'm Tasty'): Gay Sexuality in Reef Townships." In *Defiant Desire*. Edited by M. Gevisser and E. Cameron. New York: Routledge.

Medina, Andrés. 1996. *Recuentos y Figuraciones: Ensayos de Antropología Mexicana*. Mexico, D.F.: UNAM, Instituto de Investigaciones Antropológicas.

Méndez, Cecilia. 1996. "Incas Sí, Indios No: Notes on Peruvian Creole Nationalism and its Contemporary Crisis." *Journal of Latin American Studies*, 28:197–225.

Mill, John Stewart. (1865) 1977. "Considerations on Representative Government." In *Collected Works of John Stuart Mill*. Edited by J. M. Robson. Toronto: University of Toronto Press. 19: 371–577.

Miller, Nicola. 1999. *In the Shadow of the State: Intellectuals and the Quest for National Identity in Twentieth-Century Spanish America*. New York: Verso.

Mills, James H. 2000. *Madness, Cannabis and Colonialism: The 'Native-Only' Lunatic Asylums of British India 1857–1900*. Basingstoke: Macmillan.

Mills, James H., and Satadru Sen (eds.). 2004. *Confronting the Body: The Politics of Physicality in Colonial and Post-Colonial India*. London: Anthem Press.

Mines, Mattison. 1994. *Public Faces, Private Voices: Community and Individuality in South India*. Berkeley: University of California Press.

Mir, Ali, Biju Matthew and Raza Mir. 2000. "The Codes of Migration: Contours of the Global Software Market." *Cultural Dynamics*, 12(1): 5–35.

Mistry, Duxita. 1997. "Victims and the Criminal Justice System in South Africa." Paper presented at the Ninth Symposium on Victimology. Amsterdam, August 25–30, 1997.

Mitchell, Kathryn. 1997. "Transnational Subjects: Constituting the Cultural Citizens in the Era of Pacific Rim Capital." In *Ungrounded Empires*. Edited by A. Ong and D. Nonini. New York: Routledge.

Mitchell, Kathryn, and Kris Olds. 2000. "Chinese Business Networks and the Globalization of Property Markets in the Pacific Rim." In *Globalization of Chinese Business Firms*. Edited by H. Yeung and K. Olds. New York: St. Martin's Press.

Mitchell, T. 1988. *Colonising Egypt*. Cambridge: Cambridge University Press.

———. 1999. "Society, Economy and the State Effect." In *State/Culture: State Formation after the Cultural Turn*. Edited by George Steinmetz. Ithaca, N.Y.: Cornell University Press.

Mitullah, W.V., and K. Kibwana. 1998. "A Tale of Two Cities: Policy, Law, and Illegal Settlements in Kenya." In *Illegal Cities: Law and Urban Change in Developing Countries*. Edited by E. Fernandes and A. Varley. London and New York: Zed Press.

Moll, E., and G. Moll. 1994. *Common Trees of South Africa*. Cape Town: Struik.

Monenembo, T. 2000. *L'aîné des orphelins*. Paris: Seuil.

Moore, Sally Falk. 1978. *Law as Process: An Anthropological Approach*. London: Routledge.

Morales-Gomez, D., and C. Torres. 1990. *The State, Corporatist Politics, and Educational Policy Making in Mexico*. New York: Praeger.

Morales-Moreno, Luis Gerardo. 1994. "History and Patriotism in the National Museum of Mexico." *Museums and the Making of "Ourselves." The Role of Objects in National Identity*. Edited by Flora E. S. Kaplan. London and New York: Leicester University Press.

Mosse, George. 1975. *The Nationalization of the Masses: Political Symbolism and Mass Movements in Germany from the Napoleonic Wars through the Third Reich*. New York: H. Fertig.

Morgan, Edmund. 1988. *The Invention of the People: The Rise of Popular Sovereignty in England and America*. New York: Norton.

Mudimbe, V. Y. 1988. *The Invention of Africa: Gnosis, Philosophy and the Order of Knowledge*. Bloomington: University of Indiana Press.

Mufti, Aamir R. In press. "A Greater Story Writer than God: Gender, Genre and Minority in Late Colonial India." In *Subaltern Studies XI*. Edited by Partha Chatterjee and Pradeep Jeganathan. Delhi: Oxford University Press.

Munnik. L. A. P. A. 1978. "Forward." In *Plant Invaders: Beautiful But Dangerous*. Edited by C. Stirton. Cape Town: Department of Nature and Environmental Conservation.

Munro, William, A. 1998. *The Moral Economy of the State: Conservation, Community Development and State Making in Zimbabwe.* Athens, Ga.: Ohio Center for International Studies.

Murray, S., and R. Will (eds.). 1998. *Boy-Wives and Female Husbands: Studies in African Homosexualities.* New York: St Martin's Press.

Nahmad, Salomón and Thomas Weaver. 1990. "Manuel Gamio, el Primer Antropólogo Aplicado y su Relación con la Antropología Norteamericana." *America Indígena,* 50(4): 291–321.

Navaro-Yashin, Yael. 2002. *Faces of the State: Secularism and Public Life in Turkey.* Princeton, N.J.: Princeton University Press.

Niger-Thomas, M. 2000. "Women and the Arts of Smuggling in Western Cameroon." *CODESRIA Bulletin,* 2.

Nina, Daniel. 1995. *Re-thinking Popular Justice: Self-Regulation and Civil Society in South Africa.* Cape Town: Community Peace Foundation.

Nina, Daniel, and Wilfried Schärf. 2001. *The Other Law: Non-State Ordering in South Africa.* Landsdowne: Juta.

Noll, Gregor. 1999. "Rejected Asylum-Seekers: The Problem of Return." Geneva: UNHCR. *New Issues in Refugee Research* (Working Paper No. 4).

Norval, Aletta. 1996. *Deconstructing Apartheid Discourse.* London: Verso.

Nugent, Daniel. 1993. *Spent Cartridges of Revolution: An Anthropological History of Namiquipa, Chihuahua.* Chicago: University of Chicago Press.

Nugent, David. 1997. *Modernity at the Edge of Empire: State, Individual, and Nation in the Northern Peruvian Andes, 1885–1935.* Stanford: Stanford University Press.

Nunn, Frederick M. 1983. *Yesterday's Soldiers: European Military Professionalism in South America, 1890–1940.* Lincoln and London: University of Nebraska Press.

Oleart, Patricia. 1998. "Alberto Fujimori: 'The Man Peru Needed?'" In *Shining and Other Paths: War and Society in Peru 1980–95.* Edited by Stephen J. Stern. Durham, N.C., and London: Duke University Press.

Omar, Rachied. 1996. "Police, Politics and Anti-Drug Strategies: From Salt River to Salt River." In *Drugs, Gangs and People's Power: Exploring the Pagad Phenomenon.* Edited by Rashad Galant and Faik Gamieldien. Cape Town: Claremont Main Road Masjid.

Ong, Aihwa. 1987. *Spirits of Resistance and Capitalist Discipline: Factory Women in Malaysia.* Albany: State University of New York Press.

———. 1999. *Flexible Citizenship: The Cultural Logic of Transnationality.* Durham, N.C.: Duke University Press.

———. 2000. "Graduated Sovereignty in Southeast Asia." *Theory, Culture, and Society,* 17(4) (Aug.): 55–75.

———. 2003. *Buddha is Hiding: Refugees, Citizenship, the New America.* Berkeley: University of California Press.

———. 2004a. "Latitudes of Citizenship." In *People Out of Place: The Citizenship Gap.* Edited by Alison Brysk and Gershon Shafir. New York: Routledge.

———. 2004b. "The Chinese Axis: Exception, Zoning Technologies, and Variegated Sovereignty." *The East Asia Institute Journal* 4(1): 69–96.

Ong, Aihwa, and Don Nonini (eds.). 1995. *Ungrounded Empires: The Cultural Politics of Modern Chinese Transnationalism.* New York: Routledge.

Pandey, G. 1990. *The Colonial Construction of Communalism in North India*. Delhi: Oxford University Press.

Parsons, Talcott. 1967. *Sociological Theory and Modern Society*. New York: Free Press.

Pasquino, Pasquale. 1991. 'Thetrum Politicum: The Genealogy of Capital—Police and the State of Prosperity." In *The Foucault Effect. Studies in Governmentality*. Edited by Graham Burchell, Colin Gordon and Peter Miller. London: Harvester Wheatsheaf. 105–18.

Paz, Octavio. 1985. *The Labyrinth of Solitude*. New York: Grove Press.

Pérouse de Montclos, M. A. 1999. "Pétrole et conflits communautaires au Nigeria: Perspectives historiques." *Afrique contemporaine*, 190:20–38.

Pickering, Sharon. 2001. "Common Sense and Original Deviancy: News Discourses and Asylum Seekers in Australia." *Journal of Refugee Studies*, 14(2): 169–86.

Pinnock, Don. 1984. *The Brotherhoods: Street Gangs and State Control in Cape Town*. Cape Town: David Philips.

———. 1989. "Ideology and Urban Planning: Blueprints of a Garrison City." In *The Angry Divide*. Edited by Wilmot James and Mary Simons. Cape Town: David Philips.

Platt, Tristan. 1982. *Estado Boliviano y ayllu andino: Tierra y tribute en el norte de Potosí*. Lima: Instituto de Estudios Peruanos.

Pogge, Thomas. 2003. "The Influence of the Global Order on the Prospects for Genuine Democracy in Developing Countries." In *Debating Cosmopolitics*. Edited by D. Archibugi. London: Verso.

Polanyi, Karl. 1944. *The Great Transformation: The Political and Economic Origins of Our Time*. New York and Toronto: Farrar and Rinehart.

Poole, Deborah. 1988. "Landscapes of Power in a Cattle-Rustling Culture of Southern Andean Peru." *Dialectical Anthropology*, 12: 367–98.

———. 1994. "Introduction: Anthropological Perspectives on Violence and Culture—A View from the Peruvian High Provences." In *Unruly Order. Violence, Power and Cultural Identity in the High Provinces of Southern Peru*. Edited by Deborah Poole. Boulder, Colo.: Westview Press.

———. 1997. *Vision, Race and Modernity: A Visual Economy of the Andean Image World*. Princeton, N.J.: Princeton University Press.

Portal Ariosa, María Ana, and Ramírez Xóchitl. 1995. *Pensamiento Antropológico en México: Un Recorrido Histórico*. Mexico, D.F.: Universidad Autónoma Metropolitana.

Prunier, G. 2000. "Recomposition de la nation somalienne." *Le Monde diplomatique*, 553: 23.

Pufendorf, Samuel. (1673) 1991. *On the Duty of Man and Citizen According to Natural Law*. Cambridge: Cambridge University Press. (Translated by Michael Silverthorne.)

Rabinow, Paul (ed.). 1984. *The Foucault Reader*. New York: Pantheon Books.

Rajagopal, Arvind. 1997. "Hindu Immigrants in the US: Imagining Different Communities?" *Bulletin of Concerned Asian Scholars*, 51–65.

———. 2000. "Hindu Nationalism in the US: Changing Configurations of Political Practice." *Ethnic and Racial Studies*, 23(3): 467–96.

Rajaram, Prem. 2002. "Humanitarianism and Representations of the Refugee." *Journal of Refugee Studies*, 15(3): 247–64.

Ramirez Vásquez, Pedro et al. 1968. *The National Museum of Anthropology, Mexico: Art, Architecture, Archaeology, Ethnography.* New York: Harry N. Abrams and Helvetica Press.

Ramos Mendoza, Crescencio, and Teodoro Ramos Mendoza. 1983. *Proceso formativa y situación actual de las Comunidades de la Quebrada de Vilca, Huancavelica.* Huancayo: Universidad Nacional del Centro del Peru.

Rao, M.S.A., and Francine Frankel. 1990. *Dominance and State Power in India: Decline of a Social Order,* 2 vols. Delhi.

Rauch, A. 2000. *Le premier sexe: Mutations et crise de l'identité masculine.* Paris: Hachette.

Reguillo, Rossana. 1998. "Septiembre, los Caminos de la Nación." Sistema de Difusión ITESO. *Magis* 318.

Reina, Leticia (ed.). 2000. *Los Retos de la Ethnicidad en los Estados-Nación del Siglo XXI.* Mexico, D.F.: CIESAS, INI y Miguel Ángel Porrúa.

Reitzes, M. 1994. "Alien Issues." *Indicator,* 12(1): 7–11.

Republic of South Africa. 1976. *Commission of Inquiry into Matters relating to the Colored Group* (Theron Commission). Pretoria: Government Printer.

Reyntjens, Filip. 1993. "The Proof of the Pudding is in the Eating: the June 1993 Elections in Burundi." *Journal of Modern African Studies,* 31(4): 563–83.

Richardson, Dave, and R. Cowling, 1992. "Why is Mountain Fynbos Invasible and Which Species Invade?" In *Fire in South African Mountain Fynbos.* Edited by B. Van Wilgen, D. Richardson, F. Kruger, and H. van Hensbergen. Ecological Studies, 93. Berlin: Springer-Verlag.

Riesenberg, Peter, N. 1956. *Inalienability of Sovereignty in Medieval Political Thought.* New York: Columbia University Press.

Roche, Maurice. 1987. "Citizenship, Social Theory and Social Change." *Theory and Society,* 16: 363–99.

Roitman, Janet. 1998. "The Garison-Entrepôt." *Cahiers d'Etudes africaines,* 150–52, XXXVIII (2–4): 297–329.

Rojas, C. 2002. *Civilization and Violence: Regimes of Representation in Nineteenth-Century Columbia.* Minneapolis: University of Minnesota Press.

Rose, Nikolas. 1996. "The Death of the Social? Re-figuring the Territory of Government." *Economy and Society,* 25(3): 327–57.

———. 1999. *Powers of Freedom: Reforming Political Thought.* Cambridge: Cambridge University Press.

Rose-Ackerman, Susan. 1999. *Corruption and Government: Causes, Consequences and Reform.* Cambridge and New York: Cambridge University Press.

Rouse, Roger. 1995. "Thinking through Transnationalism: Notes on the Cultural Politics of Class Relations in the Contemporary United States." *Public Culture,* 7(2): 353–403.

Rousseau, Jean Jacques. 1978. *On the Social Contract.* New York: St. Martin's Press.

Rubio Goldsmith, Raquel. 1998. "Civilization, Barbarism and Norteña Gardens." *Making Worlds: Gender, Metaphor, Materiality.* Edited by Susan Ardí Aiken et al. Tucson: University of Arizona Press.

Ruggie, John Gerard. 1993. "Territoriality and beyond: problematizing modernity in international relations." *International Organization,* 47(1): 139–74.

Runciman, David. 2003. "The Concept of the State: The Sovereignty of a Fiction." In *States and Citizens: History, Theory, Prospects.* Edited by Quentin Skinner and Bo Straath. Cambridge: Cambridge University Press.

Russell y Rodríguez, Monica 1999. "Mixing it Up." Paper presented to the workshop on Race and the Politics of Mestizaje, University of Texas, Austin.

Sackey, B. M. 1997. "The Vanishing Sexual Organ Phenomenon in the Context of Ghanaian Religious Beliefs." *African Anthropology,* 4(2), 110–25.

Sahlins, Marshall. 1985. *Islands of History.* London and New York: Tavistock.

Said, Edward W. 1985. *Orientalism.* London: Penguin.

———. 1992. "Nationalism, Human Rights, and Interpretation." *Freedom and Interpretation: The Oxford Amnesty Lectures, 1992.* Edited by B. Johnson. New York: Basic Books.

Saldívar, Emiko. 2000. "Institutional Practices of *Indigenismo:* Mexico's *Instituto Nacional Indigenista.*" Paper presented to the 2000 meeting of the American Anthropological Association. San Francisco, Calif., November 15–19.

Samaniego, Carlos. 1978. "Peasant Movements at the Turn of the Century and the Rise of the Independent Farmer." In *Peasant Cooperation and Capitalist Expansion in Central Peru.* Edited by Norman Long and Bryan R. Roberts. Austin: University of Texas, Institute of Latin American Studies.

Sarkar, Tanika. 2001. *Hindu Wife, Hindu Nation: Community, Religion, and Cultural Nationalism.* New Delhi: Permanent Black.

Sartori, Giovani. 1987. *The Theory of Democracy Revisited.* Chatham, N.J.: Chatham House.

Sassen, Saskia. 1991. *The Global City: New York, London, Tokyo.* Princeton, N.J.: Princeton University Press.

———. 1996. *Losing Control? Sovereignty in an Age of Globalization.* New York: Columbia University Press.

Saxenian, AnnaLee. 1996. *Regional Advantage: Culture and Competition in Silicon Valley and Route 128.* Cambridge, Mass.: Harvard University Press.

———. 1999. *Silicon Valley's New Immigrant Entrepreneurs.* San Francisco: Public Policy Institute of California.

———. 2002. "The Silicon Valley Connection: Transnational Networks and Regional Development in Taiwan, China, and India." *Science, Technology and Society,* 7(1): 117–51.

Schafer, Boyd C. 1955. *Nationalism, Myth and Reality.* London: Gollancz.

Schärf, Wilfried. 1997a. "Specialist Courts and Community Courts." Position Paper, Commissioned by the Planning Unit, Ministry of Justice, South Africa, May 1997.

———. 1997b. "Re-Integrating Militarised Youths (Street Gangs and Self-Defence Units) into Mainstream South Africa: From Hunters to Game-Keepers?" Paper delivered to the Urban Childhood Conference. Trondheim, Norway.

———. 2001. "Police Reform and Crime Prevention in Post-Conflict Transitions: Learning from South Africa and Mozambique." In *Conflict Prevention and Peace Building in Africa: Report from the Maputo Conference, June 28–29, 2001.* Copenhagen: Danida, Ministry of Foreign Affairs.

Schärf, Wilfried, and Daniel Nina. 2001. *The Other Law: Non-State Ordering in South Africa.* Landsowne, Cape Town: Juta and Co.

Schmitt, Carl. 1950. *Der Nomos der Erde, im Volkerrecht des Jus Publicum Europaeum*. Cologne: Greven.

———. (1932) 1976. *The Concept of the Political*. New Brunswick, N.J.: Rutgers University Press.

———. (1922) 1985. *Political Theology: Four Chapters on the Concept of Sovereignty*. Cambridge, Mass., and London: MIT Press. (Translated by George Schwab).

———. 1996. "The Land Appropriation of a New World." *Telos* 109: 29–80.

Schumpeter, Joseph. 1976. *Capitalism, Socialism, and Democracy*. London: Allen And Unwin.

Secretaría de Educación Publica (SEP). 1993. *Historia de México: Primera Parte*. Mexico: SEP.

———. 1994. *Historia de México: Segunda Parte*. Mexico: SEP.

Seekings, Jeremy. 1996. "The Decline of South Africa's Civic Organizations, 1990–1996." *Critical Sociology*, 22(3): 135–57.

———. 2000. *The UDF: A History of the United Democratic Front in South Africa 1983–1991*. Cape Town: David Philip.

———. 2001. "Social Ordering and Control in the African Townships of South Africa: An Historical Overview of Extra-state Initiatives from the 1940s to the 1990s." In *The Other Law: Non-State Ordering in South Africa*. Edited by Wilfried Schärf and Daniel Nina. Landsowne, Cape Town: Juta and Co.

Sen, Satadru. 2000. *Disciplining Punishment: Colonialism and Convict Society in the Andaman Islands*. Delhi: Oxford University Press.

Sen, Sudipta. 2002. *Distant Sovereignty*. New York: Routledge.

Sesia, Paola. 1995. "*Indigenismo* and Anthropology in Post-Revolutionary Mexico: The Origins and Consolidation of a Long-lasting and Fateful Marriage." Unpublished manuscript.

Seth, Sanjai. 2000. "A 'Postcolonial World'?" *Contending Images of World Politics*. Edited by G. Fry and J. O'Hagan. London: Macmillan.

Shaw, Martin. 2002. "Post-Imperial and Quasi-Imperial: State and Empire in the Global Era." *Millennium: Journal of International Studies*, 31(2): 327–36.

Sherman, William L. 1983. "Some Aspects of Change in Guatemalan Society, 1470–1620." In *Spaniards and Indians in Southeastern Mesoamerica: Essays on the History of Ethnic Relations*. Edited by Murdo J. MacLeod and Robert Wasserstrom. Lincoln: University of Nebraska Press.

Siegel, James. 1998. *A New Criminal Type in Jakarta: Counter-revolution Today*. Durham, N.C.: Duke University Press.

Silverblatt, Irene. 1995. 'Becoming Indian in the Central Andes of Seventeenth-Century Peru." In *After Colonialism: Imperial Histories and Post-Colonial Displacements*. Edited by Gyan Prakash. Princeton, N.J.: Princeton University Press.

Simone, A. 2001. "On the Worlding of Cities in Africa." *African Studies Review*, 44(2).

Sinclair, M. 1996. "Unwilling Aliens: Forced Migrants in the New South Africa." *Indicator*, 13(3): 14–18.

Sindjoun, L. (ed.). 2000. *La biographie sociale du sexe: Genre, société et changement au Cameroun*. Paris: Karthala.

Singh, Anne-Maria. 1997. *National Crime Prevention Strategy: Changing the Face of Crime in South Africa.* Occasional Paper Series 4-97. Cape Town: Institute of Criminology, University of Cape Town.

Singha, Radhika. 1998. *A Despotism of Law: Law and Crime in Early Colonial India.* Delhi: Oxford University Press.

———. 2000. "Settle, Mobilize, Verify: Identification Practices in Colonial India." *Studies in History,* 16(2): 151–98.

Sivanandan, A. 1983. "Challenging Racism: Strategies for the '80s." *Race and Class,* 25(2): 1–11.

———. 1985. "RAT and the Degradation of Black Struggle." *Race and Class,* 26(4): 1–33.

Slater, David. 1989. *Territory and State Power in Latin America: The Peruvian Case.* Houndsmills, Basingstoke, and London: Macmillan Press.

Smith, Carol A. 1996. "Myths, Intellectuals, and Race/Class/Gender Distinctions in the Formation of Latin American Nations." Special Issue on Mestizaje in Latin America. *Journal of Latin American Anthropology,* 2(1): 148–69.

Smith, Gavin. 1989. *Livelihood and Resistance: Peasants and the Politics of Land in Peru.* Berkeley and Los Angeles: University of California Press.

Soguk, Nevzat. 1999. *States and Strangers: Refugees and Displacements of Statecraft.* Minneapolis: University of Minnesota Press.

Sommers, Marc. 1993. "Confronting the Future: The Effects of the Repatriation Program on a New Generation of Burundi Refugees." *Refuge, Canada's Periodical on Refugees,* 12(8): 25–73.

Sorel, Georges. (1908) 2000. *Reflections on Violence.* Cambridge: Cambridge University Press.

Spalding, Karen (ed.). 1982. *Essays in the Political, Economic and Social History of Colonial Latin America.* Newark: University of Delaware.

Sparks, Alistair. 1990. *The Mind of South Africa.* London: William Heinemann.

Speed, Shannon, and Jane Collier. 2000. "Limiting Indigenous Autonomy in Chiapas, Mexico: The State Government's Use of Human Rights." *Human Rights Quarterly* 22: 877–905.

Spencer, Jonathan. 2002. "The Political and Cultural Work of Nationalist Revolution in Sri Lanka." In *Elite Cultures: Anthropological Perspectives.* Edited by Stephen Nugent and Chris Shore. London: Routledge.

Spruyt, Hendrik. 1994. *The Sovereign State and its Competitors: An Analysis of Systems Change.* Princeton, N.J.: Princeton University Press.

Stacey, Judith. 1990. *Brave New Families: Domestic Upheavals in Late Twentieth-Century America.* New York: Basic Books.

Stein, Burton. 1980. *Peasant State and Society in Medieval South India.* New Delhi: Oxford University Press.

Stephen, Lynn. 2002. *Zapata Lives! Histories and Cultural Politics in Southern Mexico.* Berkeley: University of California Press.

Stern, Alexandra Minna. 2002. "From Mestizophilia to Biotypology: Racialization and Science in Mexico, 1920–1960." In *Race and Nation in Modern Latin America.* Edited by Nancy Applebaum et al. Chapel Hill: University of North Carolina Press.

Stern, Steve J. (ed.). 1987. *Resistance, Rebellion, and Consciousness in the Andean Peasant World, 18th. to 20th. Centuries.* Madison, Wis.: University of Wisconsin Press.

———. 1998. "Introduction to Part I." In *Shining and Other Paths: War and Society in Peru 1980–1995.* Edited by Steve J. Stern. Durham, N.C.: Duke University Press.

Stewart, C. C. 1976. "Southern Saharan Scholarship and the Bilad Al-Sudan." *Journal of African History,* 17(1): 73–93.

Stiansen, E., and J. I. Guyer (eds.). 1999. *Credit, Currencies and Culture: African Financial Institutions in Historical Perspective.* Stockholm: Elanders Gotab.

Stiglitz, Joseph. 1999. *Participation and Development: Perspectives from the Comprehensive Development Paradigm.* Seoul: World Bank.

Stirton C. (ed.). 1978. *Plant Invaders: Beautiful But Dangerous.* Cape Town: Department of Nature and Environmental Conservation.

Stolcke, Verena. 1995. "Talking Culture: New Boundaries, New Rhetorics of Exclusion in Europe." *Current Anthropology,* 36(1): 1–24.

Stoler, Ann Laura. 1995. *Race and the Education of Desire: Foucault's History of Sexuality and the Colonial Order of Things.* Durham, N.C., and London: Duke University Press.

———. 2002. *Carnal Knowledge and Imperial Power.* Berkeley: University of California Press.

Strang, David. 1996. "Contested Sovereignty: The Social Construction of Colonial Imperialism." In *Sovereignty as Social Construct.* Edited by Thomas Biersteker and Cynthia Weber. Cambridge: Cambridge University Press.

Sudarshan, R. 1999. "Governance of Multicultural Polities: Limits of the Rule of Law." In *Multiculturalism, Liberalism and Democracy.* Edited by Rajeev Bhargava, A. K. Bagchi, and R. Sudarshan. Delhi: Oxford University Press.

Tambiah, Stanley. 1996. *Leveling Crowds: Ethnonationalist Conflicts and Collective Violence in South Asia.* Berkeley: University of California Press.

Tansu, Ismail. 2001. *Aslinda Hic Kimse Uyumuyordu.* Ankara: Minpa Matbaacilik.

Tarlo, Emma. 2000. "Paper Truths: The Emergency and Slum Clearance Through Forgotten Files." In *Everyday Forms of State in India.* Edited by Chris Fuller and Veronique Benei. Delhi: Social Science Press.

Taussig, Michael. 1992. *The Nervous System.* New York and London: Routledge.

———. 1997. *The Magic of the State.* London and New York: Routledge.

———. 1999. *Defacement.* Stanford: Stanford University Press.

Taylor, Charles. 1994. "The Politics of Recognition." In *Multiculturalism: Examining the Politics of Recognition.* Edited by C. Taylor and A. Gutmann. Princeton, N.J.: Princeton University Press.

Taylor, P. J. 2000. "Embedded Statism and the Social Sciences II: Geographies (and Metageographies) in Globalization." *Research Bulletin 15, Environment and Planning A,* 32 (6): 1105–14.

Tayob, Abdulkader. 1996. "Islamism and Pagad: It's Location in the New South Africa." In *Drugs, Gangs and People's Power: Exploring the Pagad Phenomenon.* Edited by Rashad Galant and Faik Gamieldien. Cape Town: Claremont Main Road Masjid.

Thompson, Guy. 2002. "Liberalism and Nation-building in Mexico and Spain during the Nineteenth Century." In *Studies in the Formation of the Nation State in Latin America.* Edited by James Dunkerly. London: Institute of Latin American Studies.

Thompson, John B. 1995. *The Media and Modernity: A Social Theory of the Media.* Stanford: Stanford University Press.

Thomson, Alan. 1999. *An Introduction to African Politics.* London: Routledge.

Thomson, Janice, E. 1989. "Sovereignty in Historical Perspective: The Evolution of State Control Over Extraterritorial Violence." In *The Elusive State: International and Comparative Perspectives.* Edited by James A. Caporaso. London: Sage Publications.

Thurner, Mark. 1997. *From Two Republics to One Divided: Contradictions of Postcolonial Nation-making in Andean Peru.* Durham, N.C., and London: Duke University Press.

Tjore, Gro. 1998. *Protective Strategies in the 1990s: A Review of the Policy Discourses in UNHCR and the Executive Committee.* Bergen: CMI Report Series 1998, 3. Chr. Michelsen Institute.

Torpey, John. 2000. *The Invention of the Passport: Surveillance, Citizenship and the State.* Cambridge: Cambridge University Press.

TRC Final Report. 1998. *Final Report, Volumes 1–5: Truth and Reconciliation Commission of South Africa.* Cape Town: Juta and Co.

Turner, Brian S. 1986. *Citizenship and Capitalism: The Debate over Reformism.* London: Allen and Unwin.

———. 1990. "Outline of a Theory of Citizenship." *Sociology,* 24(2): 189–217.

Turner, Patricia. 1993. *I Heard It Through the Grapevine: Rumor in African-American Culture.* Berkeley: University of California Press.

Turner, Simon. 1998. "Representing the Past in Exile: The Politics of National History Among Burundian Refugees." *Refuge, Canada's Periodical on Refugees,* 17(6): 22–30.

———. 1999. "Angry Young Men in Camps: Gender, Age and Class Relations Among Burundian Refugees in Tanzania." *New Issues in Refugee Research* (Working Paper No. 9).

———. 2001. "The Barriers of Innocence: Humanitarian Intervention and Political Imagination in a Refugee Camp for Burundians in Tanzania." Ph.D. Dissertation. International Development Studies, Roskilde University.

———. 2002. "Dans l'œil du cyclone: Les réfugiés, l'aide et la communauté internationale en Tanzanie." *Politique Africaine,* 85: 29–45.

Twine, Francis W. 1997. *Racism in a Racial Democracy: The Maintenance of White Supremacy in Brazil.* Piscataway, N.J.: Rutgers University Press.

UNHCR. 1991. *Guidelines on the Protection of Refugee Women.* Geneva.

———. 1995. "Asylum under Threat." *Refugees,* 101 (III).

Union of South Africa. 1937. *Commission of Inquiry regarding Cape Colored Population of the Union: UG 54—1937.* Pretoria: Government Printer.

———. 1945. *Report of the Cape Colored Liquor Commission of Inquiry.* Pretoria: Government Printer.

Vallée, O. 1989. *Le prix de l'argent CFA: Heurs et malheurs de la zone franc.* Paris: Karthala.

van Beek, Martijn. 2001. "Beyond Identity Fetishism: 'Communal' Conflict in Ladakh and the Limits of Autonomy." *Cultural Anthropology,* 15(3): 525–69.

van der Gelderen, Martin. 2003. "The State and its Rivals in Early Modern Europe." In *States and Citizens: History, Theory, Prospects*. Edited by Quentin Skinner and Bo Straath. Cambridge: Cambridge University Press.

van der Veer, Peter. 1994. *Religious Nationalism: Hindus and Muslims in India*. Berkeley: University of California Press.

———. 1995. *Nation and Migration: The Politics of Space in the South Asian Diaspora*. Philadelphia: University of Pennsylvania Press.

———. 2001. *Imperial Encounters: Religion and Modernity in India and Britain*. Princeton, N.J.: Princeton University Press.

———. 2002. "Transnational Religion: Hindu and Muslim Movements." *Global Networks*, 2(2): 95–111.

———. 2003. "Postmodern India." In *Work and Social Change in Asia*. Edited by Arvind Das and Marcel van der Linden. 91–111. Delhi: Manohar.

van Rensberg, T. 1987. *An Introduction to Fynbos*. Pretoria: Department of Environment Affairs, Bulletin 61.

Van Wilgen, B. W., D. Richardson, F. Kruger, and H. van Hensbergen (eds.). *Fire in South African Mountain Fynbos*. Ecological Studies, Vol. 93, Berlin: Springer-Verlag.

van Wyk, B., and N. Gericke. 2000. *People's Plants: A Guide to Useful Plants of South Africa*. Pretoria: Briza.

Vasconcelos, José. 1979. *La Raza Cósmica*. Bilingual Edition. Los Angeles: Centro de Publicaciones, California State University. (Translated by Didier Tisdel Jaén.)

Vaughan, Mary Kay. 1997. *Cultural Politics in Revolution: Teachers, Peasants and Schools in Mexico, 1930–40*. Tucson: Arizona University Press.

Verkaaik, Oskar. 1999. "Inside the Citadel: Fun, Violence, and Religious Nationalism in Hyderabad, Pakistan." Ph.D. dissertation. University of Amsterdam.

Vevstad, Vigdis. 1993. "'Flyktning': et begrepsmessig villniss." *Juristkontakt*. 6: 2–7.

Vila, Pablo. 1999. "Identity and Empowerment on the Border." *NACLA Report on the Americas*, 33(3): 40–54.

Villoro, Luis. 1979 [1950]. *Los Grandes Momentos del Indigenismo en México*. Mexico, D.F.: 1979.

Vishwa Hindu Parishad. 1998. *The Hindu Agenda*. Delhi: Vishwa Hindu Parishad.

Visvanathan, Gauri. 1990. *Masks of Conquest*. New York: Faber and Faber.

———. 1998. *Outside the Fold: Conversion, Modernity and Belief*. Princeton, N.J.: Princeton University Press.

Wace, N. 1988. "Naturalized Plants in the Australian Landscape." In *The Australian Experience*. Edited by R. Heathcote, for the International Geographical Congress. Melbourne: Longman Chesire.

Wade, Peter. 1993. *Blackness and Race Mixture: The Dynamics of Racial Identity in Columbia*. Baltimore, Md.: Johns Hopkins University Press.

Walker, Charles F. 1999. *Smoldering Ashes: Cuzco and the Creation of Republican Peru, 1780–1840*. London and Durham, N.C.: Duke University Press.

Walker, Mack. 1971. *German Home Towns. Community, State and General Estate 1648–1871*. Ithaca, N.Y.: Cornell University Press.

Walker, Rob B. J. 1993. *Inside/Outside: International Relations as Political Theory*. Cambridge: Cambridge University Press.

———. 2002. "On the Immanence/Imminence of Empire." *Millennium: Journal of International Studies* 31(2): 337–45.

Walsh, Casey. 2000. "'Por la Grandeza de México': Manuel Gamio and Social Engineering in the Mexico–U.S. Borderlands." Paper presented to the 2000 meeting of the American Anthropological Association, San Francisco, Calif., November 15–19.

Walzer, Michael. 1983. *Spheres of Justice: A Defence of Pluralism & Equality*. New York: Basic Books.

Warman, Arturo et al. 1970. *De Eso Que Llaman Antropolgía Mexicana*. Mexico, D.F.: Editorial Nuestro Tiempo.

Warnier, J. P. 1993. *L'esprit d'entreprise au Cameroun*. Paris: Karthala.

Washbrook, David. 1978. *The Emergence of Provincial Politics: The Madras Presidency 1870–1920*. Cambridge: Cambridge University Press.

Waters, Tony. 1997. "Beyond Structural Adjustment: State and Market in a Rural Tanzanian Village." *African Studies Review*, 40(2): 59–89.

Weber, Cynthia. 1995. *Simulating Sovereignty: Intervention, State and Symbolic Exchange*. Cambridge: Cambridge University Press.

Weber, Eugen. 1977. *Peasants into Frenchmen: The Modernization of Rural France, 1870–1914*. London: Chatto and Windus.

West, Harry G., and Todd Sanders. 2003. *Transparency and Conspiracy: Ethnographies of Suspicion in the New World Order*. Durham, N.C.: Duke University Press.

Western, John. 1996. *Outcast Cape Town*. Berkeley: University of California Press.

Whitaker, Beth. 1999. "Changing Opportunities: Refugees and Host Communities in Western Tanzania.' *New Issues in Refugee Research* (Working Paper No. 11).

———. 2002. "Changing Priorities in Refugee Protection: The Rwandan Repatriation from Tanzania." *New Issues in Refugee Research* (Working Paper No. 53).

Widdifield, Stacie Graham. 1996. *The Embodiment of the National in Late Nineteenth-Century Mexican Painting*. Tucson: University of Arizona Press.

Wieviorka, Michel. 1995. *The Arena of Racism*. London: Sage.

Wikan, Unni. 1995. *Mot en ny norsk underklasse*. Oslo: Gyldendal.

Wilson, Fiona. 1979. "Propiedad e ideologia: estudio de una oligarquía en los Andes Centrales (S.XIX)." *Analisis*, 8–9: 36–54.

———. 2001. "In the Name of the State? Schools and Teachers in an Andean Province." In *State of Imagination: Ethnographic Explorations of the Postcolonial State*. Edited by Thomas Blom Hansen and Finn Stepputat. Durham, N.C., and London: Duke University Press.

———. 2003a. "Reconfiguring the Indian: Land-Labour Relations in the Postcolonial Andes." *Journal of Latin American Studies*, 35: 1–27.

———. 2004. "Indian Citizenship? The Discourse of Hygiene/Disease in 19th-century Andean Society." *Bulletin of Latin American Research* 23(2), 165–80.

Wilson, Ken. 1992. "Cults of Violence and Counterviolence in Mozambique." *Journal of Southern African Studies*, 18, 527–82.

Winder, David. 1978. "The Impact of the *Comunidad* on Local Development in the Mantaro Valley." In *Peasant Cooperation and Capitalist Expansion in Central*

Peru. Edited by Norman Long and Bryan S. Roberts. Austin: Institute of Latin American Studies, University of Texas at Austin.

Wink, Andre. 1986. *Land and Sovereignty in India: Agrarian Society and Politics under the Eighteenth-Century Maratha Swarajya.* Cambridge: Cambridge University Press.

Wolfenson, James D. 1999. *A Proposal for a Comprehensive Development Framework.* Washington, D.C.: World Bank.

Worby, Eric. 1998. "Tyranny, Parody, and Ethnic Polarity: Ritual Engagements with the State in Northwestern Zambia. *Journal of Southern African Studies,* 24(3): 560–78.

———. 2003. "The End of Modernity in Zimbabwe: Passages from Development to Sovereignty." In *Zimbabwe's Unfinished Business: Rethinking Land, State and Nation in the Context of Crisis.* Edited by Amanda Hammer, Brian Raftopoulos and Stig Jensen. Avondale, Harare: Weaver Press.

Wright, Winthrop R. 1990. *Café con leche: Race, Class and National Image in Venezuela.* Austin: University of Texas Press.

Xiang, Biao. 2001. "Structuration of Indian Information Technology Professionals' Migration to Australasia: An Ethnographic Story." *International Migration,* 39(5): 73–90.

Yang, A. 1985. *Crime and Criminality in British India.* Tucson: University of Arizona Press.

———. 2004. "The Lotah Emeutes of 1855: Caste, Religion and Prisons in North India in the Early Nineteenth Century." In *Confronting the Body.* Edited by J. Mills and S. Sen. London: Anthem Press.

Young, Crawford. 1994. *The African Colonial State in Comparative Perspective.* New Haven, Conn.: Yale University Press.

Young, Robert J. C. 1995. *Colonial Desire: Hybridity in Theory, Culture and Race.* New York: Routledge.

Zartman, William. 1994. *Collapsed States: The Disintegration and Restoration of Legitimate Authority.* Boulder, Colo.: Lynne Rienner.

Zavos, John. 2000. *The Emergence of Hindu Nationalism in India.* Delhi: Oxford University Press.

Zizek, Slavoj. 1989. *The Sublime Object of Ideology.* London and New York: Verso.

Index